Mastering GUI Progr with Python

Develop impressive cross-platform GUI applications
with PyQt

Alan D. Moore

BIRMINGHAM - MUMBAI

Mastering GUI Programming with Python

Copyright © 2019 Packt Publishing

Commissioning Editor: Richa Tripathi
Acquisition Editor: Shriram Shekhar
Content Development Editor: Digvijay Bagul
Technical Editor: Abin Sebastian
Copy Editor: Safis Editing
Project Coordinator: Prajakta Naik
Proofreader: Safis Editing
Indexer: Pratik Shirodkar
Graphics Coordinator: Jisha Chirayil
Production Coordinator: Aparna Bhagat

First published: May 2019

Production reference: 2100919

Published by Packt Publishing Ltd.
Livery Place
35 Livery Street
Birmingham
B3 2PB, UK.

ISBN 978-1-78961-290-5

www.packtpub.com

To my children—may you be inspired to create, be diligent to create well, and be bold enough to share your creations confidently with the world.

– Alan D. Moore

Packt.com

Subscribe to our online digital library for full access to over 7,000 books and videos, as well as industry leading tools to help you plan your personal development and advance your career. For more information, please visit our website.

Why subscribe?

- Spend less time learning and more time coding with practical eBooks and Videos from over 4,000 industry professionals

- Improve your learning with Skill Plans built especially for you

- Get a free eBook or video every month

- Fully searchable for easy access to vital information

- Copy and paste, print, and bookmark content

Did you know that Packt offers eBook versions of every book published, with PDF and ePub files available? You can upgrade to the eBook version at www.packt.com and as a print book customer, you are entitled to a discount on the eBook copy. Get in touch with us at customercare@packtpub.com for more details.

At www.packt.com, you can also read a collection of free technical articles, sign up for a range of free newsletters, and receive exclusive discounts and offers on Packt books and eBooks.

Contributors

About the author

Alan D. Moore is a data analyst and software developer who has been solving problems with Python since 2006. He's developed both open source and private code using frameworks such as Django, Flask, Qt, and Tkinter, and contributes to various open source Python and JavaScript projects. Alan is the author of *Python GUI Programming with Tkinter*.

Sincere thanks to my wife, Cara, for her patience and support; Caspian Moore for his prodigal knowledge of OpenGL; Emeth Moore for his awesome "Fight Fighter" graphics and unrivalled knowledge of memes; my friends and family who have been so graciously excited about a book they mostly don't understand; and to the fine people of Packt for their patience and flexibility. Most of all, thanks to God for leading me to this opportunity.

About the reviewer

Chankey Pathak is a data scientist from India. He's the author of a Python API for high-frequency trading with Morgan Stanley. He has worked with Citadel, Sophos, and Proofpoint in the past. He's also well-known in the Perl community for his contributions. He is an open source contributor and loves Linux.

Packt is searching for authors like you

If you're interested in becoming an author for Packt, please visit `authors.packtpub.com` and apply today. We have worked with thousands of developers and tech professionals, just like you, to help them share their insight with the global tech community. You can make a general application, apply for a specific hot topic that we are recruiting an author for, or submit your own idea.

Table of Contents

Section 2: Working with External Resources

Preface

In an age when the term **application developer** nearly always implies **web application developer**, the building of desktop GUI applications may seem in danger of becoming a quaint and obscure art. Yet on every forum, mailing list, and chat service where programming is discussed, I find young Python coders eager to dive into GUI toolkits so that they can start building the kind of software that any average person can readily identify as an application. The one GUI library consistently recommended to these learners, the one that is arguably Python's most exciting and most complete toolkit, is PyQt.

Despite this popularity, there have been relatively few resources available for learning PyQt. Those who wish to learn it must rely heavily on outdated books, C++ documentation, scattered blogs, or snippets of code found in mailing lists or Stack Overflow posts. There is an apparent need for a modern tutorial and reference on PyQt for the Python programmer, and this book aims to fill that need.

My first book, *Python GUI Programming with Tkinter*, focused on the rudiments of application development using Tkinter, covering core topics such as interface design, unit testing, program architecture, and packaging. In this book, I wanted to go beyond the basics, not just teaching you how to build data-driven business forms (which so many toolkits can produce, and so many other books can teach you to write), but to explore the more exciting and unique possibilities offered by PyQt: multimedia, animation, 3D graphics, image manipulation, networking, multi-threading, and more. Of course, this book doesn't shirk the business side of things either, with solid coverage of data entry forms, SQL databases, and charting.

There are two kinds of authors who write technical books. The first is the absolute expert, with infallible authority and encyclopedic knowledge of the topic at hand, who is able to draw on a deep understanding to produce explanations that perfectly address the learner's most pertinent needs.

The second kind of author is a mere mortal possessed of a reasonable familiarity with the basics, a willingness to research what is not known, and most importantly, a dogged determination to ensure that every statement asserted in print is the whole and correct truth. This author must be prepared to stop mid-sentence in the flow of writing to test claims in the interpreter or code editor; to spend hours reading documentation, mailing-list threads, code comments, and IRC logs in the pursuit of a more correct understanding; and to delete and rewrite large swathes of their work when a new fact reveals a fault in their original assumptions.

When I was asked to write a book on PyQt5, I could make no claims to being the first sort of author (nor can I now); while I had developed and maintained several PyQt applications both at work and in the open source world, my understanding of PyQt rarely strayed beyond the simple needs of my own code. So, I have aspired to be the second type, committing myself to diligent study and the painstaking process of sifting and distilling the tangled mass of available information into a text that might guide the aspiring GUI programmer toward mastery of PyQt.

As a proud father of five children, some of whom have a budding (if not blooming) interest in programming, I have worked these past six months to write a book that I could confidently and conscientiously put before them, should they wish to learn these skills. I hope, dear reader, that you sense in this text this parental enthusiasm for your growth and progress as we tackle this subject together.

Who this book is for

This book is for the intermediate Python programmer who wants to dig deep into the PyQt application framework and learn how to make powerful GUI applications. It is assumed that the reader knows the basics of Python syntax, features, and idioms such as functions, classes, and common standard library tools. It is also assumed the reader has an environment in which they are comfortable writing and executing Python code.

This book does *not* assume any prior knowledge of GUI development, other GUI toolkits, or other versions of PyQt.

What this book covers

Chapter 1, *Getting Started with PyQt*, introduces you to the Qt and PyQt libraries. You will learn how to set up your system for writing PyQt applications and be introduced to Qt Designer. You will also write the traditional Hello World application and develop a basic template for PyQt apps.

Chapter 2, *Building Forms with QtWidgets*, shows you the basics of making a PyQt GUI. You'll meet the most common input and display widgets, learn to arrange them using layouts, and learn how to validate user input. You'll put these skills into action developing a calendar GUI.

Chapter 3, *Handling Events with Signals and Slots*, focuses on PyQt's event handling and object communication system. You'll learn how to use this system to make your application respond to user input, and how to create custom signals and slots. You'll put these skills to work by completing your calendar application.

Chapter 4, *Building Applications with QMainWindow*, introduces you to the QMainWindow class, which forms the basis of our applications throughout the rest of the book. You'll also explore PyQt's standard dialog classes and the QSettings module for saving your app's configuration.

Chapter 5, *Creating Data Interfaces with Model-View Classes*, focuses on Qt's Model-View classes. You'll learn the principles of model-view design, explore the model-view classes in QtWidgets, and exercise your knowledge as we develop a CSV editor.

Chapter 6, *Styling Qt Applications*, explores the styling capabilities of PyQt widgets. You will spice up your GUI applications with custom fonts, images, and icons. You'll learn to customize colors using style objects and Qt style sheets. Finally, we'll learn how to do basic animations of style properties.

Chapter 7, *Working with Audio-Visual Using QtMultimedia*, explores the multimedia features of Qt. You will learn how to playback and record audio and video in a way that works seamlessly across platforms.

Chapter 8, *Networking with QtNetwork*, is focused on simple network communications using the QtNetwork library. You will learn to communicate over raw sockets, both **Transmission Control Protocol (TCP)** and **User Datagram Protocol (UDP)**, as well as learning to transmit and receive files and data using HTTP.

Chapter 9, *Exploring SQL with QtSQL*, introduces you to the world of SQL database programming. You will learn the basics of SQL and the SQLite database. You will then learn how your PyQt applications can use the QtSQL library to access data using raw SQL commands or Qt's SQL model-view classes.

Chapter 10, *Multithreading with QTimer and QThread*, addresses the world of multithreaded and asynchronous programming. You will learn to use timers to delay tasks on the event loop and learn how to push processes into a separate execution thread using QThread. You'll also learn how to do high-concurrency programming using QThreadPool.

`Chapter 11`, *Creating Rich Text with QTextDocument*, explores rich text and document preparation in Qt. You'll be introduced to Qt's rich text markup language, and learn how to build documents programmatically using `QTextDocument`. You'll also learn how to use Qt's printing libraries to enable document printing easily across platforms.

`Chapter 12`, *Creating 2D Graphics with Qpainter*, digs deep into two-dimensional graphics in Qt. You'll learn how to load and edit images and to create custom widgets. You'll also learn about drawing and animating with the Qt Graphics system, and create an arcade-style game.

`Chapter 13`, *Creating 3D Graphics with QtOpenGL*, introduces you to 3D graphics with OpenGL. You will learn the basics of modern OpenGL programming, and how to use PyQt widgets to display and interact with OpenGL drawings.

`Chapter 14`, *Embedding Data Plots with QtCharts*, explores Qt's built-in charting capabilities. You'll learn how to create both static and animated charts, and how to customize the colors, fonts, and styles of your charts.

`Chapter 15`, *PyQt Raspberry Pi*, focuses on the use of PyQt on the Raspberry Pi computer. You'll learn how to set up PyQt on Raspbian Linux, and how to combine the power of PyQt with the Raspberry Pi's GPIO pins to create GUI applications that interact with real-world circuitry.

`Chapter 16`, *Web Browsing with QtWebEngine*, looks at PyQt's Chromium-based web browser module. You'll explore the capabilities of this module as you build your own multi-tabbed web browser.

`Chapter 17`, *Preparing your Software for Distribution*, discusses various ways to prepare your code for sharing and distribution. We'll look at optimal project layout, packaging your source code for other Python users using `setuptools`, and building standalone executables using PyInstaller.

`Appendix A`, *Answers to Questions*, contains answers or suggestions for the questions at the end of each chapter.

`Appendix B`, *Upgrading Raspbian 9 to Raspbian 10*, explains how to upgrade a Raspberry Pi device from Raspbian 9 to Raspbian 10, for readers who are trying to follow the book before the official release of Raspbian 10.

To get the most out of this book

The reader is expected to have proficiency in the Python language, particularly Python 3. You should understand, at least in a basic sense, how to work with classes and object-oriented programming. You may find it helpful to have a passing familiarity with C++, since most of the available Qt documentation is aimed at that language.

You should have a computer running Windows, macOS, or Linux on which Python 3.7 has been installed, and on which you can install other software as needed. You should have a code editor and command-line shell with which you are comfortable. Finally, you should have access to the internet.

Each chapter of this book contains one or more example applications. Although these examples are available for download, you are encouraged to follow along, creating these applications by hand to see the intermediate stages as the applications come together.

Each chapter also contains a series of questions or a suggested project to cement your knowledge of the topic, and a selection of resources for further study on the topic. You will get the most out of each chapter if you engage your mind and creativity in solving these problems and reading the provided materials.

The code included in this book is released under the open source MIT license, which allows you to re-use the code as you see fit, provided you retain the included copyright notices. You are encouraged to use, modify, improve, and re-publish these programs.

Download the example code files

You can download the example code files for this book from your account at `www.packt.com`. If you purchased this book elsewhere, you can visit `www.packt.com/support` and register to have the files emailed directly to you.

You can download the code files by following these steps:

1. Log in or register at `www.packt.com`.
2. Select the **SUPPORT** tab.
3. Click on **Code Downloads & Errata**.
4. Enter the name of the book in the **Search** box and follow the onscreen instructions.

Once the file is downloaded, please make sure that you unzip or extract the folder using the latest version of:

- WinRAR/7-Zip for Windows
- Zipeg/iZip/UnRarX for Mac
- 7-Zip/PeaZip for Linux

The code bundle for the book is also hosted on GitHub at `https://github.com/PacktPublishing/Mastering-GUI-Programming-with-Python/tree/master`. In case there's an update to the code, it will be updated on the existing GitHub repository.

We also have other code bundles from our rich catalog of books and videos available at `https://github.com/PacktPublishing/`. Check them out!

Download the color images

We also provide a PDF file that has color images of the screenshots/diagrams used in this book. You can download it here: `http://www.packtpub.com/sites/default/files/downloads/9781789612905_ColorImages.pdf`.

Code in action

Visit the following link to check out videos of the code being run: `http://bit.ly/2M3QVrl`

Conventions used

There are a number of text conventions used throughout this book.

`CodeInText`: Indicates code words in text, database table names, folder names, filenames, file extensions, pathnames, dummy URLs, user input, and Twitter handles. Here is an example: "HTML documents are built hierarchically, with the outermost tag usually being `<html>`."

A block of code is set as follows:

```
<table border=2>
    <thead>
      <tr
bgcolor='grey'><th>System</th><th>Graphics</th><th>Sound</th></tr>
    </thead>
```

When we wish to draw your attention to a particular part of a code block, the relevant lines or items are set in bold:

```
<table border=2>
    <thead>
      <tr
bgcolor='grey'><th>System</th><th>Graphics</th><th>Sound</th></tr>
    </thead>
```

Any command-line input or output is written as follows:

```
$ python game_lobby.py
Font is Totally Nonexistent Font Family XYZ
Actual font used is Bitstream Vera Sans
```

Bold: Indicates a new term, an important word, or words that you see onscreen. For example, words in menus or dialog boxes appear in the text like this. Here is an example: "Select **System info** from the **Administration** panel."

Warnings or important notes appear like this.

Tips and tricks appear like this.

Get in touch

Feedback from our readers is always welcome.

General feedback: If you have questions about any aspect of this book, mention the book title in the subject of your message and email us at customercare@packtpub.com.

Errata: Although we have taken every care to ensure the accuracy of our content, mistakes do happen. If you have found a mistake in this book, we would be grateful if you would report this to us. Please visit www.packt.com/submit-errata, selecting your book, clicking on the Errata Submission Form link, and entering the details.

Piracy: If you come across any illegal copies of our works in any form on the Internet, we would be grateful if you would provide us with the location address or website name. Please contact us at copyright@packt.com with a link to the material.

If you are interested in becoming an author: If there is a topic that you have expertise in and you are interested in either writing or contributing to a book, please visit authors.packtpub.com.

Reviews

Please leave a review. Once you have read and used this book, why not leave a review on the site that you purchased it from? Potential readers can then see and use your unbiased opinion to make purchase decisions, we at Packt can understand what you think about our products, and our authors can see your feedback on their book. Thank you!

For more information about Packt, please visit packt.com.

Section 1: Deep Dive into PyQt 1

In this section, you will explore the core features of PyQt. By the end of this section, you should be comfortable with the basic design workflow and coding idioms involved in writing PyQt applications and feel confident in your ability to construct simple PyQt interfaces.

The following chapters are in this section:

- Chapter 1, *Getting Started with PyQt*
- Chapter 2, *Building Forms with QtWidgets*
- Chapter 3, *Handling Events with Signals and Slots*
- Chapter 4, *Building Applications with QMainWindow*
- Chapter 5, *Creating Data Interfaces with Model-View Classes*
- Chapter 6, *Styling Qt Applications*

Getting Started with PyQt 1

Welcome, Python programmer!

Python is a great language for system administration, data analysis, web services, and command-line programs; most likely you've already found Python useful in at least one of those areas. However, there is something truly satisfying about building the kind of GUI-driven application that an end user can readily identify as a program, and this skill should be in the toolbox of any master software developer. In this book, you're going to learn how you can use Python and the Qt framework to develop amazing applications—from simple data-entry forms to powerful multimedia tools.

We'll start our tour of these powerful technologies with the following topics:

- Introducing Qt and PyQt
- Creating `Hello Qt` – our first window
- Creating a PyQt application template
- Introducing Qt Designer

Technical requirements

For this chapter, and most of the rest of the book, you're going to need the following:

- A PC running **Microsoft Windows**, **Apple macOS**, or a 64-bit flavor of **GNU/Linux**.
- **Python 3**, available from `http://www.python.org`. The code in this book requires Python 3.7 or later.

- **PyQt 5.12**, which you can install from the Python Package Index using this command:

```
$ pip install --user PyQt5
```

- Linux users may also wish to install PyQt5 from their distribution's package repositories.
- **Qt Designer 4.9**, a WYSIWYG GUI building tool available from `https://www.qt.io`. See the following section for installation instructions.
- The **example code** from `https://github.com/PacktPublishing/Mastering-GUI-Programming-with-Python/tree/master/Chapter01`.

Check out the following video to see the code in action: `http://bit.ly/2M5OUeg`

Installing Qt Designer

On Windows or macOS, Qt Designer is part of the Qt Creator IDE from the Qt company. This is a free IDE that you can use for coding, though, at the time of writing, it is mainly aimed at C++ and support for Python is rudimentary. The Qt Designer component can be used regardless of whether you do your coding in Qt Creator or not.

You can download an installer for Qt Creator from `https://download.qt.io/official_releases/qtcreator/4.9/4.9.0/`.

Although the Qt company offers a similar standalone Qt installer for Linux, most Linux users will prefer to use packages from their distribution's repositories. Some distributions offer Qt Designer as a standalone application, while others include it in their Qt Creator packages.

This table shows the package that will install Qt Designer in several major distributions:

Distribution	Package name
Ubuntu, Debian, Mint	qttools5-dev-tools
Fedora, CentOS, Red Hat, SUSE	qt-creator
Arch, Manjaro, Antergos	qt5-tools

Introducing Qt and PyQt

Qt is a cross-platform application framework that was created for use with C++. Available in both commercial and open source licenses (**General Public License (GPL)** v3 and **Lesser General Public License (LGPL)** v3, specifically), it is widely used by open source projects such as KDE Plasma and Oracle VirtualBox, commercial software such as Adobe Photoshop Elements and Autodesk Maya, and even embedded software in products from companies such as LG and Panasonic. Qt is currently owned and maintained by the Qt company (https://www.qt.io).

In this book, we're going to be working with the open source release of Qt 5.12. If you're using Windows, macOS, or a major Linux distribution, you should not need to install Qt explicitly; it will be installed automatically when you install PyQt5.

 Qt is officially pronounced **cute**, though many people say, **Q T**.

PyQt5

PyQt is a Python library that allows the Qt framework to be used in Python code. It was developed by Riverbank Computing under the GPL license, although commercial licenses can be purchased for those wanting to develop proprietary applications. (Note that this is a separate license from the Qt license.) It is currently supported on Windows, Linux, UNIX, Android, macOS, and iOS.

PyQt's bindings are generated automatically by a tool called **SIP**, so, to a large extent, working with PyQt is just like working with Qt itself, only in Python. In other words, the classes, methods, and other objects are all identical in usage, apart from the language syntax.

 The Qt company has recently released **Qt for Python** (also known as **PySide2**), their own Python Qt5 library, under the terms of the LGPL. Qt for Python is functionally equivalent to PyQt5, and code can be ported between them with very few changes. This book will cover PyQt5, but what you learn can easily be applied to Qt for Python, should you need an LGPL library.

Working with Qt and PyQt

Qt is much more than a GUI library; it's an application framework. It contains dozens of modules with thousands of classes. It has classes to wrap simple data types such as dates, times, URLs, or color values. It has GUI components such as buttons, text entries, or dialog boxes. It has interfaces for hardware such as cameras or mobile sensors. It has a networking library, a threading library, and a database library. If anything, Qt is truly a second standard library!

Qt is written in C++ and designed around the needs of C++ programmers; it works well with Python, but Python programmers may find some of its concepts slightly foreign at first.

For example, Qt objects usually expect to work with data wrapped in Qt classes. A method that expects a color value won't accept a string or a tuple of RGB values; it wants a `QColor` object. A method that returns a size won't return a `(width, height)` tuple; it will return a `QSize` object. PyQt mitigates this somewhat by automatically converting some common data types (for example, strings, lists, dates, and times) between Qt objects and Python standard library types; however, there are many hundreds of Qt classes that have no analog in the Python standard library.

Qt relies heavily on named constants called **enums** or **flags** to represent things such as option settings or configuration values. For example, if you wanted to switch the state of a window between minimized, floating, or maximized, you would need to pass the window a constant that is found in the `QtCore.Qt.WindowState` enum.

Setting or retrieving values on Qt objects requires the use of **accessor** methods, sometimes known as setter and getter methods, rather than direct access to the properties.

To the Python programmer, Qt can seem to have an almost maniacal obsession with defining classes and constants, and you'll spend a lot of time early on searching the documentation to locate the item you need to configure your objects. Don't despair! You'll soon become acclimated to the Qt way of working.

Understanding Qt's documentation

Qt is such a vast and complex library that no print book could hope to document a significant portion of it in any detail. For that reason, it's important to learn how to access and understand the documentation available online. For Python programmers, this presents a minor challenge.

Qt itself is blessed with detailed and excellent documentation that documents all Qt modules and classes, including example code and high-level tutorials on coding with Qt. However, this documentation is all aimed at C++ development; all example code is in C++, and there is no indication when a methodology or approach to a problem differs for Python.

PyQt's documentation is considerably sparser. It only covers the Python-specific differences and lacks the comprehensive class reference, example code, and tutorials that make Qt's documentation great. It is an essential read for anyone working with PyQt, but it's by no means complete.

With the release of Qt for Python, there is an effort underway to port Qt's C++ documentation to Python at `https://doc-snapshots.qt.io/qtforpython/`. When finished, this will also be a valuable resource for PyQt programmers. At the time of writing, though, the effort is far from complete; in any case, there are minor differences between PyQt and Qt for Python that may make this documentation as confusing as it is helpful.

If you have a rudimentary knowledge of C++ syntax, it's not too difficult to mentally translate the Qt documentation to Python, though it can be confusing in many cases. One of the aims of this book is to close the gap for those who aren't well-versed in C++.

Core Qt modules

For the first six chapters of this book, we'll be working primarily with three Qt modules:

- `QtCore`, which contains low-level data wrapper classes, utility functions, and non-GUI core functionality
- `QtGui`, which contains GUI-specific data wrapper classes and utilities
- `QtWidgets`, which defines GUI widgets, layouts, and other high-level GUI components

Those three modules will be used in nearly any PyQt program we write. Later in the book, we will explore other modules for graphics, networking, web rendering, multimedia, and other advanced capabilities.

Creating Hello Qt – our first window

Now that you've learned about Qt5 and PyQt5, it's time to dig in and do some coding. Make sure everything is installed, open your favorite Python editor or IDE, and let's begin!

Create a `hello_world.py` file in your editor, and enter the following:

```
from PyQt5 import QtWidgets
```

We begin by importing the `QtWidgets` module. This module contains the bulk of the widget classes in Qt, as well as some other important components for GUI creation. We won't need `QtGui` or `QtCore` for such a simple application.

Next, we need to create a `QApplication` object, like this:

```
app = QtWidgets.QApplication([])
```

The `QApplication` object represents the state of our running application, and one must be created before any other Qt widgets can be created. `QApplication` is supposed to be passed a list of command-line arguments given to our script, but here we're just passing in an empty list.

Now, let's create our first widget:

```
window = QtWidgets.QWidget(windowTitle='Hello Qt')
```

In GUI toolkit terms, a **widget** refers to the visible components of the GUI, such as buttons, labels, text entries, or blank panels. The most generic widget in Qt is the `QWidget` object, which is just a blank window or panel. As we create this widget, we're settings its `windowTitle` to `'Hello Qt'`. `windowTitle` is what is known as **property**. All Qt objects and widgets have properties, which are used to configure different aspects of the widget. In this case, `windowTitle` is the name of the program window and appears in the window decorations, on the taskbar or dock, or wherever else your OS and desktop environment choose to use it.

 Unlike most Python libraries, Qt properties and methods are named using **camelCase** rather than **snake_case**.

The properties available for configuring a Qt object can be set by passing them as constructor arguments or using the appropriate setter method. Typically, this is just set plus the name of the property, so we could have written this:

```
window = QtWidgets.QWidget()
window.setWindowTitle('Hello Qt')
```

Properties can also be retrieved using the getter method, which is just the property name:

```
print(window.windowTitle())
```

Once a widget is created, we can make it appear by calling show(), as follows:

```
window.show()
```

Calling show() automatically makes window a top-level window of its own. In Chapter 2, *Building Forms with Qt Widgets*, you'll see how to place widgets inside other widgets, but, for this program, we only need one top-level widget.

The last line is a call to app.exec(), like this:

```
app.exec()
```

app.exec() begins the QApplication object **event loop.** The event loop will run forever until the application quits, processing our user interactions with the GUI. Note that the app object never refers to window, nor window to the app object. These objects are connected automatically in the background; you need only ensure that a QApplication object exists before creating any QWidget objects.

Save the hello_world.py file and run the script from your editor, or from a command line, like so:

```
python hello_world.py
```

When you run this, you should see a blank window whose title text is Hello Qt:

This isn't a terribly exciting application, but it does show us the basic workflow of any PyQt application:

1. Create a QApplication object
2. Create our main application window
3. Display our main application window
4. Call QApplication.exec() to start the event loop

 If you're experimenting with PyQt in the Python **Read-Eval-Print-Loop (REPL)**, create the QApplication object by passing in a list with a single empty string, like this: QtWidgets.QApplication(['']); otherwise, Qt will crash. Also, you don't need to call QApplication.exec() in the REPL, thanks to some special PyQt magic.

Creating a PyQt application template

hello_world.py demonstrated the bare minimum of code to get a Qt window on the screen, but it's a bit too simplistic to serve as a model for more complex applications. In this book, we're going to be creating many PyQt applications, so, to make things easier, we're going to compose a basic application template. Future chapters will refer to this template, so make sure to create it exactly as specified.

Open a new file called qt_template.py, and add in these imports:

```
import sys
from PyQt5 import QtWidgets as qtw
from PyQt5 import QtGui as qtg
from PyQt5 import QtCore as qtc
```

We'll start with importing sys, so that we can pass QApplication an actual list of script arguments; then we'll import our three main Qt modules. To save some typing, while avoiding star imports, we're going to alias them to abbreviated names. We'll be using these aliases consistently throughout the book as well.

Star imports (also called **wildcard imports**), such as `from PyQt5.QtWidgets import *`, are convenient and often seen in tutorials, but, in practice, they are best avoided. Doing this with a PyQt module will fill your namespace with hundreds of classes, functions, and constants, any of which you might accidentally overwrite with a variable name. Avoiding star imports will also help you to learn which modules contain which commonly used classes.

Next, we'll create a `MainWindow` class, as follows:

```
class MainWindow(qtw.QWidget):

    def __init__(self):
        """MainWindow constructor"""
        super().__init__()
        # Main UI code goes here

        # End main UI code
        self.show()
```

To make our `MainWindow` class, we subclass `QWidget`, then override the constructor method. Whenever we use this template in future chapters, start adding your code between the commented lines unless otherwise instructed.

Subclassing PyQt classes is a good way to approach GUI building. It allows us to customize and expand on Qt's powerful widget classes without having to reinvent the wheel. In many cases, subclassing is the only way to utilize certain classes or accomplish certain customizations.

Our constructor ends with a call to `self.show()`, so our `MainWindow` will take care of showing itself.

Always remember to call `super().__init__()` inside your child class's constructor, especially with Qt classes. Failing to do so means the parent class isn't properly set up and will undoubtedly cause very frustrating bugs.

We'll finish our template with the main code execution:

```
if __name__ == '__main__':
    app = qtw.QApplication(sys.argv)
    mw = MainWindow()
    sys.exit(app.exec())
```

In this code, we're going to create our `QApplication` object, make our `MainWindow` object, and then call `QApplication.exec()`. Although not strictly necessary, it's best practice to create the `QApplication` object at the global scope (outside of any function or class). This ensures that all Qt objects get properly closed and cleaned up when the application quits.

Notice that we're passing `sys.argv` into `QApplication()`; Qt has several default command-line arguments that can be used for debugging or to alter styles and themes. These are processed by the `QApplication` constructor if you pass in `sys.argv`.

Also, note that we're calling `app.exec()` inside a call to `sys.exit`; this is a small touch that causes the exit code of `app.exec()` to be passed to `sys.exit()`, so we pass appropriate exit codes to the OS, if the underlying Qt instance crashes for some reason.

Finally, note that we've wrapped this block in this check:

```
if __name__ == '__main__':
```

If you've never seen this before, it's a common Python idiom that simply means: only run this code if this script is called directly. By putting our main execution in this block, we could conceivably import this file into another Python script and be able to reuse our `MainWindow` class without running any of the code in this block.

If you run your template code, you should see a blank application window. In the following chapters, we'll be filling that window with various widgets and functionality.

Introducing Qt Designer

Before we wrap up our introduction to Qt, let's look at a free tool offered by the Qt company that can help us create PyQt applications—Qt Designer.

Qt Designer is a graphical **WYSIWYG GUI** designer for Qt. Using Qt Designer, you can drag and drop GUI components into an application and configure them without having to write any code at all. While it is certainly an optional tool, you may find it useful for prototyping, or preferable to hand-coding a large and complex GUI. While most of the code in this book will be hand-coded, we will be covering the use of Qt Designer with PyQt in Chapter 2, *Building Forms with Qt Widgets*, and Chapter 3, *Handling Events with Signals and Slots*.

Using Qt Designer

Let's take a moment to get familiar with how to launch and use Qt Designer:

1. Launch **Qt Creator**
2. Select **File | New File or Project**
3. Under **Files and Classes,** select **Qt**
4. Choose **Qt Designer Form**
5. Under **Choose a Template Form,** select **Widget,** then click **Next**
6. Give your form a name and click **Next**
7. Click **Finish**

You should see something that looks like this:

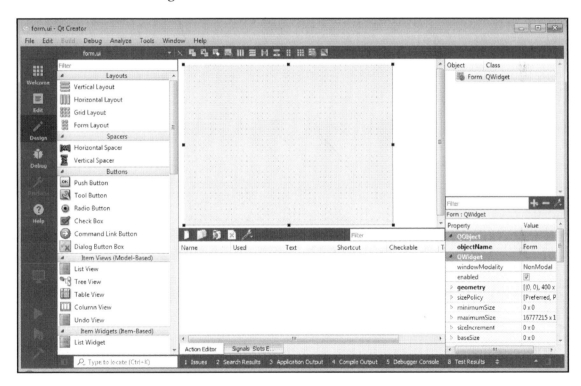

If you installed Qt Designer as a standalone application on Linux, launch it with the `designer` command or select it from your program's menu. You shouldn't need the previous steps.

Take a few minutes to test out Qt Designer:

- Drag some widgets from the left pane onto your base widget
- Resize the widgets if you wish, or select one and examine its properties in the lower-right pane
- When you've made several changes, select **Tools** | **Form Editor** | **Preview,** or hit *Alt + Shift + R*, to preview your GUI

In Chapter 2, *Building Forms with Qt Widgets*, we'll go into detail on how to use Qt Designer to build a GUI interface; for now, you can find out more information about Qt Designer from the manual at `https://doc.qt.io/qt-5/qtdesigner-manual.html`.

Summary

In this chapter, you learned about the Qt application framework and the PyQt Python bindings for Qt. We wrote a `Hello World` application and created a template for building larger Qt applications. Finally, we installed and took our first look at Qt Designer, the GUI editor.

In Chapter 2, *Building Forms with Qt Widgets*, we'll get familiar with some of the basic Qt widgets and learn how to resize and arrange them in a user interface. You'll then apply that knowledge by designing a calendar application in both code and Qt Designer.

Questions

Try these questions to test your knowledge from this chapter:

1. Qt is written in C++, a language that is very different from Python. What are some of the major differences between the two languages? How might these differences come across as we use Qt in Python?
2. GUIs are composed of widgets. Open some GUI applications on your computer and try to identify as many widgets as you can.

3. The following program crashes. Figure out why, and fix it so that it shows a
   window:

   ```
   from PyQt5.QtWidgets import *

   app = QWidget()
   app.show()
   QApplication().exec()
   ```

4. The `QWidget` class has a property called `statusTip`. Which of these are most
   likely to be the names of the accessor methods for this property?
   - a. `getStatusTip()` and `setStatusTip()`
   - b. `statusTip()` and `setStatusTip()`
   - c. `get_statusTip()` and `change_statusTip()`

5. `QDate` is a class for wrapping a calendar date. In which of the three main Qt
   modules would you expect to find it?

6. `QFont` is a class that defines a screen font. In which of the three main Qt modules
   would you expect to find it?

7. Can you recreate `hello_world.py` using Qt Designer? Make sure to set the
   `windowTitle`.

Further reading

Check out these resources for more information on Qt, PyQt, and Qt Designer:

- The **PyQt manual** at `http://pyqt.sourceforge.net/Docs/PyQt5/` is a handy
  resource for understanding PyQt's distinct aspects
- The **Qt module list** at `https://doc.qt.io/qt-5/qtmodules.html` gives a good
  rundown of the available modules in Qt
- The **QApplication** documentation at `https://doc.qt.io/qt-5/qapplication.`
  `html#QApplication` lists all the command-line switches parsed by the
  `QApplication` object
- The **QWidget** documentation at `https://doc.qt.io/qt-5/qwidget.html` shows
  the properties and methods available in the `QWidget` object
- The **Qt Designer manual** at `https://doc.qt.io/qt-5/qtdesigner-manual.html`
  will help you explore the full capabilities of Qt Designer
- If you want to understand more about C++, check out these offerings from
  Packt `https://www.packtpub.com/tech/C-plus-plus`

Building Forms with QtWidgets

2

One of the first steps in application development is prototyping your app's GUI. With a wide range of ready-to-use widgets, PyQt makes this very easy. Best of all, we can move our prototype code directly into an actual application when we're done.

In this chapter, we're going to get familiar with basic form design over the following topics:

- Creating basic QtWidgets widgets
- Placing and arranging widgets
- Validating widgets
- Building a calendar application GUI

Technical requirements

To complete this chapter, you'll need everything from Chapter 1, *Getting Started with PyQt*, plus the example code from https://github.com/PacktPublishing/Mastering-GUI-Programming-with-Python/tree/master/Chapter02.

Check out the following video to see the code in action: http://bit.ly/2M2R26r

Creating basic QtWidgets widgets

The QtWidgets module contains dozens of widgets, some simple and standard, others complex and unique. In this section, we're going to go through eight of the most common widgets and their basic usage.

Before starting this section, make a copy of your application template from Chapter 1, *Getting Started with PyQt*, and save it to a file called widget_demo.py. As we go through the examples, you can add them into your MainWindow.__init__() method to see how the objects work.

QWidget

`QWidget` is the parent class of all other widgets, so any properties and methods it has will also be available in any other widget. By itself, a `QWidget` object can be useful as a container for other widgets, a filler to fill blank areas, or as a base class for top-level windows.

Creating a widget is as simple as this:

```
# inside MainWindow.__init__()
subwidget = qtw.QWidget(self)
```

Notice we've passed `self` as an argument. If we're creating a widget to be placed on or used inside another widget class, as we are here, it's a good idea to pass a reference to the parent widget as the first argument. Specifying a parent widget will ensure that the child widget is destroyed and cleaned up when the parent is, and limit its visibility to inside the parent widget.

As you learned in `Chapter 1`, *Getting Started with PyQt*, PyQt also allows us to specify values for any of the widget's properties.

For example, we can use the `toolTip` property to set the tooltip text (which will pop up when the widget has hovered with the mouse) for this widget:

```
subwidget = qtw.QWidget(self, toolTip='This is my widget')
```

Read the C++ documentation for `QWidget` (found at `https://doc.qt.io/qt-5/qwidget.html`) and note the class's properties. Note that each property has a specified data type. In this case, `toolTip` requires `QString`. We can use a regular Unicode string whenever `QString` is required because PyQt translates it for us. For more esoteric data types, such as `QSize` or `QColor`, we would need to create the appropriate object. Be aware that these conversions are happening in the background, however, as Qt is not forgiving about data types.

For example, this code results in an error:

```
subwidget = qtw.QWidget(self, toolTip=b'This is my widget')
```

This would result in `TypeError` because PyQt won't convert a `bytes` object into `QString`. Because of this, make sure you check the data type required by a widget's properties or method calls and use a compatible type.

QWidget as a top-level window

When a `QWidget` is created without a parent and its `show()` method is called, it becomes a top-level window. When we use it as a top-level window, such as we do with our `MainWindow` instance, there are some window-specific properties we can set. Some of these are shown in the following table:

Property	Argument type	Description
windowTitle	string	The title of the window.
windowIcon	QIcon	The icon for the window.
modal	Boolean	Whether the window is modal.
cursor	Qt.CursorShape	The cursor used when this widget has hovered.
windowFlags	Qt.WindowFlags	How the OS should treat the window (dialog, tooltip, popup).

The argument type for `cursor` is an example of an enum. An enum is simply a list of named values, and Qt defines enum anywhere that a property is limited to a set of descriptive values. The argument for `windowFlags` is an example of a flag. Flags are like enums, except that they can be combined (using the pipe operator, `|`) so that multiple flags can be passed.

In this case, both the enum and flag are part of the `Qt` namespace, found in the `QtCore` module. So, for example, to set the cursor to an arrow cursor when the widget is hovered over, you'd need to find the right constant in `Qt` that refers to the arrow cursor and set the widget's `cursor` property to that value. To set flags on the window indicating to the OS that it's a `sheet` and `popup` window, you'd need to find the constants in `Qt` that represent those window flags, combine them with the pipe, and pass it as the value for `windowFlags`.

Creating such a `QWidget` window might look like this:

```
window = qtw.QWidget(cursor=qtc.Qt.ArrowCursor)
window.setWindowFlags(qtc.Qt.Sheet|qtc.Qt.Popup)
```

We'll encounter many more flags and enums as we learn to configure Qt widgets throughout the rest of this book.

QLabel

`QLabel` is a `QWidget` object configured to display simple text and images.

Creating one looks like this:

```
label = qtw.QLabel('Hello Widgets!', self)
```

Notice this time that the parent widget is specified as the second argument, while the first argument is the text of the label.

Some commonly used `QLabel` properties are shown here:

Property	Argument	Description
text	string	Text to display on the label.
margin	integer	Space (in pixels) around the text.
indent	integer	Space (in pixels) to indent the text.
wordWrap	Boolean	Whether to wrap long lines.
textFormat	Qt.TextFormat	Force plaintext or rich text, or auto-detect.
pixmap	QPixmap	An image to display instead of the text.

The label's text is stored in its `text` property so it can be accessed or changed using the related accessor methods, like this:

```
label.setText("Hi There, Widgets!")
print(label.text())
```

`QLabel` can display plaintext, rich text, or an image. Rich text in Qt uses an HTML-like syntax; by default, the label will automatically detect whether your string contains any formatting tags and display the appropriate type of text accordingly. For example, if we wanted to make our label boldface and add a margin around the text, we could do so like this:

```
label = qtw.QLabel('<b>Hello Widgets!</b>', self, margin=10)
```

We will learn more about using images, rich text, and fonts in Chapter 6, *Styling Qt Applications*, and Chapter 11, *Creating Rich Text with QTextDocument*.

QLineEdit

The QLineEdit class is a single-line text-entry widget that you might commonly use in a data-entry or login form. QLineEdit can be called with no arguments, with only a parent widget, or with a default string value as the first argument, like so:

```
line_edit = qtw.QLineEdit('default value', self)
```

There are also a number of properties we can pass in:

Property	Arguments	Description
text	string	The contents of the box.
readOnly	Boolean	Whether the field can be edited.
clearButtonEnabled	Boolean	Whether a clear button is added.
placeholderText	string	Text that will appear when the field is empty.
maxLength	integer	The maximum number of characters that can be entered.
echoMode	QLineEdit.EchoMode	Switches the way text is displayed as its entered (such as for password entry).

Let's add some properties to our line edit widget:

```
line_edit = qtw.QLineEdit(
    'default value',
    self,
    placeholderText='Type here',
    clearButtonEnabled=True,
    maxLength=20
)
```

This will populate the widget with a default text of 'default value'. It will display a placeholder string of 'Type here' when the field is empty or a small X button that clears the field when it has text in it. It also limits the number of characters that can be typed to 20.

QPushButton and other buttons

QPushButton is a simple, clickable button widget. Like QLabel and QLineEdit, it can be called with a first argument that specifies the text on the button, like so:

```
button = qtw.QPushButton("Push Me", self)
```

Some of the more useful properties we can set on `QPushButton` include the following:

Property	Arguments	Description
checkable	Boolean	Whether the button stays on when pressed.
checked	Boolean	For `checkable` buttons, whether the button is checked.
icon	QIcon	An icon image to display on the button.
shortcut	QKeySequence	A keyboard shortcut that will activate the button.

The `checkable` and `checked` properties allow us to use this button as a toggle button that reflects an on/off state, rather than just a click button that performs an action. All of these properties come from the `QPushButton` class's parent class, `QAbstractButton`. This is also the parent class of several other button classes, listed here:

Class	Description
QCheckBox	A checkbox can be Boolean for on/off or tristate for on/partially on/off.
QRadioButton	Like checkbox, but only one button among those with the same parent can be checked.
QToolButton	Special button for use on toolbar widgets.

Though each has some unique features, for the core functionality, these buttons are the same in terms of how we create and configure them.

Let's make our button checkable, check it by default, and give it a shortcut:

```
button = qtw.QPushButton(
    "Push Me",
    self,
    checkable=True,
    checked=True,
    shortcut=qtg.QKeySequence('Ctrl+p')
)
```

Note that the `shortcut` option requires us to pass in a `QKeySequence`, which is part of the `QtGui` module. This is a good example of how property arguments often need to be wrapped in some kind of utility class. `QKeySequence` encapsulates a key combination, in this case, the *Ctrl* key (or *command* key, on macOS) and *P*.

 Key sequences can be specified as a string, such as the preceding example, or by using enum values from the `QtCore.Qt` module. For example, we could write the preceding as `QKeySequence(qtc.Qt.CTRL + qtc.Qt.Key_P)`.

QComboBox

A **combobox**, also known as a dropdown or select widget, is a widget that presents a list of options when clicked on, one of which must be selected. QCombobox can optionally allow text input for custom answers by setting its `editable` property to `True`.

Let's create a QCombobox object like so:

```
combobox = qtw.QComboBox(self)
```

Right now, our `combobox` has no items in its menu. QCombobox doesn't provide a way to initialize the widget with options in the constructor; instead, we have to create the widget, then use the `addItem()` or `insertItem()` method to populate its menu with options, like so:

```
combobox.addItem('Lemon', 1)
combobox.addItem('Peach', 'Ohh I like Peaches!')
combobox.addItem('Strawberry', qtw.QWidget)
combobox.insertItem(1, 'Radish', 2)
```

The `addItem()` method takes a string for the label and a data value. As you can see, this value can be anything—an integer, a string, a Python class. This value can be retrieved for the currently selected item using the QCombobox object's `currentData()` method. It's typically a good idea—though not required—to make all the item values be of the same type.

`addItem()` will always append items to the end of the menu; to insert them earlier, use the `insertItem()` method. It works exactly the same, except that it takes an index (integer value) for the first argument. The item will be inserted at that index in the list. If we want to save time and don't need a `data` property for our items, we can also use `addItems()` or `insertItems()` to pass in a list of options.

Some other important properties for QComboBox include the following:

Property	Arguments	Description
currentData	(anything)	The data object of the currently selected item.
currentIndex	integer	The index of the currently selected item.
currentText	string	The text of the currently selected item.
editable	Boolean	Whether combobox allows text entry.
insertPolicy	QComboBox.InsertPolicy	Where entered items should be inserted in the list.

The data type for `currentData` is `QVariant`, a special Qt class that acts as a container for any kind of data. These are more useful in C++, as they provide a workaround for static typing in situations where multiple data types might be useful. PyQt automatically converts `QVariant` objects to the most appropriate Python type, so we rarely need to work directly with this type.

Let's update our `combobox` so that we can add items to the top of the dropdown:

```
combobox = qtw.QComboBox(
    self,
    editable=True,
    insertPolicy=qtw.QComboBox.InsertAtTop
)
```

Now this `combobox` will allow any text to be typed in; the text will be added to the top of the list box. The `data` property for the new items will be `None`, so this is really only appropriate if we are working with the visible strings only.

QSpinBox

In general, a spinbox is a text entry with arrow buttons designed to *spin* through a set of incremental values. `QSpinbox` is built specifically to handle either integers or discrete values (such as a combobox).

Some useful `QSpinBox` properties include the following:

Property	Arguments	Description
value	integer	The current spinbox value, as an integer.
cleanText	string	The current spinbox value, as a string (excludes the prefix and suffix).
maximum	integer	The maximum integer value of the box.
minimum	integer	The minimum value of the box.
prefix	string	A string to prepend to the displayed value.
suffix	string	A string to append to the displayed value.
singleStep	integer	How much to increment or decrement the value when the arrows are used.
wrapping	Boolean	Whether to wrap from one end of the range to the other when the arrows are used.

Let's create a `QSpinBox` object in our script, like this:

```
spinbox = qtw.QSpinBox(
    self,
    value=12,
    maximum=100,
    minimum=10,
    prefix='$',
    suffix=' + Tax',
    singleStep=5
)
```

This spinbox starts with a value of `12` and will allow entry of integers from `10` to `100`, displayed in the `$<value> + Tax` format. Note that the non-integer portion of the box is not editable. Also note that, while the increment and decrement arrows move by `5`, nothing prevents us from entering a value that is not a multiple of `5`.

`QSpinBox` will automatically ignore keystrokes that are not numeric, or that would put the value outside the acceptable range. If a value is typed that is too low, it will be auto-corrected to a valid value when the focus moves from the `spinbox`; for example, if you typed `9` into the preceding box and clicked out of it, it would be auto-corrected to `90`.

 `QDoubleSpinBox` is identical to `QSpinBox`, but designed for a decimal or floating-point numbers.

To use `QSpinBox` for discrete text values instead of integers, you need to subclass it and override its validation methods. We'll do that later in the *Validating widgets* section.

QDateTimeEdit

A close relative of the spinbox is `QDateTimeEdit`, designed for entering date-time values. By default, it appears as a spinbox that allows the user to tab through each field in the date-time value and increment/decrement it using the arrows. The widget can also be configured to use a calendar popup.

The more useful properties include the following:

Property	Arguments	Description
date	QDate or datetime.date	The date value.
time	QTime or datetime.time	The time value.
dateTime	QDateTime or datetime.datetime	The combined date-time value.
maximumDate, minimumDate	QDate or datetime.date	The maximum and minimum date enterable.
maximumTime, minimumTime	QTime or datetime.time	The maximum and minimum time enterable.
maximumDateTime, minimumDateTime	QDateTime or datetime.datetime	The maximum and minimum date-time enterable.
calendarPopup	Boolean	Whether to display the calendar popup or behave like a spinbox.
displayFormat	string	How the date-time should be formatted.

Let's create our date-time box like this:

```
datetimebox = qtw.QDateTimeEdit(
    self,
    date=qtc.QDate.currentDate(),
    time=qtc.QTime(12, 30),
    calendarPopup=True,
    maximumDate=qtc.QDate(2030, 1, 1),
    maximumTime=qtc.QTime(17, 0),
    displayFormat='yyyy-MM-dd HH:mm'
)
```

This date-time widget will be created with the following attributes:

- It will be set to 12:30 on the current date
- It will show the calendar popup when focused
- It will disallow dates after January 1st, 2030
- It will disallow times after 17:00 (5 PM) on the maximum date
- It will display date-times in the year-month-day hour-minutes format

Note that `maximumTime` and `minimumTime` only impact the `maximumDate` and `minimumDate` values, respectively. So, even though we've specified a maximum time of 17:00, nothing prevents you from entering 18:00 as long as it's before January 1st, 2030. The same concept applies to minimum dates and times.

The display format for the date-time is set using a string that contains specific substitution codes for each item. Some of the more common codes are listed here:

Code	Meaning
d	Day of the month.
M	Month number.
yy	Two-digit year.
yyyy	Four-digit year.
h	Hour.
m	Minute.
s	Second.
A	AM/PM, if used, hour will switch to 12-hour time.

Day, month, hour, minute, and second all default to omitting the leading zero. To get a leading zero, just double up the letter (for example, dd for a day with a leading zero). A complete list of the codes can be found at `https://doc.qt.io/qt-5/qdatetime.html`.

Note that all times, dates, and date-times can accept objects from the Python standard library's `datetime` module as well as the Qt types. So, our box could just as well have been created like this:

```
import datetime
datetimebox = qtw.QDateTimeEdit(
    self,
    date=datetime.date.today(),
    time=datetime.time(12, 30),
    calendarPopup=True,
    maximumDate=datetime.date(2020, 1, 1),
    minimumTime=datetime.time(8, 0),
    maximumTime=datetime.time(17, 0),
    displayFormat='yyyy-MM-dd HH:mm'
)
```

Which one you choose to use is a matter of personal preference or situational requirements. For instance, if you are working with other Python modules, the `datetime` standard library objects are going to be more compatible. If you just need to set a default value for a widget, `QDateTime` may be more convenient, since you likely already have `QtCore` imported.

If you need more control over the date and time entry, or just want to split these up, Qt has the `QTimeEdit` and `QDateEdit` widgets. They're just like this widget, except they only handle time and date, respectively.

QTextEdit

While `QLineEdit` exists for single-line strings, `QTextEdit` provides us with the capability to enter multi-line text. `QTextEdit` is much more than just a simple plaintext entry, though; it's a full-blown WYSIWYG editor that can be configured to support rich text and images.

Some of the more useful properties of `QTextEdit` are shown here:

Property	Arguments	Description
plainText	string	The contents of the box, in plaintext.
html	string	The contents of the box, as rich text.
acceptRichText	Boolean	Whether the box allows rich text.
lineWrapColumnOrWidth	integer	The pixel or column at which the text will be wrapped.
lineWrapMode	QTextEdit.LineWrapMode	Whether the line wrap uses columns or pixels.
overwriteMode	Boolean	Whether overwrite is activated; False means insert mode.
placeholderText	string	Text to display when the field is empty.
readOnly	Boolean	Whether the field is read-only.

Let's create a text edit like this:

```
textedit = qtw.QTextEdit(
    self,
    acceptRichText=False,
    lineWrapMode=qtw.QTextEdit.FixedColumnWidth,
    lineWrapColumnOrWidth=25,
    placeholderText='Enter your text here'
    )
```

This will create a plaintext editor that only allows 25 characters to be typed per line, with the phrase `'Enter your text here'` displayed when it's empty.

We'll dig in deeper to the `QTextEdit` and rich text documents in Chapter 11, *Creating Rich Text with QTextDocument*.

Placing and arranging widgets

So far, we've created a lot of widgets, but if you run the program you won't see any of them. Although our widgets all belong to the parent window, they haven't been placed on it yet. In this section, we'll learn how to arrange our widgets in the application window and set them to an appropriate size.

Layout classes

A layout object defines how child widgets are arranged on a parent widget. Qt offers a variety of layout classes, each of which has a layout strategy appropriate for different situations.

The workflow for using layout classes goes like this:

1. Create a layout object from an appropriate layout class
2. Assign the layout object to the parent widget's `layout` property using the `setLayout()` method
3. Add widgets to the layout using the layout's `addWidget()` method

You can also add layouts to a layout using the `addLayout()` method to create more complex arrangements of widgets. Let's take a tour of a few of the basic layout classes offered by Qt.

QHBoxLayout and QVBoxLayout

`QHBoxLayout` and `QVBoxLayout` are both derived from `QBoxLayout`, a very basic layout engine that simply divides the parent into horizontal or vertical boxes and places widgets sequentially as they're added. `QHBoxLayout` is oriented horizontally, and widgets are placed from left to right as added. `QVBoxLayout` is oriented vertically, and widgets are placed from top to bottom as added.

Let's try `QVBoxLayout` on our `MainWindow` widget:

```
layout = qtw.QVBoxLayout()
self.setLayout(layout)
```

Once the layout object exists, we can start adding our widgets to it using the `addWidget()` method:

```
layout.addWidget(label)
layout.addWidget(line_edit)
```

As you can see, if you run the program, the widgets are added one per line. If we wanted to add several widgets to a single line, we could nest a layout inside our layout, like this:

```
sublayout = qtw.QHBoxLayout()
layout.addLayout(sublayout)

sublayout.addWidget(button)
sublayout.addWidget(combobox)
```

Here, we've added a horizontal layout to the next cell of our main vertical layout and then inserted three more widgets to the sub-layout. These three widgets display side by side in a single line of the main layout. Most application layouts can be accomplished by simply nesting box layouts in this manner.

QGridLayout

Nested box layouts cover a lot of ground, but in some situations, you might like to arrange widgets in uniform rows and columns. This is where `QGridLayout` comes in handy. As the name suggests, it allows you to place widgets in a table-like structure.

Create a grid layout object like this:

```
grid_layout = qtw.QGridLayout()
layout.addLayout(grid_layout)
```

Adding widgets to `QGridLayout` is similar to the method for the `QBoxLayout` classes, but also requires passing coordinates:

```
grid_layout.addWidget(spinbox, 0, 0)
grid_layout.addWidget(datetimebox, 0, 1)
grid_layout.addWidget(textedit, 1, 0, 2, 2)
```

Here are the arguments for `QGridLayout.addWidget()`, in order:

1. The widget to add
2. The row number (vertical coordinate), starting from 0
3. The column number (horizontal coordinate), starting from 0

4. The row span, or how many rows the widget will encompass (optional)
5. The column span, or how many columns the widget will encompass (optional)

Thus, our `spinbox` widget is placed at row 0, column 0, which is the top left; our `datetimebox` at row 0, column 1, which is the top right; and our `textedit` at row 1, column 0, and it spans two rows and two columns.

Keep in mind that the grid layout keeps consistent widths on all columns and consistent heights on all rows. Thus, if you place a very wide widget in row 2, column 1, all widgets in all rows that happen to be in column 1 will be stretched accordingly. If you want each cell to stretch independently, use nested box layouts instead.

QFormLayout

When creating data-entry forms, it's common to have labels next to the input widgets they label. Qt provides a convenient two-column grid layout for this situation called `QFormLayout`.

Let's add a form layout to our GUI:

```
form_layout = qtw.QFormLayout()
layout.addLayout(form_layout)
```

Adding widgets can be easily done with the `addRow()` method:

```
form_layout.addRow('Item 1', qtw.QLineEdit(self))
form_layout.addRow('Item 2', qtw.QLineEdit(self))
form_layout.addRow(qtw.QLabel('<b>This is a label-only row</b>'))
```

This convenience method takes a string and a widget and automatically creates the `QLabel` widget for the string. If passed only a single widget (such as a `QLabel`), the widget spans both columns. This can be useful for headings or section labels.

`QFormLayout` is not just a mere convenience over `QGridLayout`, it also automatically provides idiomatic behavior when used across different platforms. For example, when used on Windows, the labels are left-justified; when used on macOS, the labels are right-justified, keeping with the design guidelines of the platform. Additionally, when viewed on a narrow screen (such as a mobile device), the layout automatically collapses to a single column with the labels above the input. It's definitely worthwhile to use this layout any time you have a two-column form.

Controlling widget size

If you run our demo as it currently is and expand it to fill your screen, you'll notice that each cell of the main layout gets evenly stretched to fill the screen, as shown here:

This isn't ideal. The label at the top really doesn't need to be expanded, and there is a lot of wasted space at the bottom. Presumably, if a user were to expand this window, they'd do so to get more space in input widgets like our `QTextEdit`. We need to give the GUI some guidance on how to size our widgets, and how to resize them in the event that the window is expanded or shrunk from its default size.

Controlling the size of widgets can be a bit perplexing in any toolkit, but Qt's approach can be especially confusing, so let's take it one step at a time.

We can simply set a fixed size for any widget using its `setFixedSize()` method, like this:

```
# Fix at 150 pixels wide by 40 pixels high
label.setFixedSize(150, 40)
```

`setFixedSize` accepts only pixel values, and a widget set to a fixed size cannot be altered from those pixel sizes under any circumstances. The problem with sizing a widget this way is that it doesn't account for the possibility of different fonts, different text sizes, or changes to the size or layout of the application window, which might result in the widget being too small for its contents, or needlessly large. We can make it slightly more flexible by setting `minimumSize` and `maximumSize`, like this:

```
# setting minimum and maximum sizes
line_edit.setMinimumSize(150, 15)
line_edit.setMaximumSize(500, 50)
```

If you run this code and resize the window, you'll notice `line_edit` has a bit more flexibility as the window expands and contracts. Note, however, that the widget won't shrink below its `minimumSize`, but it won't necessarily use its `maximumSize`, even if the room is available.

So, this is still far from ideal. Rather than concern ourselves with how many pixels each widget consumes, we'd prefer it be sized sensibly and fluidly with respect to its contents and role within the interface. Qt does just this using the concepts of *size hints* and *size polices*.

A size hint is a suggested size for a widget and is returned by the widget's `sizeHint()` method. This size may be based on a variety of dynamic factors; for example, the `QLabel` widget's `sizeHint()` value depends on the length and wrap of the text it contains. Because it's a method and not a property, setting a custom `sizeHint()` for a widget requires you to subclass the widget and reimplement the method. Fortunately, this isn't something we often need to do.

A size policy defines how the widget responds to a resizing request with respect to its size hint. This is set as the `sizePolicy` property of a widget. Size policies are defined in the `QtWidgets.QSizePolicy.Policy` enum, and set separately for the horizontal and vertical dimensions of a widget using the `setSizePolicy` accessor method. The available policies are listed here:

Policy	Description
Fixed	Never grow or shrink.
Minimum	Don't get smaller than `sizeHint`. Expanding isn't useful.
Maximum	Don't get larger than `sizeHint`, shrink if necessary.

Policy	Description
Preferred	Try to be `sizeHint`, but shrink if necessary. Expanding isn't useful. This is the default.
Expanding	Try to be `sizeHint`, shrink if necessary, but expand if at all possible.
MinimumExpanding	Don't get smaller than `sizeHint`, but expand if at all possible.
Ignored	Forget `sizeHint` altogether, just take up as much space as possible.

So, for example, if we'd like the spinbox to stay at a fixed width so the widget next to it can expand, we would do this:

```
spinbox.setSizePolicy(qtw.QSizePolicy.Fixed, qtw.QSizePolicy.Preferred)
```

Or, if we'd like our `textedit` widget to fill as much of the screen as possible, but never shrink below its `sizeHint()` value, we should set its policies like this:

```
textedit.setSizePolicy(
    qtw.QSizePolicy.MinimumExpanding,
    qtw.QSizePolicy.MinimumExpanding
)
```

Sizing widgets can be somewhat unpredictable when you have deeply-nested layouts; sometimes it's handy to be able to override `sizeHint()`. In Python, a quick way to do this is with Lambda functions, like this:

```
textedit.sizeHint = lambda : qtc.QSize(500, 500)
```

Note that `sizeHint()` must return a `QtCore.QSize` object, not just an integer tuple.

A final way to control the size of widgets when using a box layout is to set a `stretch` factor when adding the widget to the layout. Stretch is an optional second parameter of `addWidget()` that defines the comparative stretch of each widget.

This example shows the use of the `stretch` factor:

```
stretch_layout = qtw.QHBoxLayout()
layout.addLayout(stretch_layout)
stretch_layout.addWidget(qtw.QLineEdit('Short'), 1)
stretch_layout.addWidget(qtw.QLineEdit('Long'), 2)
```

 `stretch` only works with the `QHBoxLayout` and `QVBoxLayout` classes.

In this example, we've added a line edit with a stretch factor of 1, and a second with a stretch factor of 2. When you run this, you'll find that the second line edit is about twice the length of the first.

Keep in mind that stretch doesn't override the size hint or size policies, so depending on those factors the stretch ratios may not be exactly as specified.

Container widgets

We have seen that we can use QWidget as a container for other widgets. Qt also provides us with some special widgets that are specifically designed to contain other widgets. We'll look at two of these: QTabWidget and QGroupBox.

QTabWidget

QTabWidget, sometimes known as a **notebook widget** in other toolkits, allows us to have multiple *pages* selectable by tabs. They're very useful for breaking complex interfaces into smaller chunks that are easier for users to take in.

The workflow for using QTabWidget is as follows:

1. Create the QTabWidget object
2. Build a UI page on a QWidget or other widget class
3. Add the page to the tab widget using the QTabWidget.addTab() method

Let's try that; first, create the tab widget:

```
tab_widget = qtw.QTabWidget()
layout.addWidget(tab_widget)
```

Next, let's move the grid_layout we built under the *Placing and arranging widgets* section to a container widget:

```
container = qtw.QWidget(self)
grid_layout = qtw.QGridLayout()
# comment out this line:
#layout.addLayout(grid_layout)
container.setLayout(grid_layout)
```

Finally, let's add our container widget to a new tab:

```
tab_widget.addTab(container, 'Tab the first')
```

The second argument to `addTab()` is the title text that will appear on the tab. Subsequent tabs can be added with more calls to `addTab()`, like this:

```
tab_widget.addTab(subwidget, 'Tab the second')
```

The `insertTab()` method can also be used to add new tabs somewhere other than the end.

`QTabWidget` has a few properties we can customize, listed here:

Property	Arguments	Description
`movable`	Boolean	Whether the tabs can be reordered. The default is `False`.
`tabBarAutoHide`	Boolean	Whether the tab bar is hidden or shown when there is only one tab.
`tabPosition`	`QTabWidget.TabPosition`	Which side of the widget the tabs appear on. The default is North (top).
`tabShape`	`QTabWidget.TabShape`	The shape of the tabs. It can be rounded or triangular.
`tabsClosable`	Boolean	Whether to display a close button on the tabs.
`useScrollButtons`	Boolean	Whether to use scroll buttons when there are many tabs or to expand.

Let's amend our `QTabWidget` to have movable, triangular tabs on the left side of the widget:

```
tab_widget = qtw.QTabWidget(
    movable=True,
    tabPosition=qtw.QTabWidget.West,
    tabShape=qtw.QTabWidget.Triangular
)
```

> `QStackedWidget` is similar to the tab widget, except that it contains no built-in mechanism for switching pages. You may find it useful if you want to build your own tab-switching mechanism.

QGroupBox

`QGroupBox` provides a panel that is labeled and (depending on the platform style) bordered. It's useful for grouping related input together on a form. We create the `QGroupBox` just as we would create a `QWidget` container, except that it can have a border and a title for the box, for example:

```
groupbox = qtw.QGroupBox('Buttons')
```

```
groupbox.setLayout(qtw.QHBoxLayout())
groupbox.layout().addWidget(qtw.QPushButton('OK'))
groupbox.layout().addWidget(qtw.QPushButton('Cancel'))
layout.addWidget(groupbox)
```

Here, we create a group box with the `Buttons` title. We gave it a horizontal layout and added two button widgets.

 Notice in this example, instead of giving the layout a handle of its own as we've been doing, we create an anonymous `QHBoxLayout` and then use the widget's `layout()` accessor method to retrieve a reference to it for adding widgets. You may prefer this approach in certain situations.

The group box is fairly simple, but it does have a few interesting properties:

Property	Argument	Description
title	string	The title text.
checkable	Boolean	Whether the groupbox has a checkbox to enable/disable its contents.
checked	Boolean	Whether a checkable groupbox is checked (enabled).
alignment	QtCore.Qt.Alignment	The alignment of the title text.
flat	Boolean	Whether the box is flat or has a frame.

The `checkable` and `checked` properties are very useful for situations where you want a user to be able to disable entire sections of a form (for example, to disable the billing address part of an order form if it's the same as shipping address).

Let's reconfigure our `groupbox`, like so:

```
groupbox = qtw.QGroupBox(
    'Buttons',
    checkable=True,
    checked=True,
    alignment=qtc.Qt.AlignHCenter,
    flat=True
)
```

Notice that now the buttons can be disabled with a simple checkbox toggle, and the frame has a different look.

 If you just want a bordered widget without a label or checkbox capabilities, the `QFrame` class might be a better alternative.

Validating widgets

Although Qt provides a wide range of ready-made input widgets for things such as dates and numbers, we may find sometimes that we need a widget with very specific constraints on its input values. Such input constraints can be created using the `QValidator` class.

The workflow is like this:

1. Create a custom validator class by subclassing `QtGui.QValidator`
2. Override the `validate()` method with our validation logic
3. Assign an instance of our custom class to a widget's `validator` property

Once assigned to an editable widget, the `validate()` method will be called every time the user updates the value of the widget (for example, every keystroke in `QLineEdit`) and will determine whether the input is accepted.

Creating an IPv4 entry widget

To demonstrate widget validation, let's create a widget that validates **Internet Protocol version 4 (IPv4)** addresses. An IPv4 address must be in the format of 4 integers, each between 0 and 255, with a dot between each number.

Let's start by creating our validator class. Add this class just before the `MainWindow` class:

```
class IPv4Validator(qtg.QValidator):
    """Enforce entry of IPv4 Addresses"""
```

Next, we need to override this class's `validate()` method. `validate()` receives two pieces of information: a string that contains the proposed input and the index at which the input occurred. It will have to return a value that indicates whether the input is `Acceptable`, `Intermediate`, or `Invalid`. If the input is acceptable or intermediate, it will be accepted. If it's invalid, it will be rejected.

The value used to indicate the input state is either `QtValidator.Acceptable`, `QtValidator.Intermediate`, or `QtValidator.Invalid`.

In the Qt documentation, we're told that the validator class should only return the state constant. In PyQt, however, you actually need to return a tuple that contains the state, the string, and the position. This doesn't seem to be well-documented, unfortunately, and the error if you should forget this is not intuitive at all.

Let's start building our IPv4 validation logic as follows:

1. Split the string on the dot character:

    ```
    def validate(self, string, index):
        octets = string.split('.')
    ```

2. If there are more than 4 segments, the value is invalid:

    ```
    if len(octets) > 4:
        state = qtg.QValidator.Invalid
    ```

3. If any populated segment is not a digit string, the value is invalid:

    ```
    elif not all([x.isdigit() for x in octets if x != '']):
        state = qtg.QValidator.Invalid
    ```

4. If not every populated segment can be converted into an integer between 0 and 255, the value is invalid:

    ```
    elif not all([0 <= int(x) <= 255 for x in octets if x != '']):
        state = qtg.QValidator.Invalid
    ```

5. If we've made it this far into the checks, the value is either intermediate or valid. If there are fewer than four segments, it's intermediate:

    ```
    elif len(octets) < 4:
        state = qtg.QValidator.Intermediate
    ```

6. If there are any empty segments, the value is intermediate:

    ```
    elif any([x == '' for x in octets]):
        state = qtg.QValidator.Intermediate
    ```

7. If the value has passed all these tests, it's acceptable. We can return our tuple:

    ```
    else:
        state = qtg.QValidator.Acceptable
    return (state, string, index)
    ```

To use this validator, we just need to create an instance of it and assign it to a widget:

```
# set the default text to a valid value
line_edit.setText('0.0.0.0')
line_edit.setValidator(IPv4Validator())
```

If you run the demo now, you'll see that the line edit now constrains you to a valid IPv4 address.

Using QSpinBox for discrete values

As you learned earlier under the *Creating basic QtWidgets widgets* section, QSpinBox can be used for discrete lists of string values, much like a combobox. QSpinBox has a built-in validate() method that works just like the QValidator class' method to constrain input to the widget. To make a spinbox use discrete string lists, we need to subclass QSpinBox and override validate() and two other methods, valueFromText() and textFromValue().

Let's create a custom spinbox class that can be used to choose items from a list; just before the MainWindow class, enter this:

```python
class ChoiceSpinBox(qtw.QSpinBox):
    """A spinbox for selecting choices."""

    def __init__(self, choices, *args, **kwargs):
        self.choices = choices
        super().__init__(
            *args,
            maximum=len(self.choices) - 1,
            minimum=0,
            **kwargs
        )
```

We're subclassing qtw.QSpinBox and overriding the constructor so that we can pass in a list or tuple of choices, storing it as self.choices. Then we call the QSpinBox constructor; note that we set the maximum and minimum so that they can't be set outside the bounds of our choices. We're also passing along any extra positional or keyword arguments so that we can take advantage of all the other QSpinBox property settings.

Next, let's reimplement valueFromText(), as follows:

```python
def valueFromText(self, text):
    return self.choices.index(text)
```

The purpose of this method is to be able to return an integer index value given a string that matches one of the displayed choices. We're simply returning the list index of whatever string is passed in.

Next, we need to reimplement the complimentary method, `textFromValue()`:

```
def textFromValue(self, value):
    try:
        return self.choices[value]
    except IndexError:
        return '!Error!'
```

The purpose of this method is to translate an integer index value into the text of the matching choice. In this case, we're just returning the string at the given index. If somehow the widget gets passed a value out of range, we're returning `!Error!` as a string. Since this method is used to determine what is displayed in the box when a particular value is set, this would clearly show an error condition if somehow the value were out of range.

Finally, we need to take care of `validate()`. Just as we did with our `QValidator` class, we need to create a method that takes the proposed input and edit index and returns a tuple that contains the validation state, string value, and index.

We'll code it like this:

```
def validate(self, string, index):
    if string in self.choices:
        state = qtg.QValidator.Acceptable
    elif any([v.startswith(string) for v in self.choices]):
        state = qtg.QValidator.Intermediate
    else:
        state = qtg.QValidator.Invalid
    return (state, string, index)
```

In our method, we're returning `Acceptable` if the input string is found in `self.choices`, `Intermediate` if any choice starts with the input string (this includes a blank string), or `Invalid` in any other case.

With this class created, we can create one of our widgets in our `MainWindow` class:

```
ratingbox = ChoiceSpinBox(
    ['bad', 'average', 'good', 'awesome'],
    self
)
sublayout.addWidget(ratingbox)
```

An important difference between a `QComboBox` object and a `QSpinBox` object with text options is that the spinbox items lack a `data` property. Only the text or index can be returned. It's best used for things such as months, days of the week, or other sequential lists that translate meaningfully into integer values.

Building a calendar application GUI

It's time to put what we've learned into action and actually build a simple, functional GUI. Our goal is to build a simple calendar application that looks like this:

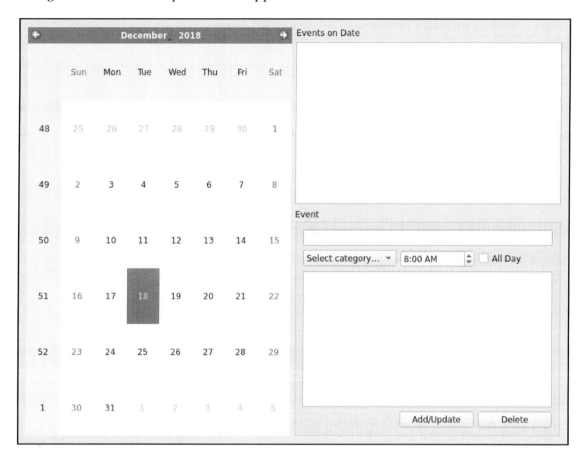

Our interface won't be functional yet; for now, we'll just focus on getting the components created and laid out as shown in the screenshot. We'll do this two ways: once using code only, and a second time using Qt Designer.

Either of these methods is valid and work fine, though as you'll see, each has advantages and disadvantages.

Building the GUI in code

Create a new file called `calendar_form.py` by copying the application template from
`Chapter 1`, *Getting Started with PyQt*.

Then we'll configure our main window; in the `MainWindow` constructor, begin with this
code:

```
self.setWindowTitle("My Calendar App")
self.resize(800, 600)
```

This code will set our window title to something appropriate and set a fixed size for our
window of 800 x 600. Note that this is just the initial size, and the user will be able to resize
the form if they wish to.

Creating the widgets

Now, let's create all of our widgets:

```
self.calendar = qtw.QCalendarWidget()
self.event_list = qtw.QListWidget()
self.event_title = qtw.QLineEdit()
self.event_category = qtw.QComboBox()
self.event_time = qtw.QTimeEdit(qtc.QTime(8, 0))
self.allday_check = qtw.QCheckBox('All Day')
self.event_detail = qtw.QTextEdit()
self.add_button = qtw.QPushButton('Add/Update')
self.del_button = qtw.QPushButton('Delete')
```

These are all of the widgets we will be using in our GUI. Most of these we have covered
already, but there are two new ones: `QCalendarWidget` and `QListWidget`.

`QCalendarWidget` is exactly what you'd expect it to be: a fully interactive calendar that can
be used to view and select dates. Although it has a number of properties that can be
configured, for our needs the default configuration is fine. We'll be using it to allow the
user to select the date to be viewed and edited.

`QListWidget` is for displaying, selecting, and editing items in a list. We're going to use it to
show a list of events saved on a particular day.

Before we move on, we need to configure our `event_category` combo box with some items to select. Here's the plan for this box:

- Have it read `Select category...` as a placeholder when nothing is selected
- Include an option called `New...` which might perhaps allow the user to enter a new category
- Include some common categories by default, such as `Work`, `Meeting`, and `Doctor`

To do this, add the following:

```
# Add event categories
self.event_category.addItems(
    ['Select category...', 'New...', 'Work',
     'Meeting', 'Doctor', 'Family']
    )
# disable the first category item
self.event_category.model().item(0).setEnabled(False)
```

`QComboBox` doesn't really have placeholder text, so we're using a trick here to simulate it. We've added our combo box items using the `addItems()` method as usual. Next, we retrieve its data model using the `model()` method, which returns a `QStandardItemModel` instance. The data model holds a list of all the items in the combo box. We can use the model's `item()` method to access the actual data item at a given index (in this case `0`) and use its `setEnabled()` method to disable it.

In short, we've simulated placeholder text by disabling the first entry in the combo box.

 We'll learn more about widget data models in `Chapter 5`, *Creating Data Interfaces with Model-View Classes*.

Building the layout

Our form is going to require some nested layouts to get everything into position. Let's break down our proposed design and determine how to create this layout:

- The application is divided into a calendar on the left and a form on the right. This suggests using `QHBoxLayout` for the main layout.
- The form on the right is a vertical stack of components, suggesting we use `QVBoxLayout` to arrange things on the right.

- The event form at the bottom right can be laid out roughly in a grid so we could use `QGridLayout` there.

We'll begin by creating the main layout and adding in the calendar:

```
main_layout = qtw.QHBoxLayout()
self.setLayout(main_layout)
main_layout.addWidget(self.calendar)
```

We want the calendar widget to fill any extra space in the layout, so we'll set its size policy accordingly:

```
self.calendar.setSizePolicy(
    qtw.QSizePolicy.Expanding,
    qtw.QSizePolicy.Expanding
)
```

Now, let's create the vertical layout on the right, and add the label and event list:

```
right_layout = qtw.QVBoxLayout()
main_layout.addLayout(right_layout)
right_layout.addWidget(qtw.QLabel('Events on Date'))
right_layout.addWidget(self.event_list)
```

In the event that there's more vertical space, we'd like the event list to fill all the available space. So, let's set its size policy as follows:

```
self.event_list.setSizePolicy(
    qtw.QSizePolicy.Expanding,
    qtw.QSizePolicy.Expanding
)
```

The next part of our GUI is the event form and its label. We could use another label here, but the design suggests that these form fields are grouped together under this heading so `QGroupBox` would be more appropriate.

So, let's create a group box with `QGridLayout` to hold our event form:

```
event_form = qtw.QGroupBox('Event')
right_layout.addWidget(event_form)
event_form_layout = qtw.QGridLayout()
event_form.setLayout(event_form_layout)
```

Finally, we need to add in our remaining widgets into the grid layout:

```
event_form_layout.addWidget(self.event_title, 1, 1, 1, 3)
event_form_layout.addWidget(self.event_category, 2, 1)
event_form_layout.addWidget(self.event_time, 2, 2,)
```

```
event_form_layout.addWidget(self.allday_check, 2, 3)
event_form_layout.addWidget(self.event_detail, 3, 1, 1, 3)
event_form_layout.addWidget(self.add_button, 4, 2)
event_form_layout.addWidget(self.del_button, 4, 3)
```

We're dividing our grid into three columns, and using the optional column-span argument to put our title and detail fields across all three columns.

And now we're done! At this point, you can run the script and see your completed form. It doesn't do anything yet, of course, but that is a topic for our Chapter 3, *Handling Events with Signals and Slots*.

Building the GUI in Qt Designer

Let's try building the same GUI, but this time we'll build it using Qt Designer.

First steps

To begin, launch Qt Designer as described in Chapter 1, *Getting Started with PyQt*, then create a new form based on a widget, like this:

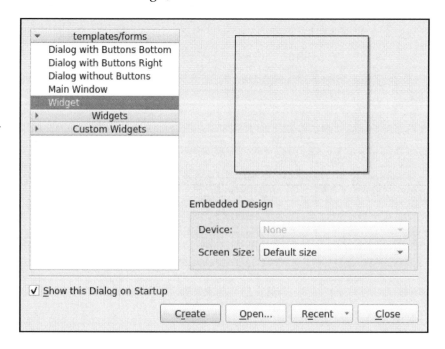

Now, click on the **Widget** and we'll configure its properties using the **Properties** panel on the right:

1. Change the object name to `MainWindow`
2. Under **Geometry**, change the Width to `800` and Height to `600`
3. Change the window title to `My Calendar App`

Next, we'll start adding in the widgets. Scroll through the widget box on the left to find the **Calendar Widget**, then drag it onto the main window. Select the calendar and edit its properties:

1. Change the name to `calendar`
2. Change the horizontal and vertical size policies to `Expanding`

To set up our main layout, right-click the main window (not on the calendar) and select **Layout | Lay Out Horizontally**. This will add a `QHBoxLayout` to the main window widget. Note that you can't do this until at least one widget is on the main window, which is why we added the calendar widget first.

Building the right panel

Now, we'll add the vertical layout for the right side of the form. Drag a **Vertical Layout** to the right of the calendar widget. Then drag a **Label Widget** into the vertical layout. Make sure the label is listed hierarchically as a child of the vertical layout, not a sibling:

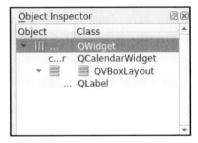

 If you are having trouble dragging the widget onto the unexpanded layout, you can also drag it into the hierarchy in the **Object Inspector** panel.

Double-click the text on the label and change it to say **Events on Date**.

Next, drag a **List Widget** onto the vertical layout so that it appears under the label. Rename it event_list and check its properties to make sure its size policies are set to Expanding.

Building the event form

Find the **Group Box** in the widget box and drag it under the list widget. Double-click the text and change it to Event.

Drag a **Line Edit** onto the group box, making sure it shows up as a child of the group box in the **Object Inspector**. Change the object name to event_title.

Now, right-click the group box and select **Lay out**, then select **Lay out in a Grid**. This will create a grid layout in the group box.

Drag a **Combo Box** onto the next line. Drag a **Time Edit** to the right of it, then a **Check Box** to the right of that. Name them event_category, event_time, and allday_check, respectively. Double-click the checkbox text and change it to All Day.

To add options to the combo box, right-click the box and select **Edit Items**. This will open a dialog where we can type in our items, so click the + button to add Select Category... like the first one, then New..., then a few random categories (such as Work, Doctor, Meeting).

Unfortunately, we can't disable the first item using Qt Designer. We'll have to handle that when we use our form in an application, which we'll discuss in Chapter 3, *Handling Events with Signals and Slots*.

Notice that adding those three widgets pushed the line edit over to the right. We need to fix the column span on that widget. Click the line edit, grab the handle on the right edge, and drag it right until it expands to the width of the group box.

Now, grab a **Text Edit** and drag it under the other widgets. Notice that it's squashed into the first column, so just as with the line edit, drag it right until it fills the whole width. Rename the text edit to event_detail.

Finally, drag two **Push Button** widgets to the bottom of the form. Make sure to drag them to the second and third columns, leaving the first column empty. Rename them add_button and del_button, changing the text to Add/Update and Delete, respectively.

Previewing the form

Save the form as `calendar_form.ui`, then press *Ctrl + R* to preview it. You should see a fully functional form, just as shown in the original screenshot. To actually use this file, we'll have to transpile it to Python code and import it into an actual script. We'll cover this in `Chapter 3`, *Handling Events with Signals and Slots*, after we've made some additional modifications to the form.

Summary

In this chapter, we covered a selection of the most popular widget classes in Qt. You learned how to create them, customize them, and add them to a form. We discussed various ways to control widget sizes and practiced building a simple application form in both Python code and the Qt Designer WYSIWYG application.

In the next chapter, we'll learn how to make this form actually do something as we explore Qt's core communication and event-handling system. Keep your calendar form handy, as we'll modify it some more and make a functional application from it.

Questions

Try these questions to test your knowledge from this chapter:

1. How would you create a `QWidget` that is fullscreen, has no window frame, and uses the hourglass cursor?
2. You're asked to design a data-entry form for a computer inventory database. Choose the best widget to use for each of the following fields:
   - **Computer make**: One of eight brands that your company purchases
   - **Processor Speed**: The CPU speed in GHz
   - **Memory amount**: The amount of RAM, in whole MB
   - **Host Name**: The computer's hostname
   - **Video make**: Whether the video hardware is Nvidia, AMD, or Intel
   - **OEM License**: Whether the computer uses an **Original Equipment Manufacturer (OEM)** license

3. The data entry form includes an `inventory number` field that requires the `XX-999-9999X` format where `X` is an uppercase letter from `A` to `Z`, excluding `O` and `I`, and `9` is a number from `0` to `9`. Can you create a validator class to validate this input?

4. Check out the following calculator form—what layouts may have been used to create it?

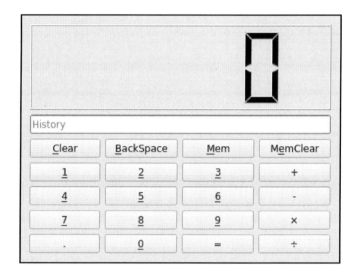

5. Referring to the preceding calculator form, how would you make the button grid take up any extra space when the form is resized?

6. The topmost widget in the calculator form is a `QLCDNumber` widget. Can you find the Qt documentation on this widget? What unique properties does it have? When might you use it?

7. Starting with your template code, build the calculator form in code.

8. Build the calculator form in Qt Designer.

Further reading

Check out the following resources for more information on the topics covered in this chapter:

- The `QWidget` properties documentation lists all the properties for `QWidget`, which are inherited by all its child classes, at `https://doc.qt.io/qt-5/qwidget.html#properties`
- The `Qt` namespace documentation lists many of the global enums used in Qt at `https://doc.qt.io/qt-5/qt.html#WindowState-enum`
- The Qt layout management tutorial provides detailed information on layouts and sizing at `https://doc.qt.io/qt-5/layout.html`
- The `QDateTime` documentation provides more information about working with dates and times in Qt at `https://doc.qt.io/qt-5/qdatetime.html`
- More information about `QCalendarWidget` can be found at `https://doc.qt.io/qt-5/qcalendarwidget.html`

3
Handling Events with Signals and Slots

Composing widgets into a nice-looking form is a good first step for designing an application, but for a GUI to be of any use, it needs to be connected to code that actually does something. In order to do this in PyQt, we need to learn about one of Qt's most vital features, **signals and slots**.

In this chapter, we'll cover the following topics:

- Signal and slot basics
- Creating custom signals and slots
- Automating our calendar form

Technical requirements

Along with the basic requirements listed in Chapter 1, *Getting Started with PyQt*, you will need your calendar-form code and Qt Designer files from Chapter 2, *Building Comprehensive Forms with QtWidgets*. You may also wish to download the example code from our GitHub repository at https://github.com/PacktPublishing/Mastering-GUI-Programming-with-Python/tree/master/Chapter03.

Check out the following video to see the code in action: http://bit.ly/2M5OFQo

Signal and slot basics

A **signal** is a special property of an object that can be emitted in response to a type of **event**. An event may be something such as a user action, a timeout, or the completion of an asynchronous method call.

Slots are object methods that can receive a signal and act in response to it. We connect signals to slots in order to configure our application's response to an event.

All classes descended from `QObject` (which accounts for most classes in Qt, including all `QWidget` classes) can send and receive signals. Each different class has its own set of signals and slots appropriate for the function of that class.

For example, `QPushButton` has a `clicked` signal that is emitted whenever the button is clicked by a user. The `QWidget` class has a `close()` slot that causes it to close if it's a top-level window. We could connect the two like this:

```
self.quitbutton = qtw.QPushButton('Quit')
self.quitbutton.clicked.connect(self.close)
self.layout().addWidget(self.quitbutton)
```

If you copy this code into our application template and run it, you'll find that clicking the **Quit** button closes the window and ends the program. The syntax for connecting a signal to a slot in PyQt5 is `object1.signalName.connect(object2.slotName)`.

You can also make connections when creating an object by passing a slot to a signal as a keyword argument. For example, the previous code could be rewritten as follows:

```
self.quitbutton = qtw.QPushButton('Quit', clicked=self.close)
self.layout().addWidget(self.quitbutton)
```

C++ and older versions of PyQt use a very different syntax for signals and slots, which uses `SIGNAL()` and `SLOT()` wrapper functions. These don't exist in PyQt5, so bear this in mind if you're following an older tutorial or non-Python documentation.

Signals can also carry data with them that slots can receive. For example, `QLineEdit` has a `textChanged` signal that sends the text entered into the widget along with the signal. The line edit also has a `setText()` slot that accepts a string argument. We could connect those like this:

```
self.entry1 = qtw.QLineEdit()
self.entry2 = qtw.QLineEdit()
self.layout().addWidget(self.entry1)
```

```
self.layout().addWidget(self.entry2)
self.entry1.textChanged.connect(self.entry2.setText)
```

In this example, we've connected the `textChanged` signal of `entry1` to the `setText()` slot of `entry2`. That means whenever the text is changed in `entry1`, it will signal `entry2` with the text entered; `entry2` will set its own text to the received string, causing it to mirror whatever is entered in `entry1`.

In PyQt5, a slot doesn't have to be an official Qt slot method; it can be any Python callable, such as a custom method or a built-in function. For example, let's connect the `entry2` widget's `textChanged` to good old `print()`:

```
self.entry2.textChanged.connect(print)
```

Now, you'll see that every change to `entry2` is printed to the console. The `textChanged` signal basically calls `print()` every time it fires, passing in the text carried with the signal.

Signals can even be connected to other signals, for example:

```
self.entry1.editingFinished.connect(lambda: print('editing finished'))
self.entry2.returnPressed.connect(self.entry1.editingFinished)
```

We've connected the `entry2` widget's `returnPressed` signal (which is emitted whenever the user presses *return/Enter* while focused on the widget) to the `entry1` widget's `editingFinished` signal, which in turn is connected to a `lambda` function that prints a message. When you connect a signal to another signal, the event and data are passed from one signal to the next. The net result is that triggering `returnPressed` on `entry2` causes `editingFinished` to be emitted by `entry1`, which in turn runs the `lambda` function.

Restrictions on signal and slot connections

While PyQt offers amazing flexibility by allowing us to connect signals to any Python callable, there are a few rules and limitations that you need to keep in mind. C++, unlike Python, is a **statically typed** language, which means that variables and function arguments must be given a type (`string`, `integer`, `float`, or one of many other types) and any value stored in the variable or passed to that function must have a matching type. This is called **type safety**.

Native Qt signals and slots are type-safe. Suppose, for instance, we tried to connect a line edit's `textChanged` signal to the button's `clicked` signal, like this:

```
self.entry1.textChanged.connect(self.quitbutton.clicked)
```

This won't work, because `textChanged` emits a string, and `clicked` emits (and therefore expects to receive) a Boolean. If you run this, you'll get an error such as this:

```
QObject::connect: Incompatible sender/receiver arguments
        QLineEdit::textChanged(QString) --> QPushButton::clicked(bool)
Traceback (most recent call last):
  File "signal_slots_demo.py", line 57, in <module>
    mw = MainWindow()
  File "signal_slots_demo.py", line 32, in __init__
    self.entry1.textChanged.connect(self.quitbutton.clicked)
TypeError: connect() failed between textChanged(QString) and clicked()
```

Slots can have multiple implementations, each with its own **signature**, allowing the same slot to take different argument types. This is called an **overloaded** slot. As long as our signal signature matches any of the overloaded slots, we can make the connection and Qt will work out which one we're connecting to.

When connecting to a slot that is a Python function, we don't have to be worried about argument types because Python is **dynamically typed** (though it's up to us to make sure our Python code does the right thing with whatever object is passed to it). As with any call to a Python function, however, we do need to make sure we pass in enough arguments to satisfy the function signature.

For example, let's add a method to our `MainWindow` class, as follows:

```
def needs_args(self, arg1, arg2, arg3):
        pass
```

This instance method needs three arguments (`self` is automatically passed). Let's try to connect a button's `clicked` signal to it:

```
self.badbutton = qtw.QPushButton("Bad")
self.layout().addWidget(self.badbutton)
self.badbutton.clicked.connect(self.needs_args)
```

This code doesn't object to the connection itself, but when you click the button, the program crashes with this error:

```
TypeError: needs_args() missing 2 required positional arguments: 'arg2' and
'arg3'
Aborted (core dumped)
```

Since the `clicked` signal only sends one argument, the function call is incomplete and it throws an exception. This can be solved by making `arg2` and `arg3` into keyword arguments (by adding default values), or by creating a wrapper function that populates them with values some other way.

Incidentally, the inverse situation—where the slot takes fewer arguments than the signal sends—is not a problem. Qt just drops the extra data from the signal.

So, for example, there is no problem connecting `clicked` to a method with no arguments, like this:

```
# inside __init__()
self.goodbutton = qtw.QPushButton("Good")
self.layout().addWidget(self.goodbutton)
self.goodbutton.clicked.connect(self.no_args)
# ...

def no_args(self):
    print('I need no arguments')
```

Creating custom signals and slots

Setting callbacks for button clicks and text changes is a common and very obvious use for signals and slots, but it is really only the beginning. At its core, the signals and slots mechanism can be seen as a way for any two objects in an application to communicate while remaining **loosely coupled**.

 Loose coupling refers to keeping the amount of information two objects need to know about each other to a minimum. It's an essential trait to preserve when designing large, complex applications because it isolates code and prevents inadvertent breakage. The opposite is tight coupling, where one object's code depends heavily on the internal structures of another.

In order to take full advantage of this functionality, we'll need to learn how to create our own custom signals and slots.

Sharing data between windows using custom signals

Suppose you have a program that pops up a form window. When the user finishes filling in the form and submits it, we need to get the entered data back to the main application class for processing. There are a few ways we could approach this; for instance, the main application could watch for click events on the pop-up window's **Submit** button, then grab the data from its fields before destroying the dialog. But that approach requires the main form to know all about the pop-up dialog's widgets, and any refactor of the popup would risk breaking code in the main application window.

Let's try a different approach using signals and slots. Open a fresh copy of our application template from Chapter 1, *Getting Started with PyQt*, and start a new class called FormWindow, like this:

```
class FormWindow(qtw.QWidget):

    submitted = qtc.pyqtSignal(str)
```

The first thing we've defined in this class is a custom signal called submitted. To define a custom signal, we need to call the QtCore.pyqtSignal() function. The arguments to pyqtSignal() are the data types our signal will be carrying, in this case, str. We can use Python type objects here, or strings naming a C++ data type ('QString', for example).

Now let's build the form by defining the __init__() method as follows:

```
def __init__(self):
    super().__init__()
    self.setLayout(qtw.QVBoxLayout())

    self.edit = qtw.QLineEdit()
    self.submit = qtw.QPushButton('Submit', clicked=self.onSubmit)

    self.layout().addWidget(self.edit)
    self.layout().addWidget(self.submit)
```

Here, we're defining a QLineEdit for data entry and a QPushButton for submitting the form. The button-click signal is bound to a method called onSubmit, which we'll define next:

```
def onSubmit(self):
    self.submitted.emit(self.edit.text())
    self.close()
```

In this method, we call the `submitted` signal's `emit()` method, passing in the contents of `QLineEdit`. This means that any connected slots will be called with the string retrieved from `self.edit.text()`.

After emitting the signal, we close the `FormWindow`.

Down in our `MainWindow` constructor, let's build an application that uses it:

```
def __init__(self):
    super().__init__()
    self.setLayout(qtw.QVBoxLayout())

    self.label = qtw.QLabel('Click "change" to change this text.')
    self.change = qtw.QPushButton("Change", clicked=self.onChange)
    self.layout().addWidget(self.label)
    self.layout().addWidget(self.change)
    self.show()
```

Here, we've created a `QLabel` and a `QPushButton` and added them to a vertical layout. When clicked, the button calls a method called `onChange()`.

The `onChange()` method looks like this:

```
def onChange(self):
    self.formwindow = FormWindow()
    self.formwindow.submitted.connect(self.label.setText)
    self.formwindow.show()
```

This method creates an instance of our `FormWindow`. It then binds our custom signal, `FormWindow.submitted`, to the `setText` slot of the label; `setText` takes a single string for an argument, and our signal sends a single string.

If you run this application, you'll see that when you submit the pop-up form window, the text in the label does indeed change.

The beauty of this design is that `FormWindow` doesn't need to know anything whatsoever about `MainWindow`, and `MainWindow` only needs to know that `FormWindow` has a `submitted` signal that emits the entered string. We could easily modify the structure and internals of either class, without causing issues for the other, as long as the same signal emits the same piece of data.

`QtCore` also contains a `pyqtSlot()` function, which we can use as a decorator to indicate that a Python function or method is intended as a slot.

For example, we can decorate our `MainWindow.onChange()` method to declare it as a slot:

```
@qtc.pyqtSlot()
def onChange(self):
    # ...
```

This is purely optional, since we can use any Python callable as a slot, though it does give us the ability to enforce type safety. For instance, if we wanted to require that `onChange()` should always receive a string, we could decorate it like this:

```
@qtc.pyqtSlot(str)
def onChange(self):
    # ...
```

If you do this and run the program, you'll see that our attempt to connect a `clicked` signal would fail:

```
Traceback (most recent call last):
  File "form_window.py", line 47, in <module>
    mw = MainWindow()
  File "form_window.py", line 31, in __init__
    self.change = qtw.QPushButton("Change", clicked=self.onChange)
TypeError: decorated slot has no signature compatible with clicked(bool)
```

Apart from imposing type safety, declaring a method as a slot reduces its memory usage and provides a small improvement in speed. So, while it's entirely optional, it may be worth doing for methods that will only ever be used as slots.

Overloading signals and slots

Just as C++ signals and slots can be overloaded to accept different argument signatures, we can overload our custom PyQt signals and slots. For instance, suppose that, if a valid integer string is entered into our pop-up window, we'd like to emit it as both a string and an integer.

To do this, we first have to redefine our signal:

```
submitted = qtc.pyqtSignal([str], [int, str])
```

Instead of just passing in a single variable type, we're passing in two lists of variable types. Each list represents the argument list of a signal signature. So, we've registered two signals here: one that sends out a string only, and one that sends out an integer and a string.

In `FormWindow.onSubmit()`, we can now examine the text in the line edit and send out the signal with the appropriate signature:

```
def onSubmit(self):
    if self.edit.text().isdigit():
        text = self.edit.text()
        self.submitted[int, str].emit(int(text), text)
    else:
        self.submitted[str].emit(self.edit.text())
    self.close()
```

Here, we test the text in `self.edit` to see whether it's a valid number string. If it is, we convert it to `int` and emit the `submitted` signal with the integer and string version of the text. The syntax for selecting a signature is to follow the signal name with square brackets containing a list of the argument types.

Back in the main window, we'll define two new methods to handle these signals:

```
@qtc.pyqtSlot(str)
def onSubmittedStr(self, string):
    self.label.setText(string)

@qtc.pyqtSlot(int, str)
def onSubmittedIntStr(self, integer, string):
    text = f'The string {string} becomes the number {integer}'
    self.label.setText(text)
```

We've created two slots—one that accepts a string and another that accepts an integer and a string. We can now connect the two signals in `FormWindow` to the appropriate slot like so:

```
def onChange(self):
    self.formwindow = FormWindow()
    self.formwindow.submitted[str].connect(self.onSubmittedStr)
    self.formwindow.submitted[int, str].connect(self.onSubmittedIntStr)
```

Run the script, and you'll find now that entering a string of digits will print a different message than an alphanumeric string.

Automating our calendar form

To see how signal and slot usage works in an actual application, let's take the calendar form that we built in Chapter 2, *Building Forms with QtWidgets*, and turn it into a working calendar application. To do this, we're going to need to make the following changes:

- The app needs a way to store events that we enter.
- The **All Day** checkbox should disable the time entry when checked.
- Selecting a day on the calendar should populate the event list with the events for that day.
- Selecting an event in the event list should populate the form with the event's details.
- Clicking **Add/Update** should update the saved event details if an event was selected, or add a new event if one was not.
- Clicking **Delete** should remove the selected event.
- If no event is selected, **Delete** should be disabled.
- Selecting **New...** as a category should open a dialog allowing us to enter a new category. If we choose to enter one, it should be selected.

We'll first go through this using our hand-coded form, then talk about how to approach the same issue using Qt Designer files.

Using our hand-coded form

To get started, copy your calendar_form.py file from Chapter 2, *Building Forms with QtWidgets*, into a new file called calendar_app.py and open it in your editor. We're going to start editing our MainWindow class and flesh it out into a complete application.

To handle storing the events, we'll just create a dict property in MainWindow, like so:

```
class MainWindow(qtw.QWidget):

    events = {}
```

We're not going to bother persisting data to disk, though you can certainly add such a feature if you wish. Each item in `dict` will use a `date` object as its key and contain a list of `dict` objects holding the details of all the events on that date. The layout of the data will look something like this:

```
events = {
    QDate:  {
        'title': "String title of event",
        'category': "String category of event",
        'time': QTime() or None if "all day",
        'detail':  "String details of event"
    }
}
```

Next, let's dig into the form automation. The easiest change to make is disabling the time entry when the **All Day** checkbox is clicked since this automation only requires dealing with built-in signals and slots.

In the __init__() method, we'll add this code:

```
self.allday_check.toggled.connect(self.event_time.setDisabled)
```

The `QCheckBox.toggled` signal is emitted whenever the checkbox is toggled on or off, and sends out a Boolean indicating whether the checkbox is (post-change) unchecked (`False`) or checked (`True`). This connects nicely to `setDisabled`, which will disable the widget on `True` or enable it on `False`.

Creating and connecting our callback methods

The rest of our required automation doesn't map to built-in Qt slots, so before we can connect any more signals, we'll need to create some methods that will be used to implement the slots. We'll create all these as methods of the `MainWindow` class.

Before we start with the callbacks, we'll create a utility method to clear out the form, which several of the callback methods will need. It looks like this:

```
def clear_form(self):
    self.event_title.clear()
    self.event_category.setCurrentIndex(0)
    self.event_time.setTime(qtc.QTime(8, 0))
    self.allday_check.setChecked(False)
    self.event_detail.setPlainText('')
```

Essentially, this method goes through the fields in our form and sets them all to default values. Unfortunately, this requires a different method call for each widget, so we just have to spell it all out.

Now let's go through the callback methods.

The populate _list () method

The first actual callback method is `populate_list()`, which looks like this:

```
def populate_list(self):
    self.event_list.clear()
    self.clear_form()
    date = self.calendar.selectedDate()
    for event in self.events.get(date, []):
        time = (
            event['time'].toString('hh:mm')
            if event['time']
            else 'All Day'
        )
        self.event_list.addItem(f"{time}: {event['title']}")
```

This will be called whenever the calendar selection is changed, and its job is to repopulate the `event_list` widget with the events from that day. It starts by clearing the list and the form. It then retrieves the selected date from the calendar widget using its `selectedDate()` method.

Then, we cycle through the list of events for the selected date's `self.events` dictionary, building a string containing the time and event title and adding it to the `event_list` widget. Note that our event time is a `QTime` object, so to use it as a string we need to convert it using its `toString()` method.

> See the `QTime` documentation at `https://doc.qt.io/qt-5/qtime.html` for details on how to format time values as strings.

To connect this method, back in `__init__()`, we add this code:

```
self.calendar.selectionChanged.connect(self.populate_list)
```

The `selectionChanged` signal is emitted whenever a new day is selected on the calendar. It does not send any data with the signal, so our callback does not expect any.

The populate _form () method

The next callback is `populate_form()`, which will be called when an event is selected and populate the event details form. It begins like this:

```
def populate_form(self):
    self.clear_form()
    date = self.calendar.selectedDate()
    event_number = self.event_list.currentRow()
    if event_number == -1:
        return
```

Here, we start by clearing the form, then retrieving the selected date from the calendar, and the selected event from the event list. When no event is selected, `QListWidget.currentRow()` returns a value of −1; in that case, we'll just return, leaving the form blank.

The remainder of the method looks like this:

```
    event_data = self.events.get(date)[event_number]

    self.event_category.setCurrentText(event_data['category'])
    if event_data['time'] is None:
        self.allday_check.setChecked(True)
    else:
        self.event_time.setTime(event_data['time'])
    self.event_title.setText(event_data['title'])
    self.event_detail.setPlainText(event_data['detail'])
```

Since the items on the list widget are displayed in the same order that they're stored in the `events` dictionary, we can use the row number of the selected item to retrieve an event from the selected date's list.

Once the data is retrieved, we just need to set each widget to the saved value.

Back in `__init__()`, we'll connect the slot like so:

```
    self.event_list.itemSelectionChanged.connect(
        self.populate_form
    )
```

`QListWidget` emits `itemSelectionChanged` whenever a new item is selected. It doesn't send any data with it, so again, our callback expects none.

The save _event () method

The `save_event()` callback will be called whenever the **Add/Update** button is pushed. It starts like this:

```
def save_event(self):
    event = {
        'category': self.event_category.currentText(),
        'time': (
            None
            if self.allday_check.isChecked()
            else self.event_time.time()
            ),
        'title': self.event_title.text(),
        'detail': self.event_detail.toPlainText()
        }
```

In this code, we are now calling the accessor methods to retrieve the values from the widgets and assign them to the appropriate keys of the event's dictionary.

Next, we'll retrieve the current event list for the selected date and determine whether this is an addition or an update:

```
date = self.calendar.selectedDate()
event_list = self.events.get(date, [])
event_number = self.event_list.currentRow()

if event_number == -1:
    event_list.append(event)
else:
    event_list[event_number] = event
```

Remember that `QListWidget.currentRow()` returns −1 if no items are selected. In which case, we want to append our new event to the list. Otherwise, we replace the selected event with our new event dictionary:

```
event_list.sort(key=lambda x: x['time'] or qtc.QTime(0, 0))
self.events[date] = event_list
self.populate_list()
```

To finish this method, we're going to sort the list using the time value. Remember that we're using `None` for an all-day event, so those will be sorted first by replacing them in the sort with a `QTime` of 0:00.

After sorting, we replace the event list for the current date with our newly sorted list and repopulate the `QListWidget` with the new list.

We'll connect the `add_button` widget's `clicked` event by adding this code to `__init__()`:

```
self.add_button.clicked.connect(self.save_event)
```

The delete _event () method

The `delete_event` method will be called whenever the **Delete** button is clicked, and it looks like this:

```
def delete_event(self):
    date = self.calendar.selectedDate()
    row = self.event_list.currentRow()
    del(self.events[date][row])
    self.event_list.setCurrentRow(-1)
    self.clear_form()
    self.populate_list()
```

Once again, we retrieve the current date and currently selected row and use them to locate the event in `self.events` that we want to delete. After deleting the item from the list, we set the list widget to no selection by setting `currentRow` to -1. Then, we clear the form and populate the list widget.

Note that we don't bother checking to see whether the currently selected row is -1, because we plan to disable the delete button when no row is selected.

This callback is pretty simple to connect to the `del_button` back in `__init__()`:

```
self.del_button.clicked.connect(self.delete_event)
```

The check _delete _btn () method

Our last callback is the simplest of all, and it looks like this:

```
def check_delete_btn(self):
    self.del_button.setDisabled(
        self.event_list.currentRow() == -1)
```

This method simply checks whether there is no event currently selected in the event list widget, and it enables or disables the delete button accordingly.

Back in `__init__()`, let's connect to this callback:

```
self.event_list.itemSelectionChanged.connect(
    self.check_delete_btn)
self.check_delete_btn()
```

We're connecting this callback to the `itemSelectionChanged` signal. Note that we've already connected that signal to another slot as well. Signals can be connected to any number of slots without a problem. We also call the method directly, so that the `del_button` will start out disabled.

Building our new category pop-up form

The last feature we want in our application is the ability to add new categories to our combo box. The basic workflow we need to implement is this:

1. When a user changes the event category, check whether they selected **New…**
2. If so, open a form in a new window that lets them type in a category
3. When the form is submitted, emit the name of the new category
4. When that signal is emitted, add a new category to the combo box and select it
5. If the user opts not to enter a new category, default the combo box to **Select Category…**

Let's start by implementing our pop-up form. This will be just like the form example we went through earlier in this chapter, and it looks like this:

```python
class CategoryWindow(qtw.QWidget):

    submitted = qtc.pyqtSignal(str)

    def __init__(self):
        super().__init__(None, modal=True)
        self.setLayout(qtw.QVBoxLayout())
        self.layout().addWidget(
            qtw.QLabel('Please enter a new catgory name:'))
        self.category_entry = qtw.QLineEdit()
        self.layout().addWidget(self.category_entry)
        self.submit_btn = qtw.QPushButton(
            'Submit',
            clicked=self.onSubmit)
        self.layout().addWidget(self.submit_btn)
        self.cancel_btn = qtw.QPushButton(
            'Cancel',
            clicked=self.close
```

```
        )
    self.layout().addWidget(self.cancel_btn)
    self.show()

@qtc.pyqtSlot()
def onSubmit(self):
    if self.category_entry.text():
        self.submitted.emit(self.category_entry.text())
    self.close()
```

This class is the same as our `FormWindow` class with the addition of a label and a **Cancel** button. The `cancel_btn` widget will call the window's `close()` method when clicked, causing the window to close without emitting any signals.

Back in `MainWindow`, let's implement a method to add a new category to the combo box:

```
def add_category(self, category):
    self.event_category.addItem(category)
    self.event_category.setCurrentText(category)
```

This method is pretty simple; it just receives a category text, adds it to the end of the combo box, and sets the combo box selection to the new category.

Now we need to write a method that will create an instance of our pop-up form whenever **New...** is selected:

```
def on_category_change(self, text):
    if text == 'New...':
        dialog = CategoryWindow()
        dialog.submitted.connect(self.add_category)
        self.event_category.setCurrentIndex(0)
```

This method takes the `text` value to which the category has been changed and checks to see whether it's **New...**. If it is, we create our `CategoryWindow` object and connect its `submitted` signal to our `add_category()` method. Then, we set the current index to 0, which is our **Select Category...** option.

Now, when `CategoryWindow` is shown, the user will either click **Cancel**, in which case the window will close and the combo box will be set to **Select Category...** where `on_category_change()` left it, or the user will enter a category and click **Submit**, in which case `CategoryWindow` will emit a `submitted` signal with the new category. The `add_category()` method will receive that new category, add it, and set the combo box to it.

Our calendar app is now complete; fire it up and give it a try!

Using Qt Designer .ui files

Now let's back up and go through that same process using the Qt Designer files we created in Chapter 2, *Building Forms with QtWidgets*. This will require a rather different approach, but the end product will be the same.

To work through this section, you'll need both your `calendar_form.ui` file from Chapter 2, *Building Forms with QtWidgets* and a second `.ui` file for the category window. You can build this form on your own as practice, or use the one included with the example code for this chapter. If you choose to build your own, make sure to name each object just as we did in the code in the last section.

Connecting slots in Qt Designer

Qt Designer has a limited capability to connect signals and slots to our GUI. For Python developers, its mainly only useful for connecting built-in Qt signals to built-in Qt slots between widgets in the same window. Connecting signals to Python callables or custom PyQt signals isn't really possible.

In the calendar GUI, we do have one example of a native Qt signal-slot connection—the `allday_check` widget is connected to the `event_time` widget. Let's look at how to connect these in Qt Designer:

1. Open the `calendar_form.ui` file in Qt Designer
2. At the lower-right side of the screen, find the **Signal/Slot Editor** panel
3. Click the + icon to add a new connection
4. Under **Sender**, open the pop-up menu and select `allday_check`
5. Under **Signal**, choose **toggled(bool)**
6. For **Receiver**, choose `event_time`
7. Finally, for **Slot**, choose **setDisabled(bool)**

The resulting entry should look like this:

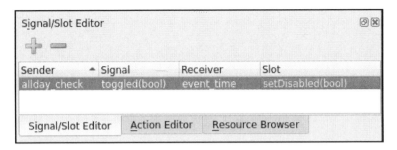

If you're building your own `category_window.ui` file, make sure you also connect the cancel button's `clicked` signal to the category window's `closed` slot.

Converting .ui files to Python

If you were to open your `calendar_form.ui` file in a text editor, you'd see that it is neither Python nor C++, but rather an XML representation of the GUI you've designed. PyQt offers us a few choices for how to use the `.ui` file in a Python application.

The first approach is to convert the XML into Python using the `pyuic5` tool included with PyQt. Open a command-line window in the directory where your `.ui` files are and run the following command:

```
$ pyuic5 calendar_form.ui
```

This will generate a file called `calendar_form.py`. If you open this file in your code editor, you'll see that it contains a single class definition for a `Ui_MainWindow` class, as follows:

```
class Ui_MainWindow(object):
    def setupUi(self, MainWindow):
        MainWindow.setObjectName("MainWindow")
        MainWindow.resize(799, 600)
        # ... etc
```

Notice that this class is not a subclass of `QWidget` or even `QObject`. By itself, this class will not display the window we built. Instead, this class will build the GUI we designed inside another widget, which we must create with code.

To do that, we'll import the class into another script, create a `QWidget` to serve as a container, and call the `setupUi()` method with our widget container as an argument.

 Don't be tempted to edit or add code to the generated Python file. If you ever want to update your GUI using Qt Designer, you'll lose all your edits when you generate the new file. Treat the generated code as if it were a third-party library.

Start by copying the PyQt app template from Chapter 1, *Getting Started with PyQt*, into the directory with `calendar_form.py` and call it `calendar_app.py`.

At the top of the file, import the `Ui_MainWindow` class like this:

```
from calendar_form import Ui_MainWindow
```

There are a few ways we can use this class, but the cleanest is to use **multiple inheritances** by adding it as a second parent class for `MainWindow`.

Update the `MainWindow` class definition like so:

```
class MainWindow(qtw.QWidget, Ui_MainWindow):
```

Note that our window's base class (the first parent class) remains `QWidget`. This base class needs to match the base class we chose when we initially designed the form (see Chapter 2, *Building Forms with QtWidgets*).

Now, inside the constructor, we can call `setupUi`, like this:

```
def __init__(self):
    super().__init__()
    self.setupUi(self)
```

If you run the application at this point, you'll see that the calendar GUI is all there, including our connection between `allday_check` and `event_time`. You can then add the remaining connections and modifications into the `MainWindow` constructor, like so:

```
# disable the first category item
self.event_category.model().item(0).setEnabled(False)
# Populate the event list when the calendar is clicked
self.calendar.selectionChanged.connect(self.populate_list)
# Populate the event form when an item is selected
self.event_list.itemSelectionChanged.connect(
    self.populate_form)
# Save event when save is hit
self.add_button.clicked.connect(self.save_event)
# connect delete button
```

```
self.del_button.clicked.connect(self.delete_event)
# Enable 'delete' only when an event is selected
self.event_list.itemSelectionChanged.connect(
    self.check_delete_btn)
self.check_delete_btn()
# check for selection of "new..." for category
self.event_category.currentTextChanged.connect(
    self.on_category_change)
```

The callback methods for this class are identical to the ones we defined in our code-only example. Go ahead and copy those into the `MainWindow` class.

Another way to use the `Ui_` class created by `pyuic5` is to instantiate it as a property of our container widget. We'll try this with our category window; add this class to the top of the file:

```
class CategoryWindow(qtw.QWidget):

    submitted = qtc.pyqtSignal(str)

    def __init__(self):
        super().__init__()
        self.ui = Ui_CategoryWindow()
        self.ui.setupUi(self)
        self.show()
```

After creating the `Ui_CategoryWindow` object as a property of `CategoryWindow`, we then call its `setupUi()` method to build the GUI on `CategoryWindow`. However, all our references to the widgets are now under the `self.ui` namespace. So, for example, `category_entry` is not `self.category_entry` but `self.ui.category_entry`. While this approach is slightly more verbose, it may help to avoid name collisions if you're building a particularly complex class.

Automatic signal and slot connections

Take another look at the `Ui_` class generated by `pyuic5` and notice the last line of code in `setupUi`:

```
QtCore.QMetaObject.connectSlotsByName(MainWindow)
```

`connectSlotsByName()` is a method that will automatically connect signals and slots by matching up signals to methods named in the `on_object_name_signal()` format, where `object_name` matches the `objectName` property of a PyQt object and `signal` is the name of one of its built-in signals.

For example, in our `CategoryWindow`, we would like to create a callback that runs when `submit_btn` is clicked (if you made your own `.ui` file, make sure you named your submit button `submit_btn`). That will happen automatically if we name the callback `on_submit_btn_clicked()`.

The code looks like this:

```
@qtc.pyqtSlot()
def on_submit_btn_clicked(self):
    if self.ui.category_entry.text():
        self.submitted.emit(self.ui.category_entry.text())
    self.close()
```

If we get the names to match up, we don't have to explicitly call `connect()` anywhere; the callback will be wired up automatically.

You can use `connectSlotsByName()` with hand-coded GUIs as well; you just need to explicitly set each widget's `objectName` property so that the method has something to match the name against. Variable names alone won't work.

Using .ui files without conversion

If you don't mind a little conversion overhead during runtime, you can actually avoid the step of manually converting your `.ui` files by converting them on the fly inside your program using PyQt's `uic` library (on which `pyuic5` is based).

Let's try this with our `MainWindow` GUI. Start by commenting out your import of `Ui_MainWindow` and importing `uic`, like so:

```
#from calendar_form import Ui_MainWindow
from PyQt5 import uic
```

Then, before your `MainWindow` class definition, call `uic.loadUiType()`, as follows:

```
MW_Ui, MW_Base = uic.loadUiType('calendar_form.ui')
```

`loadUiType()` takes a path to the `.ui` file and returns a tuple containing the generated UI class and the Qt base class on which it is based (in this case, `QWidget`).

We can then use these as the parent classes for our `MainWindow` class, like so:

```
class MainWindow(MW_Base, MW_Ui):
```

The downside of this approach is the additional conversion time, but with the added benefit of a simpler build and fewer files to maintain. This is a good approach to take during early development, when you may be iterating on your GUI design frequently.

Summary

In this chapter, you learned about Qt's inter-object communication feature, signals and slots. You learned how to use them to automate form behavior, to connect functionality to user events, and to communicate between different windows in an application.

In the next chapter, we're going to learn about `QMainWindow`, a class that simplifies building common application components. You'll learn how to quickly create menus, toolbars, and dialog, as well as how to save settings.

Questions

Try these questions to test your knowledge of this chapter:

1. Look at the following table and determine which of the connections could actually be made, and which would result in an error. You may need to look up the signatures of these signals and slots in the documentation:

#	Signal	Slot
1	QPushButton.clicked	QLineEdit.clear
2	QComboBox.currentIndexChanged	QListWidget.scrollToItem
3	QLineEdit.returnPressed	QCalendarWidget.setGridVisible
4	QLineEdit.textChanged	QTextEdit.scrollToAnchor

2. The `emit()` method does not exist on a signal object until the signal has been bound (that is, connected to a slot). Rewrite the `CategoryWindow.onSubmit()` method from our first `calendar_app.py` file to protect against the possibility of `submitted` being unbound.

3. You find an object in the Qt documentation with a slot that requires a `QString` as an argument. Can you connect your custom signal that sends Python's `str`?

4. You find an object in the Qt documentation with a slot that requires a `QVariant` as an argument. What built-in Python types could you send to this slot?

5. You're trying to create a dialog window that takes time and emits it when the user has finished editing the value. You're trying to use automatic slot connections, but your code isn't doing anything. Determine what is missing:

```
class TimeForm(qtw.QWidget):

    submitted = qtc.pyqtSignal(qtc.QTime)

    def __init__(self):
    super().__init__()
    self.setLayout(qtw.QHBoxLayout())
    self.time_inp = qtw.QTimeEdit(self)
    self.layout().addWidget(self.time_inp)

    def on_time_inp_editingFinished(self):
    self.submitted.emit(self.time_inp.time())
    self.destroy()
```

6. You've created a `.ui` file in Qt Designer for a calculator application, and you're trying to get it working in code, but it's not working. What are you doing wrong in the following source code?

```
from calculator_form import Ui_Calculator

class Calculator(qtw.QWidget):
    def __init__(self):
        self.ui = Ui_Calculator(self)
        self.ui.setupGUI(self.ui)
        self.show()
```

7. You're trying to create a new button class that emits an integer value when clicked; unfortunately, nothing happens when you click the button. Look at the following code and try to make it work:

```
class IntegerValueButton(qtw.QPushButton):

    clicked = qtc.pyqtSignal(int)

    def __init__(self, value, *args, **kwargs):
        super().__init__(*args, **kwargs)
        self.value = value
        self.clicked.connect(
            lambda: self.clicked.emit(self.value))
```

Further reading

Check out these resources for more information:

- PyQt's documentation on signal and slot support can be found here at http://pyqt.sourceforge.net/Docs/PyQt5/signals_slots.html
- PyQt's documentation on using Qt Designer can be found here at http://pyqt.sourceforge.net/Docs/PyQt5/designer.html

4
Building Applications with QMainWindow

Basic Qt widgets can take us a long way when building simple forms, but full applications include features such as menus, toolbars, dialog boxes, and other functionality that can be tedious and tricky to build from scratch. Fortunately, PyQt provides us with ready-made classes for these standard components to make building applications relatively painless.

In this chapter, we'll explore the following topics:

- The QMainWindow class
- Standard dialog boxes
- Saving settings with QSettings

Technical requirements

This chapter will require the same setup as shown in Chapter 1, *Getting Started with PyQt*. You may also wish to reference the code found in our GitHub repository at https://github.com/PacktPublishing/Mastering-GUI-Programming-with-Python/tree/master/Chapter04.

Check out the following video to see the code in action: http://bit.ly/2M5OGnq

The QMainWindow class

Up until now, we've been using the humble `QWidget` as the base class for our top-level window. This works well for simple forms, but it lacks many of the features that we might expect from an application's main window, such as menu bars or toolbars. Qt provides the `QMainWindow` class to address this need.

Make a copy of the application template from Chapter 1, *Getting Started with PyQt*, and let's make a small but crucial change:

```
class MainWindow(qtw.QMainWindow):
```

Instead of inheriting from `QWidget`, we'll inherit from `QMainWindow`. As you'll see, this will change the way we have to code our GUI, but it will also add a number of nice features to our main window.

To explore these new features, let's build a simple plain text editor. The following screenshot shows what our completed editor will look like, along with labels showing the main components of the `QMainWindow` class:

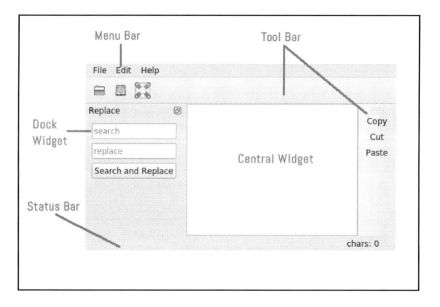

Save your updated template, copy it to a new file called `text_editor.py`, and open the new file in your code editor. Let's begin!

Setting a central widget

QMainWindow is divided into several sections, the most important of which is the **central widget**. This is a single widget that represents the main business part of the interface.

We set this by passing a reference to any widget to the QMainWindow.setCentralWidget() method, like this:

```
self.textedit = qtw.QTextEdit()
self.setCentralWidget(self.textedit)
```

There can be only one central widget, so in a more complex application (such as a data entry app, for instance) it will more likely be a QWidget object on which you've arranged a more complex GUI; for our simple text editor, a single QTextEdit widget will suffice. Notice that we do not set a layout on the QMainWindow; doing so would break the preset arrangement of components.

Adding a status bar

A **status bar** is a strip across the bottom of the application window designed for displaying short text messages and informational widgets. In Qt, a status bar is a QStatusBar object that we can assign to the main window's statusBar property.

We could create one like this:

```
status_bar = qtw.QStatusBar()
self.setStatusBar(status_bar)
status_bar.showMessage('Welcome to text_editor.py')
```

However, there's no need to go to so much trouble; the QMainWindow object's statusBar() method automatically creates a new status bar if there isn't one, or returns the existing one if there is.

So, we can reduce all that code to this:

```
self.statusBar().showMessage('Welcome to text_editor.py')
```

The showMessage() method does exactly what it says, displaying the given string in the status bar. This is by far the most common use of the status bar; however, QStatusBar objects can also contain other widgets.

For example, we can add a widget that keeps track of our character count:

```
charcount_label = qtw.QLabel("chars: 0")
self.textedit.textChanged.connect(
    lambda: charcount_label.setText(
        "chars: " +
        str(len(self.textedit.toPlainText()))
        )
    )
self.statusBar().addPermanentWidget(charcount_label)
```

This `QLabel` is updated with the number of characters entered whenever our text changes.

Note that we've added it directly to the status bar, without referencing a layout object; `QStatusBar` has its own methods for adding or inserting widgets that come in two flavors: **regular** and **permanent**. In regular mode, widgets can be covered up if the status bar is sent a long message to display. In permanent mode, they will remain visible. In this case, we used the `addPermanentWidget()` method to add `charcount_label` in permanent mode so it won't be covered up by a long text message.

 The methods for adding a widget in regular mode are `addWidget()` and `insertWidget()`; for permanent mode, use `addPermanentWidget()` and `insertPermanentWidget()`.

Creating an application menu

The **application menu** is a crucial feature for most applications, offering access to all the application's functionality in hierarchically organized drop-down menus.

We can create on easily using the `QMainWindow.menuBar()` method:

```
menubar = self.menuBar()
```

The `menuBar()` method returns a `QMenuBar` object, and as with `statusBar()`, this method will give us the window's existing menu if it exists, or simply create a new one if it doesn't.

By default, the menu is blank, but we can add submenus using the menu bar's `addMenu()` method, like so:

```
file_menu = menubar.addMenu('File')
edit_menu = menubar.addMenu('Edit')
help_menu = menubar.addMenu('Help')
```

addMenu() returns a QMenu object, which represents a drop-down submenu. The string passed into the method will be used to label the menu in the main menu bar.

> Certain platforms, such as macOS, will not display empty submenus. See the *Menus on macOS* section for more information on building menus in macOS.

To populate these menus with items, we need to create some **actions**. Actions are simply objects of the QAction class that represent things our program can do. To be useful, a QAction object needs at least a name and a callback; they can optionally define a keyboard shortcut and icon for the action.

One way to create actions is to call a QMenu object's addAction() method, like so:

```
open_action = file_menu.addAction('Open')
save_action = file_menu.addAction('Save')
```

We've created two actions called Open and Save. Neither of them actually does anything, because we haven't assigned callback methods, but if you run your application script, you'll see that the file menu does indeed have two items listed, Open and Save.

To create items that actually do something, we can pass in a second argument containing a Python callable or Qt slot:

```
quit_action = file_menu.addAction('Quit', self.destroy)
edit_menu.addAction('Undo', self.textedit.undo)
```

For cases where we want more control, it's possible to create a QAction object explicitly and add it to the menu, like so:

```
redo_action = qtw.QAction('Redo', self)
redo_action.triggered.connect(self.textedit.redo)
edit_menu.addAction(redo_action)
```

QAction objects have a triggered signal that must be connected to a callable or slot for the action to have any effect. This is handled automatically when we use the addAction() method of creating actions, but it must be done manually when creating QAction objects explicitly.

> Although not technically required, it's very important to pass in a parent widget when creating a QAction object explicitly. Failing to do so will result in the item not showing up, even when you add it to the menu.

Menus on macOS

QMenuBar wraps the OS's native menu system by default. On macOS, the native menu system has a few peculiarities that you need to be aware of:

- macOS uses a **global menu**, meaning the menu bar is not part of the application window but is attached to the bar at the top of the desktop. By default, your main window's menu bar will be used as the global menu. If you have an application with multiple main windows and you want them all to use the same menu bar, do not use QMainWindow.menuBar() to create the menu bar. Instead, create a QMenuBar object explicitly and assign it to the main window objects you create using the setMenuBar() method.
- macOS also has a number of default submenus and menu items. To access these items, simply use the same when adding a submenu. When adding a submenu see the *Further reading* section for more details on macOS menus.
- As mentioned previously, macOS will not display an empty submenu on the global menu.

If you find these issues too problematic for your application, you can always instruct Qt not to use the native menu system, like so:

```
self.menuBar().setNativeMenuBar(False)
```

This will place the menu bar in the application window as it is on other platforms and remove the platform-specific issues. However, be aware that this approach breaks the workflow typical to macOS software and users may find it jarring.

 More information about Qt menus on macOS can be found at https://doc.qt.io/qt-5/macos-issues.html#menu-bar.

Adding toolbars

A **toolbar** is a long row of buttons often used for editing commands or similar actions. Unlike main menus, toolbars are not hierarchical and the buttons are typically only labeled with an icon.

QMainWindow allows us to add multiple toolbars to our application using the addToolBar() method, like so:

```
toolbar = self.addToolBar('File')
```

The `addToolBar()` method creates and returns a `QToolBar` object. The string passed into the method becomes the toolbar's title.

We can add `QAction` objects much like we can to a `QMenu` object:

```
toolbar.addAction(open_action)
toolbar.addAction("Save")
```

Just as with a menu, we can add `QAction` objects or just the information to build an action (title, callback, and other).

Run the application; it should look something like this:

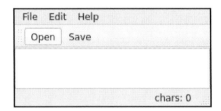

Note that the title of the toolbar is not displayed on it. However, if you right-click the toolbar area, you'll see a pop-up menu containing all the toolbar titles with checkboxes that allow you to show or hide any of the application's toolbars.

By default, toolbars can be torn from the application and left floating or docked to any of the four edges of the application. This can be disabled by setting the `movable` and `floatable` properties to `False`:

```
toolbar.setMovable(False)
toolbar.setFloatable(False)
```

You can also restrict the sides of the window to which the bar can be docked by setting its `allowedAreas` property to a combination of flags from the `QtCore.Qt.QToolBarAreas` enum.

For example, let's restrict our toolbar to the top and bottom areas only:

```
toolbar.setAllowedAreas(
    qtc.Qt.TopToolBarArea |
    qtc.Qt.BottomToolBarArea
)
```

Our toolbar currently has text-labeled buttons, but normally a toolbar would have icon-labeled buttons. To show how that works, we'll need some icons.

We can extract some icons from the built-in style, like so:

```
open_icon = self.style().standardIcon(qtw.QStyle.SP_DirOpenIcon)
save_icon = self.style().standardIcon(qtw.QStyle.SP_DriveHDIcon)
```

Don't worry about how this code works right now; a complete discussion of styles and icons will come along in Chapter 6, *Styling Qt Applications*. For now, just understand that open_icon and save_icon are QIcon objects, which is how Qt handles icons.

These can be attached to our QAction objects, which can be then attached to the toolbar, like so:

```
open_action.setIcon(open_icon)
toolbar.addAction(open_action)
```

As you can see, that looks a bit better:

Notice when you run this that the **File | Open** option in the menu also now has an icon. Because both use the open_action object, any changes we make to that action object will carry to all uses of the object.

Icon objects can be passed into the toolbar's addAction method as the first argument, like so:

```
toolbar.addAction(
    save_icon,
    'Save',
    lambda: self.statusBar().showMessage('File Saved!')
)
```

This adds a **Save** action to the toolbar with an icon and a rather useless callback. Notice that this time, the **File | Save** action in the menu did not get an icon; despite the fact that we used the same label text, calling addAction() with discrete arguments in both places results in two distinct and unrelated QAction objects.

Finally, just like with the menu, we can create `QAction` objects explicitly and add them to the toolbar, like so:

```
help_action = qtw.QAction(
    self.style().standardIcon(qtw.QStyle.SP_DialogHelpButton),
    'Help',
    self,  # important to pass the parent!
    triggered=lambda: self.statusBar().showMessage(
        'Sorry, no help yet!'
        )
)
toolbar.addAction(help_action)
```

To synchronize actions across multiple action containers (toolbars, menus, and so on), either explicitly create `QAction` objects or save the references returned from `addAction()` to make sure you're adding the same action objects in each case.

We can add as many toolbars as we wish to our application and attach them to whichever side of the application we wish. To specify a side, we have to use an alternative form of `addToolBar()`, like so:

```
toolbar2 = qtw.QToolBar('Edit')
toolbar2.addAction('Copy', self.textedit.copy)
toolbar2.addAction('Cut', self.textedit.cut)
toolbar2.addAction('Paste', self.textedit.paste)
self.addToolBar(qtc.Qt.RightToolBarArea, toolbar2)
```

To use this form of `addToolBar()`, we have to create the toolbar first then pass it in along with a `QtCore.Qt.ToolBarArea` constant.

Adding dock widgets

Dock widgets are similar to toolbars, but they sit between the toolbar areas and the central widget and are able to contain any kind of widget.

Adding a dock widget is much like explicitly creating a toolbar:

```
dock = qtw.QDockWidget("Replace")
self.addDockWidget(qtc.Qt.LeftDockWidgetArea, dock)
```

Like toolbars, dock widgets by default can be closed, floated, or moved to another side of the application. To change whether a dock widget can be closed, floated, or moved, we have to set its `features` property to a combination of `QDockWidget.DockWidgetFeatures` flag values.

For instance, let's make it so the user cannot close our dock widget, by adding this code:

```
dock.setFeatures(
    qtw.QDockWidget.DockWidgetMovable |
    qtw.QDockWidget.DockWidgetFloatable
)
```

We've set `features` to `DockWidgetMovable` and `DockWidgetFloatable`. Since `DockWidgetClosable` is missing here, the user won't be able to close the widget.

The dock widget is designed to hold a single widget that is set using the `setWidget()` method. As with our main application's `centralWidget`, we typically will set this to a `QWidget` containing some kind of form or other GUI.

Let's build a form to place in the dock widget, as follows:

```
replace_widget = qtw.QWidget()
replace_widget.setLayout(qtw.QVBoxLayout())
dock.setWidget(replace_widget)

self.search_text_inp = qtw.QLineEdit(placeholderText='search')
self.replace_text_inp = qtw.QLineEdit(placeholderText='replace')
search_and_replace_btn = qtw.QPushButton(
    "Search and Replace",
    clicked=self.search_and_replace
    )
replace_widget.layout().addWidget(self.search_text_inp)
replace_widget.layout().addWidget(self.replace_text_inp)
replace_widget.layout().addWidget(search_and_replace_btn)
replace_widget.layout().addStretch()
```

The `addStretch()` method can be called on a layout to add an expanding `QWidget` that pushes the other widgets together.

This is a fairly simple form containing two `QLineEdit` widgets and a button. When the button is clicked, it calls the main window's `search_and_replace()` method. Let's code that quickly:

```
def search_and_replace(self):
    s_text = self.search_text_inp.text()
    r_text = self.replace_text_inp.text()

    if s_text:
        self.textedit.setText(
            self.textedit.toPlainText().replace(s_text, r_text)
        )
```

This method simply retrieves the contents of the two-line edits; then, if there is content in the first, it replaces all instances of the first text with the second in the text edit's contents.

Run the program at this point and you should see our dock widget on the left side of the application, like so:

Note the icon in the upper right of the dock widget. This allows the user to detach and float the widget outside the application window.

Other QMainWindow features

Although we've covered its main components, the `QMainWindow` offers many other features and configuration options that you can explore in its documentation at `https://doc.qt.io/qt-5/qmainwindow.html`. We may touch on some of these in future chapters, as we will make extensive use of `QMainWindow` from here onward.

Standard dialog boxes

Dialog boxes are commonly required in applications, whether to ask a question, present a form or merely alert the user to some information. Qt provides a wide variety of ready-made dialog boxes for common situations, as well as the capability to define custom dialog boxes of our own. In this section, we'll look at some of the more commonly used dialog box classes and take a stab at designing our own.

QMessageBox

`QMessageBox` is a simple dialog box used mainly to display short messages or ask yes-or-no questions. The simplest way to use `QMessageBox` is to take advantage of its convenient static methods, which create and show a dialog box with minimal fuss.

The six static methods are as follows:

Function	Type	Dialog
`about()`	Modeless	Shows an **About** dialog box for your application with the given text.
`aboutQt()`	Modeless	Shows an **About** dialog box for Qt.
`critical()`	Modal	Show a critical error message with the provided text.
`information()`	Modal	Show an informational message with the provided text.
`warning()`	Modal	Show a warning message with the provided text.
`question()`	Modal	Asks the user a question.

The main difference between most of these boxes are the default icons, the default buttons, and the modality of the dialog.

Dialog boxes can be either **modal** or **modeless**. Modal dialog boxes prevent the user from interacting with any other part of the program and block program execution while displayed, and they can return a value when finished. Modeless dialog boxes do not block execution, but they also do not return a value. In the case of a modal `QMessageBox`, the return value is an `enum` constant representing the button pressed.

Let's use the `about()` method to add an **About** message to our application. First, we'll create a callback to display the dialog:

```
def showAboutDialog(self):
    qtw.QMessageBox.about(
        self,
        "About text_editor.py",
```

```
        "This is a text editor written in PyQt5."
    )
```

The **About** dialog is modeless, so it's really just a way to display information passively. The arguments are, in order, the dialog's parent widget, the dialog's window title text, and the dialog's main text.

Back in the constructor, let's add a menu action to call this method:

```
help_menu.addAction('About', self.showAboutDialog)
```

Modal dialog boxes can be used to retrieve a response from the user. For instance, we could warn the user about the unfinished nature of our editor and see whether they are really intent on using it, like so:

```
response = qtw.QMessageBox.question(
    self,
    'My Text Editor',
    'This is beta software, do you want to continue?'
)
if response == qtw.QMessageBox.No:
    self.close()
    sys.exit()
```

All modal dialog boxes return a Qt constant corresponding to the button the user pushed; by default, question() creates a dialog box with the QMessageBox.Yes and QMessageBox.No button values so we can test the response and react accordingly. The buttons presented can also be overridden by passing in a fourth argument containing multiple buttons combined with the pipe operator.

For example, we can change No to Abort, like so:

```
response = qtw.QMessageBox.question(
    self,
    'My Text Editor',
    'This is beta software, do you want to continue?',
    qtw.QMessageBox.Yes | qtw.QMessageBox.Abort
)
if response == qtw.QMessageBox.Abort:
    self.close()
    sys.exit()
```

If the static `QMessageBox` methods do not provide enough flexibility, you can also explicitly create a `QMessageBox` object, like so:

```
splash_screen = qtw.QMessageBox()
splash_screen.setWindowTitle('My Text Editor')
splash_screen.setText('BETA SOFTWARE WARNING!')
splash_screen.setInformativeText(
    'This is very, very beta, '
    'are you really sure you want to use it?'
)
splash_screen.setDetailedText(
    'This editor was written for pedagogical '
    'purposes, and probably is not fit for real work.'
)
splash_screen.setWindowModality(qtc.Qt.WindowModal)
splash_screen.addButton(qtw.QMessageBox.Yes)
splash_screen.addButton(qtw.QMessageBox.Abort)
response = splash_screen.exec()
if response == qtw.QMessageBox.Abort:
    self.close()
    sys.exit()
```

As you can see, we can set quite a few properties on the message box; these are described here:

Property	Description
windowTitle	The title printed in the taskbar and title bar of the dialog.
text	The text displayed in the dialog.
informativeText	A longer, explanatory piece of text displayed under the text string often displayed in a smaller or lighter font face.
detailedText	Text that will be hidden behind a **Show details** button and displayed in a scrolling textbox. Useful for debugging or log output.
windowModality	Used to set whether the message box is modal or modeless. Requires a QtCore.Qt.WindowModality constant.

We can also add any number of buttons to the dialog box using the `addButton()` method and then display the dialog box by calling its `exec()` method. If we configured the dialog box to be modal, this method will return the constant matching the button that was clicked.

QFileDialog

Applications commonly need to open or save files, and users need an easy way to browse and select those files. Qt provides us with the `QFileDialog` class to meet this need.

Just as with `QMessageBox`, the `QFileDialog` class contains several static methods that display an appropriate modal dialog box and return the value selected by the user.

This table shows the static methods and their intended use:

Method	Returns	Description
getExistingDirectory	String	Select an existing directory path.
getExistingDirectoryUrl	QUrl	Select an existing directory URL.
getOpenFileName	String	Select an existing filename path to open.
getOpenFileNames	List	Select multiple existing filename paths to open.
getOpenFileUrl	QUrl	Select an existing filename URL.
getSaveFileName	String	Select a new or existing filename path to save to.
getSaveFileUrl	QUrl	Select a new or existing URL.

On platforms that support it, the URL versions of these methods allow for selecting remote files and directories.

To see how file dialog boxes work, let's create the ability to open a file in our application:

```
def openFile(self):
    filename, _ = qtw.QFileDialog.getOpenFileName()
    if filename:
        try:
            with open(filename, 'r') as fh:
                self.textedit.setText(fh.read())
        except Exception as e:
            qtw.QMessageBox.critical(f"Could not load file: {e}")
```

`getOpenFileName()` returns a tuple containing the filename selected and the selected file type filter. If the user cancels the dialog, an empty string is returned for the filename, and our method will exit. If we receive a filename, we attempt to open the file and write into it the contents of our `textedit` widget.

Since we aren't using the second value returned from the method, we're assigning it to the _ (underscore) variable. This is a standard Python convention for naming variables you don't intend to use.

`getOpenFileName()` has a number of arguments for configuring the dialog, all of which are optional. In order, they are as follows:

1. The parent widget
2. The caption, used in the window title
3. The starting directory, as a path string
4. The filters available for the file type filter dropdown
5. The default selected filter
6. Option flags

For example, let's configure our file dialog:

```
filename, _ = qtw.QFileDialog.getOpenFileName(
    self,
    "Select a text file to open...",
    qtc.QDir.homePath(),
    'Text Files (*.txt) ;;Python Files (*.py) ;;All Files (*)',
    'Python Files (*.py)',
    qtw.QFileDialog.DontUseNativeDialog |
    qtw.QFileDialog.DontResolveSymlinks
)
```

 `QDir.homePath()` is a static method that returns the user's home directory.

Notice that the filters are specified as a single string; each filter is a description plus a wildcard string in parenthesis, and the filters are separated by double semi-colons. This results in a filter dropdown that looks like this:

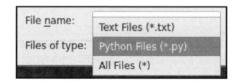

Last, of all, we can specify a collection of option flags combined using the pipe operator. In this case, we're telling Qt not to use the native OS file dialog boxes and not to resolve symbolic links (both of which it does by default). See the `QFileDialog` documentation at `https://doc.qt.io/qt-5/qfiledialog.html#Option-enum` for a complete list of option flags.

The save file dialog box works much the same way but provides an interface more appropriate for saving a file. We can implement our `saveFile()` method as follows:

```python
def saveFile(self):
    filename, _ = qtw.QFileDialog.getSaveFileName(
        self,
        "Select the file to save to...",
        qtc.QDir.homePath(),
        'Text Files (*.txt) ;;Python Files (*.py) ;;All Files (*)'
    )
    if filename:
        try:
            with open(filename, 'w') as fh:
                fh.write(self.textedit.toPlainText())
        except Exception as e:
            qtw.QMessageBox.critical(f"Could not save file: {e}")
```

Other `QFileDialog` convenience methods work the same way. As with `QMessageBox`, it's also possible to explicitly create a `QFileDialog` object, configure its properties manually, and then display it with its `exec()` method. However, this is rarely necessary as the built-in methods are adequate for most file-selection situations.

Before moving on, don't forget to add actions to call these methods back in the `MainWindow` constructor:

```python
open_action.triggered.connect(self.openFile)
save_action.triggered.connect(self.saveFile)
```

QFontDialog

Qt provides a number of other convenient selection dialog boxes similar to the `QFileDialog`; one such dialog box is the `QFontDialog`, which allows users to select and configure various aspects of a text font.

Like the other dialog box classes, this is most easily used by calling a static method to display the dialog box and return the user's selection, in this case, the `getFont()` method.

Let's add a callback method to our `MainWindow` class to set the editor font:

```python
def set_font(self):
    current = self.textedit.currentFont()
    font, accepted = qtw.QFontDialog.getFont(current, self)
    if accepted:
        self.textedit.setCurrentFont(font)
```

`getFont` takes the current font as an argument, which allows it to set the selected font to whatever is current (if you neglect to do this, the dialog box will default to the first font listed).

It returns a tuple containing the selected font and a Boolean indicating whether the user clicked **OK**. The font is returned as a `QFont` object, which encapsulates not only the font family but also the style, size, effects, and writing system of the font. Our method can pass this object back to the `QTextEdit` object's `setCurrentFont()` slot to set its font.

As with `QFileDialog`, Qt tries to use the operating system's native font dialog box if it has one; otherwise, it will use its own widget. You can force it to use the Qt version of the dialog box by passing in the `DontUseNativeDialog` option to the `options` keyword argument, as we've done here:

```
font, accepted = qtw.QFontDialog.getFont(
    current,
    self,
    options=(
        qtw.QFontDialog.DontUseNativeDialog |
        qtw.QFontDialog.MonospacedFonts
    )
)
```

We've also passed in an option here to limit the dialog box to mono-spaced fonts. See the Qt documentation on `QFontDialog` at `https://doc.qt.io/qt-5/qfontdialog.html#FontDialogOption-enum` for more information about the available options.

Other dialog boxes

Qt contains other dialog box classes for selecting colors, requesting input values, and more. All of these work more or less like the file and font dialog boxes, and they descend from the `QDialog` class. We can subclass `QDialog` ourselves to create a custom dialog box.

For example, suppose we want to have a dialog box for entering our settings. We could start building it like this:

```
class SettingsDialog(qtw.QDialog):
    """Dialog for setting the settings"""

    def __init__(self, settings, parent=None):
        super().__init__(parent, modal=True)
        self.setLayout(qtw.QFormLayout())
        self.settings = settings
        self.layout().addRow(
```

```
        qtw.QLabel('<h1>Application Settings</h1>'),
    )
    self.show_warnings_cb = qtw.QCheckBox(
        checked=settings.get('show_warnings')
    )
    self.layout().addRow("Show Warnings", self.show_warnings_cb)

    self.accept_btn = qtw.QPushButton('Ok', clicked=self.accept)
    self.cancel_btn = qtw.QPushButton('Cancel', clicked=self.reject)
    self.layout().addRow(self.accept_btn, self.cancel_btn)
```

This code isn't far removed from pop-up boxes we've made in past chapters using `QWidget`. However, by using `QDialog` we get a few things for free, namely these:

- We get `accept` and `reject` slots to which we can connect the appropriate buttons. By default, these cause the window to close and emit either an `accepted` or `rejected` signal respectively.
- We also get the `exec()` method that returns a Boolean value indicating whether the dialog box was accepted or rejected.
- We can easily set the dialog box to be modal or modeless, by passing the appropriate values to the `super()` constructor.

`QDialog` gives us a lot of flexibility on how to make use of the data entered by the user. We could use a signal to emit the data or override `exec()` to return the data, for instance.

In this case, since we're passing in a mutable `dict` object, we'll override `accept()` to alter that `dict` object:

```
def accept(self):
    self.settings['show_warnings'] = self.show_warnings_cb.isChecked()
    super().accept()
```

Back in the `MainWindow` class, let's create a property and method to use the new dialog:

```
class MainWindow(qtw.QMainWindow):

    settings = {'show_warnings': True}

    def show_settings(self):
        settings_dialog = SettingsDialog(self.settings, self)
        settings_dialog.exec()
```

Using a QDialog class is as simple as creating an instance of the dialog box class and calling exec(). Since we're editing our settings dict directly, in this case, we don't need to worry about connecting the accepted signal or using the output of exec().

Saving settings with QSettings

Applications of any reasonable size are likely to accumulate settings that need to be stored between sessions. Saving these settings usually involves a lot of tedious work with file operations and data serialization, and becomes even more complex when we want to do it in a way that works well across platforms. Qt rescues us from this work with its QtCore.QSettings class.

The QSettings class is a simple key-value data store that is automatically persisted in a platform-appropriate way. For example, on Windows, the settings are stored in the registry database, while on Linux they are placed in a plain-text configuration file under ~/.config.

Let's replace the settings dict object we created in our text editor with a QSettings object.

To create a QSettings object, we need to pass in a company name and application name, like this:

```
class MainWindow(qtw.QMainWindow):

    settings = qtc.QSettings('Alan D Moore', 'text editor')
```

These strings will determine the registry key or file path where the settings will be stored. On Linux, for example, this settings file will be saved at ~/.config/Alan D Moore/text editor.conf. On Windows, it will be stored in the registry at HKEY_CURRENT_USER\Alan D Moore\text editor\.

We can query the value of any setting using the object's value() method; for instance, we can make our startup warning dialog boxes conditional on the show _warnings setting:

```
if self.settings.value('show_warnings', False, type=bool):
    # Warning dialog code follows...
```

The arguments to value() are the key string, the default value if the key is not found, and the type keyword argument, which tells QSettings how to interpret the saved value. The type argument is crucial; not all platforms can adequately represent all data types in an unambiguous way. Boolean values, for instance, are returned as the strings true and false if the data type is not specified, both of which are True in Python.

Setting the value of a key uses the `setValue()` method, as shown here in the `SettingsDialog.accept()` method:

```
self.settings.setValue(
    'show_warnings',
    self.show_warnings_cb.isChecked()
)
```

Note that we don't have to do anything to store these values to disk; they are automatically synced to disk periodically by the Qt event loop. They are also read automatically from disk the moment the `QSettings` object is created. Simply replacing our original `settings` dict with a `QSettings` object is enough to give us persistent settings without writing a single line of file I/O code!

Limitations of QSettings

As powerful as they are, `QSettings` objects can't store just anything. All values in the settings object are stored as `QVariant` objects, so only objects that can be cast to `QVariant` can be stored. This encompasses a long list of types, including nearly any Python built-in type and most of the data classes from `QtCore`. Even function references can be stored (though not the function definitions).

Unfortunately, in the event that you try to store an object that cannot be properly stored, `QSettings.setValue()` will neither throw an exception or return an error. It will print a warning to the console and store something that will likely not be useful, for example:

```
app = qtw.QApplication([])
s = qtc.QSettings('test')
s.setValue('app', app)
# Prints: QVariant::save: unable to save type 'QObject*' (type id: 39).
```

In general, if you're storing objects that clearly represent data, you shouldn't have problems.

The other major limitation of the `QSettings` object is its inability to automatically identify the data type of some stored objects, as we saw with our Boolean value. For this reason, it's critical to pass a `type` argument when dealing with anything that is not a string value.

Summary

In this chapter, you learned about PyQt classes that help construct complete applications. You learned about the QMainWindow class, its menus, status bar, toolbars, and dock widgets. You also learned about standard dialog boxes and message boxes derived from QDialog, and how to store application settings with QSettings.

In the next chapter, we'll learn about the model-view classes in Qt, which will help us separate our concerns and create more robust application designs.

Questions

Try these questions to test your knowledge from this chapter:

1. You want to use QMainWindow with the calendar_app.py script from Chapter 3, *Handling Events with Signals and Slots*. How would you go about converting it?

2. You're working on an app and have added the submenu names to the menu bar but not populated any of them with items. Your coworker says that none of the menu names are appearing on his desktop when they test it. Your code looks correct; what is probably going on here?

3. You're developing a code editor and want to create a sidebar panel for interacting with a debugger. Which QMainWindow feature would be most appropriate for this task?

4. The following code isn't working correctly; it proceeds no matter what is clicked. Why doesn't it work, and how do you fix it?

```
answer = qtw.QMessageBox.question(
    None, 'Continue?', 'Run this program?')
if not answer:
    sys.exit()
```

5. You're building a custom dialog box by subclassing QDialog. You need to get information entered into the dialog box back to the main window object. Which of these approaches will not work?

   a. Pass in a mutable object and use the dialog's accept() method to alter its values.

   b. Override the objects accept() method and have it return a dict of the entered values.

    c. Override the dialog's `accepted` signal with one that passes along a dict of the entered values. Connect this signal to a callback in your main window class.

6. You're writing a photo editor called **SuperPhoto** on Linux. You've written the code and saved the user settings, but looking in `~/.config/` you can't find `SuperPhoto.conf`. Look at the code and determine what went wrong:

```
settings = qtc.QSettings()
settings.setValue('config_file', 'SuperPhoto.conf')
settings.setValue('default_color', QColor('black'))
settings.sync()
```

7. You're saving preferences from a settings dialog, but for some reason, the settings being saved are coming back very strangely. What is wrong here?

```
settings = qtc.QSettings('My Company', 'SuperPhoto')
settings.setValue('Default Name', dialog.default_name_edit.text)
settings.setValue('Use GPS', dialog.gps_checkbox.isChecked)
settings.setValue('Default Color', dialog.color_picker.color)
```

Further reading

For further information, please refer to the following:

- Qt's `QMainWindow` documentation can be found at `https://doc.qt.io/qt-5/qmainwindow.html`.
- Examples of using `QMainWindow` can be found at `https://github.com/pyqt/examples/tree/master/mainwindows`.
- Apple's Human Interface Guidelines for macOS include guidance on how to structure the application menus. These can be found at `https://developer.apple.com/design/human-interface-guidelines/macos/menus/menu-anatomy/`.
- Microsoft offers guidance for designing menus for Windows applications at `https://docs.microsoft.com/en-us/windows/desktop/uxguide/cmd-menus`.
- PyQt offers some examples of dialog box usage at `https://github.com/pyqt/examples/tree/master/dialogs`.
- `QMainWindow` can also be used to create **Multiple Document Interfaces (MDIs)**. For more information on how to build an MDI application, see `https://www.pythonstudio.us/pyqt-programming/multiple-document-interface-mdi.html` and the example code at `https://doc.qt.io/qt-5/qtwidgets-mainwindows-mdi-example.html`.

5
Creating Data Interfaces with Model-View Classes

The vast majority of application software is built to view and manipulate organized data. Even in applications that aren't explicitly *database applications*, there's often a need to interact with collections of data on a smaller scale, such as populating a combobox with options or displaying a hierarchy of settings. Without some sort of organizational paradigm, interactions between a GUI and a set of data can quickly become a nightmare of spaghetti code. The **model-view** pattern is one such paradigm.

In this chapter, we're going to learn about Qt's model-view widgets and how we can use them to work elegantly with data in our applications. We'll cover the following topics:

- Understanding model-view design
- Models and views in PyQt
- Building a **comma-separated values (CSV)** editor

Technical requirements

This chapter has the same technical requirements as the previous chapters. You might also wish to have the example code from `https://github.com/PacktPublishing/Mastering-GUI-Programming-with-Python/tree/master/Chapter05`.

You will also need one or two CSV files to use with our CSV editor. These can be made in any spreadsheet program and should be created with column headers as the first row.

Check out the following video to see the code in action: `http://bit.ly/2M66bnv`

Understanding model-view design

Model-view is a software application design paradigm that implements **separation of concerns**. It is based on the venerable **Model-View-Controller** (MVC) pattern but differs in that the controller and view are combined into one component.

In model-view design, the **model** is the component that holds the application data and contains the logic for retrieving, storing, and manipulating data. The **view** component presents the data to the user and provides an interface for entering and manipulating data. By separating these components of the application, we keep their interdependency to a minimum, making them much easier to reuse or refactor.

Let's go through a simple example to illustrate this process. Starting with the application template from Chapter 4, *Building Applications with QMainWindow*, let's build a simple text-file editor:

```
# This code goes in MainWindow.__init__()
form = qtw.QWidget()
self.setCentralWidget(form)
form.setLayout(qtw.QVBoxLayout())
self.filename = qtw.QLineEdit()
self.filecontent = qtw.QTextEdit()
self.savebutton = qtw.QPushButton(
  'Save',
  clicked=self.save
)

form.layout().addWidget(self.filename)
form.layout().addWidget(self.filecontent)
form.layout().addWidget(self.savebutton)
```

This is a simple form with a line edit for the filename, a text edit for the content, and a **Save** button that calls a save() method.

Let's create the save() method as follows:

```
def save(self):
  filename = self.filename.text()
  error = ''
  if not filename:
    error = 'Filename empty'
  elif path.exists(filename):
    error = f'Will not overwrite {filename}'
  else:
    try:
      with open(filename, 'w') as fh:
```

```
            fh.write(self.filecontent.toPlainText())
      except Exception as e:
        error = f'Cannot write file: {e}'
    if error:
      qtw.QMessageBox.critical(None, 'Error', error)
```

This method checks whether there is a filename entered in the line edit, makes sure the filename doesn't already exist (so you don't overwrite an important file while testing this code!), then attempts to save it. If there is an error of any kind, the method displays a QMessageBox instance to report the error.

This application works but lacks a clean separation of model and view. The same method that writes the file to disk also displays error boxes and calls input widget methods. If we were going to expand this application to any degree, the save() method would quickly become a maze of presentation logic mixed with data-handling logic.

Let's rewrite this application with separate Model and View classes.

Starting with a clean copy of the application template, let's create our Model class:

```
class Model(qtc.QObject):

  error = qtc.pyqtSignal(str)

  def save(self, filename, content):
    print("save_called")
    error = ''
    if not filename:
      error = 'Filename empty'
    elif path.exists(filename):
      error = f'Will not overwrite {filename}'
    else:
      try:
        with open(filename, 'w') as fh:
          fh.write(content)
      except Exception as e:
        error = f'Cannot write file: {e}'
    if error:
      self.error.emit(error)
```

We've built our model by subclassing `QObject`. Models should have no involvement in displaying the GUI, so there's no need to base it on `QWidget` classes. However, as the model will use signals and slots to communicate, we're using `QObject` as a base class. The model implements our `save()` method from the previous example, but with two changes:

- First, it expects user data to be passed in as arguments, having no knowledge of the widgets this data came from
- Second, it merely emits a Qt signal when an error is encountered, rather than taking any GUI-specific actions

Next, let's create our `View` class:

```
class View(qtw.QWidget):

    submitted = qtc.pyqtSignal(str, str)

    def __init__(self):
        super().__init__()
        self.setLayout(qtw.QVBoxLayout())
        self.filename = qtw.QLineEdit()
        self.filecontent = qtw.QTextEdit()
        self.savebutton = qtw.QPushButton(
            'Save',
            clicked=self.submit
        )
        self.layout().addWidget(self.filename)
        self.layout().addWidget(self.filecontent)
        self.layout().addWidget(self.savebutton)

    def submit(self):
        filename = self.filename.text()
        filecontent = self.filecontent.toPlainText()
        self.submitted.emit(filename, filecontent)

    def show_error(self, error):
        qtw.QMessageBox.critical(None, 'Error', error)
```

This class contains the same fields and field layout definitions as before. This time, however, rather than calling `save()`, our **Save** button is connected to a `submit()` callback that gathers the form data and emits it using a signal. We've also added a `show_error()` method that will display errors.

In our `MainWindow.__init__()` method, we'll bring the model and view together:

```
self.view = View()
self.setCentralWidget(self.view)

self.model = Model()

self.view.submitted.connect(self.model.save)
self.model.error.connect(self.view.show_error)
```

Here, we create an instance of the `View` class and the `Model` class and connect their signals and slots.

At this point, the model-view version of our code works identically to our original version, but with more code involved. You might well ask, what's the point? If this application was destined never to be more than it is, there might not be a point. However, applications tend to expand in functionality and, often, other applications need to reuse the same code. Consider these scenarios:

- You want to provide an alternative editing form, perhaps console-based or with more editing features
- You want to provide the option of saving to a database instead of a text file
- You're creating another application that also saves text content to files

In each of these situations, using the model-view pattern means that we don't have to start from scratch. In the first case, for example, we don't need to rewrite any file-saving code; we just need to create the user-facing code that emits the same `submitted` signal. As your code expands and your applications become more complex, this separation of concerns will help you maintain order.

Models and views in PyQt

The model-view pattern is not only useful in the design of large applications, but also on a smaller scale with widgets that contain data. Copy the application template from Chapter 4, *Building Applications with QMainWindow*, and let's look at a simple example of how model-view works on the widget level.

In the `MainWindow` class, create a list of items and add them to both the `QListWidget` and `QComboBox` objects:

```
data = [
  'Hamburger', 'Cheeseburger',
  'Chicken Nuggets', 'Hot Dog', 'Fish Sandwich'
]
# The list widget
listwidget = qtw.QListWidget()
listwidget.addItems(data)
# The combobox
combobox = qtw.QComboBox()
combobox.addItems(data)
self.layout().addWidget(listwidget)
self.layout().addWidget(combobox)
```

Because both widgets were initialized with the same list, both contain the same items. Now, let's make the list widget items editable:

```
for i in range(listwidget.count()):
  item = listwidget.item(i)
  item.setFlags(item.flags() | qtc.Qt.ItemIsEditable)
```

By iterating through the items in the list widget and setting the `Qt.ItemIsEditable` flag on each one, the widget becomes editable and we can alter the text of the items. Run the application and try editing the items in the list widget. Even though you've altered the items in the list widget, the combobox items remain unchanged. Each widget has its own internal list model, which stores a copy of the items that were originally passed in. Altering the items in one copy of the list has no effect on the other copy.

How might we keep these two lists in sync? We could connect some signals and slots or add class methods to do it, but Qt provides a better way.

`QListWidget` is actually a combination of two other Qt classes: `QListView` and `QStringListModel`. As the names imply, these are model-view classes. We can use those classes directly to build our own list widget with a discrete model and view:

```
model = qtc.QStringListModel(data)
listview = qtw.QListView()
listview.setModel(model)
```

We simply create our model class, initializing it with our list of strings, then create the view class. Finally, we connect the two using the view's `setModel()` method.

`QComboBox` doesn't have analogous model-view classes, but is nonetheless internally a model-view widget and has the capability to use an external model.

So, we can pass our `QStringListModel` to it using `setModel()`:

```
model_combobox = qtw.QComboBox()
model_combobox.setModel(model)
```

Add those widgets to your layout and try running the program again. This time, you'll see that edits to `QListView` are immediately available in the combobox, because the changes you are making are being written to the `QStringModel` object, which both widgets consult for item data.

`QTableWidget` and `QTreeWidget` also have analogous view classes: `QTableView` and `QTreeView`. However, there are no ready-made model classes that we can use with these views. Instead, we have to create our own custom model classes by subclassing `QAbstractTableModel` and `QAbstractTreeModel`, respectively.

In the next section, we'll go through how to create and use a custom model class by building our own CSV editor.

Building a CSV editor

The **comma-separated values (CSV)** is a plain-text format for storing tabular data. Any spreadsheet program can export to CSV, or you can make your own by hand in a text editor. Our program will be designed in such a way that it will open any arbitrary CSV file and display the data in `QTableView`. It is common to use the first row of a CSV to hold column headers, so our application will assume this and make that row immutable.

Creating a table model

When developing a data-driven model-view application, the model is usually the best place to begin as this is where the most complex code will be found. Once we've put this backend in place, implementing the frontend is fairly trivial.

In this case, we need to design a model that can read and write CSV data. Copy the application template from `Chapter 4`, *Building Applications with QMainWindow*, and add an import at the top for the Python `csv` library.

Now, let's start building our model by subclassing `QAbstractTableModel`:

```
class CsvTableModel(qtc.QAbstractTableModel):
    """The model for a CSV table."""

    def __init__(self, csv_file):
        super().__init__()
        self.filename = csv_file
        with open(self.filename) as fh:
            csvreader = csv.reader(fh)
            self._headers = next(csvreader)
            self._data = list(csvreader)
```

Our model will take the name of a CSV file as an argument, and will immediately open the file and read it into memory (not a great strategy for large files, but this is only an example program). We'll assume the first row is a header row, and retrieve it using the `next()` function before pulling the rest of the rows into the model's _data property.

Implementing read capabilities

To create instances of our model to display data in a view, we need to implement three methods:

- `rowCount()`, which must return the total number of rows in the table
- `columnCount()`, which must return the total number of columns in the table
- `data()`, which is used to request data from the model

`rowCount()` and `columnCount()` are easy enough in this case:

```
def rowCount(self, parent):
    return len(self._data)

def columnCount(self, parent):
    return len(self._headers)
```

The row count is just the length of the _data property, and the column count can be had by taking the length of the _headers property. Both functions are required to take a `parent` argument, but in this case, it is not used as it refers to the parent node, which is applicable only in hierarchical data.

The last required method is `data()`, which requires more explanation; `data()` looks like this:

```
def data(self, index, role):
    if role == qtc.Qt.DisplayRole:
        return self._data[index.row()][index.column()]
```

The purpose of `data()` is to return the data in a single cell of the table given the arguments `index` and `role`. Now, `index` is an instance of the `QModelIndex` class, which describes the location of a single node in a list, table, or tree structure. Every `QModelIndex` contains the following properties:

- A `row` number
- A `column` number
- A `parent` model index

In the case of a table model such as ours, we are interested in the `row` and `column` properties, which indicate the table row and column of the data cell we want. If we were dealing with hierarchical data, we'd also want the `parent` property, which would be the index of the parent node. If this were a list, we'd only care about `row`.

`role` is a constant from the `QtCore.Qt.ItemDataRole` enum. When a view requests data from a model, it passes a `role` value so that the model can return the data or metadata appropriate to the context for which it is being requested. For example, if the view makes a request using the `EditRole` role, the model should return data suitable for editing. If the view requests with the `DecorationRole` role, the model should return an icon appropriate to the cell.

> If there is no data to be returned for a particular role, `data()` should return nothing.

In this case, we're only interested in displaying the data, which is represented by the `DisplayRole` role. To actually return the data, we need to get the index's row and column and use that to pull the appropriate row and column from our CSV data.

At this point, we have a minimally functional, read-only CSV model, but there is more we can add.

Adding headers and sorting

Being able to return the data is only one piece of a model's functionality. Models also need to be able to provide other information, such as the names of the column headers or the appropriate method for sorting the data.

To implement header data in our model, we need to create a `headerData()` method:

```
def headerData(self, section, orientation, role):

  if (
    orientation == qtc.Qt.Horizontal and
    role == qtc.Qt.DisplayRole
  ):
    return self._headers[section]
  else:
    return super().headerData(section, orientation, role)
```

`headerData()` returns data on a single header given three pieces of information—the **section**, **orientation**, and **role**.

Headers can be either vertical or horizontal as determined by the orientation argument, which is specified as either the `QtCore.Qt.Horizontal` or `QtCore.Qt.Vertical` constant.

The section is an integer that indicates either the column number (for horizontal headers) or row number (for vertical headers).

The role argument, as in the `data()` method, indicates the context for which the data needs to be returned.

In our case, we're only interested in showing horizontal headers for the `DisplayRole` role. Unlike the `data()` method, the parent class method has some default logic and return values, so in any other case, we want to return the result of `super().headerData()`.

If we want to be able to sort our data, we need to implement a `sort()` method, which will look like this:

```
def sort(self, column, order):
  self.layoutAboutToBeChanged.emit()  # needs to be emitted before a sort
  self._data.sort(key=lambda x: x[column])
  if order == qtc.Qt.DescendingOrder:
    self._data.reverse()
  self.layoutChanged.emit()  # needs to be emitted after a sort
```

`sort()` takes a `column` number and `order`, which is either
`QtCore.Qt.DescendingOrder` or `QtCore.Qt.AscendingOrder`, and the aim of this
method is to sort the data accordingly. In this case, we're using Python's `list.sort()`
method to sort our data in place, using the `column` argument to determine which column of
each row will be returned for sorting. If descending order is requested, we'll use
`reverse()` to change the ordering accordingly.

`sort()` must also emit two signals:

- `layoutAboutToBeChanged` must be emitted before any sorting happens
  internally.
- `layoutChanged` must be emitted after the sorting is finished.

These two signals are used by the views to redraw themselves appropriately, so it is
important to remember to emit them.

Implementing write capabilities

Our model is read-only at this point, but because we're implementing a CSV editor, we
need to implement writing data. To begin with, we need to override some methods to
enable editing of existing data rows: `flags()` and `setData()`.

`flags()` takes a `QModelIndex` value and returns a set of `QtCore.Qt.ItemFlag` constants
for the item at the given index. These flags are used to indicate whether the item can be
selected, dragged, dropped, checked, or—most interesting to us—edited.

Our method looks like this:

```
def flags(self, index):
    return super().flags(index) | qtc.Qt.ItemIsEditable
```

Here we're adding the `ItemIsEditable` flag to the list of flags returned by the parent
class's `flags()` method, indicating that the item is editable. If we wanted to implement
logic to make only certain cells editable under certain conditions, we could do that in this
method.

For example, if we had a list of read-only indexes stored in `self.readonly_indexes`, we could write this method as follows:

```
def flags(self, index):
    if index not in self.readonly_indexes:
        return super().flags(index) | qtc.Qt.ItemIsEditable
    else:
        return super().flags(index)
```

For our application, though, we want every cell to be editable.

Now that all items in the model are marked as editable, we need to tell our model how to actually edit them. This is defined in the `setData()` method:

```
def setData(self, index, value, role):
    if index.isValid() and role == qtc.Qt.EditRole:
        self._data[index.row()][index.column()] = value
        self.dataChanged.emit(index, index, [role])
        return True
    else:
        return False
```

The `setData()` method takes the index of the item to be set, the value to set it to, and an item role. This method must take on the task of setting the data and then return a Boolean value indicating whether or not the data were successfully changed. We only want to do this if the index is valid and the role is `EditRole`.

If the data are changed, `setData()` must also emit the `dataChanged` signal. This signal is emitted whenever an item or group of items is updated with regard to any role, and so carries with it three pieces of information: the top-leftmost index that was changed, the bottom-rightmost index that was changed, and a list of the roles for each index. In our case, we're only changing one cell so we can pass our index for both ends of the cell range, and a list with a single role in it.

There's one more small change to the `data()` method that isn't required but will make things easier for the user. Go back and edit the method as follows:

```
def data(self, index, role):
    if role in (qtc.Qt.DisplayRole, qtc.Qt.EditRole):
        return self._data[index.row()][index.column()]
```

When a table cell is selected for editing, `data()` will be called with the `EditRole` role. Before this change, `data()` would return `None` when called with that role and, as a result, the data in the cell will disappear as soon as the cell is selected. By returning the data for `EditRole` as well, the user will have access to the existing data for editing.

We have now implemented the editing of existing cells, but to make our model completely editable we need to implement the insertion and removal of rows. We can do this by overriding two more methods: `insertRows()` and `removeRows()`.

The `insertRows()` method looks like this:

```
def insertRows(self, position, rows, parent):
  self.beginInsertRows(
    parent or qtc.QModelIndex(),
    position,
    position + rows - 1
  )
  for i in range(rows):
    default_row = [''] * len(self._headers)
    self._data.insert(position, default_row)
  self.endInsertRows()
```

The method takes the *position* where the insertion starts, the number of *rows* to be inserted, and the parent node index (used with hierarchical data).

Inside the method, we must put our logic between calls to `beginInsertRows()` and `endInsertRows()`. The `beginInsertRows()` method prepares the underlying object for modification, and requires three arguments:

- The `ModelIndex` object of the parent node, which is an empty `QModelIndex` for tabular data
- The position where row insertion will start
- The position where row insertion will end

We can calculate all this from the start position and the number of rows passed into the method. Once we've taken care of that, we can generate a number of rows (in the form of lists of empty strings the same length as our header list) and insert them into `self._data` at the proper index.

After the rows are inserted, we call `endInsertRows()`, which takes no arguments.

The `removeRows()` method is very similar:

```
def removeRows(self, position, rows, parent):
  self.beginRemoveRows(
    parent or qtc.QModelIndex(),
    position,
    position + rows - 1
  )
  for i in range(rows):
    del(self._data[position])
  self.endRemoveRows()
```

Once again, we need to call `beginRemoveRows()` before editing the data and `endRemoveRows()` after editing, just as we did for insertion. If we wanted to allow editing of the column structure, we could override the `insertColumns()` and `removeColumns()` methods, which work essentially the same way as the row methods. For now, we'll just stick to row editing.

At this point, our model is fully editable, but we'll add one more method that we can call to flush the data to disk, as follows:

```
def save_data(self):
  with open(self.filename, 'w', encoding='utf-8') as fh:
    writer = csv.writer(fh)
    writer.writerow(self._headers)
    writer.writerows(self._data)
```

This method simply opens our file and writes in the headers and all data rows using the Python `csv` library.

Using the model in a view

Now that our model is ready to use, let's flesh out the rest of the application to demonstrate how to use it.

To begin with, we need to create a `QTableView` widget and add it to our `MainWindow`:

```
# in MainWindow.__init__()
self.tableview = qtw.QTableView()
self.tableview.setSortingEnabled(True)
self.setCentralWidget(self.tableview)
```

As you can see, we don't have to do much to make the `QTableView` widget work with the model. Because we implemented `sort()` in the model, we'll enable sorting, but otherwise, it doesn't require much configuration.

Of course, to see any data, we need to assign a model to the view; and in order to create a model, we need a file. Let's create a callback to get one:

```
def select_file(self):
    filename, _ = qtw.QFileDialog.getOpenFileName(
        self,
        'Select a CSV file to open...',
        qtc.QDir.homePath(),
        'CSV Files (*.csv) ;; All Files (*)'
    )
    if filename:
        self.model = CsvTableModel(filename)
        self.tableview.setModel(self.model)
```

Our method uses a `QFileDialog` class to query the user for a CSV file to open. If one is chosen, it uses the CSV file to create an instance of our model class. The model class is then assigned to the view using the `setModel()` accessor method.

Back in `MainWindow.__init__()`, let's create a main menu for the application and add an `'Open'` action:

```
menu = self.menuBar()
file_menu = menu.addMenu('File')
file_menu.addAction('Open', self.select_file)
```

If you run the script now, you should be able to open a file by going to **File** | **Open** and selecting a valid CSV. You should be able to view and even edit the data, and the data should sort by column if you click a header cell.

Next, let's add the user interface components that will allow us to save our file. To begin, create a menu item that calls a `MainWindow` method called `save_file()`:

```
file_menu.addAction('Save', self.save_file)
```

Now, let's create our `save_file()` method to actually save the file:

```
def save_file(self):
    if self.model:
        self.model.save_data()
```

To save the file, all we really need to do is call the model's `save_data()` method. However, we can't connect our menu item directly to that method, because the model doesn't exist until a file is actually loaded. This wrapper method allows us to create a menu option without a model.

The last piece of functionality we want to connect is the ability to insert and remove rows. In a spreadsheet, it is often useful to be able to insert rows either above or below the selected row. So, let's create callbacks in `MainWindow` that do just that:

```
def insert_above(self):
    selected = self.tableview.selectedIndexes()
    row = selected[0].row() if selected else 0
    self.model.insertRows(row, 1, None)

def insert_below(self):
    selected = self.tableview.selectedIndexes()
    row = selected[-1].row() if selected else self.model.rowCount(None)
    self.model.insertRows(row + 1, 1, None)
```

In both methods, we're getting a list of the selected cells by calling the table view's `selectedIndexes()` method. These lists are sorted from upper-leftmost cells to lower-rightmost cells. So, for inserting above, we retrieve the row of the first index in the list (or 0 if the list is empty). For inserting below, we retrieve the row of the last index in the list (or the last index in the table if the list is empty). Finally, in both methods, we use the model's `insertRows()` method to insert one row to the appropriate location.

Removing rows is similar, as shown here:

```
def remove_rows(self):
    selected = self.tableview.selectedIndexes()
    if selected:
        self.model.removeRows(selected[0].row(), len(selected), None)
```

This time we only act if there is an active selection, and use the model's `removeRows()` method to remove the first selected row.

To make these callbacks available to the user, let's add an `'Edit'` menu back in `MainWindow`:

```
edit_menu = menu.addMenu('Edit')
edit_menu.addAction('Insert Above', self.insert_above)
edit_menu.addAction('Insert Below', self.insert_below)
edit_menu.addAction('Remove Row(s)', self.remove_rows)
```

At this point, try loading up a CSV file. You should be able to insert and remove rows in your table, edit fields, and save the result. Congratulations, you've created a CSV editor!

Summary

In this chapter, you learned about model-view programming. You learned about using models with regular widgets and about the special model-view classes in Qt. You created a custom table model and rapidly built a CSV editor by exploiting the power of model-view classes.

We will learn more advanced model-view concepts, including delegates and data mapping in Chapter 9, *Exploring SQL with QtSQL*.

In the next chapter, you'll learn about styling your PyQt applications. We'll dress up our drab forms with images, dynamic icons, fancy fonts, and colors, and we'll learn multiple approaches for controlling the overall look and feel of your Qt GUIs.

Questions

Try these questions to test your knowledge from this chapter:

1. Assuming we have a well-designed model-view application, is the following code part of a model or a view?

```
def save_as(self):
    filename, _ = qtw.QFileDialog(self)
    self.data.save_file(filename)
```

2. Can you name at least two things that a model should never do and two things that a view should never do?
3. QAbstractTableModel and QAbstractTreeModel both have *Abstract* in the name. What does *Abstract* mean in this context? Does it mean something different in C++ from what it means in Python?
4. Which model type—list, table, or tree—would best suit the following collections of data:

    - The user's recent files
    - A Windows registry hive
    - Linux syslog records
    - Blog entries
    - Personal salutations (for example, Mr., Mrs., or Dr.)
    - Distributed version control history

5. Why is the following code failing?

```
class DataModel(QAbstractTreeModel):
    def rowCount(self, node):
        if node > 2:
            return 1
        else:
            return len(self._data[node])
```

6. Your table model isn't working quite right when inserting columns. What is wrong with your `insertColumns()` method?

```
def insertColumns(self, col, count, parent):
    for row in self._data:
        for i in range(count):
            row.insert(col, '')
```

7. You would like your views to display the item data as a tooltip when hovered. How would you accomplish this?

Further reading

You might want to check out the following resources:

- The Qt documentation on model-view programming at https://doc.qt.io/qt-5/model-view-programming.html
- Martin Fowler presents an overview of **Model View Controller** (**MVC**) and related patterns at https://martinfowler.com/eaaDev/uiArchs.html

6
Styling Qt Applications

It is easy to appreciate the clean, native look that Qt effortlessly provides by default. But for less business-like applications, plain gray widgets and bog-standard fonts don't always set the right tone. Even the drabbest utility or data entry application occasionally benefits from the addition of icons or the judicious tweaking of fonts to enhance usability. Fortunately, Qt's flexibility allows us to take the look and feel of our application into our own hands.

In this chapter, we'll cover the following topics:

- Using fonts, images, and icons
- Configuring colors, style sheets, and styles
- Creating animations

Technical requirements

In this chapter, you'll need all the requirements listed in Chapter 1, *Getting Started with PyQt*, and the Qt application template from Chapter 4, *Building Applications with QMainWindow*.

Additionally, you may require PNG, JPEG, or GIF image files to work with; you can use those included in the example code at https://github.com/PacktPublishing/Mastering-GUI-Programming-with-Python/tree/master/Chapter06.

Check out the following video to see the code in action: http://bit.ly/2M5OJj6

Using fonts, images, and icons

We'll begin styling our Qt application by customizing the application's fonts, displaying some static images, and including dynamic icons. However, before we can do this, we'll need to create a **graphical user interface** (GUI) that we can work with. We'll create a game lobby dialog, which will be used for logging into an imaginary multiplayer game called **Fight Fighter**.

To do this, open a fresh copy of your application template and add the following GUI code to MainWindow.__init__():

```python
self.setWindowTitle('Fight Fighter Game Lobby')
cx_form = qtw.QWidget()
self.setCentralWidget(cx_form)
cx_form.setLayout(qtw.QFormLayout())
heading = qtw.QLabel("Fight Fighter!")
cx_form.layout().addRow(heading)

inputs = {
    'Server': qtw.QLineEdit(),
    'Name': qtw.QLineEdit(),
    'Password': qtw.QLineEdit(
        echoMode=qtw.QLineEdit.Password),
    'Team': qtw.QComboBox(),
    'Ready.': qtw.QCheckBox('Check when ready')
}
teams = ('Crimson Sharks', 'Shadow Hawks',
         'Night Terrors', 'Blue Crew')
inputs['Team'].addItems(teams)
for label, widget in inputs.items():
    cx_form.layout().addRow(label, widget)
self.submit = qtw.QPushButton(
    'Connect',
    clicked=lambda: qtw.QMessageBox.information(
        None, 'Connecting', 'Prepare for Battle!'))
self.reset = qtw.QPushButton('Cancel', clicked=self.close)
cx_form.layout().addRow(self.submit, self.reset)
```

This is fairly standard Qt GUI code that you should be familiar with by now; we're saving a few lines of code by putting our inputs in a `dict` object and adding them to the layout in a loop, but otherwise, it's relatively straightforward. Depending on your OS and theme settings, the dialog box probably looks something like the following screenshot:

As you can see, it's a nice form but it's a bit bland. So, let's explore whether we can improve the style.

Setting a font

The first thing we'll tackle is the font. Every `QWidget` class has a `font` property, which we can either set in the constructor or by using the `setFont()` accessor. The value of `font` must be a `QtGui.QFont` object.

Here is how you can create and use a `QFont` object:

```
heading_font = qtg.QFont('Impact', 32, qtg.QFont.Bold)
heading_font.setStretch(qtg.QFont.ExtraExpanded)
heading.setFont(heading_font)
```

A `QFont` object contains all the attributes that describe the way text will be drawn to the screen. The constructor can take any of the following arguments:

- A string indicating the font family
- A float or integer indicating the point size
- A `QtGui.QFont.FontWeight` constant indicating the weight
- A Boolean indicating whether the font should be italic

The remaining aspects of the font, such as the `stretch` property, can be configured using keyword arguments or accessor methods. We can also create a `QFont` object with no arguments and configure it programmatically, as follows:

```
label_font = qtg.QFont()
label_font.setFamily('Impact')
label_font.setPointSize(14)
label_font.setWeight(qtg.QFont.DemiBold)
label_font.setStyle(qtg.QFont.StyleItalic)

for inp in inputs.values():
    cx_form.layout().labelForField(inp).setFont(label_font)
```

Setting a font on a widget affects not only the widget but also all its child widgets. Therefore, we could configure the font for the entire form by setting it on `cx_form` rather than setting it on individual widgets.

Dealing with missing fonts

Now, if all platforms and **operating systems (OSes)** shipped with an infinite array of identically named fonts, this would be all you'd need to know about `QFont`. Unfortunately, that isn't the case. Most systems ship with only a handful of fonts built-in and only a few of these are universal across platforms or even different versions of a platform. Therefore, Qt has a fallback mechanism for dealing with missing fonts.

For example, suppose that we ask Qt to use a nonexistent font family, as follows:

```
button_font = qtg.QFont(
    'Totally Nonexistant Font Family XYZ', 15.233)
```

Qt will not throw an error at this call or even register a warning. Instead, after not finding the font family requested, it will fall back to its `defaultFamily` property, which utilizes the default font set in the OS or desktop environment.

The `QFont` object won't actually tell us that this has happened; if you query it for information, it will only tell you what was configured:

```
print(f'Font is {button_font.family()}')
# Prints: "Font is Totally Nonexistent Font Family XYZ"
```

To discover what font settings are actually being used, we need to pass our `QFont` object to a `QFontInfo` object:

```
actual_font = qtg.QFontInfo(button_font).family()
print(f'Actual font used is {actual_font}')
```

If you run the script, you'll see that, more than likely, your default screen font is actually being used here:

```
$ python game_lobby.py
Font is Totally Nonexistent Font Family XYZ
Actual font used is Bitstream Vera Sans
```

While this ensures that users won't be left without any text in the window, it would be nice if we could give Qt a better idea of what sort of font it should use.

We can do this by setting the font's `styleHint` and `styleStrategy` properties, as follows:

```
button_font.setStyleHint(qtg.QFont.Fantasy)
button_font.setStyleStrategy(
    qtg.QFont.PreferAntialias |
    qtg.QFont.PreferQuality
)
```

`styleHint` suggests a general category for Qt to fall back on, which, in this case, is the `Fantasy` category. Other options here include `SansSerif`, `Serif`, `TypeWriter`, `Decorative`, `Monospace`, and `Cursive`. What these options correspond to is dependent on the OS and desktop environment configuration.

The `styleStrategy` property informs Qt of more technical preferences related to the capabilities of the chosen font, such as anti-aliasing, OpenGL compatibility, and whether the size will be matched exactly or rounded to the nearest non-scaled size. The complete list of strategy options can be found at `https://doc.qt.io/qt-5/qfont.html#StyleStrategy-enum`.

After setting these properties, check the font again to see whether anything has changed:

```
actual_font = qtg.QFontInfo(button_font)
print(f'Actual font used is {actual_font.family()}'
    f' {actual_font.pointSize()}')
self.submit.setFont(button_font)
self.cancel.setFont(button_font)
```

Depending on your system's configuration, you should see different results from before:

```
$ python game_lobby.py
Actual font used is Impact 15
```

On this system, `Fantasy` has been interpreted to mean `Impact`, and the `PreferQuality` strategy flag has forced the initially odd 15.233 point size to be a nice round `15`.

At this point, depending on the fonts available on your system, your application should look as follows:

 Fonts can also be bundled with the application; see the *Using Qt resource files* section in this chapter.

Adding images

Qt offers a number of classes related to the use of images in an application, but, for simply displaying a picture in your GUI, the most appropriate is QPixmap. QPixmap is a display-optimized image class, which can load many common image formats including PNG, BMP, GIF, and JPEG.

To create one, we simply need to pass QPixmap a path to an image file:

```
logo = qtg.QPixmap('logo.png')
```

Once loaded, a QPixmap object can be displayed in a QLabel or QButton object, as follows:

```
heading.setPixmap(logo)
```

Note that labels can only display a string or a pixmap, but not both.

Being optimized for display, the QPixmap objects offer only minimal editing functionality; however, we can do simple transformations such as scaling:

```
if logo.width() > 400:
    logo = logo.scaledToWidth(
        400, qtc.Qt.SmoothTransformation)
```

In this example, we've used the pixmap's scaledToWidth() method to restrict the logo's width to 400 pixels using a smooth transformation algorithm.

> The reason why QPixmap objects are so limited is that they are actually stored in the display server's memory. The QImage class is similar but stores data in application memory, so that it can be edited more extensively. We'll explore this class more in Chapter 12, *Creating 2D Graphics with QPainter*.

QPixmap also offers the handy capability to generate simple colored rectangles, as follows:

```
go_pixmap = qtg.QPixmap(qtc.QSize(32, 32))
stop_pixmap = qtg.QPixmap(qtc.QSize(32, 32))
go_pixmap.fill(qtg.QColor('green'))
stop_pixmap.fill(qtg.QColor('red'))
```

By specifying a size in the constructor and using the fill() method, we can create a simple, colored rectangle pixmap. This is useful for displaying color swatches or to use as a quick-and-dirty image stand-in.

Using icons

Now consider an icon on a toolbar or in a program menu. When the menu item is disabled, you expect the icon to be grayed out in some way. Likewise, if a user hovers over the button or item using a mouse cursor, you might expect it to be highlighted. To encapsulate this type of state-dependent image display, Qt provides the QIcon class. A QIcon object contains a collection of pixmaps that are each mapped to a widget state.

Here is how you can create a QIcon object:

```
connect_icon = qtg.QIcon()
connect_icon.addPixmap(go_pixmap, qtg.QIcon.Active)
connect_icon.addPixmap(stop_pixmap, qtg.QIcon.Disabled)
```

After creating the icon object, we use its `addPixmap()` method to assign a `QPixmap` object to a widget state. These states include `Normal`, `Active`, `Disabled`, and `Selected`.

The `connect_icon` icon will now be a red square when disabled, or a green square when enabled. Let's add it to our submit button and add some logic to toggle the button's status:

```
self.submit.setIcon(connect_icon)
self.submit.setDisabled(True)
inputs['Server'].textChanged.connect(
    lambda x: self.submit.setDisabled(x == '')
)
```

If you run the script at this point, you'll see that the red square appears in the submit button until the `Server` field contains data, at which point it automatically switches to green. Notice that we don't have to tell the icon object itself to switch states; once assigned to the widget, it tracks any changes in the widget's state.

Icons can be used with the `QPushButton`, `QToolButton`, and `QAction` objects; the `QComboBox`, `QListView`, `QTableView`, and `QTreeView` items; and most other places where you might reasonably expect to have an icon.

Using Qt resource files

A significant problem with using image files in a program is making sure the program can find them at runtime. Paths passed into a `QPixmap` constructor or a `QIcon` constructor are interpreted as absolute (that is, if they begin with a drive letter or path separator), or as relative to the current working directory (which you cannot control). For example, try running your script from somewhere other than the code directory, as follows:

```
$ cd ..
$ python ch05/game_lobby.py
```

You'll find that your images are all missing! `QPixmap` does not complain when it cannot find a file, it just doesn't show anything. Without an absolute path to the images, you'll only be able to find them if the script is run from the exact directory to which your paths are relative.

Unfortunately, specifying absolute paths means that your program will only work from one location on the filesystem, which is a major problem if you plan to distribute it to multiple platforms.

PyQt offers us a solution to this problem in the form of a **PyQt Resource file**, which we can create using the **PyQt resource compiler** tool. The basic procedure is as follows:

1. Write an XML-format **Qt Resource Collection** file (.qrc) containing the paths of all the files that we want to include
2. Run the pyrcc5 tool to serialize and compress these files into data contained in a Python module
3. Import the resulting Python module into our application script
4. Now we can reference our resources using a special syntax

Let's step through this process—suppose that we have some team badges in the form of PNG files that we want to include in our program. Our first step is to create the resources.qrc file, which looks like the following code block:

```
<RCC>
  <qresource prefix="teams">
    <file>crimson_sharks.png</file>
    <file>shadow_hawks.png</file>
    <file>night_terrors.png</file>
    <file alias="blue_crew.png">blue_crew2.png</file>
  </qresource>
</RCC>
```

We've placed this file in the same directory as the image files listed in the script. Note that we've added a prefix value of teams. Prefixes allow you to organize resources into categories. Additionally, notice that the last file has an alias specified. In our program, we can use this alias rather than the actual name of the file to access this resource.

Now, in the command line, we'll run pyrcc5, as follows:

```
$ pyrcc5 -o resources.py resources.qrc
```

The syntax here is pyrcc5 -o outputFile.py inputFile.qrc. This command should generate a Python file containing your resource data. If you take a moment to open the file and examine it, you'll find it's mostly just a large bytes object assigned to the qt_resource_data variable.

Back in our main script, we just need to import this file in the same way as any other Python file:

```
import resources
```

The file doesn't have to be called `resources.py`; in fact, any name will suffice. You just need to import it, and the code in the file will make sure that the resources are available to Qt.

Now that the resource file is imported, we can specify pixmap paths using the resource syntax:

```python
inputs['Team'].setItemIcon(
    0, qtg.QIcon(':/teams/crimson_sharks.png'))
inputs['Team'].setItemIcon(
    1, qtg.QIcon(':/teams/shadow_hawks.png'))
inputs['Team'].setItemIcon(
    2, qtg.QIcon(':/teams/night_terrors.png'))
inputs['Team'].setItemIcon(
    3, qtg.QIcon(':/teams/blue_crew.png'))
```

Essentially, the syntax is `:/prefix/file_name_or_alias.extension`.

Because our data is stored in a Python file, we can place it inside a Python library and it will use Python's standard import resolution rules to locate the file.

Qt resource files and fonts

Resource files aren't limited to images; in fact, they can be used to include just about any kind of binary, including font files. For example, suppose that we want to include our favorite font in the program to ensure that it looks right on all platforms.

Just as with images, we start by including the font file in the `.qrc` file:

```xml
<RCC>
  <qresource prefix="teams">
    <file>crimson_sharks.png</file>
    <file>shadow_hawks.png</file>
    <file>night_terrors.png</file>
    <file>blue_crew.png</file>
  </qresource>
  <qresource prefix="fonts">
    <file>LiberationSans-Regular.ttf</file>
  </qresource>
</RCC>
```

Here, we've added a prefix of `fonts` and included a reference to the `LiberationSans-Regular.ttf` file. After running `pyrcc5` against this file, the font is bundled into our `resources.py` file.

To use this font in the code, we start by adding it to the font database, as follows:

```
libsans_id = qtg.QFontDatabase.addApplicationFont(
    ':/fonts/LiberationSans-Regular.ttf')
```

`QFontDatabase.addApplicationFont()` inserts the passed font file into the application's font database and returns an ID number. We can then use that ID number to determine the font's family string; this can be passed to `QFont`, as follows:

```
family = qtg.QFontDatabase.applicationFontFamilies(libsans_id)[0]
libsans = qtg.QFont(family)
inputs['Team'].setFont(libsans)
```

Make sure to check the license on your font before distributing it with your application! Remember that not all fonts are free to redistribute.

Our form is certainly looking more game-like now; run the application and it should look similar the following screenshot:

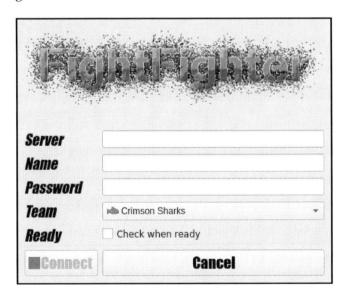

Configuring colors, style sheets, and styles

Fonts and icons have improved the look of our form, but now it's time to ditch those institutional gray tones and replace them with some color. In this section, we're going to look at three different approaches that Qt offers for customizing application colors: manipulating the **palette**, using **style sheets**, and overriding the **application style**.

Customizing colors with palettes

A palette, represented by the QPalette class, is a collection of colors and brushes that are mapped to color roles and color groups.

Let's unpack that statement:

- Here, **color** is a literal color value, represented by a QColor object
- A **brush** combines a particular color with a style, such as a pattern, gradient, or texture, and is represented by a QBrush class
- A **color role** represents the way a widget uses the color, such as in the foreground, in the background, or in the border
- The **color group** refers to the interaction state of the widget; it can be Normal, Active, Disabled, or Inactive

When a widget is painted on the screen, Qt's painting system consults the palette to determine the color and brush used to render each piece of the widget. To customize this, we can create our own palette and assign it to a widget.

To begin, we need to get a QPalette object, as follows:

```
app = qtw.QApplication.instance()
palette = app.palette()
```

While we could just create a QPalette object directly, the Qt documentation recommends that we call palette() on our running QApplication instance to retrieve a copy of the palette for the currently configured style.

You can always retrieve a copy of your QApplication object by calling QApplication.instance().

Now that we have the palette, let's start overriding some of the rules:

```
palette.setColor(
    qtg.QPalette.Button,
    qtg.QColor('#333')
)
palette.setColor(
    qtg.QPalette.ButtonText,
    qtg.QColor('#3F3')
)
```

`QtGui.QPalette.Button` and `QtGui.QPalette.ButtonText` are color role constants and, as you might guess, they represent the background and foreground colors, respectively, of all the Qt button classes. We're overriding them with new colors.

To override the color for a particular button state, we need to pass in a color group constant as the first argument:

```
palette.setColor(
    qtg.QPalette.Disabled,
    qtg.QPalette.ButtonText,
    qtg.QColor('#F88')
)
palette.setColor(
    qtg.QPalette.Disabled,
    qtg.QPalette.Button,
    qtg.QColor('#888')
)
```

In this case, we're changing the colors used when a button is in the `Disabled` state.

To apply this new palette, we have to assign it to a widget, as follows:

```
self.submit.setPalette(palette)
self.cancel.setPalette(palette)
```

`setPalette()` assigns the provided palette to the widget and all the child widgets as well. So, rather than assigning this to individual widgets, we could create a single palette and assign it to our `QMainWindow` class to apply it to all objects.

Working with QBrush objects

If we want something fancier than a solid color, then we can use a `QBrush` object. Brushes are capable of filling colors in patterns, gradients, or textures (that is, image-based patterns).

For example, let's create a brush that paints a white stipple fill:

```
dotted_brush = qtg.QBrush(
    qtg.QColor('white'), qtc.Qt.Dense2Pattern)
```

`Dense2Pattern` is one of 15 patterns available. (You can refer to `https://doc.qt.io/qt-5/qt.html#BrushStyle-enum` for the full list.) Most of these are varying degrees of stippling, cross-hatching, or alternating line patterns.

Patterns have their uses, but gradient-based brushes are perhaps more interesting for modern styling. However, creating one is a little more involved, as shown in the following code:

```
gradient = qtg.QLinearGradient(0, 0, self.width(), self.height())
gradient.setColorAt(0, qtg.QColor('navy'))
gradient.setColorAt(0.5, qtg.QColor('darkred'))
gradient.setColorAt(1, qtg.QColor('orange'))
gradient_brush = qtg.QBrush(gradient)
```

To use a gradient in a brush, we first have to create a gradient object. Here, we've created a `QLinearGradient` object, which implements a basic linear gradient. The arguments are the starting and ending coordinates for the gradient, which we've specified as the top-left (0, 0), and the bottom-right (width, height) of the main window.

 Qt also offers the `QRadialGradient` and `QConicalGradient` classes for additional gradient options.

After creating the object, we then specify color stops using `setColorAt()`. The first argument is a float value between 0 and 1 that specifies the percentage between the start and finish, and the second argument is the `QColor` object that the gradient should be at that point.

After creating the gradient, we pass it to the `QBrush` constructor to create a brush that paints with our gradient.

We can now apply our brushes to a palette using the `setBrush()` method, as follows:

```
window_palette = app.palette()
window_palette.setBrush(
    qtg.QPalette.Window,
    gradient_brush
)
window_palette.setBrush(
    qtg.QPalette.Active,
    qtg.QPalette.WindowText,
    dotted_brush
)
self.setPalette(window_palette)
```

Just as with `QPalette.setColor()`, we can assign our brush with or without specifying a specific color group. In this case, our gradient brush will be used to paint the main window regardless of its state, but our dotted brush will only be used when the widget is active (that is, the currently active window).

Customizing the appearance with Qt Style Sheets (QSS)

For developers who have worked with web technologies, styling an application using palette, brush, and color objects may seem verbose and unintuitive. Fortunately, Qt offers you an alternative known as QSS, which is very similar to the **Cascading Style Sheets (CSS)** used in web development. It is an easy way to apply some simple changes to our widgets.

You can use QSS as follows:

```
stylesheet = """
QMainWindow {
    background-color: black;
}
QWidget {
    background-color: transparent;
    color: #3F3;
}
QLineEdit, QComboBox, QCheckBox {
    font-size: 16pt;
}"""
self.setStyleSheet(stylesheet)
```

Here, a style sheet is just a string containing style directives, which we can assign to a widget's `styleSheet` property.

The syntax, which should be familiar to anyone who has worked with CSS, is as follows:

```
WidgetClass {
    property-name: value;
    property-name2: value2;
}
```

If you run the program at this point, you'll find, to your dismay, that (depending on your system theme) it may look something like the following screenshot:

Here, the interface has mostly gone black apart from the text and images. Our buttons and checkbox, in particular, are indistinguishable from the background. So, why did this happen?

Well, when you add a QSS style to a widget class, the style change carries down to all its subclasses. Since we styled `QWidget`, all the other `QWidget` derived classes (such as `QCheckbox` and `QPushButton`) inherited this style.

Let's fix this by overriding the styles for those subclasses, as follows:

```
stylesheet += """
QPushButton {
    background-color: #333;
}
QCheckBox::indicator:unchecked {
    border: 1px solid silver;
    background-color: darkred;
}
```

```
QCheckBox::indicator:checked {
    border: 1px solid silver;
    background-color: #3F3;
}
"""
self.setStyleSheet(stylesheet)
```

Just as with CSS, applying a style to a more specific class overrides the more general case. For example, our `QPushButton` background color overrides the `QWidget` background color.

Note the use of colons with `QCheckBox`—the double colon in QSS allows us to reference a subelement of a widget. In this case, this is the indicator portion of the `QCheckBox` class (as opposed to its label portion). We can also use a single colon to reference a widget state, as, in this case, we're setting a different style depending on whether or not the checkbox is checked or unchecked.

If you wanted to restrict a change to a particular class only and not any of its subclasses, simply add a period (.) to the name, as follows:

```
stylesheet += """
.QWidget {
    background: url(tile.png);
}
"""
```

This preceding example also demonstrates how to use images in QSS. Just like in CSS, we can provide a file path that is wrapped in the `url()` function.

> QSS also accepts resource paths if you've serialized your images with `pyrcc5`.

If you want to apply a style to a particular widget rather than a whole class of widgets, there are two ways to do so.

The first method is to rely on the `objectName` property, as follows:

```
self.submit.setObjectName('SubmitButton')
stylesheet += """
#SubmitButton:disabled {
    background-color: #888;
    color: darkred;
}
"""
```

In our style sheet, an object name must be preceded by a

symbol to identify it as an object name rather than a class.

The other way to set styles on individual widgets is to call t

he widget's setStyleSheet() method with some style sheet directives, as follows:

```
for inp in ('Server', 'Name', 'Password'):
    inp_widget = inputs[inp]
    inp_widget.setStyleSheet('background-color: black')
```

If we want to apply a style directly to the widget we're calling, we don't need to specify class names or object names; we can simply pass in the properties and values.

Having made all these changes, our application now looks a lot more like a game GUI:

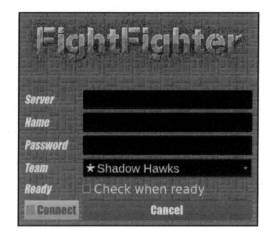

The downside of QSS

As you can see, QSS is a very powerful styling method and is accessible for any developer who has worked with web development; however, it does have some disadvantages.

QSS is an abstraction over the palette and style objects and must be translated to the actual system. This makes them slower for large applications, and it also means that there is no default style sheet that you can retrieve and edit – you're starting from scratch each time.

As we've already seen, QSS can have unpredictable results when applied to high-level widgets, since it inherits through the class hierarchy.

Finally, bear in mind that QSS is a modest subset of CSS 2.0 with a few additions or changes—it is not CSS. Therefore, transitions, animations, flexbox containers, relative units, and other modern CSS goodies are completely absent. So, while web developers may find its basic syntax familiar, the limited set of options may be frustrating and its different behaviors confusing.

Customizing the appearance with QStyle

Palettes and style sheets can take us a long way towards customizing the look of a Qt application, and for most cases, that's all you'll ever need. To really dig into the heart of a Qt application's appearance, we need to understand the style system.

Every running instance of a Qt application has a single style, which is in charge of telling the graphics system how to draw each widget or GUI component. Styles are dynamic and pluggable, so that different OS platforms have different styles, and users can install their own Qt styles to use in Qt applications. This is how Qt applications are able to have a native look on different OSes.

In `Chapter 1`, *Getting Started with PyQt*, we learned that `QApplication` should be passed a copy of `sys.argv` when created, so that it can process some Qt-specific arguments. One such argument is `-style`, which allows the user to set a custom style for their Qt application.

For example, let's run the calendar application from `Chapter 3`, *Handling Events with Signals and Slots*, with the `Windows` style:

```
$ python3 calendar_app.py -style Windows
```

Now try it using the `Fusion` style, as follows:

```
$ python3 calendar_app.py -style Fusion
```

Notice the difference in appearance, especially in the input controls.

Capitalization counts with styles; **windows** is not a valid style, whereas **Windows** is!

The styles that are available on common OS platforms are shown in the following table:

OS	Styles
Windows 10	windowsvista, Windows, and Fusion
macOS	macintosh, Windows, and Fusion
Ubuntu 18.04	Windows and Fusion

 On many Linux distributions, additional Qt styles are available from the package repositories. A list of currently installed styles can be obtained by calling QtWidgets.QStyleFactory.keys().

Styles can also be set inside the application itself. In order to retrieve a style class, we need to use the QStyleFactory class, as follows:

```
if __name__ == '__main__':
    app = qtw.QApplication(sys.argv)
    windows_style = qtw.QStyleFactory.create('Windows')
    app.setStyle(windows_style)
```

QStyleFactory.create() will attempt to find an installed style with the given name and return a QCommonStyle object; if the style requested is not found, then it will return None. The style object can then be used to set the style property of our QApplication object. (A value of None will just cause it to use the default.)

 If you plan to set a style inside the application, it's best to do it as early as possible before any widgets are drawn to avoid visual glitches.

Customizing Qt styles

Building a Qt style is an involved process that requires a deep understanding of Qt's widgets and painting system, and few developers will ever need to create one. We might, however, want to override some aspects of the running style to accomplish some things that aren't possible through manipulation of the palette or style sheets. We can do this by subclassing QtWidgets.QProxyStyle.

A proxy style is an overlay that we can use to override methods of the actual style that's running. In this way, it doesn't matter what actual style the user chooses, our proxy style's methods (where implemented) will be used instead.

For example, let's create a proxy style that forces all the screen text to be in uppercase, as follows:

```
class StyleOverrides(qtw.QProxyStyle):

    def drawItemText(
            self, painter, rect,
            flags, palette, enabled,
            text, textRole
    ):
        """Force uppercase in all text"""
        text = text.upper()
        super().drawItemText(
            painter, rect, flags,
            palette, enabled, text,
            textRole
        )
```

`drawItemText()` is the method called on the style whenever text must be drawn to the screen. It receives a number of arguments, but the one we're most concerned with is the `text` argument that is to be drawn. We're simply going to intercept this text and make it uppercase before passing all the arguments back to `super().drawTextItem()`.

This proxy style can then be applied to our `QApplication` object in the same way as any other style:

```
if __name__ == '__main__':
    app = qtw.QApplication(sys.argv)
    proxy_style= StyleOverrides()
    app.setStyle(proxy_style)
```

If you run the program at this point, you'll see that all the text is now uppercase. Mission accomplished!

Drawing widgets

Now let's try something a bit more ambitious. Let's change all our `QLineEdit` entry boxes to a green rounded rectangle outline. So, how do we go about doing this in a proxy style?

The first step is to figure out what element of the widget we're trying to modify. These can be found as enum constants of the `QStyle` class, and they're divided into three main classes:

- `PrimitiveElement`, which includes fundamental, non-interactive GUI elements such as frames or backgrounds
- `ControlElement`, which includes interactive elements such as buttons or tabs
- `ComplexControl`, which includes complex interactive elements such as combo boxes and sliders

Each of these classes of items is drawn by a different method of `QStyle`; in this case, it turns out that we want to modify the `PE_FrameLineEdit` element, which is a primitive element (as indicated by the `PE_` prefix). This type of element is drawn by `QStyle.drawPrimitive()`, so we'll need to override that method in our proxy style.

Add this method to `StyleOverrides`, as follows:

```
def drawPrimitive(
    self, element, option, painter, widget
):
    """Outline QLineEdits in Green"""
```

To control the drawing of an element, we need to issue commands to its `painter` object, as follows:

```
self.green_pen = qtg.QPen(qtg.QColor('green'))
self.green_pen.setWidth(4)
if element == qtw.QStyle.PE_FrameLineEdit:
    painter.setPen(self.green_pen)
    painter.drawRoundedRect(widget.rect(), 10, 10)
else:
    super().drawPrimitive(element, option, painter, widget)
```

Painter objects and the drawing will be fully covered in Chapter 12, *Creating 2D Graphics with QPainter*, but, for now, understand that the preceding code draws a green rounded rectangle if the `element` argument matches `QStyle.PE_FrameLineEdit`. Otherwise, it passes the arguments to the superclass's `drawPrimitive()` method.

Notice that we do not call the superclass method after drawing our rectangle. If we did, then the superclass would draw its style-defined widget element on top of our green rectangle.

As you can see in this example, while working with QProxyStyle is considerably more esoteric than using palettes or style sheets, it does give us almost limitless control over how our widgets appear.

 It doesn't matter whether you use QSS or styles and palettes to restyle an application; however, it is highly advised that you stick to one or the other. Otherwise, your style modifications can fight with one another and give unpredictable results across platforms and desktop settings.

Creating animations

Nothing quite adds a sophisticated edge to a GUI like the tasteful use of animations. Dynamic GUI elements that fade smoothly between changes in color, size, or position can add a modern touch to any interface.

Qt's animation framework allows us to create simple animations on our widgets using the QPropertyAnimation class. In this section, we'll explore how to use this class to spice up our game lobby with some animations.

 Because Qt style sheets override another widget- and palette-based styling, you will need to comment out all the style sheet code for these animations to work correctly.

Basic property animations

A QPropertyAnimation object is used to animate a single Qt property of a widget. The class automatically creates an interpolated series of steps between two numeric property values and applies the changes over time.

For example, let's animate our logo so that it scrolls out from left to right. You can begin by adding a property animation object, as follows:

```
self.heading_animation = qtc.QPropertyAnimation(
    heading, b'maximumSize')
```

`QPropertyAnimation` requires two arguments: a widget (or another type of `QObject` class) to be animated, and a `bytes` object indicating the property to be animated (note that this is a `bytes` object and not a string).

Next, we need to configure our animation object as follows:

```
self.heading_animation.setStartValue(qtc.QSize(10, logo.height()))
self.heading_animation.setEndValue(qtc.QSize(400, logo.height()))
self.heading_animation.setDuration(2000)
```

At the very least, we need to set a `startValue` value and an `endValue` value for the property. Naturally, these values must be of the data type required by the property. We can also set `duration` in milliseconds (the default is 250).

Once configured, we just need to tell the animation to start, as follows:

```
self.heading_animation.start()
```

There are a few requirements that limit what `QPropertyAnimation` objects can do:

- The object to be animated must be a `QObject` subclass. This includes all widgets but excludes some Qt classes such as `QPalette`.
- The property to be animated must be a Qt property (not just a Python member variable).
- The property must have read-and-write accessor methods that require only a single value. For example, `QWidget.size` can be animated but not `QWidget.width`, because there is no `setWidth()` method.
- The property value must be one of the following types: `int`, `float`, `QLine`, `QLineF`, `QPoint`, `QPointF`, `QSize`, `QSizeF`, `QRect`, `QRectF`, or `QColor`.

Unfortunately, for most widgets, these limitations exclude a number of aspects that we might want to animate—in particular, colors. Fortunately, we can work around this.

Animating colors

As you learned earlier in this chapter, widget colors are not properties of the widget – rather they are properties of the palette. The palette cannot be animated, because `QPalette` is not a subclass of `QObject`, and because `setColor()` requires more than just a single value.

Colors are something that we'd like to animate, though; to make that happen, we need to subclass our widget and make its color settings into Qt properties.

Let's do that with a button; start a new class at the top of the script, as follows:

```
class ColorButton(qtw.QPushButton):

    def _color(self):
        return self.palette().color(qtg.QPalette.ButtonText)

    def _setColor(self, qcolor):
        palette = self.palette()
        palette.setColor(qtg.QPalette.ButtonText, qcolor)
        self.setPalette(palette)
```

Here, we have a `QPushButton` subclass with accessor methods for the palette's `ButtonText` color. However, note that these are Python methods; in order to animate this property, we need `color` to be an actual Qt property. To correct this, we'll use the `QtCore.pyqtProperty()` function to wrap our accessor methods and create a property on the underlying Qt object.

You can do this as follows:

```
color = qtc.pyqtProperty(qtg.QColor, _color, _setColor)
```

The property name we use will be the name of the Qt property. The first argument passed is the data type required by the property, and the next two arguments are the getter and setter methods.

`pyqtProperty()` can also be used as a decorator, as follows:

```
@qtc.pyqtProperty(qtg.QColor)
def backgroundColor(self):
    return self.palette().color(qtg.QPalette.Button)

@backgroundColor.setter
def backgroundColor(self, qcolor):
    palette = self.palette()
    palette.setColor(qtg.QPalette.Button, qcolor)
    self.setPalette(palette)
```

Notice that, in this approach, both methods must be named identically using the property name we intend to create.

Now that our properties are in place, we need to replace our regular `QPushButton` objects with `ColorButton` objects:

```
# Replace these definitions
# at the top of the MainWindow constructor
self.submit = ColorButton(
    'Connect',
    clicked=lambda: qtw.QMessageBox.information(
        None,
        'Connecting',
        'Prepare for Battle!'))
self.cancel = ColorButton(
    'Cancel',
    clicked=self.close)
```

With these changes made, we can animate the color values, as follows:

```
self.text_color_animation = qtc.QPropertyAnimation(
    self.submit, b'color')
self.text_color_animation.setStartValue(qtg.QColor('#FFF'))
self.text_color_animation.setEndValue(qtg.QColor('#888'))
self.text_color_animation.setLoopCount(-1)
self.text_color_animation.setEasingCurve(
    qtc.QEasingCurve.InOutQuad)
self.text_color_animation.setDuration(2000)
self.text_color_animation.start()
```

This works like a charm. We've also added a couple of additional configuration settings here:

- `setLoopCount()` will set how many times the animation restarts. A value of -1 will make it loop forever.
- `setEasingCurve()` changes the curve along which the values are interpolated. We've chosen `InOutQuad`, which slows the rate of the start and finish of the animation.

Now, when you run the script, note that the color fades from white to gray and then immediately loops back to white. If we want an animation to move from one value to another and then smoothly back again, we can use the `setKeyValue()` method to put a value in the middle of the animation:

```
self.bg_color_animation = qtc.QPropertyAnimation(
    self.submit, b'backgroundColor')
self.bg_color_animation.setStartValue(qtg.QColor('#000'))
self.bg_color_animation.setKeyValueAt(0.5, qtg.QColor('darkred'))
self.bg_color_animation.setEndValue(qtg.QColor('#000'))
```

```
self.bg_color_animation.setLoopCount(-1)
self.bg_color_animation.setDuration(1500)
```

In this case, our start and end values are the same, and we've added a value at 0.5 (50% of the way through the animation) set to a second color. This animation will fade from black to dark red and back again. You can add as many key values as you wish and make quite complex animations.

Using animation groups

As we add more and more animations to a GUI, we may find it necessary to group them together so that we can control the animations as a group. This can be done using the animation group classes, QParallelAnimationGroup and QSequentialAnimationGroup.

Both of these classes allow us to add multiple animations to the group and start, stop, pause, and resume the animations as a group.

For example, let's group our button animations as follows:

```
self.button_animations = qtc.QParallelAnimationGroup()
self.button_animations.addAnimation(self.text_color_animation)
self.button_animations.addAnimation(self.bg_color_animation)
```

QParallelAnimationGroup plays all animations in parallel whenever its start() method is called. In contrast, QSequentialAnimationGroup will playback its animations one at a time in the order added, as shown in the following code block:

```
self.all_animations = qtc.QSequentialAnimationGroup()
self.all_animations.addAnimation(self.heading_animation)
self.all_animations.addAnimation(self.button_animations)
self.all_animations.start()
```

By adding animation groups to other animation groups as we've done here, we can choreograph complex arrangements of animations into one object that can be started, stopped, or paused altogether.

Comment out all the other animation start() calls and launch the script. Note that the button animations start only after the heading animation has finished.

 We will explore more uses of QPropertyAnimation in *Chapter 12, 2D Graphics with QPainter.*

Summary

In this chapter, we learned how to customize the look and feel of a PyQt application. We also learned how to manipulate screen fonts and add images. Additionally, we learned how to package image and font resources in a way that is resilient to path changes. We also explored how to alter the color and appearance of the application using palettes and style sheets, and how to override style methods to implement nearly limitless style changes. Finally, we explored widget animation using Qt's animation framework and learned how to add custom Qt properties to our classes so that we can animate them.

In the next chapter, we're going to explore the world of multimedia applications using the QtMultimedia library. You'll learn how to work with cameras to take pictures and videos, how to display video content, and how to record and playback audio.

Questions

Try these questions to test your knowledge from this chapter:

1. You are preparing to distribute your text editor application, and want to ensure that the user is given a monospaced font by default, no matter what platform they use. What two ways can you use to accomplish this?
2. As closely as possible, try to mimic the following text using QFont:

3. Can you explain the difference between QImage, QPixmap, and QIcon?
4. You have defined the following .qrc file for your application, run pyrcc5, and imported the resource library in your script. How would you load this image into QPixmap?

```
<RCC>
  <qresource prefix="foodItems">
    <file alias="pancakes.png">pc_img.45234.png</file>
  </qresource>
</RCC>
```

5. Using `QPalette`, how would you tile the background of a `QWidget` object with the `tile.png` image?

6. You are trying to make a delete button pink using QSS, but it's not working. What is wrong with your code?

```
deleteButton = qtw.QPushButton('Delete')
form.layout().addWidget(deleteButton)
form.setStyleSheet(
    form.styleSheet() + 'deleteButton{ background-color: #8F8; }'
)
```

7. Which style sheet string will turn the background colors of your `QLineEdit` widget black?

```
stylesheet1 = "QWidget {background-color: black; }"
stylesheet2 = ".QWidget {background-color: black; }"
```

8. Build a simple app with a combo box that allows you to change the Qt style to any style installed on your system. Include some other widgets so that you can see how they look in the different styles.

9. You feel very happy about learning how to style PyQt apps and want to create a `QProxyStyle` class that will force all pixmaps in a GUI to be `smile.gif`. How would you do this? Hint: You will need to research some other drawing methods of `QStyle` than the ones discussed in this chapter.

10. The following animation doesn't work; figure out why it doesn't work:

```
class MyWidget(qtw.QWidget):
    def __init__(self):
        super().__init__()
        animation = qtc.QPropertyAnimation(
            self, b'windowOpacity')
        animation.setStartValue(0)
        animation.setEndValue(1)
        animation.setDuration(10000)
        animation.start()
```

Further reading

For further information, please refer to the following:

- A more detailed description of how fonts are resolved can be found in the QFont documentation at https://doc.qt.io/qt-5/qfont.html#details
- This Qt styling example in C++ (https://doc.qt.io/qt-5/qtwidgets-widgets-styles-example.html) demonstrates how to create a comprehensive Qt Proxy Style
- The overview of the Qt's animation framework at https://doc.qt.io/qt-5/animation-overview.html offers additional details on how to use property animations and what their limitations are

2
Section 2: Working with External Resources

Now that you understand the basics of building a PyQt GUI, it's time to venture into the outside world. In this section, you will learn how to connect your PyQt applications to external resources, such as networks and databases.

The following chapters are in this section:

- Chapter 7, *Working with Audio-Visual Using QtMultimedia*
- Chapter 8, *Networking with QtNetwork*
- Chapter 9, *Exploring SQL with QtSQL*

7
Working with Audio-Visual Using QtMultimedia

Whether in games, communications, or media production applications, audio and video content is often a crucial part of modern applications. When working with native APIs, even the simplest **audio-visual (AV)** applications can be quite complicated, especially when supporting multiple platforms. However, fortunately for us, Qt provides us with a simple cross-platform multimedia API in the form of `QtMultimedia`. With `QtMultimedia`, we can easily work with audio content, video content, or devices such as cameras and radios.

In this chapter, we'll use `QtMultimedia` to explore the following topics:

- Simple audio playback
- Recording and playing audio
- Recording and playing video

Technical requirements

In addition to the basic PyQt setup described in Chapter 1, *Getting Started with PyQt*, you will need to make sure the `QtMultimedia` and `PyQt.QtMultimedia` libraries are installed. If you installed PyQt5 using `pip`, then it should already be installed. Linux users who are using their distro's package manager should check that these packages are installed.

You may also want to download the code from our GitHub repository at https://github.com/PacktPublishing/Mastering-GUI-Programming-with-Python/tree/master/Chapter07, which contains not only the example code but the audio data used for these examples.

If you want to create your own audio files to work with, you might want to install the free Audacity sound editor at `https://www.audacityteam.org/`.

Finally, you will get the most out of this chapter if your computer has a working audio system, microphone, and webcam. If it does not, then some of the examples will not work for you.

Check out the following video to see the code in action: `http://bit.ly/2Mjr8vx`

Simple audio playback

Quite often, applications need to playback sounds in response to GUI events, as you might do in a game or just to provide audio feedback for user actions. For this application, `QtMultimedia` offers the `QSoundEffect` class. `QSoundEffect` is limited to playing back uncompressed audio, so it works with **Pulse Code Modulation (PCM)**, **Waveform data (WAV)** files but not MP3 or OGG files. The trade-off is that it is low-latency and very efficient with resources, so while it's not useful as a general-purpose audio player, it is perfect for fast playback of sound effects.

To demonstrate `QSoundEffect`, let's build a phone dialer. Copy the application template from Chapter 4, *Building Applications with QMainWindow*, into a new file called `phone_dialer.py` and open it in your editor.

Let's start by importing the `QtMultimedia` library, as follows:

```
from PyQt5 import QtMultimedia as qtmm
```

Importing `QtMultimedia` will be a necessary first step for all the examples in this chapter, and we will consistently use `qtmm` as an alias for it.

We'll also import a `resources` library containing the necessary WAV data:

```
import resources
```

This `resources` file contains a collection of **Dial Tone Multi-Frequency (DTMF)** tones. These are the tones generated by telephones when dialing, and we've included 0 through to 9, *, and #. We've included this file in the example code; alternatively, you can create your own `resources` file from your own audio samples (you can refer to Chapter 6, *Styling Qt Applications*, for information on how to do this).

You can generate DTMF tones using the free Audacity sound editor. To do so, select **Generate | DTMF** from Audacity's main menu.

Once that's in place, we're going to create a `QPushButton` subclass that plays a sound effect when it is clicked on, as follows:

```
class SoundButton(qtw.QPushButton):

    def __init__(self, wav_file, *args, **kwargs):
        super().__init__(*args, **kwargs)
        self.wav_file = wav_file
        self.player = qtmm.QSoundEffect()
        self.player.setSource(qtc.QUrl.fromLocalFile(wav_file))
        self.clicked.connect(self.player.play)
```

As you can see, we've modified the constructor to take a sound file path as an argument. This value is converted to `QUrl` and passed into our `QSoundEffect` object using the `setSource()` method. Finally, the `QSoundEffect.play()` method triggers playback of the sound, so we've connected it to the button's `clicked` signal. This is all it takes to create our `SoundButton` object.

Back in the `MainWindow.__init__()` method, let's create some `SoundButton` objects and arrange them in the GUI:

```
        dialpad = qtw.QWidget()
        self.setCentralWidget(dialpad)
        dialpad.setLayout(qtw.QGridLayout())

        for i, symbol in enumerate('123456789*0#'):
            button = SoundButton(f':/dtmf/{symbol}.wav', symbol)
            row = i // 3
            column = i % 3
            dialpad.layout().addWidget(button, row, column)
```

We've set up the resource file so that each DTMF tone can be accessed by its symbol under the `dtmf` prefix; for example, `':/dtmf/1.wav'` refers to the DTMF tone for 1. In this way, we can just iterate through a string of symbols and create a `SoundButton` object for each, which we add to a three-column grid.

That's all there is to it; run this program and push the buttons. It should sound just like dialing a phone!

Recording and playing audio

QSoundEffect is adequate for dealing with simple event sounds, but for more advanced audio projects we're going to need something with more capabilities. Ideally, we want the ability to load more formats, control various aspects of the playback, and record new sounds.

In this section, we're going to focus on two classes that provide these features:

- The QMediaPlayer class, which is like a virtual media player device that can load audio or video content
- The QAudioRecorder class, which manages the recording of audio data to a disk

To see these classes in action, we're going to build a sampling soundboard.

The initial setup

First, make a fresh copy of the application template and call it soundboard.py. Then, import QtMultimedia as you did for the last project, and let's layout the main interface.

Inside the MainWindow constructor, add in the following code:

```
rows = 3
columns = 3
soundboard = qtw.QWidget()
soundboard.setLayout(qtw.QGridLayout())
self.setCentralWidget(soundboard)
for c in range(columns):
    for r in range(rows):
        sw = SoundWidget()
        soundboard.layout().addWidget(sw, c, r)
```

All we're doing here is creating an empty central widget, adding a grid layout, and then filling it with 3 rows and 3 columns of SoundWidget objects.

Implementing sound playback

Our SoundWidget class is going to be a QWidget object that manages a single sound sample. When finished, it will allow us to load or record an audio sample, play it back looped or as a one-shot, and control its volume and playback position.

Above the `MainWindow` constructor, let's create the class and give it a layout:

```
class SoundWidget(qtw.QWidget):

    def __init__(self):
        super().__init__()
        self.setLayout(qtw.QGridLayout())
        self.label = qtw.QLabel("No file loaded")
        self.layout().addWidget(self.label, 0, 0, 1, 2)
```

The first thing we've added is a label that will display the name of the sample file the widget has loaded. The next thing we need is a button to control the playback. Instead of just a plain push button, let's apply some of our styling skills to create a custom button that can switch between being a **Play** button and a **Stop** button.

Start a `PlayButton` class above the `SoundWidget` class, as follows:

```
class PlayButton(qtw.QPushButton):
    play_stylesheet = 'background-color: lightgreen; color: black;'
    stop_stylesheet = 'background-color: darkred; color: white;'

    def __init__(self):
        super().__init__('Play')
        self.setFont(qtg.QFont('Sans', 32, qtg.QFont.Bold))
        self.setSizePolicy(
            qtw.QSizePolicy.Expanding,
            qtw.QSizePolicy.Expanding
        )
        self.setStyleSheet(self.play_stylesheet)
```

Back in the `SoundWidget` class, we'll add a `PlayButton` object, as follows:

```
        self.play_button = PlayButton()
        self.layout().addWidget(self.play_button, 3, 0, 1, 2)
```

Now that we have a control button, we need to create the `QMediaPlayer` object that will play the sample, as follows:

```
        self.player = qtmm.QMediaPlayer()
```

You can think of `QMediaPlayer` as the software equivalent to a hardware media player such as a CD or Blu-ray player. Just like a hardware media player has **Play**, **Pause**, and **Stop** buttons, the `QMediaPlayer` object has `play()`, `stop()`, and `pause()` slots to control the playback of the media.

Let's connect our dual-function `PlayButton` object to the player. We'll do this by way of an instance method called `on_playbutton()`:

```
self.play_button.clicked.connect(self.on_playbutton)
```

Here is how `SoundWidget.on_playbutton()` will look:

```
def on_playbutton(self):
    if self.player.state() == qtmm.QMediaPlayer.PlayingState:
        self.player.stop()
    else:
        self.player.play()
```

This method examines the player object's `state` property, which returns a constant indicating whether the player is playing, has paused, or has stopped. If the player is currently playing, we stop it—if not, we ask it to play.

Since our button is switching between a play and stop button, let's update its label and appearance. `QMediaPlayer` emits a `stateChanged` signal when its state changes, which we can send to our `PlayButton` object, as follows:

```
self.player.stateChanged.connect(self.play_button.on_state_changed)
```

Back in the `PlayButton` class, let's handle that signal, as follows:

```
def on_state_changed(self, state):
    if state == qtmm.QMediaPlayer.PlayingState:
        self.setStyleSheet(self.stop_stylesheet)
        self.setText('Stop')
    else:
        self.setStyleSheet(self.play_stylesheet)
        self.setText('Play')
```

Here, `stateChanged` passes along the new state of the media player, which we use to set the button to its play or stop appearance.

Loading the media

Just as a hardware media player requires a CD, a DVD, or a Blu-ray disc loaded into it to actually play anything back, our `QMediaPlayer` also needs some kind of content loaded before it can play any audio. Let's explore how to load a sound from a file.

Start by adding a button to the `SoundWidget` layout, as follows:

```
self.file_button = qtw.QPushButton(
    'Load File', clicked=self.get_file)
self.layout().addWidget(self.file_button, 4, 0)
```

This button calls to the `get_file()` method, which looks like this:

```
def get_file(self):
    fn, _ = qtw.QFileDialog.getOpenFileUrl(
        self,
        "Select File",
        qtc.QDir.homePath(),
        "Audio files (*.wav *.flac *.mp3 *.ogg *.aiff);; All files (*)"
    )
    if fn:
        self.set_file(fn)
```

This method simply calls `QFileDialog` to retrieve a file URL and then passes it along to another method, `set_file()`, which we'll write next. We've set the filter to look for five common audio file types, but feel free to add more if you have audio in a different format—`QMediaPlayer` is quite flexible in what it can load.

Note that we're calling `getOpenFileUrl()`, which returns a `QUrl` object rather than a file path string. `QMediaPlayer` prefers working with `QUrl` objects so this will save us a conversion step.

The `set_file()` method is where we'll finally load our media into the player:

```
def set_file(self, url):
    content = qtmm.QMediaContent(url)
    self.player.setMedia(content)
    self.label.setText(url.fileName())
```

Before we can pass the URL to our media player, we have to wrap it in a `QMediaContent` class. This provides the player with the API it needs to playback the content. Once wrapped, we can use `QMediaPlayer.setMedia()` to load it up, and then it's ready for playback. You can visualize this process as putting audio data onto a CD (the `QMediaContent` object), and then loading that CD into a CD player (using `setMedia()`).

As a last touch, we've retrieved the filename of the loaded file and put it in the label.

Tracking the playback position

At this point, our soundboard can load and play samples, but it would be nice to see and control the position of playback, particularly for long samples. QMediaPlayer allows us to retrieve and control the playback position through signals and slots, so let's look into that from our GUI.

Start by creating a QSlider widget, as follows:

```
self.position = qtw.QSlider(
    minimum=0, orientation=qtc.Qt.Horizontal)
self.layout().addWidget(self.position, 1, 0, 1, 2)
```

QSlider is a widget that we haven't looked at yet; it's just a slider control that can be used to input integers between a minimum and maximum value.

Now connect the slider and player, as follows:

```
self.player.positionChanged.connect(self.position.setSliderPosition)
        self.player.durationChanged.connect(self.position.setMaximum)
        self.position.sliderMoved.connect(self.player.setPosition)
```

The QMediaPlayer class reports its position in integers representing the number of milliseconds from the start of the file so that we can connect the positionChanged signal to the slider's setSliderPosition() slot.

However, we also need to adjust the slider's maximum position so that it matches the duration of the sample, otherwise, the slider won't know what percentage the value represents. Therefore, we've connected the player's durationChanged signal (which is emitted whenever new content is loaded into the player) to the slider's setMaximum() slot.

Finally, we'd like to be able to control the playback position using the slider, so we set the sliderMoved signal to the player's setPosition() slot. Note that we definitely want to use sliderMoved and not valueChanged (which QSlider emits when the value is changed by the user *or* by an event), because the latter would create a feedback loop when the media player changes the position.

These connections are all we need for our slider to work. Now you can run the program and load up a long sound; you'll see that the slider tracks the playback position and can be moved around before or during playback to alter the position.

Looping the audio

Playing our samples in one-shots is neat, but we'd also like to loop them. Looping audio in a QMediaPlayer object requires a slightly different approach. Instead of loading a QMediaContent object directly, we need to first add it to a QMediaPlayList object. We can then tell the playlist to loop.

Back in our set_file() method, we need to make the following changes to our code:

```
def set_file(self, url):
    self.label.setText(url.fileName())
    content = qtmm.QMediaContent(url)
    #self.player.setMedia(content)
    self.playlist = qtmm.QMediaPlaylist()
    self.playlist.addMedia(content)
    self.playlist.setCurrentIndex(1)
    self.player.setPlaylist(self.playlist)
```

A playlist can, of course, have multiple files loaded, but, in this case, we only want one. We load the QMediaContent object into the playlist using the addMedia() method and then point the playlist to that file using the setCurrentIndex() method. Note that the playlist won't automatically point to any item by default. This means that if you skip this last step, then nothing will happen when you try to play the playlist.

Finally, we use the media player's setPlaylist() method to add the playlist.

Now that our content is in a playlist, we'll create a checkbox to switch looping on and off:

```
self.loop_cb = qtw.QCheckBox(
    'Loop', stateChanged=self.on_loop_cb)
self.layout().addWidget(self.loop_cb, 2, 0)
```

As you can see, we're connecting the checkbox's stateChanged signal to a callback method; the method will be as follows:

```
def on_loop_cb(self, state):
    if state == qtc.Qt.Checked:
        self.playlist.setPlaybackMode(
            qtmm.QMediaPlaylist.CurrentItemInLoop)
    else:
        self.playlist.setPlaybackMode(
            qtmm.QMediaPlaylist.CurrentItemOnce)
```

The `playbackMode` property of the `QMediaPlaylist` class is very similar to the track mode button on a CD player, which can be used to switch between repeat, shuffle, or sequential play. There are five playback modes, as shown in the following table:

Mode	Description
CurrentItemOnce	Play the current track once and stop.
CurrentItemInLoop	Play the current item repeatedly.
Sequential	Play all the items in the order and then stop.
Loop	Play all the items in the order and then repeat.
Random	Play all the items in a random order.

In this method, we're switching between `CurrentItemOnce` and `CurrentItemInLoop` depending on whether the checkbox is checked. Since our playlist only has one item, the remaining modes aren't meaningful.

As a final touch, we'll clear the checkbox on loading a new file. So, add this to the end of `set_file()`:

```
self.loop_cb.setChecked(False)
```

At this point, you should be able to run the program and loop the sample. Note that looping audio using this method may not guarantee a seamless loop; depending on your platform and system capabilities, there may be a small gap between iterations of the loop.

Setting the volume

Our final playback feature will be volume control. To allow us to control the playback level, `QMediaPlayer` has a `volume` parameter that accepts values from `0` (muted) to `100` (full volume).

We'll simply add another slider widget to control the volume, as follows:

```
self.volume = qtw.QSlider(
    minimum=0,
    maximum=100,
    sliderPosition=75,
    orientation=qtc.Qt.Horizontal,
    sliderMoved=self.player.setVolume
)
self.layout().addWidget(self.volume, 2, 1)
```

After setting the minimum and maximum values accordingly, we just need to connect `sliderMoved` to the media player's `setVolume()` slot. That's all there is to it!

 For smoother volume control, the Qt documentation recommends converting the slider's linear scale to a logarithmic scale. We recommend that you read `https://doc.qt.io/qt-5/qaudio.html#convertVolume` and see whether you can do this yourself.

Implementing recording

The audio recording in Qt is facilitated by the `QAudioRecorder` class. Just as the `QMediaPlayer` class was analogous to a media playback device, the `QAudioRecorder` class is analogous to a media recording device such as a digital audio recorder (or, if you're of the author's generation, a tape recorder). The recorder is controlled using the `record()`, `stop()`, and `pause()` methods, much like the media player object.

Let's add a recorder object to our `SoundWidget`, as follows:

```
self.recorder = qtmm.QAudioRecorder()
```

To control the recorder, we'll create another dual-function button class that is similar to the play button that we previously created:

```
class RecordButton(qtw.QPushButton):

    record_stylesheet = 'background-color: black; color: white;'
    stop_stylesheet = 'background-color: darkred; color: white;'

    def __init__(self):
        super().__init__('Record')

    def on_state_changed(self, state):
        if state == qtmm.QAudioRecorder.RecordingState:
            self.setStyleSheet(self.stop_stylesheet)
            self.setText('Stop')
        else:
            self.setStyleSheet(self.record_stylesheet)
            self.setText('Record')
```

Just as with the `PlayButton` class, we're switching the appearance of the button whenever a new `state` value is received from the recorder's `stateChanged` signal. In this case, we're looking for the recorder's `RecordingState` state.

Let's add a `RecordButton()` method to our widget, as follows:

```
self.record_button = RecordButton()
self.recorder.stateChanged.connect(
    self.record_button.on_state_changed)
self.layout().addWidget(self.record_button, 4, 1)
self.record_button.clicked.connect(self.on_recordbutton)
```

We've connected the `clicked` signal to an `on_recordbutton()` method, which will handle the starting and stopping of the audio recording.

This method is as follows:

```
def on_recordbutton(self):
    if self.recorder.state() == qtmm.QMediaRecorder.RecordingState:
        self.recorder.stop()
        url = self.recorder.actualLocation()
        self.set_file(url)
```

The first thing that we'll do is check the state of the recorder. If it's currently recording, then we'll stop it by calling `recorder.stop()`, which not only stops the recording but writes the recorded data to an audio file on a disk. We can then get the location of that file by calling the recorder's `actualLocation()` method. This method returns a `QUrl` object, which we can pass directly to `self.set_file()` to set our playback to the newly recorded file.

Make sure that you use `actualLocation()` to get the location of the file. The recording location can be configured using `setLocation()`, and this value is available from the `location()` accessor. However, Qt may fall back to a default setting if the configured location is invalid or non-writable. `actualLocation()` returns the URL where the file was actually saved.

If we're not currently recording, we'll tell the recorder to start recording by calling `recorder.record()`:

```
    else:
        self.recorder.record()
```

When `record()` is called, the audio recorder begins recording audio in the background and will continue to do so until `stop()` is called.

Before we can playback our recorded files, we need to make one fix to `set_file()`. At the time of writing, the `QAudioRecorder.actualLocation()` method neglects to add a scheme value to the URL, so we'll need to specify this manually:

```
def set_file(self, url):
    if url.scheme() == '':
        url.setScheme('file')
    content = qtmm.QMediaContent(url)
    #...
```

 In `QUrl` terms, the `scheme` object indicates the protocol of the URL, such as HTTP, HTTPS, or FTP. Since we're accessing local files, the scheme should be `'file'`.

If the default settings of `QAudioRecorder` work correctly on your system, then you should be able to record and playback audio. However, that's a big *if*; it is more than likely that you'll need to do some configuration on the audio recorder object to get things working. Let's look at how to do that next.

Examining and configuring the recorder

Even if the `QAudioRecorder` class worked well for you, you might wonder whether there's a way to control the type and quality of the audio that it records, what source it records the audio from, and what location it writes the audio files to.

In order to configure these things, we first have to know what your system supports, as support for different audio recording features can be dependent on hardware, drivers, or operating system capabilities. `QAudioRecorder` has methods that can provide information about the capabilities that are available.

The following script will display information about supported audio features on your system:

```
from PyQt5.QtCore import *
from PyQt5.QtMultimedia import *

app = QCoreApplication([])
r = QAudioRecorder()
print('Inputs: ', r.audioInputs())
print('Codecs: ', r.supportedAudioCodecs())
print('Sample Rates: ', r.supportedAudioSampleRates())
print('Containers: ', r.supportedContainers())
```

You can run this script on your system and get a list of the supported `Inputs`, `Codecs`, `Sample Rates`, and `container` formats. For instance, on a typical Microsoft Windows system, your results will probably be as follows:

```
Inputs:    ['Microhpone (High Defnition Aud']
Codecs:    ['audio/pcm']
Sample Rates:    ([8000, 11025, 16000, 22050, 32000,
                44100, 48000, 88200, 96000, 192000], False)
Containers:    ['audio/x-wav', 'audio/x-raw']
```

To configure the input source for a `QAudioRecorder` object, you need to pass the name of the audio input to the `setAudioInput()` method, as follows:

```
self.recorder.setAudioInput('default:')
```

The actual name of the input may be different on your system. Unfortunately, `QAudioRecorder` will not throw an exception or register an error when you set an invalid audio input—it will simply fail to record any audio. So, if you decide to customize this attribute, take pains to ensure that the value is valid first.

To change the output file that is recorded, we need to call `setOutputLocation()`, as follows:

```
sample_path = qtc.QDir.home().filePath('sample1')
self.recorder.setOutputLocation(
    qtc.QUrl.fromLocalFile(sample_path))
```

Note that `setOutputLocation()` requires a `QUrl` object and not a file path. Once set, Qt will try to use this location for recording audio. However, as mentioned previously, it will revert to a platform-specific default if this location is not available.

The container format is the type of file that holds the audio data. For example, `audio/x-wav` is the container used for WAV files. We can set this value in the record object using the `setContainerFormat()` method, as follows:

```
self.recorder.setContainerFormat('audio/x-wav')
```

The value of this property should be a string returned by `QAudioRecorder.supportedContainers()`. Using an invalid value will result in an error when you try to record.

Setting the codec, sample rate, and quality requires a new object called a `QAudioEncoderSettings` object. The following example demonstrates how to create and configure a `settings` object:

```
settings = qtmm.QAudioEncoderSettings()
settings.setCodec('audio/pcm')
settings.setSampleRate(44100)
settings.setQuality(qtmm.QMultimedia.HighQuality)
self.recorder.setEncodingSettings(settings)
```

In this case, we've configured our audio to high-quality encoding at `44100` Hz using the PCM codec.

Understand that not all codecs are compatible with all container types. If you pick two incompatible types, Qt will print errors to the console and the recording will fail, but it will not otherwise crash or throw an exception. It's up to you to do the proper research and testing to make sure that you are picking compatible settings.

Depending on the codec chosen, there may be other settings you can set on your `QAudioEncoderSettings` object. You can consult the Qt documentation at `https://doc.qt.io/qt-5/qaudioencodersettings.html` for more information.

Configuring audio settings can be very tricky, especially as support varies widely from system to system. It's best to let Qt use its default settings when you can, or let the user configure these settings using values obtained from the support detection methods of `QAudioRecorder`. Whatever you do, don't hardcode settings or options if you cannot guarantee that the systems running your software will support them.

Recording and playing video

Once you understand how to work with audio in Qt, working with video is only a small step up in terms of complexity. Just as with audio, we'll use a player object to load and playback content, and a recorder object to record it. However, with video, we'll need to add in a few extra components to handle the visualization of the content and to initialize the source device.

In order to understand how it works, we're going to build a video-logging application. Copy the application template from `Chapter 4`, *Building Applications with QMainWindow*, to a new file called `captains_log.py` and we'll start coding.

Building the basic GUI

The **Captain's Log** application will allow us to record videos from a webcam to a timestamped file in a preset directory and play them back. Our interface will feature a list of past logs on the right and a preview/playback area on the left. We'll have a tabbed interface so that the user can swap between playback and recording mode.

Inside `MainWindow.__init__()`, start laying out the basic GUI as follows:

```
base_widget = qtw.QWidget()
base_widget.setLayout(qtw.QHBoxLayout())
notebook = qtw.QTabWidget()
base_widget.layout().addWidget(notebook)
self.file_list = qtw.QListWidget()
base_widget.layout().addWidget(self.file_list)
self.setCentralWidget(base_widget)
```

Next, we'll add a toolbar to hold the transport controls:

```
toolbar = self.addToolBar("Transport")
record_act = toolbar.addAction('Rec')
stop_act = toolbar.addAction('Stop')
play_act = toolbar.addAction('Play')
pause_act = toolbar.addAction('Pause')
```

We want our application to only display log videos, so we need to isolate our recordings to a unique directory rather than using the record's default location. Using `QtCore.QDir`, we'll create and store a custom location in a cross-platform way, as follows:

```
self.video_dir = qtc.QDir.home()
if not self.video_dir.cd('captains_log'):
    qtc.QDir.home().mkdir('captains_log')
    self.video_dir.cd('captains_log')
```

This creates the `captains_log` directory under your home directory (if it doesn't exist) and sets the `self.video_dir` object to point to that directory.

We now need a method to scan this directory for videos and populate the list widget:

```
def refresh_video_list(self):
    self.file_list.clear()
    video_files = self.video_dir.entryList(
        ["*.ogg", "*.avi", "*.mov", "*.mp4", "*.mkv"],
        qtc.QDir.Files | qtc.QDir.Readable
    )
    for fn in sorted(video_files):
        self.file_list.addItem(fn)
```

`QDir.entryList()` returns a list of the contents of our `video_dir`. This first argument is a list of filters for common video file types so that non-video files won't be listed in our log list (feel free to add whatever formats your OS prefers), and the second is a set of flags that will limit the entries returned to readable files. Once retrieved, these files are sorted and added to the list widget.

Back in `__init__()`, let's call this function to refresh the list:

```
self.refresh_video_list()
```

You may want to drop a video file or two in that directory to make sure they're being read and added to the list widget.

Video playback

Our old friend `QMediaPlayer` can handle video playback as well as audio. However, just as a Blu-ray player needs to be connected to a TV or monitor to display what it's playing, `QMediaPlayer` needs to be connected to a widget that will actually display the video. The widget we need is the `QVideoWidget` class, which is found in the `QtMultimediaWidgets` module.

To use it, we'll need to import `QMultimediaWidgets`, as follows:

```
from PyQt5 import QtMultimediaWidgets as qtmmw
```

To connect our `QMediaPlayer()` method to a `QVideoWidget()` method, we set the player's `videoOutput` property, as follows:

```
self.player = qtmm.QMediaPlayer()
self.video_widget = qtmmw.QVideoWidget()
self.player.setVideoOutput(self.video_widget)
```

This is easier than hooking up your Blu-ray player, right?

Now we can add the video widget to our GUI and connect the transport to our player:

```
notebook.addTab(self.video_widget, "Play")
play_act.triggered.connect(self.player.play)
pause_act.triggered.connect(self.player.pause)
stop_act.triggered.connect(self.player.stop)
play_act.triggered.connect(
    lambda: notebook.setCurrentWidget(self.video_widget))
```

As a final touch, we've added a connection to switch back to the **Play** tab whenever the **Play** button is clicked on.

The last thing we need to do to enable playback is to connect the selecting of a file in the file list to the loading and playing of the video in the media player.

We'll do that in a callback called `on_file_selected()`, as follows:

```
def on_file_selected(self, item):
    fn = item.text()
    url = qtc.QUrl.fromLocalFile(self.video_dir.filePath(fn))
    content = qtmm.QMediaContent(url)
    self.player.setMedia(content)
    self.player.play()
```

The callback receives `QListWidgetItem` from `file_list` and extracts the `text` parameter, which should be the name of the file. We pass this to the `filePath()` method of our `QDir` object to get a full path to the file and build a `QUrl` object from this (remember that `QMediaPlayer` works with URLs, not file paths). Finally, we wrap the content in a `QMediaContent` object, load it into the player, and hit `play()`.

Back in `__init__()`, let's connect this callback to our list widget:

```
self.file_list.itemDoubleClicked.connect(
    self.on_file_selected)
self.file_list.itemDoubleClicked.connect(
    lambda: notebook.setCurrentWidget(self.video_widget))
```

Here, we're connecting `itemDoubleClicked`, which passes the item that's been clicked on to the slot just as our callback expects. Note that we're also connecting the action to a `lambda` function to switch to the video widget. This is so that if the user double-clicks on a file while on the **Record** tab, they will be able to watch it without manually switching back to the **Play** tab.

At this point, your player is capable of playing videos. Drop a few video files in your `captains_log` directory if you haven't already and see if they play.

Video recording

To record videos, we first need a source. In Qt, this source must be a subclass of `QMediaObject`, which can include an audio source, a media player, a radio, or—as we'll be using in this program—a camera.

Qt 5.12 currently does not support video recording on Windows, only macOS, and Linux. For more information about the current state of multimedia support on Windows, please see `https://doc.qt.io/qt-5/qtmultimedia-windows.html`.

Cameras themselves are represented as `QCamera` objects in Qt. To create a working `QCamera` object, though, we need to first get a `QCameraInfo` object. The `QCameraInfo` object contains information about a physical camera attached to the computer. A list of these objects can be obtained from the `QtMultimedia.QCameraInfo.availableCameras()` method.

Let's put this together into a method that will find a camera on your system and return a `QCamera` object for it:

```
def camera_check(self):
    cameras = qtmm.QCameraInfo.availableCameras()
    if not cameras:
        qtw.QMessageBox.critical(
            self,
            'No cameras',
            'No cameras were found, recording disabled.'
        )
    else:
        return qtmm.QCamera(cameras[0])
```

`availableCameras()` should return a list of `QCameraInfo` objects if you have one or more cameras attached to your system. If it does not, then we'll display an error and return nothing; if it does, then we pass the info object to the `QCamera` constructor and return an object representing the camera.

Back in `__init__()`, we'll use the following function to acquire a camera object:

```
self.camera = self.camera_check()
if not self.camera:
    self.show()
    return
```

If there is no camera, then none of the remaining code in this method will work, so we'll just show the window and return.

Before we use our camera, we need to tell it what we want it to capture. Cameras can capture still images or video content, which are configured by the camera's `captureMode` property.

Here, we set it to video using the `QCamera.CaptureVideo` constant:

```
self.camera.setCaptureMode(qtmm.QCamera.CaptureVideo)
```

Before we hit record, we'd like to be able to preview what the camera is capturing (after all, the captain needs to make sure their hair looks good for posterity). `QtMultimediaWidgets` has a special widget just for this purpose called `QCameraViewfinder`.

We'll add one and connect our camera to it as follows:

```
self.cvf = qtmmw.QCameraViewfinder()
self.camera.setViewfinder(self.cvf)
notebook.addTab(self.cvf, 'Record')
```

The camera is now created and configured, so we need to activate it by calling the `start()` method:

```
self.camera.start()
```

If you run the program at this point, you should see a real-time display of what your camera is capturing on the **Record** tab.

The final piece of this puzzle is the recorder object. In the case of video, we use the `QMediaRecorder` class to create a video recording object. This class is actually the parent of the `QAudioRecorder` class we used in our soundboard and works much the same way.

Let's create our recorder object, as follows:

```
self.recorder = qtmm.QMediaRecorder(self.camera)
```

Note that we pass in our camera object to the constructor. You must pass `QMediaObject` (of which `QCamera` is a subclass) whenever you are creating a `QMediaRecorder` property. This property cannot be set later, nor can the constructor be called without it.

Just as with our audio recorder, we can configure various settings about the video we capture. This is done by creating a `QVideoEncoderSettings` class and passing it to the recorder's `videoSettings` property:

```
settings = self.recorder.videoSettings()
settings.setResolution(640, 480)
settings.setFrameRate(24.0)
settings.setQuality(qtmm.QMultimedia.VeryHighQuality)
self.recorder.setVideoSettings(settings)
```

It's important to understand that if you set a configuration that your camera doesn't support, then the recording will likely fail and you may see errors in the console:

```
CameraBin warning: "not negotiated"
CameraBin error: "Internal data stream error."
```

To make sure that this doesn't happen, we can query our recorder object to see which settings are supported just as we did with the audio settings. The following script will print supported codecs, frame rates, resolutions, and containers to the console for each detected camera on your system:

```python
from PyQt5.QtCore import *
from PyQt5.QtMultimedia import *

app = QCoreApplication([])

for camera_info in QCameraInfo.availableCameras():
    print('Camera: ', camera_info.deviceName())
    camera = QCamera(camera_info)
    r = QMediaRecorder(camera)
    print('\tAudio Codecs: ', r.supportedAudioCodecs())
    print('\tVideo Codecs: ', r.supportedVideoCodecs())
    print('\tAudio Sample Rates: ', r.supportedAudioSampleRates())
    print('\tFrame Rates: ', r.supportedFrameRates())
    print('\tResolutions: ', r.supportedResolutions())
    print('\tContainers: ', r.supportedContainers())
    print('\n\n')
```

Bear in mind that, on some systems, the results returned may be empty. When in doubt, it may be best to either experiment or accept whatever the default settings provide.

Now that our recorder is ready, we need to connect the transport and enable it to record. Let's start by writing a callback method for recording:

```python
def record(self):
    # create a filename
    datestamp = qtc.QDateTime.currentDateTime().toString()
    self.mediafile = qtc.QUrl.fromLocalFile(
        self.video_dir.filePath('log - ' + datestamp)
    )
    self.recorder.setOutputLocation(self.mediafile)
    # start recording
    self.recorder.record()
```

This callback has two jobs—to create and set the filename to record to, and to start the recording. We're using our QDir object again in conjunction with a QDateTime class to generate a filename containing the date and time when the record was pressed. Note that we don't add a file extension to the filename. This is because QMediaRecorder will do this automatically based on the type of file it has been configured to create.

The recording is started by simply calling record() on the QMediaRecorder object. It will record video in the background until the stop() slot is called.

Back in __init__(), let's finish things up by wiring in the transport controls as follows:

```
record_act.triggered.connect(self.record)
record_act.triggered.connect(
    lambda: notebook.setCurrentWidget(self.cvf)
)
pause_act.triggered.connect(self.recorder.pause)
stop_act.triggered.connect(self.recorder.stop)
stop_act.triggered.connect(self.refresh_video_list)
```

We're connecting the record action to our callback and to a lambda function, which switches to the recording tab. We're then connecting the pause and stop actions directly to the recorder's pause() and stop() slots. Finally, when the video stops recording, we will want to refresh the file list to display the new file, so we connect stop_act to the refresh_video_list() callback.

And that's all we need; dust your webcam's lens, fire up this script, and start keeping track of your stardates!

Summary

In this chapter, we explored the capabilities of the QtMultimedia and QMultimediaWidgets modules. You learned how to play back low-latency sound effects with QSoundEffect, and how to play and record a variety of media formats using QMediaPlayer and QAudioRecorder. Finally, we created a video recording and playback application using QCamera, QMediaPlayer, and QMediaRecorder.

In the next chapter, we'll connect to the wider world by exploring Qt's networking features. We'll work with low-level networking with sockets and higher-level networking with the QNetworkAccessManager.

Questions

Try these questions to test your knowledge from this chapter:

1. Using `QSoundEffect`, you've written a utility for a call center that allows them to review recorded phone calls. They're moving to a new phone system that stores the audio calls as MP3 files. Do you need to make any changes to your utility?

2. `cool_songs` is a Python list containing path strings to your favorite songs. What do you need to do to play these songs back in a random order?

3. You have installed the `audio/mpeg` codec on your system, but the following code isn't working. Find out what's wrong with it:

   ```
   recorder = qtmm.QAudioRecorder()
   recorder.setCodec('audio/mpeg')
   recorder.record()
   ```

4. Run `audio_test.py` and `video_test.py` on several different Windows, macOS, and Linux systems. How is the output different? Are there any items supported across all systems?

5. The properties of the `QCamera` class include several control objects, which allow you to manage different aspects of the camera. One of these is `QCameraFocus`. Investigate `QCameraFocus` in the Qt documentation at https://doc.qt.io/qt-5/qcamerafocus.html and write a simple script that shows a viewfinder and lets you adjust the digital zoom.

6. You've noticed the audio being recorded to your **Captain's Log** video log is quite loud. You want to add a control to adjust it; how would you do this?

7. Implement a dock widget in `captains_log.py` that allows you to control as many aspects of the audio and video recording as you can. You can include things such as focus, zoom, exposure, white balance, frame rate, resolution, audio volume, audio quality, and more.

Further reading

You can check the following references for further information:

- You can get an overview of the Qt Multimedia system and its capabilities at `https://doc.qt.io/qt-5/multimediaoverview.html`.
- The official PyQt `QtMultimedia` and `QtMultimediaWidgets` examples can be found at `https://github.com/pyqt/examples/tree/master/multimedia` and `https://github.com/pyqt/examples/tree/master/multimediawidgets`. They provide more example code of using PyQt for media capture and playback.

8
Networking with QtNetwork

Humans are social creatures and, increasingly, so are the software systems we create. As useful as computers are on their own, they are far more useful when connected to other computers. Whether on a small local switch or the global internet, engaging with other systems over a network is crucial functionality for much modern software. In this chapter, we're going to explore the networking capabilities offered by Qt and how to use them within PyQt5.

In particular, we'll cover the following topics:

- Low-level networking with sockets
- HTTP communications with `QNetworkAccessManager`

Technical requirements

You will, as in other chapters, need a basic Python and PyQt5 setup as described in `Chapter 1`, *Getting Started with PyQt*, and you will benefit from downloading the example code from our GitHub repository at `https://github.com/PacktPublishing/Mastering-GUI-Programming-with-Python/tree/master/Chapter08`.

In addition, you will want access to at least one other Python-equipped computer on the same local area network.

Check out the following video to see the code in action: `http://bit.ly/2M5xqid`

Low-level networking with sockets

Nearly every modern network uses the **internet protocol suite**, also known as **TCP/IP**, to facilitate connections between computers or other devices. TCP/IP is a set of protocols that manage the transmission of raw data over the network. The most common way to work with TCP/IP directly in code is with a **socket API**.

A socket is a file-like object that represents a single point of network connectivity for the system. Every socket has a **host address**, **network port**, and **transmission protocol**.

The host address, also known as an **IP address**, is a set of numbers used to identify a single network host on a network. Although backbone systems rely on the IPv6 protocol, most personal computers still use the older IPv4 address, which consists of four numbers between 0 and 255 separated by a dot. You can find the address of your system using GUI tools, or by typing one of the following commands into a command-line terminal:

OS	Command
Windows	ipconfig
macOS	ifconfig
Linux	ip address

Port is simply a number from 0 to 65535. Although you can create a socket with any port number, certain port numbers are assigned to common services; these are called **well-known ports**. For example, HTTP servers are typically assigned to port 80, and SSH is typically on port 22. On many operating systems, administrative or root privileges are required to create a socket on ports less than 1024.

An official list of well-known ports can be found at https://www.iana.org/assignments/service-names-port-numbers/service-names-port-numbers.xhtml.

Transmission protocols include **Transmission Control Protocol** (TCP) and **User Datagram Protocol** (UDP). TCP is a stateful connection between two systems. You can think of it as a phone call—a connection is established, information is exchanged, and at some definite point the connection is disconnected. Because of its statefulness, TCP ensures that all transmitted packets are received. UDP, on the other hand, is a stateless protocol. Think of it like using a walkie-talkie—users transmit a message, which receivers may or may not receive in whole or in part, and an explicit connection is never established. UDP is comparatively lightweight and often used for broadcast messages since it doesn't require a connection to a specific host.

The QtNetwork module provides us with classes to establish TCP and UDP socket connections. To understand how they work, we're going to construct two chat systems—one using UDP, the other using TCP.

Building a chat GUI

Let's begin by creating a basic GUI form that we can use for both versions of the chat application. Start with the application template from Chapter 4, *Building Applications with QMainWindow*, and add this class:

```
class ChatWindow(qtw.QWidget):

    submitted = qtc.pyqtSignal(str)

    def __init__(self):
        super().__init__()

        self.setLayout(qtw.QGridLayout())
        self.message_view = qtw.QTextEdit(readOnly=True)
        self.layout().addWidget(self.message_view, 1, 1, 1, 2)
        self.message_entry = qtw.QLineEdit()
        self.layout().addWidget(self.message_entry, 2, 1)
        self.send_btn = qtw.QPushButton('Send', clicked=self.send)
        self.layout().addWidget(self.send_btn, 2, 2)
```

The GUI is pretty simple, just a text edit to display the conversation, a line edit to enter a message, and a button to send. We've also implemented a signal we can emit whenever the user submits a new message.

The GUI will also have two methods:

```
    def write_message(self, username, message):
        self.message_view.append(f'<b>{username}: </b> {message}<br>')

    def send(self):
        message = self.message_entry.text().strip()
        if message:
            self.submitted.emit(message)
            self.message_entry.clear()
```

The `send()` method, triggered by the `send_btn` button, emits our `submitted` signal containing the text in the line edit, and the `write_message()` method which receives a `username` and `message` and writes it to the text edit using some simple formatting.

Down in the `MainWindow.__init__()` method, add in this code:

```
self.cw = ChatWindow()
self.setCentralWidget(self.cw)
```

Finally, before we can do any networking code, we need to add an `import` for `QtNetwork`. Add it to the top of the file, like this:

```
from PyQt5 import QtNetwork as qtn
```

This code will be the base code for both our UDP and TCP chat applications, so save one copy of this file as `udp_chat.py` and another as `tcp_chat.py`. We'll complete each application by creating a backend object for the form.

Building a UDP chat client

UDP is most commonly used in broadcast applications on local networks, so to demonstrate this, we're going to make our UDP chat a local-network-only broadcast chat. That means that any computer on a local network running a copy of this application will be able to view and participate in the conversation.

We'll start by creating our backend class, which we'll call `UdpChatInterface`:

```
class UdpChatInterface(qtc.QObject):

    port = 7777
    delimiter = '||'
    received = qtc.pyqtSignal(str, str)
    error = qtc.pyqtSignal(str)
```

Our backend inherits `QObject` so that we can use Qt signals, of which we've defined two—a `received` signal that we'll emit when a message is received, and an `error` signal that we'll emit when an error happens. We've also defined a port number to use, and a `delimiter` string. The `delimiter` string will be used to separate the username and message when we serialize our message for transmission; so, when the user `alanm` sends the message `Hello World`, our interface will send the string `alanm||Hello World` out on the wire.

Only one application can be bound to a port at one time; if you already have an application using port 7777, you should change this number to something else between 1024 and 65535. On Windows, macOS, and older Linux systems, the netstat command can be used to show which ports are in use. On newer Linux systems, the ss command can be used.

Now start an __init__() method:

```
def __init__(self, username):
    super().__init__()
    self.username = username

    self.socket = qtn.QUdpSocket()
    self.socket.bind(qtn.QHostAddress.Any, self.port)
```

After calling super() and storing the username variable, our first order of business is to create and configure a QUdpSocket object. Before we can use the socket, it must be **bound** to a localhost address and a port number. QtNetwork.QHostAddress.Any represents all addresses on the local system so our socket will be listening and sending on port 7777 on all local interfaces.

To use the socket, we have to handle its signals:

```
        self.socket.readyRead.connect(self.process_datagrams)
        self.socket.error.connect(self.on_error)
```

Socket objects have two signals that we're interested in watching. The first is readyRead, and it's emitted whenever data is received by the socket. We're going to handle that signal in a method called process_datagrams(), which we'll write in a moment.

The error signal is emitted when there is an error of any kind, which we'll handle in an instance method called on_error().

Let's start with that error handler since it's relatively simple:

```
def on_error(self, socket_error):
    error_index = (qtn.QAbstractSocket
                    .staticMetaObject
                    .indexOfEnumerator('SocketError'))
    error = (qtn.QAbstractSocket
                .staticMetaObject
                .enumerator(error_index)
                .valueToKey(socket_error))
    message = f"There was a network error: {error}"
    self.error.emit(message)
```

This method has a little bit of Qt magic in it. Network errors are defined in the `SocketError` enum of the `QAbstractSocket` class (the parent class of `UdpSocket`). Unfortunately, if we just try to print the error, we get the integer value of the constant. To actually get a meaningful string, we're going to dig into the `staticMetaObject` associated with `QAbstractSocket`. We first get the index of the enum class containing the error constants, then use `valueToKey()` to convert our socket error integer into its constant name. This trick can be used with any Qt enum to retrieve a meaningful name rather than just its integer value.

One that's been retrieved, we simply format the error in a message and emit it in our `error` signal.

Now let's tackle `process_datagrams()`:

```
def process_datagrams(self):
    while self.socket.hasPendingDatagrams():
        datagram = self.socket.receiveDatagram()
        raw_message = bytes(datagram.data()).decode('utf-8')
```

A single UDP transmission is known as a **datagram**. When a datagram is received by our socket, it is stored in a buffer and the `readyRead` signal is emitted. As long as that buffer has datagrams waiting, the socket's `hasPendingDatagrams()` will return `True`. Thus, we loop continually while there are pending datagrams, calling the socket's `receiveDatagram()` method, which returns and removes the next datagram waiting in the buffer until all the datagrams are retrieved.

The datagram object returned by `receiveDatagram()` is a `QByteArray`, the Qt equivalent of a Python `bytes` object. Since our program is transmitting strings, rather than binary objects, we can just convert the `QByteArray` to a Unicode string. The fastest way to do this is to first cast it to a `bytes` object, then use the `decode()` method to convert it to UTF-8 Unicode text.

Now that we have our raw string, we need to check it to make sure it came from another instance of `udp_chat.py`, then split it out into its `username` and `message` components:

```
if self.delimiter not in raw_message:
    continue
username, message = raw_message.split(self.delimiter, 1)
self.received.emit(username, message)
```

If the raw text received by the socket doesn't contain our `delimiter` string, it's most likely from some other program or a corrupt packet, and we'll just skip it. Otherwise, we'll split it at the first instance of the `delimiter` into the `username` and `message` strings, then emit those strings with the `received` signal.

The final thing our chat client needs is a method to send a message, which we'll implement in the `send_message()` method:

```
def send_message(self, message):
    msg_bytes = (
        f'{self.username}{self.delimiter}{message}'
    ).encode('utf-8')
    self.socket.writeDatagram(
        qtc.QByteArray(msg_bytes),
        qtn.QHostAddress.Broadcast,
        self.port
    )
```

This method starts by formatting the passed message with our configured username using the `delimiter` string, then encodes the formatted string as a `bytes` object.

Next, we write the datagram to our socket object using the `writeDatagram()` method. This method takes a `QByteArray` (to which we have cast our `bytes` object) and a destination address and port. Our destination is specified as `QHostAddress.Broadcast`, which indicates that we want to use the broadcast address, and the port is, of course, the one we defined in our class variable.

 The **broadcast address** is a reserved address on a TCP/IP network which, when used, indicates that the transmission should be received by all hosts.

Let's summarize what we've done in this backend:

- When a message is sent, it is prefixed with the username and broadcast as a byte array to all hosts on the network on port 7777.
- When a message is received on port 7777, it is converted from a byte array to a string. The message and username are split and emitted in a signal.
- When an error occurs, the error number is converted to an error string and emitted with an error signal.

Now we just need to hook our backend into the frontend form.

Connecting signals

Back in our `MainWindow` constructor, we need to finish up our application by creating a `UdpChatInterface` object and connecting its signals:

```
username = qtc.QDir.home().dirName()
self.interface = UdpChatInterface(username)
self.cw.submitted.connect(self.interface.send_message)
self.interface.received.connect(self.cw.write_message)
self.interface.error.connect(
    lambda x: qtw.QMessageBox.critical(None, 'Error', x))
```

Before creating the interface, we're determining the `username` by grabbing the name of the current user's home directory. This is a bit of a hack, but it works well enough for our purposes here.

Next, we create our interface object and connect the chat window `submitted` signal to its `send_message()` slot.

We then connect the interface's `received` signal to the chat window's `write_message()` method, and the `error` signal to a lambda function that shows the error in a `QMessageBox`.

With everything wired up, we're ready to test.

Testing the chat

To test this chat system, you'll need two computers with Python and PyQt5 installed running on the same local area network. You may need to disable the systems' firewalls or open UPD port 7777 before proceeding.

Once you've done that, copy `udp_chat.py` to both machines and launch it. Type a message on one machine; it should show up in the chat window on both machines, looking something like this:

Notice that the systems also pick up and react to their own broadcast messages, so we don't need to worry about echoing our own messages in the text area.

UDP is certainly simple to work with, but it has many limitations. For example, UDP broadcasts cannot usually be routed outside a local network, and the lack of stateful connection means that there is no way to know whether a transmission was received or lost. In the *Building a TCP chat client* section, we'll build a TCP version of our chat that doesn't have these issues.

Building a TCP chat client

TCP is a stateful transmission protocol, meaning that a connection is established and maintained until the transmission is complete. TCP is also primarily a one-to-one connection between hosts, which we generally implement using a **client-server** design. Our TCP chat application will make a direct connection between two network hosts and will contain both a client component that will connect to other instances of the app and a server component that will handle incoming client connections.

In the `tcp_chat.py` file you created earlier, start a TCP chat interface class like so:

```
class TcpChatInterface(qtc.QObject):

    port = 7777
    delimiter = '||'
    received = qtc.pyqtSignal(str, str)
    error = qtc.pyqtSignal(str)
```

So far, this is identical to the UDP interface apart from the name. Now let's create the constructor:

```
    def __init__(self, username, recipient):
        super().__init__()
        self.username = username
        self.recipient = recipient
```

As before, the interface object takes a `username`, but we've added a `recipient` argument as well. Since TCP requires a direct connection to another host, we need to specify which remote host we want to connect to.

Now we need to create the server component that will listen for incoming connections:

```
self.listener = qtn.QTcpServer()
self.listener.listen(qtn.QHostAddress.Any, self.port)
self.listener.acceptError.connect(self.on_error)

self.listener.newConnection.connect(self.on_connection)
self.connections = []
```

`listener` is a `QTcpServer` object. `QTcpServer` enables our interface to receive incoming connections from TCP clients on the given interface and port, which in this case we've set to any local interface on port `7777`.

When there is an error with an incoming connection, the server object emits an `acceptError` signal, which we connect to an `on_error()` method. These are the same kind of errors that `UdpSocket` emits, so we can copy the `on_error()` method from `udp_chat.py` and handle them identically.

The `newConnection` signal is emitted whenever a new connection comes into the server; we're going to handle that in a method called `on_connection()`, which looks like this:

```
def on_connection(self):
    connection = self.listener.nextPendingConnection()
    connection.readyRead.connect(self.process_datastream)
    self.connections.append(connection)
```

The server's `nextPendingConnection()` method returns the next waiting connection as a `QTcpSocket` object. Like `QUdpSocket`, `QTcpSocket` emits a `readyRead` signal when it receives data. We'll connect this signal to a `process_datastream()` method.

Finally, we'll save a reference to our new connection in the `self.connections` list.

Working with data streams

While UDP sockets work with datagrams, TCP sockets work with **data streams**. As the name implies, data streams involve a flow of data rather than discrete units. TCP transmissions are sent as a stream of network packets that may or may not arrive in the correct order, and it's up to the receiver to correctly reassemble the data received. To make this process easier, we can wrap our socket in a `QtCore.QDataStream` object, which provides a generic interface for reading and writing data from file-like sources.

Let's begin our method like this:

```
def process_datastream(self):
    for socket in self.connections:
        self.datastream = qtc.QDataStream(socket)
        if not socket.bytesAvailable():
            continue
```

We're iterating through the connected sockets and passing each to a `QDataStream` object. The `socket` object has a `bytesAvailable()` method that tells us how many bytes of data are queued up to be read. If this number is zero, we're going to continue to the next connection in the list.

If not, we'll read from the data stream:

```
raw_message = self.datastream.readQString()
if raw_message and self.delimiter in raw_message:
    username, message = raw_message.split(self.delimiter, 1)
    self.received.emit(username, message)
```

`QDataStream.readQString()` attempts to pull a string from the data stream and return it. Despite the name, in PyQt5 this method actually returns a Python Unicode string, not a `QString`. It's important to understand that this method *only* works if a `QString` was sent with the original packet. If some other object was sent (a raw byte string, an integer, and so on), `readQString()` will return `None`.

The `QDataStream` has methods for writing and reading a variety of data types. See its documentation at https://doc.qt.io/qt-5/qdatastream. html.

Once we have the transmission as a string, we check for the `delimiter` string in the raw message and, if found, split the raw message and emit the `received` signal.

Sending data over TCP

`QTcpServer` has handled the reception of messages; now we need to implement sending messages. To do this, we first need to create a `QTcpSocket` object to be our client socket.

Let's add this to the end of `__init__()`:

```
self.client_socket = qtn.QTcpSocket()
self.client_socket.error.connect(self.on_error)
```

We've created a default `QTcpSocket` object and connected its `error` signal to our error handling method. Note that we don't need to bind this socket because it won't be listening.

To use the client socket, we'll create a `send_message()` method; just as with our UDP chat, this method will start by formatting the message it into the raw transmission string:

```
def send_message(self, message):
    raw_message = f'{self.username}{self.delimiter}{message}'
```

Now we need to connect to the remote host with which we're going to communicate:

```
socket_state = self.client_socket.state()
if socket_state != qtn.QAbstractSocket.ConnectedState:
    self.client_socket.connectToHost(
        self.recipient, self.port)
```

The socket's `state` property can tell us whether our socket is connected to a remote host. The `QAbstractSocket.ConnectedState` state indicates that our client is connected to a server. If it's not, we call the socket's `connectToHost()` method to establish the connection to our recipient host.

Now that we can be fairly certain we've connected, let's send the message. To do this, we once again turn to the `QDataStream` object to handle the delicate aspects of communicating with our TCP socket.

Begin by creating a new data stream attached to the client socket:

```
self.datastream = qtc.QDataStream(self.client_socket)
```

Now we can write a string to the data stream using its `writeQString()` method:

```
self.datastream.writeQString(raw_message)
```

It's important to understand that objects can be pulled from the data stream only in the order we sent them. For instance, if we wanted to prefix the string with its length so that the recipient can check it for corruption, we might do this:

```
self.datastream.writeUInt32(len(raw_message))
self.datastream.writeQString(raw_message)
```

Our `process_datastream()` method would then have to be adjusted accordingly:

```
def process_datastream(self):
    #...
    message_length = self.datastream.readUInt32()
    raw_message = self.datastream.readQString()
```

The last thing we need to do in `send_message()` is emit our message locally so that the local display can show it. Since this isn't a broadcast message, our local TCP server won't hear the messages being sent out.

Add this at the end of `send_message()`:

```
self.received.emit(self.username, message)
```

Let's summarize how this backend operates:

- We have a TCP server component:
  - The TCP server object listens for connections from remote hosts on port 7777
  - When one is received, it stores the connection as a socket and waits for data from that socket
  - When data is received, it is read from the socket using a data stream, interpreted, and emitted
- We have a TCP client component:
  - When a message needs to be sent, it is first formatted
  - Then the connection state is checked, and one is established if necessary
  - Once the connection state is ensured, the message is written to the socket using a data stream

Connecting our backend and testing

Back in `MainWindow.__init__()`, we need to add the relevant code to create our interface and connect the signals:

```
recipient, _ = qtw.QInputDialog.getText(
    None, 'Recipient',
    'Specify of the IP or hostname of the remote host.')
if not recipient:
    sys.exit()

self.interface = TcpChatInterface(username, recipient)
self.cw.submitted.connect(self.interface.send_message)
self.interface.received.connect(self.cw.write_message)
self.interface.error.connect(
    lambda x: qtw.QMessageBox.critical(None, 'Error', x))
```

Since we need a recipient, we'll ask the user using a `QInputDialog`. This dialog class allows you to easily query a user for a single value. In this case, we're asking for the IP address or hostname of the other system. This value we pass to the `TcpChatInterface` constructor.

The rest of the code is essentially the same as the UDP chat client.

To test this chat client, you'll need to run one copy on another computer on the same network or on an address you can reach from your own network. When you launch the client, specify the IP or hostname of the other machine. Once both clients are running, you should be able to send messages back and forth. If you launch the client on a third machine, note that you won't see the messages, since they are being directed to a single machine only.

HTTP communications with QNetworkAccessManager

HyperText Transfer Protocol (HTTP) is the protocol on which the World Wide Web is built, and arguably the most important communications protocol of our time. We could certainly implement our own HTTP communications on top of sockets, but Qt has already done the work for us. The `QNetworkAccessManager` class implements an object that can transmit HTTP requests and receive HTTP replies. We can use this class to create applications that communicate with web services and APIs.

Simple downloading

To demonstrate the basic use of `QNetworkAccessManager`, we're going to build a simple command-line HTTP download tool. Open a blank file called `downloader.py` and let's start with some imports:

```
import sys
from os import path
from PyQt5 import QtNetwork as qtn
from PyQt5 import QtCore as qtc
```

Since we aren't doing a GUI here, we don't need `QtWidgets` or `QtGui`, just `QtNetwork`, and `QtCore`. We'll also use the standard library `path` module for some filesystem-based operations.

Let's create a `QObject` subclass for our download engine:

```
class Downloader(qtc.QObject):

    def __init__(self, url):
        super().__init__()
        self.manager = qtn.QNetworkAccessManager(
            finished=self.on_finished)
        self.request = qtn.QNetworkRequest(qtc.QUrl(url))
        self.manager.get(self.request)
```

Inside our download engine, we're creating a `QNetworkAccessManager` and connecting its `finished` signal to a callback called `on_finish()`. The `finished` signal is emitted when the manager completes a network transaction and has a reply ready to process, which it includes with the signal.

Next, we create a `QNetworkRequest` object. `QNetworkRequest` represents the HTTP request that we're sending to the remote server and contains all the information we're going to send. In this case, we just need the URL that has been passed into the constructor.

Finally, we tell our network manager to execute the request using `get()`. The `get()` method sends our request using the HTTP GET method, which is typically used for requesting information for download. The manager will send this request and await a reply.

When the reply comes, it will be sent to our `on_finished()` callback:

```
    def on_finished(self, reply):
        filename = reply.url().fileName() or 'download'
        if path.exists(filename):
            print('File already exists, not overwriting.')
            sys.exit(1)
        with open(filename, 'wb') as fh:
            fh.write(reply.readAll())
        print(f"{filename} written")
        sys.exit(0)
```

The `reply` object here is a `QNetworkReply` instance, which contains the data and metadata received from the remote server.

We first try to determine a filename, which we'll use for saving the file. The reply's `url` property contains the URL to which the original request was made, and we can query the URL's `fileName` property. Sometimes this is empty, though, so we'll fall back to the `'download'` string.

Next, we'll check whether the filename already exists on our system. For safety, we exit if it does, so that you don't destroy important files on your system testing this demo.

Finally, we extract the data from the reply using its `readAll()` method, writing this data to a local file. Notice that we open the file in `wb` mode (write-binary) since `readAll()` returns binary data in the form of a `QByteAarray` object.

The main execution code for our `Downloader` class comes last:

```
if __name__ == '__main__':
    if len(sys.argv) < 2:
        print(f'Usage: {sys.argv[0]} <download url>')
        sys.exit(1)
    app = qtc.QCoreApplication(sys.argv)
    d = Downloader(sys.argv[1])
    sys.exit(app.exec_())
```

Here, we're just getting the first argument from the command line and passing it into our `Downloader` object. Notice that we use `QCoreApplication` rather than `QApplication`; this class is used when you want to create a command-line Qt application. It's otherwise the same as `QApplication`.

In a nutshell, using `QNetworkAccessManager` is as simple as this:

- Create a `QNetworkAccessManager` object
- Create a `QNetworkRequest` object
- Pass the request to the manager's `get()` method
- Handle the reply in a callback connected to the manager's `finished` signal

Posting data and files

Retrieving data with a GET request is fairly simple HTTP; for a deeper exploration of HTTP communications with PyQt5, we're going to build a utility that will allow us to send POST requests with arbitrary key-value and file data to a remote URL. This utility might be useful for testing web APIs, for example.

Building the GUI

Starting with a copy of your Qt application template from Chapter 4, *Building Applications with QMainWindow*, let's add our main GUI code into the MainWindow.__init__() method:

```
widget = qtw.QWidget(minimumWidth=600)
self.setCentralWidget(widget)
widget.setLayout(qtw.QVBoxLayout())
self.url = qtw.QLineEdit()
self.table = qtw.QTableWidget(columnCount=2, rowCount=5)
self.table.horizontalHeader().setSectionResizeMode(
    qtw.QHeaderView.Stretch)
self.table.setHorizontalHeaderLabels(['key', 'value'])
self.fname = qtw.QPushButton(
    '(No File)', clicked=self.on_file_btn)
submit = qtw.QPushButton('Submit Post', clicked=self.submit)
response = qtw.QTextEdit(readOnly=True)
for w in (self.url, self.table, self.fname, submit, response):
    widget.layout().addWidget(w)
```

This is a simple form built on a QWidget object. There is a line input for the URL, a table widget for entering key-value pairs, and a button that will be used to trigger a file dialog and store the selected filename.

After that, we have a submit button for sending the request and a read-only text edit that will display the returned results.

The fname button calls on_file_btn() when clicked, which looks like this:

```
def on_file_btn(self):
    filename, accepted = qtw.QFileDialog.getOpenFileName()
    if accepted:
        self.fname.setText(filename)
```

This method simply calls a QFileDialog function to retrieve a filename to open. In order to keep things simple, we're taking the slightly unorthodox approach of storing the filename as our QPushButton text.

The final MainWindow method is submit(), which is called when the submit button is clicked. We'll come back to that method after writing our web backend since its operation depends on how we define that backend.

The POSTing backend

Our web posting backend will be based on a `QObject` simply so that we can use signals and slots.

Begin by subclassing `QObject` and creating a signal:

```
class Poster(qtc.QObject):

    replyReceived = qtc.pyqtSignal(str)
```

The `replyReceived` will be emitted when we receive a reply from the server to which we're posting and will carry with it the body of the reply as a string.

Now let's create the constructor:

```
def __init__(self):
    super().__init__()
    self.nam = qtn.QNetworkAccessManager()
    self.nam.finished.connect(self.on_reply)
```

Here, we're creating our `QNetworkAccessManager` object and connecting its `finished` signal to a local method called `on_reply()`.

The `on_reply()` method will look like this:

```
def on_reply(self, reply):
    reply_bytes = reply.readAll()
    reply_string = bytes(reply_bytes).decode('utf-8')
    self.replyReceived.emit(reply_string)
```

Recall that the `finished` signal carries with it a `QNetworkReply` object. We can call its `readAll()` method to get the body of the reply as a `QByteArray`. Just as we did with our raw socket data, we first cast this to a `bytes` object, then use the `decode()` method to convert it to UTF-8 Unicode data. Finally, we'll emit our `replyReceived` signal with the string from the server.

Now we need a method that will actually post our key-value data and file to a URL. We'll call it `make_request()`, and it begins as follows:

```
def make_request(self, url, data, filename):
    self.request = qtn.QNetworkRequest(url)
```

Just as with a GET request, we start by creating a `QNetworkRequest` object from the provided URL. Unlike the GET request, however, our POST request carries a data payload. To carry this payload, we need to create a special object that we can send with the request.

There are a few ways that an HTTP request can format a data payload, but the most common way to transmit a file over HTTP is to use a **Multipart Form** request. This kind of request contains both key-value data and byte-encoded file data and is what you would get from submitting an HTML form containing a mix of input widgets and file widgets.

To perform this kind of request in PyQt, we will begin by creating a `QtNetwork.QHttpMultiPart` object, like so:

```
self.multipart = qtn.QHttpMultiPart(
    qtn.QHttpMultiPart.FormDataType)
```

There are different types of multipart HTTP messages, and we define which type we want by passing a `QtNetwork.QHttpMultiPart.ContentType` enum constant to the constructor. The type we need for transmitting file and form data together is `FormDataType`, which we've used here.

The HTTP multipart object is a container for `QHttpPart` objects, each of which represents a component of our data payload. We need to create these parts from the data passed into this method and add them to our multipart object.

Let's start with our key-value pairs:

```
for key, value in (data or {}).items():
    http_part = qtn.QHttpPart()
    http_part.setHeader(
        qtn.QNetworkRequest.ContentDispositionHeader,
        f'form-data; name="{key}"'
    )
    http_part.setBody(value.encode('utf-8'))
    self.multipart.append(http_part)
```

Each HTTP part has a header and a body. The header contains metadata about the part, including its **Content-Disposition**—in other words, what it contains. In the case of form data, that would be `form-data`.

So, for each key-value pair in the `data` dictionary, we're creating a single `QHttpPart` object, setting the Content-Disposition header to `form-data` with a `name` argument set to the key. Finally, we set the body of the HTTP part to our value (encoded as a byte string) and add the HTTP part to our multipart object.

To include our file, we need to do something similar:

```
if filename:
    file_part = qtn.QHttpPart()
    file_part.setHeader(
        qtn.QNetworkRequest.ContentDispositionHeader,
```

```
        f'form-data; name="attachment"; filename="{filename}"'
    )
    filedata = open(filename, 'rb').read()
    file_part.setBody(filedata)
    self.multipart.append(file_part)
```

This time, our Content-Disposition header is still set to `form-data`, but also includes a `filename` argument set to the name of our file. The body of the HTTP part is set to the contents of the file. Note that we open the file in `rb` mode, meaning that its binary contents will be read as a `bytes` object rather than interpreting it as plaintext. This is important as `setBody()` expects bytes rather than Unicode.

Now that our multipart object is built, we can call the `post()` method of our `QNetworkAccessManager` object to send the request with the multipart data:

```
self.nam.post(self.request, self.multipart)
```

Back in `MainWindow.__init__()`, let's create a `Poster` object to work with:

```
self.poster = Poster()
self.poster.replyReceived.connect(self.response.setText)
```

Since `replyReceived` emits the reply body as a string, we can connect it directly to `setText` in our response widget to view the server's response.

Finally, it's time to create our `submit()` callback:

```
def submit(self):
    url = qtc.QUrl(self.url.text())
    filename = self.fname.text()
    if filename == '(No File)':
        filename = None
    data = {}
    for rownum in range(self.table.rowCount()):
        key_item = self.table.item(rownum, 0)
        key = key_item.text() if key_item else None
        if key:
            data[key] = self.table.item(rownum, 1).text()
    self.poster.make_request(url, data, filename)
```

Remember that `make_request()` wants `QUrl`, a `dict` of the key-value pairs, and a filename string; so, this method simply goes through each widget, extracting and formatting the data, then passes it to `make_request()`.

Testing the utility

If you have access to a server that accepts POST requests and file uploads, you can certainly use that to test your script; if not, you can also use the `sample_http_server.py` script included with the example code for this chapter. This script requires only Python 3 and the standard library and will echo back your POST request to you.

Launch the server script in a console window, then in a second console run your `poster.py` script and do the following:

- Enter `http://localhost:8000` for the URL
- Add a few arbitrary key-value pairs to the table
- Select a file (probably a not-very-large text file, such as one of your Python scripts) to upload
- Click **Submit Post**

You should see a printout of your request in both the server console window and in the response text edit on the GUI. It should look like this:

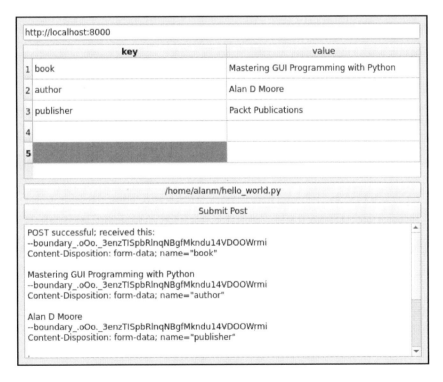

To summarize, handling a POST request with QNetworkAccessManager involves the following:

- Creating a QNetworkAccessManager and connecting its finished signal to a method that will process a QNetworkReply
- Creating a QNetworkRequest pointed to the target URL
- Creating a data payload object, such as a QHttpMultiPart object
- Passing the request and data payload to the QNetworkAccessManager object's post() method

Summary

In this chapter, we explored connecting our PyQt applications to the network. You learned how to do low-level programming with sockets, including both a UDP broadcast application and TCP client-server application. You also learned how to interact with HTTP services using QNetworkAccessManager, beginning with simple downloading and ending with the uploading of complex multi-part form and file data.

The next chapter will explore the use of SQL databases to store and retrieve data. You will learn how to build and query a SQL database, how to integrate SQL commands into your applications using the QtSQL module, and how to use SQL model-view components to quickly build data-driven GUI applications.

Questions

Try these questions to test your knowledge from this chapter:

1. You are designing an application that will emit a status message to the local network, which you will monitor with administrator tools. What kind of socket object would be a good choice?

2. Your GUI class has a QTcpSocket object called self.socket. You've connected its readyRead signal to the following method, but it's not working. What's happening, and how can you fix it?

```
def on_ready_read(self):
    while self.socket.hasPendingDatagrams():
        self.process_data(self.socket.readDatagram())
```

3. Use `QTcpServer` to implement a simple service that listens on port `8080` and prints any requests received. Make it reply to the client with a byte string of your choice.

4. You're creating a download function for your application to retrieve a large data file for import into your application. The code does not work. Read the code and decide what you're doing wrong:

```
def download(self, url):
  self.manager = qtn.QNetworkAccessManager(
      finished=self.on_finished)
  self.request = qtn.QNetworkRequest(qtc.QUrl(url))
  reply = self.manager.get(self.request)
  with open('datafile.dat', 'wb') as fh:
      fh.write(reply.readAll())
```

5. Modify your `poster.py` script so that it sends the key-value data as JSON rather than HTTP form data.

Further reading

For further information, please refer to the following:

- More information on the datagram packet structure can be found at `https://en.wikipedia.org/wiki/Datagram`.
- With the ever-increasing focus on security and privacy in network communications, it's important to know how to work with SSL. See `https://doc.qt.io/qt-5/ssl.html` for an overview of the `QtNetwork` facilities for working with SSL.
- The **Mozilla Developer Network** has a large number of resources for understanding HTTP and its various standards and protocols at `https://developer.mozilla.org/en-US/docs/Web/HTTP`.

Exploring SQL with Qt SQL 9

For about 40 years, **relational databases** managed with the **structured query language** (commonly known as SQL) have been the de facto standard technology for storing, retrieving, and analyzing the world's data. Whether you are creating business applications, games, web applications, or something else, if your application deals with a large amount of data, you will almost certainly be working with SQL. While Python has many modules available for connecting to a SQL database, Qt's `QtSql` module provides us with powerful and convenient classes for integrating SQL data into PyQt applications.

In this chapter, you'll learn how to build database-driven PyQt applications as we cover the following topics:

- SQL basics
- Performing SQL queries with Qt
- Using SQL with model-view widgets

Technical requirements

Apart from the basic setup you've been using since `Chapter 1`, *Getting Started with PyQt*, you will want the example code found in the GitHub repository at `https://github.com/PacktPublishing/Mastering-GUI-Programming-with-Python/tree/master/Chapter09`.

You may also find it helpful to have a copy of **SQLite** to practice the SQL examples. SQLite is free and can be downloaded from `https://sqlite.org/download.html`.

Check out the following video to see the code in action: `http://bit.ly/2M5xu1r`

SQL basics

Before we jump into what `QtSql` has to offer, you will need to be familiar with the basics of SQL. This section will give you a quick overview of how to create, populate, alter, and query data in a SQL database. If you already know SQL, you may want to skip ahead to the PyQt part of this chapter.

SQL is a very different language from Python in syntax and structure. It is a **declarative** language, meaning that we describe the results we want rather than the procedures used to get them. To interact with a SQL database, we execute **statements**. Each statement is made up of a SQL **command** followed by a series of **clauses**, each of which further describes the results desired. Statements are terminated with a semicolon.

Although SQL is standardized, all SQL database implementations provide their own alterations and extensions to the standard language. We're going to be learning the SQLite dialect of SQL, which is reasonably close to standard SQL.

 Unlike Python, SQL is generally a case-insensitive language; however, it is a long-standing convention to write SQL keywords in all uppercase letters. This helps them to stand out from data and object names. We will follow this convention in the book, but it is optional for your code.

Creating tables

SQL databases are made of relations, also known as **tables**. A table is a two-dimensional data structure made of rows and columns. Each row in the table represents a single item about which we have information, and each column represents a type of information we are storing.

Tables are defined using the CREATE TABLE command, like so:

```
CREATE TABLE coffees (
        id  INTEGER PRIMARY KEY,
        coffee_brand TEXT NOT NULL,
        coffee_name TEXT NOT NULL,
        UNIQUE(coffee_brand, coffee_name)
        );
```

The CREATE TABLE statement is followed by a table name and a list of column definitions. In this example, coffees is the name of the table we're creating, and the column definitions are inside the parentheses. Each column has a name, a data type, and any number of **constraints** that describe valid values.

In this case, we have three columns:

- id is an integer column. It's marked as the **primary key**, which means it will be a unique value that can be used to identify the row.
- coffee_brand and coffee_name are both text columns with a NOT NULL constraint, meaning they cannot have NULL for a value.

Constraints can also be defined on multiple columns. The UNIQUE constraint added after the fields is not a field, but a table-level constraint that makes sure the combination of coffee _brand and coffee _name is unique for each row.

 NULL is the SQL equivalent of Python's None. It indicates the absence of information.

SQL databases, at a minimum, support text, numeric, date, time, and binary object data types; but it's not uncommon for different database implementations to extend SQL with additional data types, such as currency or IP address types. Many databases also have SMALL and BIG variants of numeric types, allowing the developer to fine-tune the amount of storage space used by a column.

As useful as simple two-dimensional tables are, the real power of a SQL database is in joining multiple, related tables together, for example:

```
CREATE TABLE roasts (
        id INTEGER PRIMARY KEY,
        description TEXT NOT NULL UNIQUE,
        color TEXT NOT NULL UNIQUE
        );

CREATE TABLE coffees (
        id   INTEGER PRIMARY KEY,
        coffee_brand TEXT NOT NULL,
        coffee_name TEXT NOT NULL,
        roast_id INTEGER REFERENCES roasts(id),
        UNIQUE(coffee_brand, coffee_name)
        );

CREATE TABLE reviews (
```

```
id INTEGER PRIMARY KEY,
coffee_id REFERENCES coffees(id),
reviewer TEXT NOT NULL,
review_date DATE NOT NULL DEFAULT CURRENT_DATE,
review TEXT NOT NULL
);
```

The `roast_id` column in `coffees` holds values that match the primary keys of `roasts`, as indicated by the REFERENCES constraint. Rather than having to rewrite the description and color of a roast in every coffee record, each `coffees` record simply points to a row in `roasts` that holds the information about the roast of that coffee. In the same way, the `reviews` table contains the `coffee_id` column, which refers to an individual `coffees` entry. These relationships are called **foreign key relationships** since the field refers to the key from another table.

Modeling data in multiple, related tables like this reduces duplication and enforces data **consistency**. Imagine if the data in all three tables were combined into one table of coffee reviews—it would be possible for two reviews of the same coffee product to have different roasts specified. That shouldn't be possible, and with relational data tables, it isn't.

Inserting and updating data

Once tables are created, we can add new rows of data using an INSERT statement using this syntax:

```
INSERT INTO table_name(column1, column2, ...)
    VALUES (value1, value2, ...), (value3, value4, ...);
```

For example, let's insert some rows into `roasts` :

```
INSERT INTO roasts(description, color) VALUES
    ('Light', '#FFD99B'),
    ('Medium', '#947E5A'),
    ('Dark', '#473C2B'),
    ('Burnt to a Crisp', '#000000');
```

In this example, we're providing a `description` and `color` value for each new record in the `roasts` table. The VALUES clause contains a list of tuples, each of which represents a row of data. The number and data types of the values in these tuples *must* match the number and data types of the columns specified.

Note that we didn't include all the columns—id is missing. Any fields we don't specify in an INSERT statement will get a default value, which is NULL unless we specify otherwise.

In SQLite, an INTEGER PRIMARY KEY field has special behavior in which its default value is automatically incremented on each insert. Therefore, the id values resulting from this query will be 1 for Light, 2 for Medium, 3 for Dark, and 4 for Burnt to a Crisp.

This is important to know, since we need that key value to insert records into our coffees table:

```
INSERT INTO coffees(coffee_brand, coffee_name, roast_id) VALUES
    ('Dumpy''s Donuts', 'Breakfast Blend', 2),
    ('Boise''s Better than Average', 'Italian Roast', 3),
    ('Strawbunks', 'Sumatra', 2),
    ('Chartreuse Hillock', 'Pumpkin Spice', 1),
    ('Strawbunks', 'Espresso', 3),
    ('9 o''clock', 'Original Decaf', 2);
```

 Unlike Python, SQL string literals *must* use single quotes only. A double-quoted string is interpreted as the name of a database object, such as a table or column. To escape a single quote in a string, use two of them, as we've done in the preceding query.

Because of our foreign key constraint, it is impossible to insert a row in coffees that contains a roast_id that doesn't exist in roasts. For example, this would return an error:

```
INSERT INTO coffees(coffee_brand, coffee_name, roast_id) VALUES
    ('Minwell House', 'Instant', 48);
```

Note that we can insert NULL in the roast_id field; unless the column was defined with a NOT NULL constraint, NULL is the only value that doesn't have to obey the foreign key constraint.

Updating existing rows

To update existing rows in a table, you use the UPDATE statement, like so:

```
UPDATE coffees SET roast_id = 4 WHERE id = 2;
```

The SET clause is followed by a list of value assignments for the fields you want to change, and the WHERE clause describes conditions that must be true if a particular row is to be updated. In this case, we're going to change the value of the roast_id column to 4 for the record where the id column is 2.

SQL uses a single equals sign for both assignment and equality operations. It does not ever use the double-equals sign that Python uses.

Update operations can also affect multiple records, like this:

```
UPDATE coffees SET roast_id = roast_id + 1
    WHERE coffee_brand LIKE 'Strawbunks';
```

In this case, we're incrementing the `roast_id` value on all the `Strawbunks` coffees by setting it equal to `roast_id + 1`. Whenever we reference a column's value in a query like this, the value will be that of the column in the same row.

Selecting data

Probably the most important operation in SQL is the `SELECT` statement, which is used to retrieve data. A simple `SELECT` statement looks like this:

```
SELECT reviewer, review_date
FROM reviews
WHERE   review_date > '2019-03-01'
ORDER BY reviewer DESC;
```

The `SELECT` command is followed by a list of fields, or by the `*` symbol, which means *all fields*. The `FROM` clause defines the source of the data; in this case, the `reviews` table. The `WHERE` clause, once again, defines conditions that must be true for the rows to be included. In this case, we'll only include reviews newer than March 1, 2019, by comparing each row's `review_date` field (which is a `DATE` type) to the string `'2019-03-01'` (which SQLite will convert to a `DATE` to make the comparison). Finally, the `ORDER BY` clause determines the sorting of the result set.

Table joins

`SELECT` statements always return a single table of values. Even if your result set has only a single value, it will be in a table of one row and one column, and there is no way to return multiple tables from a single query. However, we can pull data from multiple tables by combining the data into a single table.

This can be done using a JOIN in the FROM clause, for example:

```
SELECT coffees.coffee_brand,
    coffees.coffee_name,
    roasts.description AS roast,
    COUNT(reviews.id) AS reviews
FROM coffees
    JOIN roasts ON coffees.roast_id = roasts.id
    LEFT OUTER JOIN reviews ON reviews.coffee_id = coffees.id
GROUP BY coffee_brand, coffee_name, roast
ORDER BY reviews DESC;
```

In this case, our FROM clause contains two JOIN statements. The first joins coffees to roasts by matching the roast_id field in coffees to the id field in roasts. The second joins the reviews table by matching the coffee_id column in reviews to the id column in coffees.

The joins are slightly different: notice that the reviews join is a LEFT OUTER JOIN. This means that we're including rows from coffees that don't have any matching reviews records; a default JOIN is an INNER join, meaning only rows with matching records in both tables will be shown.

We're also using an **aggregate function** in this query, COUNT(). The COUNT() function merely tallies up the matching rows. An aggregate function requires that we specify a GROUP BY clause listing the fields that will be the basis of the aggregation. In other words, for each unique combination of coffee_brand, coffee_name, and roast, we'll get a tally of the review records in the database. Other standard aggregate functions include SUM (for summing all matching values), MIN (for returning the minimum of all matching values), and MAX (for returning the maximum of all matching values). Different database implementations also include their own custom aggregate functions.

SQL subqueries

A SELECT statement can be embedded in another SQL statement by putting it in parentheses. This is called a **subquery**. Exactly where it can be embedded depends on what kind of data the query is expected to return:

- If the statement will return a single row and column, it can be embedded wherever a single value is expected
- If the statement will return a single column with multiple rows, it can be embedded wherever a list of values is expected

- If the statement will return multiple rows and columns, it can be embedded wherever a table of values is expected

Consider this query:

```
SELECT coffees.coffee_brand, coffees.coffee_name
FROM coffees
    JOIN (
    SELECT * FROM roasts WHERE id > (
        SELECT id FROM roasts WHERE description = 'Medium'
            )) AS dark_roasts
    ON coffees.roast_id = dark_roasts.id
WHERE coffees.id IN (
    SELECT coffee_id FROM reviews WHERE reviewer = 'Maxwell');
```

We have three subqueries here. The first is located in the FROM clause:

```
(SELECT * FROM roasts WHERE id > (
    SELECT id FROM roasts WHERE description = 'Medium'
        )) AS dark_roasts
```

Because it begins with SELECT *, we can be sure it will return a table of data (or no data, but that's moot). Therefore, it can be used in the FROM clause, since a table is expected here. Note that we need to give the subquery a name using the AS keyword. This is required when using a subquery in the FROM clause.

This subquery contains its own subquery:

```
SELECT id FROM roasts WHERE description = 'Medium'
```

This query is reasonably certain to give us a single value, so we're using it where a single value is expected; in this case, as an operand of a greater-than expression. If, for some reason, this query returned multiple rows, our query would return an error.

Our final subquery is in the WHERE clause:

```
SELECT coffee_id FROM reviews WHERE reviewer = 'Maxwell'
```

This expression is guaranteed to return only one column but may return multiple rows. We're therefore using it as an argument to the IN keyword, which expects a list of values.

Subqueries are powerful, but can also cause slowdown and, sometimes, errors if our assumptions about the data are incorrect.

Learning more

We've only touched on the basics of SQL here, but this should be enough to get you started creating and using simple databases, and covers the SQL we'll be using in this chapter. See the *Further reading* section at the end of the chapter for more in-depth SQL resources. In the next section, you'll see how to combine your knowledge of SQL with PyQt to create data-driven applications.

Performing SQL queries with Qt

Working with different SQL implementations can be frustrating: not only are there slight differences in the SQL syntax, but the Python libraries used to connect to them are often inconsistent in the various methods they implement. While, in some ways, it's less convenient than the better-known Python SQL libraries, QtSQL does provide us with a single abstracted API for working with a variety of database products in a consistent way. When leveraged properly, it can also save us a large amount of code.

To learn how to work with SQL data in PyQt, we're going to build a graphical frontend for the coffee database we created in the *SQL basics* section of this chapter.

 A complete version of this database can be created from the sample code using this command:
`$ sqlite3 coffee.db -init coffee.sql`. You will need to create this database file before the frontend will work.

Building a form

Our coffee database has three tables: a list of coffee products, a list of roasts, and a table of reviews for the products. Our GUI will be designed as follows:

- It will have a list of coffee brands and products
- When we double-click an item in the list, it will open a form that will show all the information about the coffee and all the reviews associated with that product
- It will allow us to add new products and new reviews or edit any existing information

Let's start by copying your basic PyQt application template from Chapter 4, *Building Applications with QMainWindow* to a file called coffee_list1.py. Then, add an import for QtSQL like so:

```
from PyQt5 import QtSql as qts
```

Now we're going to create a form to display information about our coffee product. The basic form looks like this:

```
class CoffeeForm(qtw.QWidget):

    def __init__(self, roasts):
        super().__init__()
        self.setLayout(qtw.QFormLayout())
        self.coffee_brand = qtw.QLineEdit()
        self.layout().addRow('Brand: ', self.coffee_brand)
        self.coffee_name = qtw.QLineEdit()
        self.layout().addRow('Name: ', self.coffee_name)
        self.roast = qtw.QComboBox()
        self.roast.addItems(roasts)
        self.layout().addRow('Roast: ', self.roast)
        self.reviews = qtw.QTableWidget(columnCount=3)
        self.reviews.horizontalHeader().setSectionResizeMode(
            2, qtw.QHeaderView.Stretch)
        self.layout().addRow(self.reviews)
```

This form has fields for the brand, name, and roast of the coffee, plus a table widget for showing the reviews. Note that the constructor requires roasts, which is a list of roasts for the combo box; we want to get these from the database, not hardcode them into the form, since new roasts might get added to the database.

This form is also going to need a way to display a coffee product. Let's create a method that will take coffee data and review it, and populate the form with it:

```
    def show_coffee(self, coffee_data, reviews):
        self.coffee_brand.setText(coffee_data.get('coffee_brand'))
        self.coffee_name.setText(coffee_data.get('coffee_name'))
        self.roast.setCurrentIndex(coffee_data.get('roast_id'))
        self.reviews.clear()
        self.reviews.setHorizontalHeaderLabels(
            ['Reviewer', 'Date', 'Review'])
        self.reviews.setRowCount(len(reviews))
        for i, review in enumerate(reviews):
            for j, value in enumerate(review):
                self.reviews.setItem(i, j, qtw.QTableWidgetItem(value))
```

This method assumes that `coffee_data` is a `dict` object containing the brand, name, and roast ID and that `reviews` is a list of tuples containing the review data. It simply goes through those data structures and populates each field with the data.

Down in `MainWindow.__init__()`, let's start the main GUI:

```
self.stack = qtw.QStackedWidget()
self.setCentralWidget(self.stack)
```

We'll be using `QStackedWidget` to swap between our coffee list and coffee form widgets. Recall that this widget is similar to `QTabWidget` but without the tabs.

Before we can build more of our GUI, we need to get some information from the database. Let's talk about how to connect to a database with `QtSQL`.

Connecting and making simple queries

To use a SQL database with `QtSQL`, we first have to establish a connection. There are three steps to this:

- Create the connection object
- Configure the connection object
- Open the connection

In `MainWindow.__init__()`, let's create our database connection:

```
self.db = qts.QSqlDatabase.addDatabase('QSQLITE')
```

Rather than directly creating a `QSqlDatabase` object, we create one by calling the static `addDatabase` method with the name of the database driver we're going to use. In this case, we're using Qt's SQLite3 driver. Qt 5.12 comes with nine drivers built-in, including ones for MySQL (`QMYSQL`), PostgreSQL (`QPSQL`), and ODBC connections (including Microsoft SQL Server) (`QODBC`). A complete list can be found at https://doc.qt.io/qt-5/qsqldatabase. html#QSqlDatabase-2.

Once our database object is created, we need to configure it with any required connection settings, such as the host, user, password, and database name. For SQLite, we only need to specify a filename, as shown here:

```
self.db.setDatabaseName('coffee.db')
```

Some of the properties we can configure include the following:

- hostName—The hostname or IP of the database server
- port—The network port on which the database service is listening
- userName—The username to connect with
- password—The password to authenticate with
- connectOptions—A string of additional connection options

All of these can be configured or queried using the usual accessor method (for example, hostName() and setHostName()). If you're working with something other than SQLite, consult its documentation to see what settings you need to configure.

Once our connection object is configured, we can open the connection using the open() method. This method returns a Boolean value, indicating whether or not the connection succeeded. If it failed, we can find out why by checking the connection object's lastError property.

This code demonstrates how we might do that:

```
if not self.db.open():
    error = self.db.lastError().text()
    qtw.QMessageBox.critical(
        None, 'DB Connection Error',
        'Could not open database file: '
        f'{error}')
    sys.exit(1)
```

Here, we call self.db.open() and, if it fails, we retrieve the error from lastError and display it in a dialog. The lastError() call returns a QSqlError object, which holds data and metadata about the error; to extract the actual error text, we call its text() method.

Getting information about the database

Once our connection is actually connected, we can use it to start inspecting the database. For example, the tables() method lists all tables in the database. We can use this to check that all required tables are present as follows, for example:

```
required_tables = {'roasts', 'coffees', 'reviews'}
tables = self.db.tables()
missing_tables = required_tables - set(tables)
if missing_tables:
    qtw.QMessageBox.critica(
        None, 'DB Integrity Error'
```

```
                'Missing tables, please repair DB: '
                f'{missing_tables}')
        sys.exit(1)
```

Here, we compare the tables that exist in the database to a set of the required tables. If we find any missing, we'll show an error and exit.

set objects are like lists, except that all items in them are unique, and they allow for some useful comparisons. In this situation, we're subtracting sets to find out whether there are any items in required_tables that aren't in tables.

Making simple queries

Interacting with our SQL database relies on the QSqlQuery class. This class represents a request to the SQL engine and can be used to prepare, execute, and retrieve data and metadata about a query.

We can make a SQL query to the database by using our database object's exec() method:

```
query = self.db.exec('SELECT count(*) FROM coffees')
```

The exec() method creates a QSqlQuery object from our string, executes it, and returns it to us. We can then retrieve the results of our query from the query object:

```
query.next()
count = query.value(0)
print(f'There are {count} coffees in the database.')
```

It's important to get a mental model of what's happening here, because it's not terribly intuitive. As you know, SQL queries always return a table of data, even if there is just one row and one column. QSqlQuery has an implicit *cursor* that will be pointed at a row of the data. Initially, this cursor is pointed nowhere, but calling the next() method moves it to the next available row of data, which, in this case, is the first row. The value() method is then used to retrieve the value of a given column in the currently selected row (value(0) will retrieve the first column, value(1) the second, and so on).

So, what's happening here is something like this:

- The query is executed and populated with data. The cursor points nowhere.
- We call next() to point the cursor at the first row.
- We call value(0) to retrieve the value from the first column of the row.

To retrieve a list or table of data from a `QSqlQuery` object, we just need to repeat those last two steps until `next()` returns `False` (meaning that there is not the next row to point to). For example, we need a list of the coffee roasts to populate our form, so let's retrieve that:

```
query = self.db.exec('SELECT * FROM roasts ORDER BY id')
roasts = []
while query.next():
    roasts.append(query.value(1))
```

In this case, we've asked a query to get all the data from the `roasts` table and order it by `id`. Then, we call `next()` on our query object until it returns `False`; each time, extracting the value of the second field (`query.value(1)`) and appending it to our `roasts` list.

Now that we have that data, we can create our `CoffeeForm` and add it to the application:

```
self.coffee_form = CoffeeForm(roasts)
self.stack.addWidget(self.coffee_form)
```

In addition to retrieving values using `value()`, we can retrieve an entire row by calling the `record()` method. This returns a `QSqlRecord` object containing data for the current row (or an empty record, if no row is pointed at). We'll use `QSqlRecord` later in this chapter.

Prepared queries

Quite often, data needs to be passed into a SQL query from an application. For example, we need to write a method that looks up a single coffee by ID number so that we can display it in our form.

We could start writing that method something like this:

```
def show_coffee(self, coffee_id):
    query = self.db.exec(f'SELECT * FROM coffees WHERE id={coffee_id}')
```

In this situation, we're using a format string to put the `coffee_id` value directly into our query. Do not do this!

Using string formatting or concatenation to build SQL queries can lead to something called a **SQL injection vulnerability**, in which passing a specially crafted value can expose or destroy data in the database. In this case, we're assuming that `coffee_id` is going to be an integer, but suppose a malicious user is able to send this function a string like this:

```
0; DELETE FROM coffees;
```

Our string formatting would evaluate this and generate the following SQL statement:

```
SELECT * FROM coffees WHERE id=0; DELETE FROM coffees;
```

The result would be that all the rows in our `coffees` table would be deleted! While this may seem trivial or absurd in this context, SQL injection vulnerabilities are behind many of the data breaches and hacking scandals you read about in the news. It's important to be defensive when working with important data (and what's more important than coffee?).

The proper way to do this query and protect your database from such vulnerabilities is to use a prepared query. A **prepared query** is a query that contains variables to which we can bind values. The database driver will then properly escape our values so that they are not accidentally interpreted as SQL code.

This version of the code uses a prepared query:

```
query1 = qts.QSqlQuery(self.db)
query1.prepare('SELECT * FROM coffees WHERE id=:id')
query1.bindValue(':id', coffee_id)
query1.exec()
```

Here, we've explicitly created an empty `QSqlQuery` object connected to our database. Then, we passed a SQL string to the `prepare()` method. Notice the `:id` string used in our query; the colon indicates that this is a variable. Once we have the prepared query, we can begin binding the variables in the query to variables in our code using `bindValue()`. In this case, we've bound the `:id` SQL variable to our `coffee_id` Python variable.

Once our query is prepared and the variables are bound, we call its `exec()` method to execute it.

Once executed, we can extract the data from the query object just as we've done before:

```
query1.next()
coffee = {
    'id': query1.value(0),
    'coffee_brand': query1.value(1),
    'coffee_name': query1.value(2),
    'roast_id': query1.value(3)
}
```

Let's try the same approach to retrieve the coffee's review data:

```
query2 = qts.QSqlQuery()
query2.prepare('SELECT * FROM reviews WHERE coffee_id=:id')
query2.bindValue(':id', coffee_id)
query2.exec()
```

```
        reviews = []
        while query2.next():
            reviews.append((
                query2.value('reviewer'),
                query2.value('review_date'),
                query2.value('review')
            ))
```

Notice that we did not pass the database connection object to the `QSqlQuery` constructor this time. Since we only have one connection, it's not necessary to pass the database connection object to `QSqlQuery`; `QtSQL` will automatically use our default connection in any method call that requires a database connection.

Also notice that we're using the column names, rather than their numbers, to fetch the values from our `reviews` table. This works just as well, and is a much friendlier approach, especially in tables with many columns.

We'll finish off this method by populating and showing our coffee form:

```
        self.coffee_form.show_coffee(coffee, reviews)
        self.stack.setCurrentWidget(self.coffee_form)
```

Note that prepared queries are only able to introduce *values* into a query. You cannot, for example, prepare a query like this:

```
        query.prepare('SELECT * from :table ORDER BY :column')
```

If you want to build queries containing variable tables or column names, you'll have to resort to string formatting, unfortunately. In such cases, be aware of the potential for SQL injection and take extra precautions to ensure that the values being interpolated are what you think they are.

Using QSqlQueryModel

Populating data into a table widget manually seems like an awful chore; if you recall Chapter 5, *Creating Data Interfaces with Model-View Classes*, Qt provides us with model-view classes that do the boring work for us. We could subclass `QAbstractTableModel` and create a model that is populated from a SQL query, but fortunately, `QtSql` already provides this in the form of `QSqlQueryModel`.

As the name suggests, `QSqlQueryModel` is a table model that uses a SQL query for its data source. We'll use one to create our coffee products list, like so:

```
coffees = qts.QSqlQueryModel()
coffees.setQuery(
    "SELECT id, coffee_brand, coffee_name AS coffee "
    "FROM coffees ORDER BY id")
```

After creating our model, we set its `query` property to a SQL `SELECT` statement. The model's data will be drawn from the table returned by this query.

 Just as with `QSqlQuery`, we don't need to explicitly pass a database connection because there's only one. If you did have multiple database connections active, you should pass the one you want to use to `QSqlQueryModel()`.

Once we have the model, we can use it in `QTableView`, like this:

```
self.coffee_list = qtw.QTableView()
self.coffee_list.setModel(coffees)
self.stack.addWidget(self.coffee_list)
self.stack.setCurrentWidget(self.coffee_list)
```

Just as we did in `Chapter 5`, *Creating Data Interfaces with Model-View Classes*, we've created `QTableView` and passed the model to its `setModel()` method. Then, we added the table view to the stacked widget and set it as the currently visible widget.

By default, the table view will use the column names from the query as the header labels. We can override this by using the model's `setHeaderData()` method, like so:

```
coffees.setHeaderData(1, qtc.Qt.Horizontal, 'Brand')
coffees.setHeaderData(2, qtc.Qt.Horizontal, 'Product')
```

Keep in mind that the `QSqlQueryModel` object is in read-only mode, so there is no way to set this table view to editable in order to change details about our coffee list. We'll look at how to have an editable SQL model in the next section, *Using model-view widgets without SQL*. First, though, let's finish our GUI.

Finishing the GUI

Now that our application has both the list and the form widgets, let's enable some navigation between them. First, create a toolbar button to switch from the coffee form to the list:

```
navigation = self.addToolBar("Navigation")
navigation.addAction(
    "Back to list",
    lambda: self.stack.setCurrentWidget(self.coffee_list))
```

Next, we'll configure our list so that double-clicking an item will show the coffee form with that coffee record in it. Remember that our `MainView.show_coffee()` method expects the coffee's id value, but the list widget's `itemDoubleClicked` signal carries the model index of the click. Let's create a method on `MainView` to translate one to the other:

```
def get_id_for_row(self, index):
    index = index.siblingAtColumn(0)
    coffee_id = self.coffee_list.model().data(index)
    return coffee_id
```

Since `id` is in column 0 of the model, we retrieve the index of column 0 from whatever row was clicked using `siblingAtColumn(0)`. Then we can retrieve the id value by passing that index to `model().data()`.

Now that we have this, let's add a connection for the `itemDoubleClicked` signal:

```
self.coffee_list.doubleClicked.connect(
    lambda x: self.show_coffee(self.get_id_for_row(x)))
```

At this point, we have a simple, read-only application for our coffee database. We can certainly keep going with the current approach of using SQL queries to manage our data, but Qt provides a more elegant approach. We'll explore that approach in the next section.

Using model-view widgets without SQL

Having used `QSqlQueryModel` in the last section, you might wonder whether this approach can be further generalized to just access tables directly and avoid having to write SQL queries altogether. You also might wonder if we can get around the read-only limitations of `QSqlQueryModel`. The answer to both questions is *yes*, thanks to `QSqlTableModel` and `QSqlRelationalTableModels`.

To see how these work, let's back up and start over with our application:

1. Start with a fresh template copy, calling it `coffee_list2.py`. Add the import for `QtSql` and the database connection code from the first application. Now let's start building using table models. For simple situations where we want to create a model from a single database table, we can use `QSqlTableModel`:

```
self.reviews_model = qts.QSqlTableModel()
self.reviews_model.setTable('reviews')
```

2. The `reviews_model` is now a read-write table model for the `reviews` table. Just as we used our CSV table model to edit our CSV file in Chapter 5, *Creating Data Interfaces with Model-View Classes*, we can use this model to view and edit the `reviews` table. For tables that need to look up values from joined tables, we can use`QSqlRelationalTableModel`:

```
self.coffees_model = qts.QSqlRelationalTableModel()
self.coffees_model.setTable('coffees')
```

3. Once again, we have a table model that can be used to view and edit the data in the SQL table; this time, the `coffees` table. However, the `coffees` table has a `roast_id` column that references the `roasts` table. `roast_id` is not meaningful to the application user, who would much rather work with the roast's `description` column. To replace `roast_id` with `roasts.description` in our model, we can use the `setRelation()` function to join the two tables together, like so:

```
self.coffees_model.setRelation(
    self.coffees_model.fieldIndex('roast_id'),
    qts.QSqlRelation('roasts', 'id', 'description')
)
```

This method takes two arguments. The first is the column number of the main table that we're joining, which we can fetch by name using the model's `fieldIndex()` method. The second is a `QSqlRelation` object, which represents a foreign key relationship. The arguments it takes are the table name (`roasts`), the related column in the joined table (`roasts.id`), and the field to display for this relationship (`description`).

The result of setting this relationship is that our table view will use the related `description` column from `roasts` in place of the `roast_id` value when we join our `coffee_model` to a view.

4. Before we can join the model to the view, there's one more step we need to take:

```
self.mapper.model().select()
```

Whenever we configure or reconfigure a `QSqlTableModel` or
`QSqlRelationalTableModel`, we must call its `select()` method. This causes
the model to generate and run a SQL query to refresh its data and make it
available to views.

5. Now that our model is ready, we can try it in a view:

```
self.coffee_list = qtw.QTableView()
self.coffee_list.setModel(self.coffees_model)
```

6. Running the program at this point, you should get something like this:

	id	coffee_brand	coffee_name	description
1	1	Dumpy's Donuts	Breakfast Blend	Medium
2	2	Boise's Better than Average	Italian Roast	Burnt to a Crisp
3	3	Strawbunks	Sumatra	Burnt to a Crisp
4	4	Chartreuse Hillock	Pumpkin Spice	Light
5	6	9 o'clock	Original Decaf	Medium

Notice that, thanks to our relational table model, we have a `description` column
containing the description of the roast in place of the `roast_id` column. Just what we
wanted.

Also note that, at this point, you can view and edit any of the values in the coffee
list. `QSqlRelationalTableModel` is read/write by default, and we do not need to make
any adjustments to the view to make it editable. However, it could use some improvement.

Delegates and data mapping

While we can edit the list, we can't yet add or remove items in the list; let's add that
capability before we move on to the coffee form itself.

Start by creating some toolbar actions pointing to `MainView` methods:

```
toolbar = self.addToolBar('Controls')
toolbar.addAction('Delete Coffee(s)', self.delete_coffee)
toolbar.addAction('Add Coffee', self.add_coffee)
```

Now we'll write the `MainView` methods for those actions:

```
def delete_coffee(self):
    selected = self.coffee_list.selectedIndexes()
    for index in selected or []:
        self.coffees_model.removeRow(index.row())

def add_coffee(self):
    self.stack.setCurrentWidget(self.coffee_list)
    self.coffees_model.insertRows(
        self.coffees_model.rowCount(), 1)
```

To delete a row from the model, we can call its `removeRow()` method, passing in the row number desired. This, we can obtain from the `selectedIndexes` property. To add a row, we call the model's `insertRows()` method. This code should be familiar, from `Chapter 5, Creating Data Interfaces with Model-View Classes`.

Now, if you run the program and try to add a row, notice that you get what is essentially a `QLineEdit` in each cell for entering the data. This is fine for text fields such as coffee brand and product name, but for the roast description, it makes more sense to have something that constrains us to the proper values, such as a combo box.

In Qt's model-view system, the object that decides what widget to draw for a piece of data is called a **delegate**. The delegate is a property of the view, and by setting our own delegate object we can control how data is presented for viewing or editing.

In the case of a view backed by `QSqlRelationalTableModel`, we can take advantage of a ready-made delegate called `QSqlRelationalDelegate`, as follows:

```
self.coffee_list.setItemDelegate(qts.QSqlRelationalDelegate())
```

`QSqlRelationalDelegate` automatically provides a combo box for any field for which a `QSqlRelation` has been set. With this simple change, you should find that the `description` column now presents you with a combo box containing the available description values from the `roasts` table. Much better!

Data mapping

Now that our coffee list is in good shape, it's time to deal with the coffee form, which will allow us to display and edit the details of individual products and their reviews

Let's start with the GUI code for the coffee details part of the form:

```python
class CoffeeForm(qtw.QWidget):

    def __init__(self, coffees_model, reviews_model):
        super().__init__()
        self.setLayout(qtw.QFormLayout())
        self.coffee_brand = qtw.QLineEdit()
        self.layout().addRow('Brand: ', self.coffee_brand)
        self.coffee_name = qtw.QLineEdit()
        self.layout().addRow('Name: ', self.coffee_name)
        self.roast = qtw.QComboBox()
        self.layout().addRow('Roast: ', self.roast)
```

This section of the form is the exact same information that we displayed in the coffee list, except now we're displaying just a single record, using a series of distinct widgets. Connecting our `coffees` table model to a view was straightforward, but how can we connect a model to a form like this? One answer is with a `QDataWidgetMapper` object.

The purpose of `QDataWidgetMapper` is to map fields from a model to widgets in a form. To see how it works, let's add one to `CoffeeForm`:

```python
self.mapper = qtw.QDataWidgetMapper(self)
self.mapper.setModel(coffees_model)
self.mapper.setItemDelegate(
    qts.QSqlRelationalDelegate(self))
```

The mapper sits between the model and the form's fields, translating the columns between them. In order to ensure that data is written properly from the form widgets to the relational fields in the model, we also need to set an `itemDelegate` of the proper type, in this case, `QSqlRelationalDelegate`.

Now that we have a mapper, we need to define the field mappings using the `addMapping` method:

```python
self.mapper.addMapping(
    self.coffee_brand,
    coffees_model.fieldIndex('coffee_brand')
)
self.mapper.addMapping(
    self.coffee_name,
```

```
        coffees_model.fieldIndex('coffee_name')
    )
    self.mapper.addMapping(
        self.roast,
        coffees_model.fieldIndex('description')
    )
```

The `addMapping()` method takes two arguments: a widget and a model column number. We're using the model's `fieldIndex()` method to retrieve these column numbers by name, but you could also just use integers here.

Before we can use our combo box, we need to populate it with options. To do this, we need to retrieve the `roasts` model from our relational model and pass it to the combo box:

```
    roasts_model = coffees_model.relationModel(
        self.coffees_model.fieldIndex('description'))
    self.roast.setModel(roasts_model)
    self.roast.setModelColumn(1)
```

The `relationalModel()` method can be used to retrieve an individual table model back from our `coffees_model` object by passing in the field number. Notice we retrieve the field number by asking for the field index of `description`, not `roast_id`. In our relational model, `roast_id` has been replaced with `description`.

While the coffee list `QTableView` can display all records at once, our `CoffeeForm` is designed to show only one record at a time. For this reason, `QDataWidgetMapper` has the concept of a *current record* and will populate the widgets only with the data of the current record.

In order to display data in our form, then, we need to control the record that the mapper is pointed to. The `QDataWidgetMapper` class has five methods to navigate through the table of records:

Method	Description
toFirst()	Go to the first record in the table.
toLast()	Go to the last record in the table.
toNext()	Advance to the next record in the table.
toPrevious()	Go back to the previous record.
setCurrentIndex()	Go to a specific row number.

Since our user is selecting an arbitrary coffee from the list to navigate to, we are going to use the last method, setCurrentIndex(). We'll use this in our show_coffee() method, like so:

```
def show_coffee(self, coffee_index):
    self.mapper.setCurrentIndex(coffee_index.row())
```

setCurrentIndex() takes a single integer value that corresponds to the row number in the model. Note that this is not the same as the coffee's id value, which we used in the previous version of the application. We're working strictly with model index values at this point.

Now that we have our working CoffeeForm, let's create one back in MainView and connect it to our coffee list's signals:

```
self.coffee_form = CoffeeForm(
    self.coffees_model,
    self.reviews_model
)
self.stack.addWidget(self.coffee_form)
self.coffee_list.doubleClicked.connect(
    self.coffee_form.show_coffee)
self.coffee_list.doubleClicked.connect(
    lambda: self.stack.setCurrentWidget(self.coffee_form))
```

Since we're using indexes instead of row numbers, we can just connect our doubleClicked signal directly to the form's show_coffee() method. We'll also connect it to a lambda function to change the current widget to the form.

While we're here, let's go ahead and create a toolbar action to return to the list:

```
toolbar.addAction("Back to list", self.show_list)
```

The associated callback looks like this:

```
def show_list(self):
    self.coffee_list.resizeColumnsToContents()
    self.coffee_list.resizeRowsToContents()
    self.stack.setCurrentWidget(self.coffee_list)
```

To accommodate possible changes to the data that may have happened while editing in CoffeeForm, we'll call resizeColumnsToContents() and resizeRowsToContents(). Then, we simply set the stack widget's current widget to coffee_list.

Filtering data

The last thing we need to take care of in this application is the review section of the coffee form:

1. The reviews model, remember, is QSqlTableModel, which we pass into the CoffeeForm constructor. We can easily bind it to QTableView, like this:

    ```python
    self.reviews = qtw.QTableView()
    self.layout().addRow(self.reviews)
    self.reviews.setModel(reviews_model)
    ```

2. This adds a table of reviews to our form. Before moving on, let's take care of some cosmetic issues with the view:

    ```python
    self.reviews.hideColumn(0)
    self.reviews.hideColumn(1)
    self.reviews.horizontalHeader().setSectionResizeMode(
        4, qtw.QHeaderView.Stretch)
    ```

    The first two columns of the table are the id and coffee_id, both of which are implementation details we don't need to display for the user. The last line of code causes the fourth field (review) to expand to the right-hand edge of the widget.

    If you run this, you'll see we have a slight problem here: we don't want to see *all* the reviews in the table when we view a coffee's record. We only want to display the ones that are associated with the current coffee product.

3. We can do this by applying a **filter** to the table model. In the show_coffee() method, we'll add the following code:

    ```python
    id_index = coffee_index.siblingAtColumn(0)
    self.coffee_id = int(self.coffees_model.data(id_index))
    self.reviews.model().setFilter(f'coffee_id = {self.coffee_id}')
    self.reviews.model().setSort(3, qtc.Qt.DescendingOrder)
    self.reviews.model().select()
    self.reviews.resizeRowsToContents()
    self.reviews.resizeColumnsToContents()
    ```

    We begin by extracting the selected coffee's id number from our coffee model. This may not be the same as the row number, which is why we are consulting the value from column 0 of the selected row. We're going to save it as an instance variable because we may need it later.

4. Next, we call the review model's `setFilter()` method. This method takes a string that it will quite literally append to a `WHERE` clause in the query used to select data from the SQL table. Likewise, `setSort()` will set the `ORDER BY` clause. In this case, we're sorting by the review date, with the most recent first.

Unfortunately, there is no way to use a bound variable in `setFilter()`, so if you want to insert a value, you must use string formatting. As you have learned, this opens you up to SQL injection vulnerabilities, so be *very* careful about how you insert data. In this example, we've cast `coffee_id` to an `int` to make sure it's not SQL injection code.

After setting our filter and sort properties, we need to call `select()` to apply them. Then, we can resize our rows and columns to the new content. Now, the form should only show reviews for the currently selected coffee.

Using a custom delegate

The reviews table contains a column with a date; while we can certainly edit dates using a regular `QLineEdit`, it would be nicer if we could use the more appropriate `QDateEdit` widget. Unlike the situation with our coffee list view, Qt doesn't have a ready-made delegate that will do this for us. Fortunately, we can easily create our own delegate:

1. Above the `CoffeeForm` class, let's define a new delegate class:

```
class DateDelegate(qtw.QStyledItemDelegate):

    def createEditor(self, parent, option, proxyModelIndex):
        date_inp = qtw.QDateEdit(parent, calendarPopup=True)
        return date_inp
```

The delegate class inherits `QStyledItemDelegate`, and its `createEditor()` method is responsible for returning the widget that will be used for editing the data. In this case, we simply need to create `QDateEdit` and return it. We can configure the widget any way that we deem appropriate; for instance, we've enabled the calendar popup here.

Note that we're passing along the `parent` argument—this is critical! If you don't explicitly pass the parent widget, your delegate widget will pop up in its own top-level window.

For our purposes in the reviews table, this is all that we need to change. In more complex scenarios, there are a few other methods you might need to override:

- The `setModelData()` method is responsible for extracting data from the widget and passing it to the model. You might override this if the raw data from the widget needs to be converted or prepped in some way before being updated in the model.
- The `setEditorData()` method is responsible for retrieving data from the model and writing it to the widget. You might override this if the model data isn't in the right format for the widget to understand.
- The `paint()` method draws the editing widget to the screen. You might override this to build a custom widget or to change the appearance of the widget depending on the data. If you override this method, you might also need to override `sizeHint()` and `updateEditorGeometry()` to make sure enough space is provided for your custom widget.

2. Once we've created our custom delegate class, we need to tell our table view to use it:

```
self.dateDelegate = DateDelegate()
self.reviews.setItemDelegateForColumn(
    reviews_model.fieldIndex('review_date'),
    self.dateDelegate)
```

In this case, we've created an instance of `DateDelegate` and told the `reviews` view to use it for the `review_date` column. Now, when you edit the review date, you'll get `QDateEdit` with a calendar popup.

Inserting custom rows in a table view

The last feature we want to implement is adding and deleting rows in our review table:

1. We'll start with some buttons:

```
self.new_review = qtw.QPushButton(
    'New Review', clicked=self.add_review)
self.delete_review = qtw.QPushButton(
    'Delete Review', clicked=self.delete_review)
self.layout().addRow(self.new_review, self.delete_review)
```

2. The callback for deleting rows is straightforward enough:

```
def delete_review(self):
    for index in self.reviews.selectedIndexes() or []:
        self.reviews.model().removeRow(index.row())
    self.reviews.model().select()
```

Just as we did with `MainView.coffee_list`, we just iterate through the selected indexes and remove them by row number.

3. Adding new rows presents a problem: we can add rows, but we need to make sure they're set to use the currently selected `coffee_id`. To do this, we'll use a `QSqlRecord` object. This object represents a single row from `QSqlTableModel`, and can be created using the model's `record()` method. Once we have an empty `record` object, we can populate it with values and write it back to the model. Our callback starts like this:

```
def add_review(self):
    reviews_model = self.reviews.model()
    new_row = reviews_model.record()
    defaults = {
        'coffee_id': self.coffee_id,
        'review_date': qtc.QDate.currentDate(),
        'reviewer': '',
        'review': ''
    }
    for field, value in defaults.items():
        index = reviews_model.fieldIndex(field)
        new_row.setValue(index, value)
```

To begin with, we extract an empty record from the `reviews_model` by calling `record()`. It's important to do this from the model, as it will be prepopulated with all the model's fields. Next, we need to set the values. By default, all fields are set to `None` (SQL `NULL`), so we'll need to override this if we want a default value or if our fields have a `NOT NULL` constraint.

In this case, we're setting `coffee_id` to the currently shown coffee ID (good thing we saved that as an instance variable, eh?) and `review_date` to the current date. We're also setting `reviewer` and `review` to empty strings because they have `NOT NULL` constraints. Note that we're leaving `id` as `None`, because inserting a `NULL` on a field will cause it to use its default value (which, in this case, will be an auto-incremented integer).

4. After setting up the `dict`, we iterate through it and write the values to the record's fields. Now we need to insert this prepared record into the model:

```
inserted = reviews_model.insertRecord(-1, new_row)
if not inserted:
    error = reviews_model.lastError().text()
    print(f"Insert Failed: {error}")
reviews_model.select()
```

`QSqlTableModel.insertRecord()` takes the index of insertion (-1 means the end of the table) and the record to insert, and returns a simple Boolean value indicating whether insertion was successful. If it failed, we can query the model for the error text by calling `lastError().text()`.

5. Finally, we call `select()` on the model. This will repopulate the view with our inserted record and allow us to edit the remaining fields.

At this point, our application is fully functional. Take some time to insert new records and reviews, edit records, and delete them.

Summary

In this chapter, you learned about SQL databases and how to use them with PyQt. You learned the basics of creating a relational database with SQL, how to connect to the database with the `QSqlDatabase` class, and how to execute queries on the database. You also learned how to build elegant database applications without having to write SQL by using the SQL model-view classes available in `QtSql`.

In the next chapter, you're going to learn how to create asynchronous applications that can deal with slow workloads without locking up your application. You'll learn the effective use of the `QTimer` class, as well as how to safely utilize `QThread`. We'll also cover the use of `QTheadPool` to enable high-concurrency processing.

Questions

Try these questions to test your knowledge of this chapter:

1. Compose a SQL CREATE statement that builds a table to hold television schedule listings. Make sure it has fields for date, time, channel, and program name. Also make sure it has a primary key and constraints to prevent nonsensical data (such as two shows at the same time on the same channel, or a show with no time or date).

2. The following SQL query is returning a syntax error; can you fix it?

   ```
   DELETE * FROM my_table IF category_id == 12;
   ```

3. The following SQL query doesn't work correctly; can you fix it?

   ```
   INSERT INTO flavors(name) VALUES ('hazelnut', 'vanilla',
   'caramel', 'onion');
   ```

4. The documentation for QSqlDatabase can be found at https://doc.qt.io/qt-5/qsqldatabase.html. Read up on how you can work with multiple database connections; for example, a read-only and read/write connection to the same database. How would you create two connections and make specific queries to each?

5. Using QSqlQuery, write code to safely insert the data in the dict object into the coffees table:

   ```
   data = {'brand': 'generic', 'name': 'cheap coffee',
       'roast': 'light'}
   # Your code here:
   ```

6. You've created a QSqlTableModel object and attached it to a QTableView. You know there is data in the table, but it is not showing in the view. Look at the code and decide what is wrong:

   ```
   flavor_model = qts.QSqlTableModel()
   flavor_model.setTable('flavors')
   flavor_table = qtw.QTableView()
   flavor_table.setModel(flavor_model)
   mainform.layout().addWidget(flavor_table)
   ```

7. The following is a callback attached to the `textChanged` signal of `QLineEdit`. Explain why this is not a good idea:

```
def do_search(self, text):
    self.sql_table_model.setFilter(f'description={text}')
    self.sql_table_model.select()
```

8. You decide you'd rather have colors than names in the `roasts` combo boxes in your coffee list. What changes would you need to make to accomplish this?

Further reading

Check out these resources for more information:

- A guide to the SQL language used in SQLite can be found at `https://sqlite.org/lang.html`
- An overview of the `QtSQL` module and its use can be found at `https://doc.qt.io/qt-5/qtsql-index.html`

3
Section 3: Unraveling Advanced Qt Implementations

In this final section, you will jump into the more advanced functionality offered by PyQt. You'll tackle multithreading, 2D and 3D graphics, rich-text documents, printing, data plotting, and web browsing. You'll learn how to work with PyQt on the Raspberry Pi, and how to structure and deploy your code to desktop systems. By the end of this section, you will have all the tools and techniques that you need in your arsenal to build beautiful GUIs using PyQt.

The following chapters are in this section:

Multithreading with QTimer and QThread
10

Despite the ever-increasing power of computer hardware, programs are still often called upon to perform tasks that take seconds, if not minutes, to complete. While such delays may be due to factors outside the programmer's control, it nevertheless reflects poorly on an application to become unresponsive while background tasks are running. In this chapter, we're going to learn about some tools that can help us to retain our application's responsiveness by deferring heavy operations or moving them out of the thread entirely. We'll also learn how to use a multithreaded application design to speed up these operations on multicore systems.

This chapter is broken into the following topics:

- Delayed actions with `QTimer`
- Multithreading with `QThread`
- High concurrency with `QThreadPool` and `QRunner`

Technical requirements

This chapter requires only the basic Python and PyQt5 setup you've been using throughout the book. You can also reference the example code at `https://github.com/PacktPublishing/Mastering-GUI-Programming-with-Python/tree/master/Chapter10`.

Check out the following video to see the code in action: `http://bit.ly/2M6iSP1`

Delayed actions with QTimer

Being able to delay action in a program is useful in a variety of situations. For example, let's say that we want a modeless **pop-up** dialog that closes itself after a defined number of seconds rather than waiting for a user to click on a button.

We will start by subclassing QDialog:

```
class AutoCloseDialog(qtw.QDialog):

    def __init__(self, parent, title, message, timeout):
        super().__init__(parent)
        self.setModal(False)
        self.setWindowTitle(title)
        self.setLayout(qtw.QVBoxLayout())
        self.layout().addWidget(qtw.QLabel(message))
        self.timeout = timeout
```

Having saved a timeout value, we now want to override the dialog box's show() method so that it closes after that number of seconds.

A naive approach might be as follows:

```
    def show(self):
        super().show()
        from time import sleep
        sleep(self.timeout)
        self.hide()
```

Python's time.sleep() function will halt program execution for the number of seconds we pass in as an argument. At first glance, it appears like this should do what we want—that is, show the window, pause for timeout seconds, and then hide the window.

So, let's add some code in our MainWindow.__init__() method to test it:

```
        self.dialog = AutoCloseDialog(
            self,
            "Self-destructing message",
            "This message will self-destruct in 10 seconds",
            10
        )
        self.dialog.show()
```

If you run the program, you'll find that things don't go quite as expected. Since this dialog is modeless, it should appear alongside our main window and not block anything. Additionally, since we called `show()` before calling `sleep()`, it should display itself before pausing. Instead, you most likely got a blank and frozen dialog window that paused the entire program for the duration of its existence. So, what's happening here?

Remember from `Chapter 1`, *Getting Started with PyQt*, that Qt programs have an **event loop**, which is started when we call `QApplication.exec()`. When we call a method such as `show()`, which involves many behind-the-scenes actions such as painting widgets and communicating with the window manager, these tasks aren't executed immediately. Instead, they are placed in a task queue. The event loop works through this task queue one job at a time until it's empty. This process is **asynchronous**, so a call to the `QWidget.show()` method doesn't wait for the window to be shown before it returns; it merely places the tasks involved in showing the widget on the event queue and returns.

Our call to the `time.sleep()` method creates an immediate blocking delay in the program, halting all other processing until the function exits. This includes halting the Qt event loop, which means that all of those drawing operations that are still in the queue won't happen. In fact, no events will be processed until `sleep()` completes. This is why the widget was not fully drawn, and why the program did not continue while `sleep()` was executing.

In order to work correctly, we need to place our `hide()` call on the event loop, so that our call to `AutoCloseDialog.show()` can return immediately and let the event loop handle hiding the dialog, in the same way that it handles showing it. But we don't want to do this right away—we want to delay its execution on the event queue until a certain amount of time has passed. This is what the `QtCore.QTimer` class can do for us.

Single shot timers

`QTimer` is a simple `QObject` subclass that can emit a `timeout` signal after a certain period of time.

The simplest way to defer a single action with `QTimer` is to use the `QTimer.singleShot()` static method, as follows:

```
def show(self):
    super().show()
    qtc.QTimer.singleShot(self.timeout * 1000, self.hide)
```

`singleShot()` takes two arguments: an interval in milliseconds and a callback function. In this case, we're calling the `self.hide()` method after a number of `self.timeout` seconds (we will multiply by 1,000 to convert this into milliseconds).

Running this script again, you should now see your dialog behaving as expected.

Repeating timers

Sometimes in an application, we need to repeat an action at specified intervals, such as autosaving a document, polling a network socket, or nagging a user incessantly to give the application a 5-star review in the app store (well, maybe not that one).

`QTimer` can handle this too, as you can see from the following code block:

```
interval_seconds = 10
self.timer = qtc.QTimer()
self.timer.setInterval(interval_seconds * 1000)
self.interval_dialog = AutoCloseDialog(
    self, "It's time again",
    f"It has been {interval_seconds} seconds "
    "since this dialog was last shown.", 2000)
self.timer.timeout.connect(self.interval_dialog.show)
self.timer.start()
```

In this example, we're creating a `QTimer` object explicitly rather than using the static `singleShot()` method. Then, we're using the `setInterval()` method to configure a timeout interval in milliseconds. When that interval has passed, the timer object will emit a `timeout` signal. By default, the `QTimer` object will repeatedly issue the `timeout` signal every time reaches the end of the specified interval. You can use the `setSingleShot()` method to convert it into a single shot as well, though, in general, it's easier to use the static method that we demonstrated in the *Single shot timers* section.

After creating the `QTimer` object and configuring the interval, we just connect its `timeout` signal to the `show()` method of another `AutoCloseDialog` object and then start the timer by calling the `start()` method.

We can also stop the timer and restart it again:

```
toolbar = self.addToolBar('Tools')
toolbar.addAction('Stop Bugging Me', self.timer.stop)
toolbar.addAction('Start Bugging Me', self.timer.start)
```

The `QTimer.stop()` method stops the timer and the `start()` method will start it again from the beginning. It's worth noting that there is no `pause()` method here; the `stop()` method will clear any current progress and the `start()` method will start over from the configured interval.

Getting information from timers

`QTimer` has a few methods that we can use to extract information about the state of the timer. For example, let's keep our user updated on how things are going with the following lines of code:

```
self.timer2 = qtc.QTimer()
self.timer2.setInterval(1000)
self.timer2.timeout.connect(self.update_status)
self.timer2.start()
```

We've set up yet another timer that will call `self.update_status()` once every second. `update_status()` will then query the first time for information, as follows:

```
def update_status(self):
    if self.timer.isActive():
        time_left = (self.timer.remainingTime() // 1000) + 1
        self.statusBar().showMessage(
            f"Next dialog will be shown in {time_left} seconds.")
    else:
        self.statusBar().showMessage('Dialogs are off.')
```

The `QTimer.isActive()` method tells us whether a timer is currently running, while `remainingTime()` tells us how many milliseconds remain until the next `timeout` signal.

Running this program now, you should see a status update about your next dialog box.

Limitations of timers

While timers allow us to defer actions to the event queue and can help to prevent awkward pauses in our programs, it's important to understand that functions connected to the `timeout` signal are still executed in—and will therefore block—the main execution thread.

For example, suppose that we have a long blocking method, as follows:

```
def long_blocking_callback(self):
    from time import sleep
    self.statusBar().showMessage('Beginning a long blocking function.')
    sleep(30)
    self.statusBar().showMessage('Ending a long blocking function.')
```

You might think that calling this method from a single shot timer will prevent it from locking up your application. Let's test that theory by adding this code to `MainView.__init__()`:

```
qtc.QTimer.singleShot(1, self.long_blocking_callback)
```

Calling `singleShot()` with a 1 millisecond delay is a simple way of scheduling an event almost immediately. So, does it work?

Well, no, it doesn't; if you run the program, then you'll see that it locks up for 30 seconds. Despite the fact that we deferred the action, it's still a long blocking action that will freeze up the program when it runs. It may be that we can play with the delay value to make sure it's deferred to a more opportune moment (such as after the application has painted itself or after a splash screen displays), but sooner or later, the application will have to freeze and become unresponsive while the task runs.

There is a solution to such a problem, however; in the next section, *Multithreading with QThread*, we'll look at how to push heavy, blocking tasks like this to another thread so that our program can keep running without freezing.

Multithreading with QThread

Waiting is sometimes unavoidable. Whether querying the network, accessing a filesystem, or running a complex computation, sometimes a program just needs time to complete a process. While we're waiting, though, there's no reason for our GUI to become completely unresponsive. Modern systems with multiple CPU cores and threading technology allow us to run concurrent processes, and there's no reason why we can't take advantage of this to make responsive GUIs. Although Python has its own threading library, Qt offers us the `QThread` object, which can be used to build multithreaded applications easily. It has the additional advantage of being integrated into Qt and being compatible with signals and slots.

In this section, we'll build a somewhat slow file searching tool and then use `QThread` to ensure that the GUI remains responsive.

The SlowSearcher file search engine

In order to talk effectively about threading, we first require a slow process that can be run on a separate thread. Open a new copy of the Qt application template and call it file_searcher.py.

Let's begin by implementing a file searching engine:

```
class SlowSearcher(qtc.QObject):

    match_found = qtc.pyqtSignal(str)
    directory_changed = qtc.pyqtSignal(str)
    finished = qtc.pyqtSignal()

    def __init__(self):
        super().__init__()
        self.term = None
```

We're calling this SlowSearcher because it's going to be deliberately non-optimized. It starts with defining a few signals, as follows:

- The match_found signal will be emitted when a filename matches the search term and will contain the matched filename
- The directory_changed signal will be emitted whenever we start searching in a new directory
- The finished signal will be emitted when the whole filesystem tree has been searched

Finally, we override __init__() just to define an instance variable called self.term.

Next, we'll create a setter method for term:

```
def set_term(self, term):
    self.term = term
```

If you're wondering why we're bothering with such a simple setter method when we could just set the variable directly, the reason for this will soon become apparent as we discuss some of the limitations of QThread.

Now, we'll create the searching methods, as follows:

```
def do_search(self):
    root = qtc.QDir.rootPath()
    self._search(self.term, root)
    self.finished.emit()
```

This method will be the slot that we call to start off the search process. It begins by locating the root directory as a `QDir` object and then calls the `_search()` method. Once `_search()` returns, it emits the `finished` signal.

The actual `_search()` method is as follows:

```
def _search(self, term, path):
    self.directory_changed.emit(path)
    directory = qtc.QDir(path)
    directory.setFilter(directory.filter() |
        qtc.QDir.NoDotAndDotDot | qtc.QDir.NoSymLinks)
    for entry in directory.entryInfoList():
        if term in entry.filePath():
            print(entry.filePath())
            self.match_found.emit(entry.filePath())
        if entry.isDir():
            self._search(term, entry.filePath())
```

`_search()` is a recursive search method. It begins by emitting the `directory_changed` signal to indicate that we're searching in a new directory and then creates a `QDir` object for the current path. Next, it sets the `filter` property so that, when we query the `entryInfoList()` method, it won't include symbolic links or the `.` and `..` shortcuts (this is to avoid infinite loops in the search). Finally, we iterate the contents of the directory retrieved by `entryInfoList()` and emit a `match_found` signal for each matched item. For each directory found, we run the `_search()` method on it.

In this way, our method will recurse through all of the directories on the filesystem, looking for matches to our search term. This is not the most optimized approach, and intentionally so. Depending on your hardware, platform, and the number of files on your drive, this search can take anywhere from a few seconds to several minutes to complete, so it's perfect for looking at how threading can help an application that must execute a slow process.

 In multithreading terminology, a class that performs the actual work is referred to as a `Worker` class. `SlowSearcher` is an example of a `Worker` class.

A non-threaded searcher

To implement a searching application, let's add a GUI form for entering a search term and displaying the search results.

Let's call it `SearchForm`, as follows:

```
class SearchForm(qtw.QWidget):

    textChanged = qtc.pyqtSignal(str)
    returnPressed = qtc.pyqtSignal()

    def __init__(self):
        super().__init__()
        self.setLayout(qtw.QVBoxLayout())
        self.search_term_inp = qtw.QLineEdit(
            placeholderText='Search Term',
            textChanged=self.textChanged,
            returnPressed=self.returnPressed)
        self.layout().addWidget(self.search_term_inp)
        self.results = qtw.QListWidget()
        self.layout().addWidget(self.results)
        self.returnPressed.connect(self.results.clear)
```

This GUI only contains a `QLineEdit` widget for entering a term and a `QListWidget` widget for displaying the results. We're forwarding the `QLineEdit` widget's `returnPressed` and `textChanged` signals to identically named signals on the `SearchForm` object so that we can connect them more easily in our `MainView` method. We've also connected `returnPressed` to the list widget's `clear` slot so that starting a new search clears the results area.

The `SearchForm()` method will also require a method to add a new item:

```
    def addResult(self, result):
        self.results.addItem(result)
```

This is simply a convenience method so that, once again, the main application doesn't have to directly manipulate the widgets in the form.

In our `MainWindow.__init__()` method, we can create a searcher and form object and connect them, as follows:

```
        form = SearchForm()
        self.setCentralWidget(form)
        self.ss = SlowSearcher()
        form.textChanged.connect(self.ss.set_term)
```

```
form.returnPressed.connect(self.ss.do_search)
self.ss.match_found.connect(form.addResult)
```

After creating the `SlowSearcher` and `SearchForm` objects and setting the form as the central widget, we connect the appropriate signals together, as follows:

- The form's `textChanged` signal, which emits the string entered, is connected to the searcher's `set_term()` setter method.
- The form's `returnPressed` signal is connected to the searcher's `do_search()` method to trigger the search.
- The searcher's `match_found` signal, which carries the pathname found, is connected to the form's `addResult()` method.

Finally, let's add two `MainWindow` methods to keep the user informed about the status of the search:

```
def on_finished(self):
    qtw.QMessageBox.information(self, 'Complete', 'Search complete')

def on_directory_changed(self, path):
    self.statusBar().showMessage(f'Searching in: {path}')
```

The first will show a status indicating that the search is finished, while the second will show a status indicating the current path that the searcher is searching.

Back in `__init__()`, these will be connected to the searcher, as follows:

```
self.ss.finished.connect(self.on_finished)
self.ss.directory_changed.connect(self.on_directory_changed)
```

Testing our non-threaded search application

Our expectation with this script is that, as we search through directories on the system, we'll get a steady printout of search results to the results area, as well as constant updates on the current directory being searched in the status bar.

If you run it, however, you'll find that this is not what actually happens. Instead, the moment the search starts, the GUI freezes up. Nothing is shown in the status bar and no entries appear in the list widget, even though matches are being printed to the console. Only when the search finally finishes do the results appear and the status gets updated.

To fix this, we need to introduce threading.

So, why does the program print to the console in real time but not update our GUI in real time? It's because `print()` is synchronous—it executes as soon as it's called and does not return until the text is written to the console. Our GUI methods, however, are asynchronous—they are queued in the Qt event queue and will not execute until the main event loop finishes executing the `SlowSearcher.search()` method.

Adding threads

A **thread** is an independent code execution context. By default, all of our code runs in a single thread, so we refer to it as a **single-threaded** application. Using the `QtCore.QThread` class, we can create new threads and move portions of our code to them, making it a **multithreaded** application.

You can use the `QThread` object as follows:

```
self.searcher_thread = qtc.QThread()
self.ss.moveToThread(self.searcher_thread)
self.ss.finished.connect(self.searcher_thread.quit)
self.searcher_thread.start()
```

We start by creating a `QThread` object, and then use the `SlowSearcher.moveToThread()` method to move our `SlowSearcher` object to the new thread. `moveToThread()` is a `QObject` method inherited by any class that subclasses `QObject`.

Next, we connect the searcher's `finished` signal to the thread's `quit` slot; this will cause the thread to stop executing when the search is finished. Since the search thread isn't part of our main execution thread, it must have some way to quit on its own or it will continue to run after the search is over.

Finally, we need to call the search thread's `start()` method to begin executing the code and allow our main thread to interact with the `SlowSearcher` object.

This code needs to be inserted after the `SlowSearcher` object is created, but before any signals or slots are connected to it (we'll discuss why in the *Threading tips and caveats* section).

Since we're quitting the thread after each search, we need to restart the thread each time a new search is started. We can do this by using the following connection:

```
form.returnPressed.connect(self.searcher_thread.start)
```

This is all that is needed to use a thread. Run the script again and you'll see that the GUI is updated as the search progresses.

Let's recap the process, as follows:

1. Create an instance of the `Worker` class of your `QObject` object
2. Create a `QThread` object
3. Use the `Worker` class' `moveToThread()` method to move it to the new thread
4. Connect any other signals and slots
5. Call the thread's `start()` method

An alternate method

Although the `moveToThread()` method of working with `QThread` is the preferred approach recommended by the documentation, there is another way that works perfectly well and, in some way, simplifies our code. This approach is to create our `Worker` class by subclassing `QThread` and overriding the `run()` method using our worker code.

For example, create a copy of `SlowSearcher` and alter it as follows:

```
class SlowSearcherThread(qtc.QThread):
    # rename "do_search()" to "run()":

    def run(self):
        root = qtc.QDir.rootPath()
        self._search(self.term, root)
        self.finished.emit()

    # The rest of the class is the same
```

Here, we've altered only three things:

- We've renamed the class to `SlowSearcherThread`.
- We've changed the parent class to `QThread`.
- We've renamed `do_search()` to `run()`.

Our `MainWindow.__init__()` method will now be considerably simpler:

```
form = SearchForm()
self.setCentralWidget(form)
self.ss = SlowSearcherThread()
form.textChanged.connect(self.ss.set_term)
form.returnPressed.connect(self.ss.start)
self.ss.match_found.connect(form.addResult)
self.ss.finished.connect(self.on_finished)
self.ss.directory_changed.connect(self.on_directory_changed)
```

Now, we only need to connect `returnPressed` to `SlowSearcher.start()`. The `start()` method creates the new thread and executes the object's `run()` method inside the new thread. This means that, by overriding that method, we can effectively place that code in a new thread.

 Always remember to implement `run()` but call `start()`. Don't get this mixed up, or your multithreading won't work!

While there are some valid use cases for such an approach, it can create subtle problems with the thread ownership of the object's data. Even though a `QThread` object provides a control interface for a secondary thread, the object itself lives in the main thread. When we call `moveToThread()` on a `worker` object, we can be assured that the `worker` object is moved entirely to the new thread. However, when the `worker` object is a subclass of `QThread`, those `QThread` parts must remain in the main thread even though the executed code is moved to the new thread. This can lead to subtle bugs as it is difficult to untangle which parts of the `worker` object are in which thread.

Ultimately, unless you have clear reasons for subclassing `QThread5`, you should use `moveToThread()`.

Threading tips and caveats

The previous example may have made multithreaded programming seem simple, but that's because the code was carefully designed to avoid some of the problems that can arise when working with threads. In reality, retrofitting multithreading on a single-threaded application can be much more difficult.

One common problem is when a `worker` object gets stuck in the main thread, causing us to lose the benefits of multithreading. This can happen in a few ways.

For example, in our original threading script (the one that used `moveToThread()`), we had to move the worker to the thread before connecting any signals. If you try moving the threading code after the signal connections, you will find that the GUI locks up as though you hadn't used a thread.

The reason this happens is that our worker's methods are Python methods and connecting to them creates a connection in Python, which must persist in the main thread. One way around this is to use the `pyqtSlot()` decorator to make the worker's methods into true Qt slots, as follows:

```
@qtc.pyqtSlot(str)
def set_term(self, term):
    self.term = term

@qtc.pyqtSlot()
def do_search(self):
    root = qtc.QDir.rootPath()
    self._search(self.term, root)
    self.finished.emit()
```

Once you do this, the order won't matter because the connections will exist entirely between the Qt objects rather than between the Python objects.

You can also trap a `worker` object in the main thread by calling one of its methods directly in the main thread:

```
# in MainView__init__():
self.ss.set_term('foo')
self.ss.do_search()
```

Placing the preceding lines in __init__() will cause the GUI to remain hidden until a filesystem search for `foo` has completed. Sometimes, this issue can be subtle; for example, the following `lambda` callback suggests that we are simply connecting the signal directly to the slot:

```
form.returnPressed.connect(lambda: self.ss.do_search())
```

However, this connection breaks threading because the `lambda` function is itself part of the main thread and, therefore, the call to `search()` will be executed in the main thread.

Unfortunately, this limitation also means that you cannot use a `MainWindow` method as a slot to call the worker methods either; for example, we cannot run the following code in `MainWindow`:

```
def on_return_pressed(self):
    self.searcher_thread.start()
    self.ss.do_search()
```

Using this as a callback for `returnPressed` rather than connecting the signal to the `worker` object's methods individually causes the threading to fail and the GUI to lock.

In short, it's best to constrain your interactions with the `worker` object to pure Qt signal and slot connections with no intermediate functions.

High concurrency with QThreadPool and QRunner

`QThreads` are ideal for putting a single long process into the background, especially when we want to communicate with that process using signals and slots. Sometimes, however, what we need to do is run a number of computationally intensive operations in parallel using as many threads as possible. This can be done with `QThread`, but a better alternative is found in `QThreadPool` and `QRunner`.

`QRunner` represents a single runnable task that we want our worker threads to perform. Unlike `QThread`, it is not derived from `QObject` and cannot use signals and slots. However, it is very efficient and is much simpler to use when you want many threads.

The `QThreadPool` object's job is to manage a queue of `QRunner` objects, spinning up new threads to execute the objects as compute resources become available.

To demonstrate how to work with this, let's build a file hashing utility.

The file hasher GUI

Our file hasher utility will take a source directory, a destination file, and a number of threads to use. It will use the number of threads to calculate the MD5 hash of each file in the directory and then write the information out to the destination file as it does so.

A **hashing function** such as MD5 is used to calculate a unique, fixed-length binary value from any arbitrary piece of data. Hashes are often used to determine the authenticity of a file since any change to the file will result in a different hash value.

Make a clean copy of your Qt template from Chapter 4, *Building Applications with QMainWindow*, calling it `hasher.py`.

Then, we'll start with our GUI form class, as follows:

```
class HashForm(qtw.QWidget):

    submitted = qtc.pyqtSignal(str, str, int)

    def __init__(self):
        super().__init__()
        self.setLayout(qtw.QFormLayout())
        self.source_path = qtw.QPushButton(
            'Click to select...', clicked=self.on_source_click)
        self.layout().addRow('Source Path', self.source_path)
        self.destination_file = qtw.QPushButton(
            'Click to select...', clicked=self.on_dest_click)
        self.layout().addRow('Destination File', self.destination_file)
        self.threads = qtw.QSpinBox(minimum=1, maximum=7, value=2)
        self.layout().addRow('Threads', self.threads)
        submit = qtw.QPushButton('Go', clicked=self.on_submit)
        self.layout().addRow(submit)
```

This form is very similar to the forms we've designed in previous chapters, with a `submitted` signal to publish the data, `QPushButton` objects to store the selected files, a spin box to select the number of threads, and another push button to submit the form.

The file button callbacks will be as follows:

```
    def on_source_click(self):
        dirname = qtw.QFileDialog.getExistingDirectory()
        if dirname:
            self.source_path.setText(dirname)

    def on_dest_click(self):
        filename, _ = qtw.QFileDialog.getSaveFileName()
        if filename:
            self.destination_file.setText(filename)
```

Here, we're using `QFileDialog` static functions (which you learned about in `Chapter 5`, *Creating Data Interfaces with Model-View Classes*) to retrieve a directory name to examine and a filename that we'll use to save the output to.

Finally, our `on_submit()` callback is as follows:

```python
def on_submit(self):
    self.submitted.emit(
        self.source_path.text(),
        self.destination_file.text(),
        self.threads.value()
    )
```

This callback simply gathers the data from our widgets and publishes it with the `submitted` signal.

In `MainWindow.__init__()`, create a form and make it the central widget:

```python
form = HashForm()
self.setCentralWidget(form)
```

That takes care of our GUI, so let's now build the backend.

A hash runner

The `HashRunner` class will represent a single instance of the actual task that we're going to perform. For each file that we need to process, we'll create a unique `HashRunner` instance so its constructor will need to receive an input filename and an output filename as arguments. Its task will be to calculate the MD5 hash of the input file and append it along with the input filename to the output file.

We'll start it by subclassing `QRunnable`:

```python
class HashRunner(qtc.QRunnable):

    file_lock = qtc.QMutex()
```

The first thing we do is create a `QMutex` object. In multithreading terminology, a **mutex** is an object shared between threads that can be locked or unlocked.

You can think of a mutex in the same way as the door of a single-user restroom facility; suppose that Bob attempts to enter the restroom and lock the door. If Alice is in the restroom already, then the door won't open, and Bob will have to wait patiently outside until Alice has unlocked the door and exited the restroom. Then, Bob will be able to enter and lock the door.

Likewise, when a thread attempts to lock a mutex that another thread has already locked, it has to wait until the first thread has finished and unlocked the mutex before it can acquire the lock.

In `HashRunner`, we're going to use our `file_lock` mutex to ensure that two threads don't attempt to write to the output file at the same time. Note that this object is created in the class definition so it will be shared by all instances of `HashRunner`.

Now, let's create the `__init__()` method:

```
def __init__(self, infile, outfile):
    super().__init__()
    self.infile = infile
    self.outfile = outfile
    self.hasher = qtc.QCryptographicHash(
        qtc.QCryptographicHash.Md5)
    self.setAutoDelete(True)
```

The object will receive paths to the input file and output file and store them as instance variables. It also creates an instance of `QtCore.QCryptographicHash`. This object is able to calculate various cryptographic hashes of data, such as MD5, SHA-256, or Keccak-512. A complete list of hashes supported by this class can be found at https://doc.qt.io/qt-5/ qcryptographichash.html.

Finally, we set the `autoDelete` property of the class to `True`. This property of `QRunnable` will cause the object to be deleted whenever the `run()` method returns, saving us memory and resources.

The actual work done by the runner is defined in the `run()` method:

```
def run(self):
    print(f'hashing {self.infile}')
    self.hasher.reset()
    with open(self.infile, 'rb') as fh:
        self.hasher.addData(fh.read())
    hash_string = bytes(self.hasher.result().toHex()).decode('UTF-8')
```

Our function starts by printing a message to the console and resetting the QCryptographicHash object, clearing out any data that might be in it.

We then read the binary contents of our file into the hash object using the addData() method. The hash value can be calculated and retrieved as a QByteArray object from the hash object using the result() method. We then convert the byte array into a hexadecimal string using the toHex() method and then into a Python Unicode string by way of a bytes object.

Now all that's left is to write this hash string to the output file. This is where our mutex object comes in.

Traditionally, the way to use the mutex is as follows:

```
try:
    self.file_lock.lock()
    with open(self.outfile, 'a', encoding='utf-8') as out:
        out.write(f'{self.infile}\t{hash_string}\n')
finally:
    self.file_lock.unlock()
```

We call the mutex's lock() method inside a try block and then perform our file operation. Inside the finally block, we call the unlock method. The reason this is done inside the try and finally blocks is so that the mutex is sure to be released even if something goes wrong with the file method.

In Python, however, whenever we have an operation like this that has initialization and cleanup code, it is best to use a **context manager** object in conjunction with the with keyword. PyQt provides us with such an object: QMutexLocker.

We can use this object as follows:

```
with qtc.QMutexLocker(self.file_lock):
    with open(self.outfile, 'a', encoding='utf-8') as out:
        out.write(f'{self.infile}\t{hash_string}\n')
```

This method is much cleaner. By using the mutex context manager, we are assured that anything done inside the with block is done by only one thread at a time, and other threads will wait until the object finishes.

Creating the thread pool

The final piece of this application will be a `HashManager` object. The job of this object is to take the form output, locate the files to be hashed, and then start up a `HashRunner` object for each file.

It will begin like this:

```
class HashManager(qtc.QObject):

    finished = qtc.pyqtSignal()

    def __init__(self):
        super().__init__()
        self.pool = qtc.QThreadPool.globalInstance()
```

We've based the class on `QObject` so that we can define a `finished` signal. This signal will be emitted when all of the runners have completed their tasks.

In the constructor, we're creating our `QThreadPool` object. Rather than creating a new object, however, we're using the `globalInstance()` static method to access the global thread pool object that already exists in every Qt application. You don't have to do this, but it is sufficient for most applications and removes some complexities involved in having multiple thread pools.

The real work of this class will happen in a method we'll call `do_hashing`:

```
@qtc.pyqtSlot(str, str, int)
def do_hashing(self, source, destination, threads):
    self.pool.setMaxThreadCount(threads)
    qdir = qtc.QDir(source)
    for filename in qdir.entryList(qtc.QDir.Files):
        filepath = qdir.absoluteFilePath(filename)
        runner = HashRunner(filepath, destination)
        self.pool.start(runner)
```

This method is designed to be hooked directly to the `HashForm.submitted` signal, so we've made it a slot with a matching signal. It begins by setting the thread pool's maximum number of threads (as defined by the `maxThreadCount` property) to the number received in the function call. Once this is set, we can queue up any number of `QRunnable` objects in the thread pool, but only `maxThreadCount` threads will actually be started up concurrently.

Next, we'll use the `QDir` object's `entryList()` method to iterate through the files in the directory and create a `HashRunner` object for each one. The runner object is then passed to the thread pool's `start()` method, which adds it to the pool's work queue.

At this point, all of our runners are running in separate execution threads, but we'd like to emit a signal when they are done. Unfortunately, there is no signal built-in to `QThreadPool` to tell us this, but the `waitForDone()` method will continue to block until all of the threads are done.

So, add the following code to `do_hashing()`:

```
self.pool.waitForDone()
self.finished.emit()
```

Back in `MainWindow.__init__()`, let's create our manager object and add our connections:

```
self.manager = HashManager()
self.manager_thread = qtc.QThread()
self.manager.moveToThread(self.manager_thread)
self.manager_thread.start()
form.submitted.connect(self.manager.do_hashing)
```

After creating our `HashManager`, we move it to a separate thread using `moveToThread()`. This is because our `do_hashing()` method is going to block until all of the runners are completed, and we don't want the GUI to freeze up while waiting for that to happen. Had we left out the last two lines of `do_hashing()`, this wouldn't be necessary (but we'd also never know when it was done).

In order to get feedback on what's happening, let's add two more connections:

```
form.submitted.connect(
    lambda x, y, z: self.statusBar().showMessage(
        f'Processing files in {x} into {y} with {z} threads.'))
self.manager.finished.connect(
    lambda: self.statusBar().showMessage('Finished'))
```

The first connection will set the status when the form is submitted, indicating details about the job that is commencing; the second will notify us when the job is done.

Testing the script

Go ahead and launch this script and let's see how it works. Point your source directory at a folder full of large files, such as DVD images, archive files, or video files. Leave the threads' spin box at its default setting and click on **Go**.

Notice from the console output that the files are being hashed two at a time. As soon as one completes, another one starts until all of the files have been hashed.

Try it again, but this time bump the threads up to four or five. Notice that more files are being processed at once. As you play with this value, you may also notice that there is a point of diminishing returns, especially as you approach the number of cores in your CPU. This is an important lesson about parallelization—sometimes, too much causes the performance to drop.

Threading and the Python GIL

No discussion of multithreading in Python is complete without addressing the **global interpreter lock (GIL)**. The GIL is part of the memory management system in the official Python implementation (CPython). Essentially, it is like the mutex that we used in our `HashRunner` class—just as a `HashRunner` class has to acquire the `file_lock` mutex before it can write to the output, any thread in a Python application must acquire the GIL before it can execute any Python code. In other words, only one thread can execute Python code at a time.

At first glance, this may appear to make multithreading in Python a futile pursuit; after all, what's the point of creating multiple threads if only one thread can execute Python code at a time?

The answer involves two exceptions to the GIL requirement:

- The long-running code can be **CPU-bound** or **I/O-bound**. CPU-bound means that most of the processing time is spent running heavy CPU operations, such as cryptographic hashing. I/O-bound operations are those that spend most of their time waiting on **input/output (I/O)** calls, such as writing a large file to a disk or reading data from a network socket. When a thread makes an I/O call and begins waiting on a response, it releases the GIL. Therefore, if our worker code is mostly I/O-bound, we can benefit from multithreading because other code can run while we wait on the I/O operation to finish.

- CPU-bound code also releases the GIL if the code is running outside of Python. In other words, if we use a C or C++ function or object to perform a CPU-bound operation, then the GIL is released and only reacquired when the next Python operation is run.

This is why our `HashRunner` works; its two heaviest operations are as follows:

- Reading the large file from disk (which is an I/O-bound operation)
- Hashing the file contents (which is handled inside of the `QCryptographicHash` object—a C++ object that operates outside of Python)

If we were to implement a hashing algorithm in pure Python instead, then we'd likely find that our multithreaded code actually ran slower than even a single-threaded implementation.

Ultimately, multithreading is not a magic bullet to speed up the code in Python; it must be carefully planned out to avoid problems with the GIL and the pitfalls that we discussed in the *Threading tips and caveats* section. With proper care, however, it can help us to create fast and responsive programs.

Summary

In this chapter, you learned how to keep your application responsive when running a slow code. You learned how to use `QTimer` to defer actions to a later time, either as a one-time or repeating action. You learned how to push code to another thread using `QThread`, both by using `moveToThread()` and by subclassing `QThread`. Finally, you learned how to use `QThreadPool` and `QRunnable` to build highly concurrent data processing applications.

In `Chapter 11`, *Creating Rich Text with QTextDocument*, we're going to take a look at working with rich text in PyQt. You'll learn how to define rich text using an HTML-like markup and how to inspect and manipulate documents using the `QDocument` API. You'll also learn how to take advantage of Qt's printing support to bring documents into the real world.

Questions

Try answering these questions to test your knowledge from this chapter:

1. Create code to call the `self.every_ten_seconds()` method every 10 seconds.

2. The following code uses `QTimer` incorrectly. Can you fix it?

```
timer = qtc.QTimer()
timer.setSingleShot(True)
timer.setInterval(1000)
timer.start()
while timer.remainingTime():
    sleep(.01)
run_delayed_command()
```

3. You've created the following word-counting `Worker` class and want to move it to another thread to prevent large documents from slowing the GUI. But it's not working—what do you need to change about this class?

```
class Worker(qtc.QObject):

    counted = qtc.pyqtSignal(int)

    def __init__(self, parent):
        super().__init__(parent)
        self.parent = parent

    def count_words(self):
        content = self.parent.textedit.toPlainText()
        self.counted.emit(len(content.split()))
```

4. The following code is blocking rather than running in a separate thread. Why is this the case?

```
class Worker(qtc.QThread):

    def set_data(data):
        self.data = data

    def run(self):n
        start_complex_calculations(self.data)

class MainWindow(qtw.QMainWindow):

    def __init__(self):
        super().__init__()
```

```
form = qtw.QWidget()
self.setCentralWidget(form)
form.setLayout(qtw.QFormLayout())

worker = Worker()
line_edit = qtw.QLineEdit(textChanged=worker.set_data)
button = qtw.QPushButton('Run', clicked=worker.run)
form.layout().addRow('Data:', line_edit)
form.layout().addRow(button)
self.show()
```

5. Will this `Worker` class run correctly? If not, why?

```
class Worker(qtc.QRunnable):

    finished = qtc.pyqtSignal()

    def run(self):
        calculate_navigation_vectors(30)
        self.finished.emit()
```

6. The following code is a `run()` method from a `QRunnable` class designed for processing large data files output from scientific equipment. The files consist of millions of long rows of space-delimited numbers. Is this code likely to be slowed down by the Python GIL? Could you make it less likely that the GIL will interfere?

```
def run(self):
    with open(self.file, 'r') as fh:
        for row in fh:
            numbers = [float(x) for x in row.split()]
            if numbers:
                mean = sum(numbers) / len(numbers)
                numbers.append(mean)
        self.queue.put(numbers)
```

7. The following is a `run()` method from a `QRunnable` class in a multithreaded TCP Server application you're writing. All of the threads share a server socket instance accessed through `self.datastream`. This code is not thread-safe, however. What do you need to do to fix it?

```
def run(self):
    message = get_http_response_string()
    message_len = len(message)
    self.datastream.writeUInt32(message_len)
    self.datastream.writeQString(message)
```

Further reading

For further information, please refer to the following:

- A **semaphore** is similar to a mutex but allows for an arbitrary number of locks to be taken rather than just a single lock. You can read more about Qt's implementation, the `QSemaphore` class, at `https://doc.qt.io/qt-5/qsemaphore.html`
- David Beazley's talk from PyCon 2010, available at `https://www.youtube.com/watch?v=Obt-vMVdM8s`, provides deeper insight into the operation of the Python GIL

11
Creating Rich Text with QTextDocument

Whether drafting business memos in a word processor, writing a blog entry, or generating reports, much of the world's computing involves the creation of text documents. Most of these applications require the ability to produce not just plain alphanumeric strings, but rich text as well. Rich text (as opposed to plain text) means text that includes styles and formatting features such as font faces, colors, lists, tables, and images.

In this chapter, we're going to learn how PyQt allows us to work with rich text by covering the following topics:

- Creating rich text using markup
- Manipulating rich text using `QTextDocument`
- Printing rich text

Technical requirements

For this chapter, you'll need the basic Python and Qt setup you've been using since `Chapter 1`, *Getting Started with PyQt*. You might like to have the example code that can be found at `https://github.com/PacktPublishing/Mastering-GUI-Programming-with-Python/tree/master/Chapter11` as a reference.

Check out the following video to see the code in action: `http://bit.ly/2M5P4Cq`

Creating rich text using markup

Every application that supports rich text must have some format to represent that text in memory and when saving it to a file. Some formats use custom binary code, such as the .doc and .rtf files used by older versions of Microsoft Word. In other cases, a plain-text **markup language** is used. In a markup language, special strings called **tags** indicate the placement of rich text features. Qt takes the markup approach and represents rich text using a subset of **hypertext markup language (HTML)** version 4.

Rich text markup in Qt is rendered by the QTextDocument object, and as such it is only usable on widgets that use QTextDocument to store their contents. This includes the QLabel, QTextEdit, and QTextBrowser widgets. In this section, we're going to create a demo script to explore the syntax and capabilities of this markup language.

Given the popularity and ubiquity of web development, it's likely that you already know a bit about HTML; in case you don't, the following section will act as a quick introduction.

HTML basics

An HTML document is composed of text content interspersed with tags to indicate non-plain text features. A tag is simply a word enclosed in angle brackets, as follows:

```
<sometag>This is some content</sometag>
```

Notice the </sometag> code at the end of the preceding example. This is called a **closing tag**, and it's simply like the opening tag but with a forward slash (/) before the tag name. Closing tags are generally only used for tags that enclose (or have the ability to enclose) text content.

Consider the following example:

```
Text can be <b>bold<b> <br>
Text can be <em>emphasized</em> <br>
Text can be <u>underlined</u> <hr>
```

The b, em, and u tags require a closing tag because they enclose a portion of the content and indicate a change in appearance. The br and hr tags (*break* and *horizontal rule*, respectively) simply indicate non-textual items to include in the document, so they have no closing tags.

If you want to see what any of these examples look like, you can copy them into a text file and open them in your web browser. Also, check out the `html_examples.html` file in the example code.

Sometimes, complex structures are created by nesting tags, such as in the following list:

```
<ol>
  <li> Item one</li>
  <li> Item two</li>
  <li> Item three</li>
</ol>
```

Here, the `ol` tag starts an ordered list (a list that uses sequential numbers or letters, rather than bullet characters). Each item in the list is indicated by the `li` (list item) tag. Note that when nesting tags use a closing tag, the tags must be closed in the correct order, as follows:

```
<b><i>This is right</i></b>
<b><i>This is wrong!</b></i>
```

The preceding incorrect example would not work because the inner tag (`<i>`) was closed after the outer tag (`<b>`).

HTML tags can have attributes, which are key-value pairs that are used to configure the tag, as shown in the following example:

```
<img src="my_image.png" width="100px" height="20px">
```

The preceding tag is an `img` (image) tag that's used for showing images. Its attributes are `src` (indicating the image file path), `width` (indicating the width to display the image), and `height` (indicating the height to display).

HTML attributes are space-delimited, so don't put commas between them. Values can be quoted using single or double-quotes, or left unquoted if they contain no spaces or other confusing characters (such as a closing angle bracket); in general, however, it's usually best to double-quote them. In Qt HTML, sizes are usually specified in `px` (pixels) or `%` (percent), though in modern web HTML, other units are commonly used.

Style sheet syntax

Modern HTML is styled using **Cascading Style Sheets (CSS)**. You learned about CSS in Chapter 6, *Styling Qt Applications*, when we discussed QSS. To review, CSS allows you to make declarations about the way a tag will look, as follows:

```
b {
    color: red;
    font-size: 16pt;
}
```

The preceding CSS directive will make all the content inside bold tags (between <b> and </b>) appear in a red 16 point font.

Certain tags can also have modifiers, for example:

```
a:hovered {
    color: green;
    font-size: 16pt;
}
```

The preceding CSS applies to <a> (anchor) tag contents, but *only* when the anchor is hovered over by the mouse pointer. Modifiers like this are also called **pseudo-classes**.

Semantic versus cosmetic tags

Some HTML tags describe how a piece of content should appear. We call these **cosmetic** tags. For example, the <i> tag indicates that text should be printed in an italic font. Consider, though, that italics are used in modern printing for many reasons—to emphasize a word, to indicate a title of a published work, or to indicate that a phrase is from a foreign language. To differentiate between these uses, HTML also has *semantic* tags. For example, <em> means emphasis, and will result in italic text in most situations. But unlike the <i> tag, it also indicates *why* the text should be italic. Older versions of HTML generally focused on cosmetic tags, whereas newer versions focus increasingly on semantic tags.

Qt's rich-text HTML supports a few semantic tags, but they are merely aliases for equivalent cosmetic tags.

There is much more to the modern HTML and CSS that's used on web pages than we've described here, but what we've covered is sufficient for understanding the limited subset used by Qt widgets. If you want to learn more, take a look at the resources under the, *Further reading* section at the end of this chapter.

Structure and heading tags

To experiment with rich text markup, we're going to write an advertisement for our next big game, *Fight Fighter 2*, and view it in a QTextBrowser. To begin, get a copy of the application template from `Chapter 4`, *Building Applications with QMainWindow*, and call it `qt_richtext_demo.py`.

In `MainWindow.__init__()`, add in a `QTextBrowser` object as the main widget, like so:

```
main = qtw.QTextBrowser()
self.setCentralWidget(main)
with open('fight_fighter2.html', 'r') as fh:
    main.insertHtml(fh.read())
```

`QTextBrowser` is based on `QTextEdit`, but is read-only and preconfigured to navigate hypertext links. After creating the text browser, we open the `fight_fighter2.html` file and insert its contents into the browser using the `insertHtml()` method. Now, we can edit `fight_fighter2.html` and see how it is rendered in PyQt.

Open `fight_fighter2.html` in your editor and begin with the following code:

```
<qt>
  <body>
    <h1>Fight Fighter 2</h1>
    <hr>
```

HTML documents are built hierarchically, with the outermost tag usually being `<html>`. However, we can also use `<qt>` as the outermost tag when passing HTML to a `QTextDocument`-based widget, which is a good idea as it reminds us that we're writing the Qt-supported subset of HTML, not actual HTML.

Inside that, we have a `<body>` tag. This tag is also optional, but it will make styling easier down the road.

Next, we've got a title inside an `<h1>` tag. The *H* here stands for heading, and tags `<h1>` through `<h6>` indicate section headings from the outermost to the innermost. This tag will be rendered in a larger and bolder font, indicating that it is the title of the section.

Following the heading, we have an `<hr>` tag to add a horizontal line. By default, `<hr>` produces a single-pixel-thick black line, but that can be customized using style sheets.

Let's add the following regular text content:

```
<p>Everything you love about fight-fighter, but better!</p>
```

The `<p>` tag, or paragraph tag, indicates a block of text. It is not strictly necessary to enclose text content in paragraph tags, but understand that HTML does not respect new lines by default. If you want to get distinct paragraphs separated by line breaks, you need to enclose them in paragraph tags. (You can also insert `<br>` tags, but the paragraph tag is considered a cleaner approach as it is more semantic.)

Next, add the first child heading, as follows:

```
<h2>About</h2>
```

Any child section under `<h1>` should be `<h2>`; any child section inside `<h2>` should be `<h3>`, and so on. Heading tags are examples of semantic tags, and indicate the level of the document hierarchy.

Never select heading levels based on the appearance they produce—for example, don't use `<h4>` under `<h1>` just because you want smaller header text. Use them semantically and adjust the look using styles (see the *Fonts, colors, images, and styles*, section for more information).

Typography tags

Qt rich text supports many tags for altering the basic appearance of the text, as follows:

```
<p>Fight fighter 2 is the <i>amazing</i> sequel to <u>Fight Fighter</u>,
an <s>intense</s> ultra-intense multiplayer action game from <b>FightSoft
Software, LLC</b>.</p>
```

In this example, we've used the following tags:

Tag	Result
`<i>`	*Italic*
`<b>`	**Bold**
`<u>`	Underlined
`<s>`	Strikethrough

These are cosmetic tags, and each of them alters the appearance of the text inside the tag as indicated. In addition to these tags, some lesser-used tags for the sizing and position of text are supported, including the following:

```
<p>Fight Fighter 2's new Ultra-Action<sup>TM</sup> technology delivers
low-latency combat like never before.   Best of all, at only
$1.99<sub>USD</sub>, you <big>Huge Action</big> for a <small>tiny</small>
price.</p>
```

In the preceding example, we can see the `<sup>` and `<sub>` tags, which provide superscript and subscript text, respectively, and the `<big>` and `<small>` tags, which provide slightly bigger or smaller fonts.

Hyperlinks

Hyperlinks can also be added to Qt rich text using the `<a>` (anchor) tag, as follows:

```
<p>Download it today from
<a href='http://www.example.com'>Example.com</a>!</p>
```

The exact behavior of hyperlinks varies according to the widget displaying the hyperlink and the settings of the widget.

The QTextBrowser by default will attempt to navigate to a hyperlink within the widget; keep in mind, however, that these links will only work if they are resource URLs or local file paths. `QTextBrowser` lacks a network stack and cannot be used to browse the internet.

It can, however, be configured to open URLs in an external browser; back in the Python script, add the following line of code to `MainWindow.__init__()`:

```
main.setOpenExternalLinks(True)
```

This utilizes `QDesktopServices.openUrl()` to open the anchor's `href` value in the desktop's default browser. You should configure this setting whenever you want to support external hyperlinks in a document.

External hyperlinks can also be configured on `QLabel` widgets, but not within a `QTextEdit` widget.

Documents can also use hyperlinks for navigating within a document itself, as follows:

```
<p><a href='#Features'>Read about the features</a></p>

<br><br><br><br><br><br>

<a name='Features'></a>
<h2>Features</h2>
<p>Fight Fighter 2 is so amazing in so many ways:</p>
```

Here, we've added an anchor pointing to #Features (with a pound sign), followed by a number of breaks to simulate more content. When a user clicks the link, it will scroll the browser widget to the anchor tag with a name (not href) attribute of Features (without the pound sign).

This feature can be useful for doing things such as providing a navigable table of contents.

Lists and tables

Lists and tables are very useful for presenting orderly information in a way that users can quickly parse.

An example of a list is as follows:

```
<ul type=square>
  <li>More players at once!  Have up to 72 players.</li>
  <li>More teams!  Play with up to 16 teams!</li>
  <li>Easier installation!  Simply:<ol>
    <li>Copy the executable to your system.</li>
    <li>Run it!</li>
  </ol></li>
  <li>Sound and music! &gt;16 Million colors on some systems!</li>
</ul>
```

Lists in Qt rich text can be of the ordered or unordered variety. In the preceding example, we have an unordered list (<ul>). The optional type attribute allows you to specify what kind of bullets should be used. In this case, we've chosen square; other options for unordered lists include circle and disc.

Each item in a list is specified using the <li> (list item) tag. We can also nest a list inside a list item to make a sublist. In this case, we've added an ordered list, which will use sequential numbers to indicate new items. Ordered lists also accept the type attribute; valid values are a (lower case letters), A (upper case letters), or 1 (sequential numbers).

> in the last bullet item is an example of an HTML entity. These are special codes that are used to display HTML special characters such as angle brackets, or non-ASCII characters, such as the copyright symbol. Entities start with an ampersand and end with a colon and contain a string indicating the character to display. The gt, in this case, stands for *greater than*. An official list of entities can be found at https://dev.w3.org/html5/html-author/charref, though not all may be supported by QTextDocument.

Creating HTML tables is somewhat more involved, as it requires many levels of nesting. The hierarchy for table tags is as follows:

- The table itself is defined by a <table> tag
- The heading portion of the table is defined by the <thead> tag
- Each row of the table (header or data) is defined by a <tr> (table row) tag
- Within each row, table cells are defined by either a <th> (table heading) tag or a <td> (table data) tag

Let's start a table with the following code:

```
<table border=2>
  <thead>
    <tr bgcolor='grey'>
    <th>System</th><th>Graphics</th><th>Sound</th></tr>
  </thead>
```

In the preceding example, we've started with the opening <table> tag. The border attribute specifies a width for the table border in pixels; in this case, we want a two-pixel border. Keep in mind that this border goes around each cell and does not collapse (that is, merge with an adjacent cell's border), so in actuality, we'll have a four-pixel border between each cell. Table borders can have different styles; by default, the *ridge* style is used, so this border will be shaded to look slightly three-dimensional.

Inside the <thead> section, there is a table row filled with table heading cells. By setting the bgcolor attribute of the row, we can change the background color of all the header cells to grey.

Now, let's add some data rows with the following code:

```
<tr><td>Windows</td><td>DirectX 3D</td><td>24 bit PCM</td></tr>
<tr><td>FreeDOS</td><td>256 color</td><td>8 bit Adlib PCM</td></tr>
<tr><td>Commodore 64</td><td>256 color</td><td>SID audio</td></tr>
<tr><td>TRS80</td>
  <td rowspan=2>Monochrome</td>
```

```
      <td rowspan=2>Beeps</td>
    </tr>
    <tr><td>Timex Sinclair</td></tr>
    <tr>
      <td>BBC Micro</td>
      <td colspan=2 bgcolor='red'>No support</td>
    </tr>
  </table>
```

In the preceding example, the rows contain <td> cells for the actual table data. Note that we can use the rowspan and colspan attributes on individual cells to make them take up additional rows and columns, and the bgcolor attribute can also be applied to individual cells.

 It's possible to wrap the data rows in a <tbody> tag to differentiate it from the <thead> section, but this doesn't actually have any useful impact in Qt rich text HTML.

Fonts, colors, images, and styles

Rich text fonts can be set using the <font> tag, as follows:

```
<h2>Special!</h2>

<p>
  <font face='Impact' size=32 color='green'>Buy Now!</font>
  and receive <tt>20%</tt> off the regular price plus a
  <font face=Impact size=16 color='red'>Free sticker!</font>
</p>
```

<font> may be unfamiliar to those who have learned more modern HTML, as it was deprecated in HTML 5. As you can see, though, it can be used to set the face, size, and color attributes of the text enclosed in the tags.

The <tt> (typewriter type) tag is shorthand for using mono-spaced fonts and is useful for presenting things like inline code, keyboard shortcuts, and terminal output.

If you prefer to use more modern CSS-style font configuration, this can be done by setting the `style` attribute on a block-level tag like `<div>`, as follows:

```
<div style='font-size: 16pt; font-weight: bold; color: navy;
        background-color: orange; padding: 20px;
        text-align: center;'>
        Don't miss this exciting offer!
</div>
```

Within the `style` attribute, you can set any of the supported CSS values to be applied to that block.

Document-wide styles

Qt rich text documents do *not* support HTML `<style>` tags or `<link>` tags for setting a document-wide style sheet. Instead, you can use the `setDefaultStyleSheet()` method of the `QTextDocument` object to set a CSS style sheet that will be applied to all viewed documents.

Back in `MainWindow.__init__()`, add the following:

```
main.document().setDefaultStyleSheet(
    'body {color: #333; font-size: 14px;} '
    'h2 {background: #CCF; color: #443;} '
    'h1 {background: #001133; color: white;} '
)
```

Note, however, that this must be added *before* the HTML is inserted into the widget. The `defaultStyleSheet` method is only applied to newly inserted HTML.

Also note that certain aspects of the appearance are not properties of the document, but of the widget. Notably, the background color of the document cannot be set by altering the body's styles.

Instead, set the widget's style sheet, as follows:

```
main.setStyleSheet('background-color: #EEF;')
```

Keep in mind that the widget's style sheet uses QSS, whereas the document's style sheet uses CSS. The difference is minimal, but could come into play in certain situations.

Images

An image can be inserted using the `<img>` tag, as follows:

```
<div>
  <img src=logo.png width=400 height=100 />
</div>
```

The `src` attribute should be a file or resource path to an image file supported by Qt (see Chapter 6, *Styling Qt Applications*, for more information about image format support). The `width` and `height` attributes can be used to force a certain size.

Differences between Qt rich text and Web HTML

If you have any experience in web design or development, you have no doubt already noted several differences between Qt's rich text markup and the HTML used in modern web browsers. It's important to keep these in mind as you create rich text, so let's go over the main differences.

First, Qt rich text is based on HTML 4 and CSS 2.1; as you have seen, it includes some deprecated tags, such as `<font>`, and excludes many of the more modern tags, such as `<section>` or `<figure>`.

Furthermore, Qt rich text is based on only a subset of those specifications, so it lacks support for many tags. For example, there are no input- or form-related tags, such as `<select>` or `<textarea>`.

`QTextDocument` is also less forgiving than most web browser renderers when it comes to syntax errors and case. For example, when setting a default style sheet, the case of the tag name needs to match the case used in the document, or the style won't apply. In addition, failing to use block-level tags (such as `<p>`, `<div>`, and so on) around content can lead to unpredictable results.

In short, it's best not to think of Qt rich text markup as true HTML, but rather as a similar but separate markup language. If you have any questions about whether a particular tag or style directive is supported, consult the support reference at https://doc.qt.io/qt-5/richtext-html-subset.html.

Manipulating rich text using QTextDocument

In addition to allowing us to specify rich text in markup, Qt provides us with an API to create and manipulate rich text programmatically. This API is called the **Qt Scribe Framework**, and it's built around the `QTextDocument` and `QTextCursor` classes.

To demonstrate how to create a document using the `QTextDocument` and `QTextCursor` classes, we're going to build a simple invoice generator application. Our application will take data from a widget form and use it to generate a rich text document programmatically.

Creating the invoice application GUI

Get a fresh copy of our PyQt application template and call it `invoice_maker.py`. We'll begin our application by creating the GUI elements, and then develop the method that will actually build the document.

Start your script with a data entry form class, as follows:

```
class InvoiceForm(qtw.QWidget):

    submitted = qtc.pyqtSignal(dict)

    def __init__(self):
        super().__init__()
        self.setLayout(qtw.QFormLayout())
        self.inputs = dict()
        self.inputs['Customer Name'] = qtw.QLineEdit()
        self.inputs['Customer Address'] = qtw.QPlainTextEdit()
        self.inputs['Invoice Date'] = qtw.QDateEdit(
            date=qtc.QDate.currentDate(), calendarPopup=True)
        self.inputs['Days until Due'] = qtw.QSpinBox(
            minimum=0, maximum=60, value=30)
        for label, widget in self.inputs.items():
            self.layout().addRow(label, widget)
```

Like with most of the forms we've created, this class is based on `QWidget` and starts by defining a `submitted` signal to carry a dictionary of the form's values. Here, we have also added various inputs to `QFormLayout` to enter basic invoice data such as customer name, customer address, and invoice date.

Next, we'll add `QTableWidget` for entering the invoice's line items, as follows:

```
self.line_items = qtw.QTableWidget(
    rowCount=10, columnCount=3)
self.line_items.setHorizontalHeaderLabels(
    ['Job', 'Rate', 'Hours'])
self.line_items.horizontalHeader().setSectionResizeMode(
    qtw.QHeaderView.Stretch)
self.layout().addRow(self.line_items)
for row in range(self.line_items.rowCount()):
    for col in range(self.line_items.columnCount()):
        if col > 0:
            w = qtw.QSpinBox(minimum=0)
            self.line_items.setCellWidget(row, col, w)
```

Each row of this table widget contains a description of the task, the rate for the work, and the number of hours worked. Because the values in the last two columns are numbers, we're using the table widget's `setCellWidget()` method to replace the default `QLineEdit` widgets in those cells with `QSpinBox` widgets.

Finally, we'll add a `submit` button with the following code:

```
submit = qtw.QPushButton('Create Invoice', clicked=self.on_submit)
self.layout().addRow(submit)
```

The `submit` button calls an `on_submit()` method, which starts as follows:

```
def on_submit(self):
    data = {
        'c_name': self.inputs['Customer Name'].text(),
        'c_addr': self.inputs['Customer Address'].toPlainText(),
        'i_date': self.inputs['Invoice Date'].date().toString(),
        'i_due': self.inputs['Invoice Date'].date().addDays(
            self.inputs['Days until Due'].value()).toString(),
        'i_terms': '{} days'.format(
            self.inputs['Days until Due'].value())
    }
```

This method is simply going to extract the values that are entered into the form, make a few calculations, and emit the resulting data `dict` with the `submitted` signal. Here, we started by grabbing the values from each of the form's input widgets into a Python dictionary using the appropriate method for each widget.

Next, we need to retrieve the line items' data, as follows:

```
data['line_items'] = list()
for row in range(self.line_items.rowCount()):
    if not self.line_items.item(row, 0):
        continue
    job = self.line_items.item(row, 0).text()
    rate = self.line_items.cellWidget(row, 1).value()
    hours = self.line_items.cellWidget(row, 2).value()
    total = rate * hours
    row_data = [job, rate, hours, total]
    if any(row_data):
        data['line_items'].append(row_data)
```

For each row in the table widget that has a description, we're going to retrieve all the data, calculate a total cost by multiplying the rate and hours, and append all the data to the list in our data dictionary.

Finally, we'll calculate a grand total cost and append that with the following code:

```
data['total_due'] = sum(x[3] for x in data['line_items'])
self.submitted.emit(data)
```

After summing the cost in each line, we will add it to the data dictionary and emit our submitted signal with the data.

This takes care of our form class, so let's set up the main application layout in MainWindow. Down in MainWindow.__init__(), add the following code:

```
main = qtw.QWidget()
main.setLayout(qtw.QHBoxLayout())
self.setCentralWidget(main)

form = InvoiceForm()
main.layout().addWidget(form)

self.preview = InvoiceView()
main.layout().addWidget(self.preview)

form.submitted.connect(self.preview.build_invoice)
```

The main widget is given a horizontal layout to contain the form and the view widget for the formatted invoice. We then connect the form's submitted signal to a build_invoice() method, which we will create on the view object.

This is the main GUI and logic for the application; now all that's left to do is create our InvoiceView class.

Building InvoiceView

The `InvoiceView` class is where all the hard work takes place; we will base it on a read-only `QTextEdit` widget, and it will contain a `build_invoice()` method that, when called with a dictionary of data, will construct a formatted invoice document using the Qt Scribe framework.

Let's start with the constructor, as shown in the following example:

```python
class InvoiceView(qtw.QTextEdit):

    dpi = 72
    doc_width = 8.5 * dpi
    doc_height = 11 * dpi

    def __init__(self):
        super().__init__(readOnly=True)
        self.setFixedSize(qtc.QSize(self.doc_width, self.doc_height))
```

To begin, we've defined class variables for the document's width and height. We've chosen these values to give us the aspect ratio of a standard US letter-sized document at a reasonable size for the average computer monitor. Inside the constructor, we use the calculated value to set a fixed size for the widget. This is all we need to do in the constructor, so it's now time to get to the real work—building a document.

Let's begin with `build_invoice()`, as follows:

```python
    def build_invoice(self, data):
        document = qtg.QTextDocument()
        self.setDocument(document)
        document.setPageSize(qtc.QSizeF(self.doc_width, self.doc_height))
```

As you can see in the preceding example, the method starts by creating a fresh `QTextDocument` object and assigning it to the view's `document` property. Then, the `pageSize` property is set using the document dimensions calculated in the class definition. Note that our QTextEdit-based view already has a `document` object that we could retrieve, but we're creating a fresh object so that the method will start with an empty document each time it is called.

Editing documents with `QTextDocument` may feel a bit backward from the way we have been creating GUI forms, where we typically create objects, and then configure and place them on the layout.

Instead, the `QTextDocument` workflow is more like a word processor:

- There is a `cursor` that always points to some location in the document
- There is an active text style, paragraph style, or another block-level style whose settings will be applied to whatever is entered
- To add content, users start by positioning the cursor, configuring the styles, and finally creating the content

So, clearly, the first step is to get a reference to the cursor; do this with the following code:

```
cursor = qtg.QTextCursor(document)
```

The `QTextCursor` object is the tool that we use to insert content, and it has many methods for inserting different types of elements into the document.

For example, at this point, we could just start inserting text content, as follows:

```
cursor.insertText("Invoice, woohoo!")
```

However, before we start writing content to our document, we should build a basic document framework to work within. To do this, we need to understand how `QTextDocument` objects are structured.

The QTextDocument structure

Just like an HTML document, a `QTextDocument` object is a hierarchical structure. It is made up of **frames**, **blocks**, and **fragments**, which are defined as follows:

- A frame is represented by the `QTextFrame` object, and is a rectangular region of a document that can contain any type of content, including other frames. At the top of our hierarchy is the **root frame**, which contains all the document's contents.
- A block, represented by the `QTextBlock` object, is a region of text surrounded by line breaks, such as a paragraph or a list item.
- A fragment, represented by the `QTextFragment` object, is a contiguous region of text inside a block that shares a common text formatting. For example, if you have a sentence containing a word in bold, that represents three text fragments: the sentence before the bold word, the bold word, and the sentence after the bold word.
- Other items, such as tables, lists, and images, are subclassed from one of these preceding classes.

We're going to organize our document by inserting a set of sub-frames under the root frame so that we can easily navigate to the section of the document we want to work on. Our document will have the following four frames:

- The **logo frame** will contain the company logo and contact information
- The **customer address frame** will hold the customer name and address
- The **terms frame** will hold a list of the invoice terms and conditions
- The **line items frame** will hold a table of the line-items and totals

Let's create some text frames to outline the structure of our document. We'll start by saving a reference to the root frame so that we can easily return to it after creating a sub-frame, as follows:

```
root = document.rootFrame()
```

Now that we have that, we can retrieve a cursor position for the end of the root frame at any point by calling the following command:

```
cursor.setPosition(root.lastPosition())
```

The cursor's `setPosition()` method places our cursor at any given position, and the root frame's `lastPosition()` method retrieves the position at the end of the root frame.

Now, let's define the first sub-frame, as follows:

```
logo_frame_fmt = qtg.QTextFrameFormat()
logo_frame_fmt.setBorder(2)
logo_frame_fmt.setPadding(10)
logo_frame = cursor.insertFrame(logo_frame_fmt)
```

A frame must be created with a `QTextFrameFormat` object defining its format, so before we can write the frame, we have to define our formatting. Unfortunately, the frame format's properties cannot be set using keyword arguments, so we must configure it using setter methods instead. In this example, we've set a two-pixel border around the frame, as well as ten pixels of padding.

Once the format object is created, we call the cursor's `insertFrame()` method to create a new frame with our configured format.

`insertFrame()` returns the `QTextFrame` object created, and also positions our document's cursor inside the new frame. Since we aren't ready to add content to this frame, and we don't want to create the next frame inside of it, we need to return to the root frame before creating the next frame by using the following code:

```
cursor.setPosition(root.lastPosition())
cust_addr_frame_fmt = qtg.QTextFrameFormat()
cust_addr_frame_fmt.setWidth(self.doc_width * .3)
cust_addr_frame_fmt.setPosition(qtg.QTextFrameFormat.FloatRight)
cust_addr_frame = cursor.insertFrame(cust_addr_frame_fmt)
```

In the preceding example, we're using the frame format to set the width of this frame to one-third of the width of the document and to make it float to the right. *Floating* a document frame means that it will be pushed to one side of the document and other content will flow around it.

Now, we'll add the terms frame, as follows:

```
cursor.setPosition(root.lastPosition())
terms_frame_fmt = qtg.QTextFrameFormat()
terms_frame_fmt.setWidth(self.doc_width * .5)
terms_frame_fmt.setPosition(qtg.QTextFrameFormat.FloatLeft)
terms_frame = cursor.insertFrame(terms_frame_fmt)
```

This time, we're going to make the frame half of the document's width and float it to the left.

> In theory, these two frames should be next to each other. In practice, due to a quirk in the `QTextDocument` class' rendering, the top of the second frame will be a line below the top of the first one. This is OK for our demo, but if you need actual columns, use a table instead.

Finally, let's add the frame to hold our line items table, as follows:

```
cursor.setPosition(root.lastPosition())
line_items_frame_fmt = qtg.QTextFrameFormat()
line_items_frame_fmt.setMargin(25)
line_items_frame = cursor.insertFrame(line_items_frame_fmt)
```

Once again, we've moved the cursor back to the root frame and inserted a new frame. This time, the format adds a margin of 25 pixels to the frame.

Note that we don't have to do any special configuration of the `QTextFrameFormat` objects if we don't want to, but we *do* have to create one for each frame, and we *do* need to set up any configuration on them *before* creating the new frame. Note that it's also possible to reuse frame formats if you have many frames with the same configuration.

Character formats

Just like frames must be created with a frame format, text content must be created with a **character format**, which defines properties such as the font and alignment of the text. Before we start adding content to our frames, we should define some common character formats to use for different parts of the document.

This is done using the QTextCharFormat class, as follows:

```
std_format = qtg.QTextCharFormat()

logo_format = qtg.QTextCharFormat()
logo_format.setFont(
    qtg.QFont('Impact', 24, qtg.QFont.DemiBold))
logo_format.setUnderlineStyle(
    qtg.QTextCharFormat.SingleUnderline)
logo_format.setVerticalAlignment(
    qtg.QTextCharFormat.AlignMiddle)

label_format = qtg.QTextCharFormat()
label_format.setFont(qtg.QFont('Sans', 12, qtg.QFont.Bold))
```

In the preceding example, we've created the following three formats:

- std_format, which will be used for regular text. We aren't changing anything from the default settings.
- logo_format, which will be used for our company logo. We're customizing its font and adding an underline, as well as setting its vertical alignment.
- label_format, which will be used for labels; they will be in 12-point font and bold.

Note that QTextCharFormat allows you to make many font configurations directly using setter methods, or you can even configure a QFont object to assign to the format. We'll use these three formats when we add our text content for the remainder of the document.

Adding basic content

Now, let's add some basic content to our logo_frame with the following command:

```
cursor.setPosition(logo_frame.firstPosition())
```

Just like we called the root frame's `lastPosition` method to get the position at its end, we can call the logo frame's `firstPosition()` method to get the position at the beginning of the frame. Once there, we can insert content, such as a logo image, as follows:

```
cursor.insertImage('nc_logo.png')
```

Images can be inserted just like this—by passing a path to the image as a string. However, this method offers little in the way of configuration, so let's try a slightly more involved approach:

```
logo_image_fmt = qtg.QTextImageFormat()
logo_image_fmt.setName('nc_logo.png')
logo_image_fmt.setHeight(48)
cursor.insertImage(logo_image_fmt, qtg.QTextFrameFormat.FloatLeft)
```

By using a `QTextImageFormat` object, we can configure various aspects of the image first, such as its height and width, then add it along with an enum constant specifying its positioning policy. In this case, `FloatLeft` will cause the image to align to the left of the frame, and subsequent text will wrap around it.

Now, let's write the following text in the block:

```
cursor.insertText('    ')
cursor.insertText('Ninja Coders, LLC', logo_format)
cursor.insertBlock()
cursor.insertText('123 N Wizard St, Yonkers, NY 10701', std_format)
```

Using our `logo_format`, we have written a text fragment containing the company name and then inserted a new block so, we can add another fragment containing the address on another line. Note that passing a character format is optional; if we don't do it, the fragment will be inserted with the currently active format, just as it is in a word processor.

That takes care of our logo, so now let's deal with the customer address block, as follows:

```
cursor.setPosition(cust_addr_frame.lastPosition())
```

Text blocks can have formats just like frames and characters. Let's create a text block format to use with our customer address using the following code:

```
address_format = qtg.QTextBlockFormat()
address_format.setAlignment(qtc.Qt.AlignRight)
address_format.setRightMargin(25)
address_format.setLineHeight(
    150, qtg.QTextBlockFormat.ProportionalHeight)
```

Text block formats allow you to change the sort of settings you'd change in a paragraph of text: margins, line heights, indents, and alignment. Here, we've set the text alignment to the right-aligned, a right margin of 25 pixels, and the line-height to 1.5 lines. There are multiple ways to specify the height in `QTextDocument`, and the second argument to `setLineHeight()` determines how the value passed in will be interpreted. In this case, we're using the `ProportionalHeight` mode, which interprets the value as a percentage of the line-height.

We can pass our block format object to any `insertBlock` call, as follows:

```
cursor.insertBlock(address_format)
cursor.insertText('Customer:', label_format)
cursor.insertBlock(address_format)
cursor.insertText(data['c_name'], std_format)
cursor.insertBlock(address_format)
cursor.insertText(data['c_addr'])
```

Each time we insert a block, it's like starting a new paragraph. Our multi-line address string will be inserted as one paragraph, but note that it will still be spaced to 1.5 lines.

Inserting a list

Our invoice terms will be presented as an unordered bullet list. Ordered and unordered lists can be inserted into `QTextDocument` using the cursor's `insertList()` method, as follows:

```
cursor.setPosition(terms_frame.lastPosition())
cursor.insertText('Terms:', label_format)
cursor.insertList(qtg.QTextListFormat.ListDisc)
```

The argument for `insertList()` can be either a `QTextListFormat` object or a constant from the `QTextListFormat.Style` enum. In this case, we're using the latter, specifying that we want a list with disc-style bullets.

Other options for list formats include `ListCircle` and `ListSquare` for unordered lists, and `ListDecimal`, `ListLowerAlpha`, `ListUpperAlpha`, `ListUpperRoman`, and `ListLowerRoman` for ordered lists.

Now, we'll define some items to insert into our list, as follows:

```
term_items = (
    f'<b>Invoice dated:</b> {data["i_date"]}',
    f'<b>Invoice terms:</b> {data["i_terms"]}',
```

```
    f'<b>Invoice due:</b> {data["i_due"]}',
)
```

Note that we're using markup in the preceding example, rather than raw strings. You can still use markup when creating a document with QTextCursor; however, you'll need to tell the cursor it's inserting HTML rather than plain text by calling insertHtml() rather than insertText(), as shown in the following example:

```
for i, item in enumerate(term_items):
    if i > 0:
        cursor.insertBlock()
    cursor.insertHtml(item)
```

After calling insertList(), our cursor is positioned inside the first list item, so we now need to call insertBlock() to get to subsequent items (we don't want to do this for the first item, since we're already in a bullet point, hence the if i > 0 check).

Unlike insertText(), insertHtml() does not accept a character format object. You have to rely on your markup to determine the formatting.

Inserting a table

The last thing we're going to insert in our invoice is a table containing our line items. QTextTable is a subclass of QTextFrame, and just like a frame, we'll need to create a format object for it before we can create the table itself.

The class we need is the QTextTableFormat class:

```
table_format = qtg.QTextTableFormat()
table_format.setHeaderRowCount(1)
table_format.setWidth(
    qtg.QTextLength(qtg.QTextLength.PercentageLength, 100))
```

Here, we've configured the headerRowCount property, which indicates that the first row is a header row and should be repeated at the top of each page. This is equivalent to putting the first row in a <thead> tag in markup.

We're also setting the width, but instead of using pixel values, we're making use of a QTextLength object. This class is somewhat confusingly named because it doesn't refer specifically to the length of text, but rather to any generic length you might need in QTextDocument. QTextLength objects can be of the percentage, fixed, or variable type; in this case, we're specifying PercentageLength with a value of 100, or 100%.

Now, let's insert our table with the following code:

```
headings = ('Job', 'Rate', 'Hours', 'Cost')
num_rows = len(data['line_items']) + 1
num_cols = len(headings)

cursor.setPosition(line_items_frame.lastPosition())
table = cursor.insertTable(num_rows, num_cols, table_format)
```

When inserting a table into QTextDocument, we not only need to define a format, but also a number of rows and columns. To do that, we've created a tuple of the headers, then calculated the rows and columns by taking the length of the line item list (adding 1 for the header row), and the length of the headers tuple.

We then need to position the cursor in the line items frame and insert our table. Just like other insert methods, insertTable() positions our cursor inside the inserted item, in the first column of the first row.

We can now insert our heading row with the following code:

```
for heading in headings:
    cursor.insertText(heading, label_format)
    cursor.movePosition(qtg.QTextCursor.NextCell)
```

Up to this point, we've been positioning the cursor by passing an exact position to setPosition(). QTextCursor objects also have a movePosition() method which can take a constant from the QTextCursor.MoveOperation enum. This enum defines constants representing about two dozen different cursor movements, such as StartOfLine, PreviousBlock, and NextWord. In this case, the NextCell movement takes us to the next cell in a table.

We can use the same idea to insert our data, like this:

```
for row in data['line_items']:
    for col, value in enumerate(row):
        text = f'${value}' if col in (1, 3) else f'{value}'
        cursor.insertText(text, std_format)
        cursor.movePosition(qtg.QTextCursor.NextCell)
```

In this case, we're iterating every column of every row in the data list and using insertText() to add the data to the cell. If the column number is 1 or 3, that is, a monetary value, we need to add a currency symbol to the display.

We also need to add one more row to hold the grand total for the invoice. To add an extra row in our table, we can use the following `QTextTable.appendRows()` method:

```
table.appendRows(1)
```

To position our cursor into a particular cell in the new row, we can use the table object's `cellAt()` method to retrieve a `QTableCell` object, then use that object's `lastCursorPosition()` method, which returns a new cursor positioned at the end of the cell, as follows:

```
cursor = table.cellAt(num_rows, 0).lastCursorPosition()
cursor.insertText('Total', label_format)
cursor = table.cellAt(num_rows, 3).lastCursorPosition()
cursor.insertText(f"${data['total_due']}", label_format)
```

That's the last bit of content we need to write to the invoice document, so let's go ahead and test it out.

Finishing and testing

Now, if you run your application, fill in the fields, and hit **Create Invoice**, you should see something like the following screenshot:

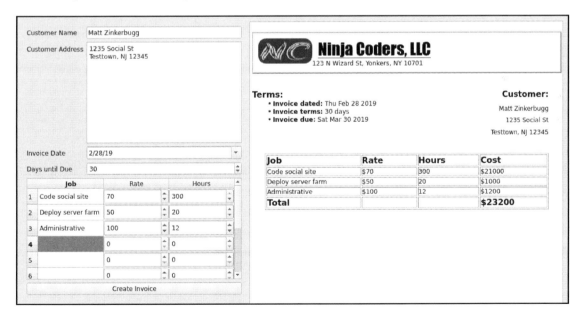

Looking good! Of course, that invoice won't do us much good if we can't print or export it. So, in the next section, we'll look at how to handle the printing of documents.

Printing rich text

Nothing strikes terror into the hearts of programmers like being asked to implement printer support. The act of turning pristine digital bits into ink on paper is messy in real life and can be just as messy in the software world. Fortunately, Qt provides the `QtPrintSupport` module, a cross-platform print system that can easily turn `QTextDocument` into hard-copy format, no matter what OS we're using.

Updating the Invoice app for print support

Readers outside the United States almost certainly groaned when we hard-coded the dimensions of our document to 8.5×11, but never fear—we're going to make some changes that will allow us to set the size based on a user's selection of document sizes.

In the `InvoiceView` class, create the following new method, `set_page_size()`, to set the page size:

```
def set_page_size(self, qrect):
    self.doc_width = qrect.width()
    self.doc_height = qrect.height()
    self.setFixedSize(qtc.QSize(self.doc_width, self.doc_height))
    self.document().setPageSize(
        qtc.QSizeF(self.doc_width, self.doc_height))
```

This method will receive a `QRect` object, from which it will extract width and height values to update the document's settings, the widget's fixed size, and the document's page size.

Down in `MainWindow.__init__()`, add a toolbar to control printing and set up the following actions:

```
print_tb = self.addToolBar('Printing')
print_tb.addAction('Configure Printer', self.printer_config)
print_tb.addAction('Print Preview', self.print_preview)
print_tb.addAction('Print dialog', self.print_dialog)
print_tb.addAction('Export PDF', self.export_pdf)
```

We'll implement each of these callbacks as we walk through how to set up each aspect of the print process.

Configuring the printer

Printing begins with a `QtPrintSupport.QPrinter` object, which represents a printed document in memory. The basic workflow of printing in PyQt is as follows:

1. Create a `QPrinter` object
2. Configure the `QPrinter` object using its methods or printer configuration dialogs
3. Print `QTextDocument` to the `QPrinter` object
4. Pass the `QPrinter` object to the operating system's print dialog, from which the user can print using a physical printer

In `MainWindow.__init__()`, let's create our `QPrinter` object, as follows:

```
self.printer = qtps.QPrinter()
self.printer.setOrientation(qtps.QPrinter.Portrait)
self.printer.setPageSize(qtg.QPageSize(qtg.QPageSize.Letter))
```

Once the printer is created, we can configure a wide number of properties; here, we've simply set the orientation and page size (to the US letter defaults, once again, but feel free to change this to your preferred paper size).

Anything you can configure in a printer settings dialog can be configured via the `QPrinter` method, but ideally, we'd rather let the user make these decisions. So, let's implement the following `printer_config()` method:

```
def printer_config(self):
    dialog = qtps.QPageSetupDialog(self.printer, self)
    dialog.exec()
```

The `QPageSetupDialog` object is a `QDialog` subclass that presents all the options that are available for the `QPrinter` object. We pass into it our `QPrinter` object, which causes any changes that have been made in the dialog to be applied to that printer object. On Windows and macOS, Qt will use the OS-provided print dialogs by default; on other platforms, a Qt-specific dialog will be used.

Now that the user can configure paper size, we need to allow the page size used by `InvoiceView` to reset after each change. So, let's add the following method to `MainWindow`:

```
def _update_preview_size(self):
    self.preview.set_page_size(
        self.printer.pageRect(qtps.QPrinter.Point))
```

The `QPrinter.pageRect()` method extracts a `QRect` object, defining the configured page size. Since our `InvoiceView.set_page_size()` method accepts a `QRect`, we just need to pass this object along to it.

Note that we've passed a constant into `pageRect()`, indicating that we want the size in **points**. A point is 1/72 of an inch, so our widget size will be 72 × the physical page size in inches. You can request the page rectangle in a variety of units (including millimeters, picas, inches, and so on) if you want to do your own calculations to scale the widget's size.

 Unfortunately, the `QPrinter` object is not a `QObject` descendant, so that we cannot use signals to determine when its parameters were changed.

Now, add a call to `self._update_preview_size()` to the end of `printer_config()`, so that it will be called whenever the user configures the page. You'll find that if you change the size of the paper in the printer configuration dialog, your preview widget will resize accordingly.

Printing a page

Before we can physically print a document, we have to first print `QTextDocument` to the `QPrinter` object. This is done by passing the printer object to the document's `print()` method.

We'll create the following method to do that for us:

```
def _print_document(self):
    self.preview.document().print(self.printer)
```

Note that this doesn't actually cause your printing device to start putting ink on the page – it just loads the document into the `QPrinter` object.

To actually print it to paper, a printer dialog is needed; so, add the following method to `MainView`:

```
def print_dialog(self):
    self._print_document()
    dialog = qtps.QPrintDialog(self.printer, self)
    dialog.exec()
    self._update_preview_size()
```

In this method, we first call our internal method to load the document into the `QPrinter` object, then pass the object to a `QPrintDialog` object, which we execute by calling its `exec()` method. This will display the printing dialog, which the user can then use to send the document off to a physical printer.

 If you don't need the printing dialog to block program execution, you can call its `open()` method instead. We're blocking in the preceding example so we can perform actions once the dialog is closed.

After the dialog has closed, we call `_update_preview_size()` to grab the new paper size and update our widget and document. In theory, we could connect the dialog's `accepted` signal to that method, but in practice, there are some race conditions that may cause this to fail.

Print previewing

Nobody likes to waste paper by printing something that isn't right, so we should add a `print_preview` function. `QPrintPreviewDialog` exists for this purpose and works very much like other printing dialogs, as follows:

```python
def print_preview(self):
    dialog = qtps.QPrintPreviewDialog(self.printer, self)
    dialog.paintRequested.connect(self._print_document)
    dialog.exec()
    self._update_preview_size()
```

Once again, we just need to pass the printer object to the dialog's constructor and call `exec()`. We also need to connect the dialog's `paintRequested` signal to a slot that will update the document in `QPrinter` so that the dialog can make sure the preview is up to date. Here, we've connected it to our `_print_document()` method, which does exactly what is required.

Exporting to PDF

In this paperless digital age, the PDF file has replaced the hard copy for many purposes, so an easy export to PDF function is always a good thing to add. `QPrinter` can do this for us easily.

Add the following `export_pdf()` method to `MainView`:

```python
def export_pdf(self):
    filename, _ = qtw.QFileDialog.getSaveFileName(
        self, "Save to PDF", qtc.QDir.homePath(), "PDF Files (*.pdf)")
    if filename:
        self.printer.setOutputFileName(filename)
        self.printer.setOutputFormat(qtps.QPrinter.PdfFormat)
        self._print_document()
```

Here, we're going to start by asking the user for a filename. If they provide one, we'll configure our `QPrinter` object with the filename, set the output format to `PdfFormat`, and then print the document. When writing to a file, `QTextDocument.print()` will take care of writing the data and saving the file for us, so we don't need to do anything else here.

That covers all your printing needs for the invoice program! Take some time to test this functionality and see how it works with your printers.

Summary

In this chapter, you mastered working with rich text documents in PyQt5. You learned how to use Qt's HTML subset to add rich text formatting in the `QLabel`, `QTextEdit`, and `QTextBrowser` widgets. You worked through constructing a QTextDocument programmatically using the `QTextCursor` interface. Finally, you learned how to bring your `QTextDocument` objects into the real world using Qt's printing support module.

In `Chapter 12`, *Creating 2D Graphics with QPainter*, you'll learn some advanced concepts of two-dimensional graphics. You'll learn to work with `QPainter` objects to create graphics, build custom widgets, and create an animation.

Questions

Try these questions to test your knowledge from this chapter:

1. The following HTML isn't displaying as you'd hoped. Find as many errors as you can:

```html
<table>
<thead background=#EFE><th>Job</th><th>Status</th></thead>
<tr><td>Backup</td>
<font text-color='green'>Success!</font></td></tr>
```

```
<tr><td>Cleanup<td><font text-style='bold'>Fail!</font></td></tr>
</table>
```

2. What is wrong with the following Qt HTML snippets?

```
<p>There is nothing <i>wrong</i> with your television
<b>set</p></b>
<table><row><data>french fries</data>
<data>$1.99</data></row></table>
<font family='Tahoma' color='#235499'>Can you feel the
<strikethrough>love</strikethrough>code tonight?</font>
<label>Username</label><input type='text' name='username'></input>
<img source='://mypix.png'>My picture</img>
```

3. This snippet is supposed to implement a table of contents. Why doesn't it work correctly?

```
<ul>
  <li><a href='Section1'>Section 1</a></li>
  <li><a href='Section2'>Section 2</a></li>
</ul>
<div id=Section1>
  <p>This is section 1</p>
</div>
<div id=Section2>
  <p>This is section 2</p>
</div>
```

4. Using QTextCursor, add a sidebar to the right-hand side of your document. Explain how you would go about this.

5. You are trying to create a document with QTextCursor. It should have a top and bottom frame; in the top frame, there should be a title, and in the bottom frame, an unordered list. Correct the following code so that it does that:

```
document = qtg.QTextDocument()
cursor = qtg.QTextCursor(document)
top_frame = cursor.insertFrame(qtg.QTextFrameFormat())
bottom_frame = cursor.insertFrame(qtg.QTextFrameFormat())

cursor.insertText('This is the title')
cursor.movePosition(qtg.QTextCursor.NextBlock)
cursor.insertList(qtg.QTextListFormat())
for item in ('thing 1', 'thing 2', 'thing 3'):
    cursor.insertText(item)
```

6. You're creating your own `QPrinter` subclass to add a signal when the page size changes. Will the following code work?

```
class MyPrinter(qtps.QPrinter):

    page_size_changed = qtc.pyqtSignal(qtg.QPageSize)

    def setPageSize(self, size):
        super().setPageSize(size)
        self.page_size_changed.emit(size)
```

7. `QtPrintSupport` contains a class called `QPrinterInfo`. Using this class, print a list of the names, makes, models, and default page sizes of all of the printers on your system.

Further reading

For further information, please refer to the following links:

- Qt's overview of the Scribe framework can be found at `https://doc.qt.io/qt-5/richtext.html`
- Advanced document layouts can be defined using the `QAbstractTextDocumentLayout` and `QTextLine` classes; information about how to use these classes can be found at `https://doc.qt.io/qt-5/richtext-layouts.html`
- An overview of Qt's printing system can be found at `https://doc.qt.io/qt-5/qtprintsupport-index.html`

12
Creating 2D Graphics with QPainter

We've already seen that Qt provides a vast array of widgets with extensive styling and customization capabilities. There are times, however, when we need to take direct control of what is being drawn on the screen; for example, we might like to edit an image, create a unique widget, or build an interactive animation. At the core of all these tasks in Qt sits a humble, hardworking object known as QPainter.

In this chapter, we're going to explore Qt's **two-dimensional (2D)** graphics capabilities in three sections:

- Image editing with QPainter
- Custom widgets with QPainter
- Animating 2D graphics with QGraphicsScene

Technical requirements

This chapter requires the basic Python and PyQt5 setup that you've been using throughout the book. You may also wish to download the example code from https://github.com/PacktPublishing/Mastering-GUI-Programming-with-Python/tree/master/Chapter12.

You will also need the psutil library, which you can install from PyPI using the following command:

```
$ pip install --user psutil
```

Finally, it would be helpful to have some images on hand that you can use for sample data.

Check out the following video to see the code in action: http://bit.ly/2M5xzlL

Image editing with QPainter

Images can be edited in Qt using a `QPainter` object to draw on a `QImage` object. In Chapter 6, *Styling Qt Applications*, you learned about the `QPixmap` object, which is a display-optimized object representing a graphical image. The `QImage` object is a similar object, which is optimized for editing rather than display. To demonstrate how we can draw on a `QImage` object using `QPainter`, we're going to build a classic meme generator application.

The meme generator GUI

Create a copy of your Qt application template from Chapter 4, *Building Applications with QMainWindow*, and call it `meme_gen.py`. We will begin by building the GUI form for our meme generator.

The editing form

Before we create the actual form, we're going to simplify our code slightly by creating some custom button classes: a `ColorButton` class for setting colors, a `FontButton` class for setting fonts, and an `ImageFileButton` class for selecting images.

The `ColorButton` class begins like this:

```
class ColorButton(qtw.QPushButton):

    changed = qtc.pyqtSignal()

    def __init__(self, default_color, changed=None):
        super().__init__()
        self.set_color(qtg.QColor(default_color))
        self.clicked.connect(self.on_click)
        if changed:
            self.changed.connect(changed)
```

This button inherits `QPushButton` but makes a few changes. We've defined a `changed` signal to track when the value of the button changes and added a keyword option so that this signal can be connected using keywords, just like built-in signals.

We've also added the ability to specify a default color, which will be passed to a `set_color` method:

```
def set_color(self, color):
    self._color = color
    pixmap = qtg.QPixmap(32, 32)
    pixmap.fill(self._color)
    self.setIcon(qtg.QIcon(pixmap))
```

This method stores the passed color value in an instance variable and then generates a `pixmap` object of the given color to use as a button icon (we saw this technique in Chapter 6, *Styling Qt Applications*).

The button's `clicked` signal is connected to an `on_click()` method:

```
def on_click(self):
    color = qtw.QColorDialog.getColor(self._color)
    if color:
        self.set_color(color)
        self.changed.emit()
```

This method opens `QColorDialog`, allowing the user to choose a color and, if one is selected, it sets its color and emits the `changed` signal.

The `FontButton` class will be nearly identical to the preceding class:

```
class FontButton(qtw.QPushButton):

    changed = qtc.pyqtSignal()

    def __init__(self, default_family, default_size, changed=None):
        super().__init__()
        self.set_font(qtg.QFont(default_family, default_size))
        self.clicked.connect(self.on_click)
        if changed:
            self.changed.connect(changed)

    def set_font(self, font):
        self._font = font
        self.setFont(font)
        self.setText(f'{font.family()} {font.pointSize()}')
```

Similar to the color button, it defines a `changed` signal that can be connected through a keyword. It takes a default family and size, which is used to generate a default `QFont` object stored in the button's _font property using the `set_font()` method.

The set_font() method also changes the button's font and text to the selected family and size.

Finally, the on_click() method handles the button clicks:

```
def on_click(self):
    font, accepted = qtw.QFontDialog.getFont(self._font)
    if accepted:
        self.set_font(font)
        self.changed.emit()
```

Similar to the color button, we're displaying a QFontDialog dialog box and, if the user selects a font, setting the button's font accordingly.

Finally, the ImageFileButton class will be very much like the preceding two classes:

```
class ImageFileButton(qtw.QPushButton):

    changed = qtc.pyqtSignal()

    def __init__(self, changed=None):
        super().__init__("Click to select...")
        self._filename = None
        self.clicked.connect(self.on_click)
        if changed:
            self.changed.connect(changed)

    def on_click(self):
        filename, _ = qtw.QFileDialog.getOpenFileName(
            None, "Select an image to use",
            qtc.QDir.homePath(), "Images (*.png *.xpm *.jpg)")
        if filename:
            self._filename = filename
            self.setText(qtc.QFileInfo(filename).fileName())
            self.changed.emit()
```

The only difference here is that the dialog is now a getOpenFileName dialog that allows the user to select PNG, XPM, or JPEG files.

QImage can actually handle a wide variety of image files. You can find these at https://doc.qt.io/qt-5/qimage.html#reading-and-writing-image-files or by calling QImageReader.supportedImageFormats(). We've shortened the list here for brevity.

Now that these classes are created, let's build a form for editing the meme's properties:

```
class MemeEditForm(qtw.QWidget):

    changed = qtc.pyqtSignal(dict)

    def __init__(self):
        super().__init__()
        self.setLayout(qtw.QFormLayout())
```

This form will be very similar to those that we have created in previous chapters, but, rather than using a submitted signal for when the form is submitted, the changed signal will be triggered whenever any form item is changed. This will allow us to display any changes in real-time rather than requiring a button push.

Our first control will be to set the filename of the source image:

```
        self.image_source = ImageFileButton(changed=self.on_change)
        self.layout().addRow('Image file', self.image_source)
```

We're going to be linking the changed signal (or something similar) on each widget to a method called on_change(), which will gather up the data in the form and emit the changed signal of MemeEditForm.

First, though, let's add fields to control the text itself:

```
        self.top_text = qtw.QPlainTextEdit(textChanged=self.on_change)
        self.bottom_text = qtw.QPlainTextEdit(textChanged=self.on_change)
        self.layout().addRow("Top Text", self.top_text)
        self.layout().addRow("Bottom Text", self.bottom_text)
        self.text_color = ColorButton('white', changed=self.on_change)
        self.layout().addRow("Text Color", self.text_color)
        self.text_font = FontButton('Impact', 32, changed=self.on_change)
        self.layout().addRow("Text Font", self.text_font)
```

Our memes will have separate text drawn at the top and bottom of the images, and we've used our ColorButton and FontButton classes to create inputs for the text's color and font. Once again, we're connecting an appropriate changed signal from each widget to an on_changed() instance method.

Let's finish up the form GUI by adding controls to draw background boxes for the text:

```
self.text_bg_color = ColorButton('black', changed=self.on_change)
self.layout().addRow('Text Background', self.text_bg_color)
self.top_bg_height = qtw.QSpinBox(
    minimum=0, maximum=32,
    valueChanged=self.on_change, suffix=' line(s)')
self.layout().addRow('Top BG height', self.top_bg_height)
self.bottom_bg_height = qtw.QSpinBox(
    minimum=0, maximum=32,
    valueChanged=self.on_change, suffix=' line(s)')
self.layout().addRow('Bottom BG height', self.bottom_bg_height)
self.bg_padding = qtw.QSpinBox(
    minimum=0, maximum=100, value=10,
    valueChanged=self.on_change, suffix=' px')
self.layout().addRow('BG Padding', self.bg_padding)
```

These fields allow the user to add opaque backgrounds behind the text in case the image is too colorful for it to be readable. The controls allow you to change the number of lines for the top and bottom backgrounds, the color of the boxes, and the padding.

That takes care of the form layout, so now we'll deal with the on_change() method:

```
def get_data(self):
    return {
        'image_source': self.image_source._filename,
        'top_text': self.top_text.toPlainText(),
        'bottom_text': self.bottom_text.toPlainText(),
        'text_color': self.text_color._color,
        'text_font': self.text_font._font,
        'bg_color': self.text_bg_color._color,
        'top_bg_height': self.top_bg_height.value(),
        'bottom_bg_height': self.bottom_bg_height.value(),
        'bg_padding': self.bg_padding.value()
    }

def on_change(self):
    self.changed.emit(self.get_data())
```

First, we define a get_data() method, which assembles a dict object of values from the form's widgets and returns them. This will be useful if we need to pull data from the form explicitly, rather than rely on a signal. The on_change() method retrieves this dict object and emits it with the changed signal.

The main GUI

With the form widget created, let's now assemble our main GUI.

Let's start with `MainView.__init__()`:

```
self.setWindowTitle('Qt Meme Generator')
self.max_size = qtc.QSize(800, 600)
self.image = qtg.QImage(
    self.max_size, qtg.QImage.Format_ARGB32)
self.image.fill(qtg.QColor('black'))
```

We're going to begin by setting a window title and then defining a maximum size for our generated meme image. We'll use this to create our `QImage` object. Since we haven't got an image file at program launch time, we'll just generate a black placeholder image that is of the maximum size, which we do using the `fill()` method—just as we did with our pixmaps. However, when creating a blank `QImage` object, we need to specify an image format to use for the generated image. In this case, we're using the ARGB32 format, which can be used to make full-color images with transparency.

We'll use this image as we create the main GUI layout:

```
mainwidget = qtw.QWidget()
self.setCentralWidget(mainwidget)
mainwidget.setLayout(qtw.QHBoxLayout())
self.image_display = qtw.QLabel(pixmap=qtg.QPixmap(self.image))
mainwidget.layout().addWidget(self.image_display)
self.form = MemeTextForm()
mainwidget.layout().addWidget(self.form)
self.form.changed.connect(self.build_image)
```

This GUI is a simple two-panel layout featuring a `QLabel` object on the left for displaying our meme image, and the `MemeTextForm()` method on the right for editing it. We've connected the form's `changed` signal to a `MainWindow` method called `build_image()`, which will contain our main drawing logic. Note that we cannot display a `QImage` object in a `QLabel` object directly; we must convert it to a `QPixmap` object first.

Drawing with QImage

Now that our GUI is squared away, it's time to create `MainView.build_image()`. This method will contain all of the image manipulation and painting methods.

We'll begin by adding the following code:

```
def build_image(self, data):
    if not data.get('image_source'):
        self.image.fill(qtg.QColor('black'))
    else:
        self.image.load(data.get('image_source'))
        if not (self.max_size - self.image.size()).isValid():
            # isValid returns false if either dimension is negative
            self.image = self.image.scaled(
                self.max_size, qtc.Qt.KeepAspectRatio)
```

Our first task is to set up the base image of our meme. If we don't have an image_source value in the form data, then we'll just fill our QImage object with the color black, providing us a blank canvas for the rest of the drawing. If we do have an image source, then we can load in the selected image by passing its file path to QImage.load(). In the event that our loaded image is larger than the maximum size, we will want to scale it down so that it is smaller than the maximum width and height while keeping the same aspect ratio.

A quick way to check whether the image is too large in either dimension is to subtract its size from our maximum size. If either the width or the height is larger than the maximum, then one of the dimensions will be negative, which makes the QSize object produced by the subtraction expression invalid.

The QImage.scaled() method will return a new QImage object, which has been scaled to the provided QSize object. By specifying KeepAspectRatio, our width and height will be scaled separately so that the resulting size has an identical aspect ratio to the original.

Now that we have our image, we can start painting on it.

The QPainter object

At last, we get to meet the QPainter class! QPainter can be thought of as a little robot that lives inside your screen—to whom we can provide a brush and a pen, and issue drawing commands.

Let's create our painting robot:

```
painter = qtg.QPainter(self.image)
```

The painter's constructor is passed a reference to the object on which it will paint. The object to be painted must be a subclass of QPaintDevice; in this case, we're passing a QImage object, which is such a class. The passed object will be the painter's canvas on which the painter will draw when we issue drawing commands.

To see how basic painting works, let's start with our top and bottom background blocks. We'll first figure out the boundaries of the rectangles that we need to paint:

```
font_px = qtg.QFontInfo(data['text_font']).pixelSize()
top_px = (data['top_bg_height'] * font_px) + data['bg_padding']
top_block_rect = qtc.QRect(
    0, 0, self.image.width(), top_px)
bottom_px = (
    self.image.height() - data['bg_padding']
    - (data['bottom_bg_height'] * font_px))
bottom_block_rect = qtc.QRect(
    0, bottom_px, self.image.width(), self.image.height())
```

The coordinates used by QPainter start from the upper-left side of the painting surface. Therefore, the coordinates (0, 0) are the upper-left side of the screen, and (width, height) will be the lower-right of the screen.

To calculate the height of our top rectangle, we've multiplied the number of lines desired by the pixel height of our selected font (which we obtained from QFontInfo; see Chapter 6, *Styling Qt Applications*, for more information about using QFontInfo). Finally, we add in the padding amount. We end up with a rectangle that starts at the origin ((0, 0)) and ends on a point that is at the full width and height of the image of our box. These coordinates are used to create a QRect object representing the box area.

For the bottom box, we will need to calculate from the bottom of the image; this means that we must first calculate the height of the rectangle and then *subtract* it from the height of the box. Then, we construct a rectangle that starts at that coordinate on the left-side and extends to the bottom-right.

QRect coordinates must always be defined from upper-left to bottom-right.

Now that we have our rectangles, let's draw them:

```
painter.setBrush(qtg.QBrush(data['bg_color']))
painter.drawRect(top_block_rect)
painter.drawRect(bottom_block_rect)
```

QPainter has a number of drawing functions for creating lines, circles, polygons, and other shapes. In this case, we're using drawRect(), which draws a rectangle. To define the fill of this rectangle, we've set the painter's brush property to a QBrush object, which is set to our selected background color. The painter's brush value determines the color and pattern with which it will fill any shape.

In addition to drawRect(), QPainter contains a number of other drawing methods, as follows:

Method	For drawing
drawEllipse()	Circles and ellipses
drawLine()	Straight lines
drawRoundedRect()	Rectangle with rounded corners
drawPolygon()	Polygons of any kind
drawPixmap()	QPixmap objects
drawText()	Text

To place our meme text on the image, we need to use drawText():

```
painter.setPen(data['text_color'])
painter.setFont(data['text_font'])
flags = qtc.Qt.AlignHCenter | qtc.Qt.TextWordWrap
painter.drawText(
    self.image.rect(), flags | qtc.Qt.AlignTop, data['top_text'])
painter.drawText(
    self.image.rect(), flags | qtc.Qt.AlignBottom,
    data['bottom_text'])
```

Before we draw the text, we need to give the painter a QPen object to define the text color and a QFont object to define the font used. The painter's QPen determines the color used for text, shape outlines, lines, and points drawn by our painter.

To control where the text is drawn on the image, we could use the first argument to drawText(), which is a QRect object defining the bounding box for our text. However, since we don't know how many lines of text we're dealing with, we're just going to use the entire image as a bounding box and use vertical alignment to determine whether the text is written at the top or bottom.

Behaviors such as alignment and word-wrap are configured using flag values from the `QtCore.Qt.TextFlag` and `QtCore.Qt.AlignmentFlag` enums. In this case, we're specifying the center alignment and word wrap for both the top and bottom text, and then adding the vertical alignment option inside the `drawText()` call.

The last argument to `drawText()` is the actual text, which we've pulled from our `dict` data.

Now that we've drawn our text, the final thing we need to do is set the image in our image display label:

```
self.image_display.setPixmap(qtg.QPixmap(self.image))
```

At this point, you should be able to start up the program and create an image. Go ahead and try it out!

Saving our image

After creating a snazzy meme image, our user probably wants to save it so that they can upload it to their favorite social media website. To enable that, let's head back to `MainWindow.__init_()` and create a toolbar:

```
toolbar = self.addToolBar('File')
toolbar.addAction("Save Image", self.save_image)
```

You could, of course, do this using the menu options or another widget. In any case, we need to define the `save_image()` method called by this action:

```
def save_image(self):
    save_file, _ = qtw.QFileDialog.getSaveFileName(
        None, "Save your image",
        qtc.QDir.homePath(), "PNG Images (*.png)")
    if save_file:
        self.image.save(save_file, "PNG")
```

To save a `QImage` file to disk, we need to call its `save()` method with a file path string and a second string defining the image format. In this case, we're going to retrieve a save location using `QFileDialog.getSaveFileName()` and save it in the PNG format.

If you run your meme generator, you should find that it looks something like the following screenshot:

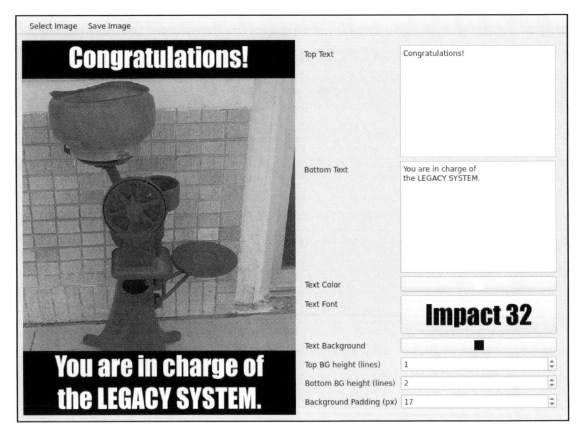

As an additional exercise, try thinking up some other things that you'd like to draw on a meme and add this capability to the code.

Custom widgets with QPainter

QPainter is not merely a specialized tool for drawing on images; it's actually the workhorse that draws all the graphics for all the widgets in Qt. In other words, every pixel of every widget you see in your PyQt application was drawn by a QPainter object. We can take control of QPainter to create a purely custom widget.

To explore this idea, let's create a CPU monitor application. Get a fresh copy of the Qt application template and call it cpu_graph.py, and then we'll begin.

Building a GraphWidget

Our CPU monitor will display real-time CPU activity using an area graph. The graph will be enhanced by a color gradient, which will show higher values in a different color from lower values. The graph will only show a configured number of values at one time, scrolling old values off to the left side of the widget as new ones are added from the right.

To accomplish this, we need to build a custom widget. We'll call it GraphWidget, and begin it as follows:

```
class GraphWidget(qtw.QWidget):
    """A widget to display a running graph of information"""

    crit_color = qtg.QColor(255, 0, 0)    # red
    warn_color = qtg.QColor(255, 255, 0)   # yellow
    good_color = qtg.QColor(0, 255, 0)   # green

    def __init__(
        self, *args, data_width=20,
        minimum=0, maximum=100,
        warn_val=50, crit_val=75, scale=10,
        **kwargs
    ):
        super().__init__(*args, **kwargs)
```

The custom widget begins with some class properties to define colors for *good, warning,* and *critical* values. Feel free to change these if you prefer.

Our constructor takes a number of keyword arguments, as follows:

- data_width: This refers to how many values will be displayed at a time
- minimum and maximum: The minimum and maximum values to be displayed
- warn_val and crit_val: These are threshold values for color changes
- Scale: This refers to how many pixels will be used on each data point

Our next step is to save all of these values as instance properties:

```
        self.minimum = minimum
        self.maximum = maximum
        self.warn_val = warn_val
        self.scale = scale
        self.crit_val = crit_val
```

To store our values, we require something like a Python `list` but constrained to a fixed number of items. Python's `collections` module offers the perfect object for this: the `deque` class.

Let's import this class at the top of our code block:

```
from collections import deque
```

The `deque` class can take a `maxlen` argument, which will limit its length. When new items are appended to the `deque` class, pushing it beyond its `maxlen` value, old items will be dropped from the beginning of the list to keep it under the limit. This is perfect for our graph since we only want to display a fixed number of data points in the graph at one time.

We'll create our `deque` class as follows:

```
self.values = deque([self.minimum] * data_width, maxlen=data_width)
self.setFixedWidth(data_width * scale)
```

`deque` can take a `list` as an argument, which will be used to initialize its data. In this case, we're initializing it with a `list` of `data_width` items containing our minimum value and setting the `maxlen` value of the `deque` class to `data_width`.

You can create a list of *N* items quickly in Python by multiplying a list of 1 item by *N*, as we've done here; for example, `[2] * 4` will create a list of `[2, 2, 2, 2]`.

We finish off the `__init__()` method by setting the fixed width of the widget to `data_width * scale`, which represents the total number of pixels that we want to display.

Next, we need a method to add a new value to our `deque` class, which we'll call `add_value()`:

```
def add_value(self, value):
    value = max(value, self.minimum)
    value = min(value, self.maximum)
    self.values.append(value)
    self.update()
```

The method begins by constraining our value between the minimum and maximum values and then appending it to the `deque` object. This has the additional effect of popping the first item off the beginning of the `deque` object so that it remains at the `data_width` value.

Finally, we call `update()`, which is a `QWidget` method that tells the widget to redraw itself. We'll handle this drawing process next.

Painting the widget

The `QWidget` class, just like `QImage`, is a subclass of `QPaintDevice`; as such, we can use a `QPainter` object to draw directly onto the widget. When a widget gets a request to redraw itself (similar to how we issued our call to `update()`), it calls its `paintEvent()` method. We can override this method with our own drawing commands to define a custom look for our widget.

Let's start the method as follows:

```
def paintEvent(self, paint_event):
    painter = qtg.QPainter(self)
```

`paintEvent()` will be called with one argument, a `QPaintEvent` object. This object contains information about the event that requested the repaint – most notably, the region and rectangle that needs to be redrawn. For a complex widget, we can use this information to only redraw requested parts. For our simple widget, we're going to ignore this information and just redraw the whole thing.

We've defined a painter object that is pointed to the widget itself, so any commands we issue to the painter will be drawn on our widget. Let's start by creating a background:

```
brush = qtg.QBrush(qtg.QColor(48, 48, 48))
painter.setBrush(brush)
painter.drawRect(0, 0, self.width(), self.height())
```

Just as we did in our meme generator, we're defining a brush, giving it to our painter, and drawing a rectangle.

Notice that we're using an alternate form of `drawRect()` here, which takes coordinates directly instead of a `QRect` object. Many of the `QPainter` object's drawing functions have alternate versions that take slightly different types of arguments for flexibility.

Next, let's draw some dotted lines to show where the thresholds for warning and critical are. To do this, we're going to need to translate a raw data value to a *y* coordinate on the widget. Since this will need to happen often, let's create a convenient method to convert values to *y* coordinates:

```
def val_to_y(self, value):
    data_range = self.maximum - self.minimum
    value_fraction = value / data_range
    y_offset = round(value_fraction * self.height())
    y = self.height() - y_offset
    return y
```

To convert a value to a *y* coordinate, we need to first determine what fraction of the data range the value represents. We then multiply that fraction by the height of the widget to determine how many pixels it should be from the bottom of the widget. Then, because pixel coordinates count *down* from the top, we have to subtract our offset from the height of the widget to determine the *y* coordinate.

Back in `paintEvent()`, let's use this method to draw a warning threshold line:

```
pen = qtg.QPen()
pen.setDashPattern([1, 0])
warn_y = self.val_to_y(self.warn_val)
pen.setColor(self.warn_color)
painter.setPen(pen)
painter.drawLine(0, warn_y, self.width(), warn_y)
```

Since we're drawing a line, we need to set the painter's `pen` property. The `QPen.setDashPattern()` method allows us to define a dash pattern for the line by passing it a list of `1` and `0` values, representing drawn or not-drawn pixels. In this case, our pattern will alternate between a drawn pixel and an empty pixel.

With the pen created, we use our new conversion method to convert our `warn_val` value to a *y* coordinate and set the color of the pen to `warn_color`. We hand the configured pen to our painter and instruct it to draw a line across the width of the widget at the *y* coordinate that we calculated.

The same approach can be used to draw our critical threshold line:

```
crit_y = self.val_to_y(self.crit_val)
pen.setColor(self.crit_color)
painter.setPen(pen)
painter.drawLine(0, crit_y, self.width(), crit_y)
```

We can reuse our QPen object, but remember that any time we make changes to a pen or brush, we have to reassign it to the painter. The painter is passed a copy of the pen or brush, so the changes that we make to the object *after* assigning it to a painter are not implicitly passed along to the pen or brush that is used.

In Chapter 6, *Styling Qt Applications*, you learned how to make a gradient object and apply it to a QBrush object. We'll want to use a gradient in this application to draw our data values so that high values are red at the top, medium values are yellow, and low values are green.

Let's define a QLinearGradient gradient object as follows:

```
gradient = qtg.QLinearGradient(
    qtc.QPointF(0, self.height()), qtc.QPointF(0, 0))
```

This gradient will go from the bottom of the widget (self.height()) to the top (0). This is important to remember because, as we define the color stops, a 0 location indicates the start of the gradient (which is at the bottom of the widget) and a 1 location will indicate the end of the gradient (which is at the top).

We'll set our color stops as follows:

```
gradient.setColorAt(0, self.good_color)
gradient.setColorAt(
    self.warn_val/(self.maximum - self.minimum),
    self.warn_color)
gradient.setColorAt(
    self.crit_val/(self.maximum - self.minimum),
    self.crit_color)
```

Similar to how we calculated the *y* coordinates, here, we're determining the fraction of the data range represented by the warning and critical values by dividing them by the difference between the minimum and maximum values. This fraction is what setColorAt() needs for its first argument.

Now that we have a gradient, let's set up our painter for drawing the data:

```
brush = qtg.QBrush(gradient)
painter.setBrush(brush)
painter.setPen(qtc.Qt.NoPen)
```

To make our area graph look smooth and cohesive, we don't want any outlines on the chart sections. To stop `QPainter` from outlining shapes, we're setting our pen to a special constant: `QtCore.Qt.NoPen`.

To create our area chart, each data point is going to be represented by a quadrilateral, where the upper-right corner will be the current data point and the upper left corner will be the previous data point. The width will be equal to the `scale` property we set in the constructor.

Since we're going to need a *previous* value for each data point, we need to start with a bit of bookkeeping:

```
self.start_value = getattr(self, 'start_value', self.minimum)
last_value = self.start_value
self.start_value = self.values[0]
```

The first thing we need to do is to determine a starting value. Since we need a value *before* our current value, our first item needs a place to start drawing. We're going to create an instance variable called `start_value`, which persists between calls to `paintEvent` and stores the value, to begin with. We then assign that to `last_value`, which is a local variable that will be used to remember the previous value for each iteration of the loop. Finally, we update the start value for the *next* call to `paintEvent` as the first value of the `deque` object.

Now, let's start looping through the data and calculating x and y values for each point:

```
for indx, value in enumerate(self.values):
    x = (indx + 1) * self.scale
    last_x = indx * self.scale
    y = self.val_to_y(value)
    last_y = self.val_to_y(last_value)
```

The two *x* coordinates for the polygon will be (1) the index of the value multiplied by the scale, and (2) the scale multiplied by the index of the value plus one. For the *y* values, we pass the current and last values to our conversion method. These four values will give us the ability to draw a four-sided shape representing a change from one point of data to the next.

To draw that shape, we're going to use something called a QPainterPath object. In digital graphics, a **path** is an object built from individual line segments or shapes combined together. The QPainterPath object allows us to create a unique shape by drawing each side individually in code.

Let's start drawing our path object using the x and y data we've calculated:

```
path = qtg.QPainterPath()
path.moveTo(x, self.height())
path.lineTo(last_x, self.height())
path.lineTo(last_x, last_y)
path.lineTo(x, y)
```

To draw a path, we begin by creating a QPainterPath object. We then use its moveTo() method to set a starting point for drawing. We then connect the four corners of the path using the lineTo() method to draw a straight line between the points. The last connection between our end and start points is made automatically.

Note that we're not actually drawing on the screen at this point; we're merely defining an object that our painter can paint to the screen using its current brush and pen.

Let's draw this object:

```
painter.drawPath(path)
last_value = value
```

We've finished out the method by painting the path and updating the last value to the current value. Of course, this path, which is made of straight lines, is rather dull—we could have just used the painter's drawPolygon() method for this. The real power of using a QPainterPath object is to take advantage of some of its non-linear drawing methods.

For example, if we want our chart to be smooth and rounded rather than jagged, then we can draw the last line (which is the top of the shape) using a **cubic Bezier curve** rather than a straight line:

```
#path.lineTo(x, y)
c_x = round(self.scale * .5) + last_x
c1 = (c_x, last_y)
c2 = (c_x, y)
path.cubicTo(*c1, *c2, x, y)
```

A cubic Bezier curve uses two control points to define its curve. Each control point *pulls* a segment of the line towards it—the first control point pulling the first half of the line, and the second control point pulling the second half of the line:

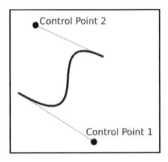

We're setting the first control point at the last *y* value and the second control point at the current *y* value—both of these are halfway between the start and end *x* values. This gives us an *S* curve on the upward slopes and a reverse *S* curve on the downward slopes, resulting in softer peaks and valleys.

After setting up the GraphWidget object in an application, you can try switching between the curve and line commands to see the difference.

Using GraphWidget

Our graph widget is finished, so let's head down to MainWindow and use it.

Start by creating your widget and making it the central widget:

```
self.graph = GraphWidget(self)
self.setCentralWidget(self.graph)
```

Next, let's create a method that will read the current CPU usage and send it to GraphWidget. To do this, we'll need to import the cpu_percent function from the psutil library:

```
from psutil import cpu_percent
```

Now we can write our graph-updating method as follows:

```
def update_graph(self):
    cpu_usage = cpu_percent()
    self.graph.add_value(cpu_usage)
```

The `cpu_percent()` function returns an integer from 0 to 100, reflecting the current CPU utilization on your computer. This is perfect for sending directly to our `GraphWidget`, whose default range is 0 to 100.

Now we just need to call this method periodically to update the graph; back in `MainWindow.__init__()`, add the following code:

```
self.timer = qtc.QTimer()
self.timer.setInterval(1000)
self.timer.timeout.connect(self.update_graph)
self.timer.start()
```

This is just a `QTimer` object, which you learned about in `Chapter 10`, *Multithreading with QTimer and QThread*, set to call `update_graph()` on a one-second interval.

If you run the application now, you should get something like this:

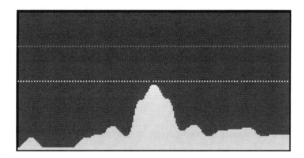

Notice the smooth peaks created by our Bezier curves. If you switch back to the straight-line code, you'll see those peaks sharpen up.

If your CPU is too powerful to provide an interesting activity graph, try the following changes to `update_graph()` for a better test of the widget:

```
def update_graph(self):
    import random
    cpu_usage = random.randint(1, 100)
    self.graph.add_value(cpu_usage)
```

This will just spit out random values between `1` and `100` and should make for some fairly chaotic results.

Seeing this CPU graph animated in real-time might make you wonder about the animation capabilities of Qt. In the next section, we'll learn how to create 2D animations in Qt using `QPainter` in conjunction with the Qt Graphics View framework.

Animating 2D graphics with QGraphicsScene

Painting on a `QPaintDevice` object works well for simple widgets and image editing, but in situations where we want to draw a large number of 2D objects, and possibly animate them in real-time, we need a more powerful object. Qt provides the Graphics View Framework, an item-based model-view framework for composing complex 2D graphics and animations.

To explore how this framework operates, we're going to create a game called **Tankity Tank Tank Tank**.

First steps

This tank game will be a two-player combat game modeled after the kind of simple action game you might find on a classic 1980s game system. One player will be at the top of the screen, one at the bottom, and the two tanks will move constantly from left to right while each player tries to shoot the other with a single bullet.

To get started, copy your Qt application template to a new file called `tankity_tank_tank_tank.py`. Starting just after the `import` statements at the top of the file, we'll add a few constants:

```
SCREEN_WIDTH = 800
SCREEN_HEIGHT = 600
BORDER_HEIGHT = 100
```

These constants will be used throughout the game code to calculate sizes and locations. In fact, we'll use two of them right away in `MainWindow.__init__()`:

```
self.resize(qtc.QSize(SCREEN_WIDTH, SCREEN_HEIGHT))
self.scene = Scene()
view = qtw.QGraphicsView(self.scene)
self.setCentralWidget(view)
```

This is all the code we're going to add into `MainWindow`. After resizing the window to our width and height constants, we'll create two objects, as follows:

- The first is a `Scene` object. This is a custom class we're going to create, subclassed from `QGraphicsScene`. `QGraphicsScene` is the model in this model-view framework and represents a 2D scene containing a variety of graphics items.
- The second is the `QGraphicsView` object, which is the view component of the framework. This widget's job is simply to render the scene and display it for the user.

Our `Scene` object is going to contain most of the code for the game, so we will build that part next.

Making a scene

The `Scene` class will be the main stage for our game and will manage all the various objects involved in the game, such as the tanks, bullets, and walls. It will also display the scores and keep track of other game logic.

Let's start it as follows:

```
class Scene(qtw.QGraphicsScene):

    def __init__(self):
        super().__init__()
        self.setBackgroundBrush(qtg.QBrush(qtg.QColor('black')))
        self.setSceneRect(0, 0, SCREEN_WIDTH, SCREEN_HEIGHT)
```

The first thing we've done here is to paint our scene black by setting the `backgroundBrush` property. This property, naturally, takes a `QBrush` object, which it will use to fill the background of the scene. We've also set the `sceneRect` property, which describes the size of the scene, to a `QRect` object set to our width and height constants.

To begin placing objects on the scene, we can use one of its many add methods:

```
wall_brush = qtg.QBrush(qtg.QColor('blue'), qtc.Qt.Dense5Pattern)
floor = self.addRect(
    qtc.QRectF(0, SCREEN_HEIGHT - BORDER_HEIGHT,
               SCREEN_WIDTH, BORDER_HEIGHT),
    brush=wall_brush)
ceiling = self.addRect(
    qtc.QRectF(0, 0, SCREEN_WIDTH, BORDER_HEIGHT),
    brush=wall_brush)
```

Here, we've used `addRect()` to draw two rectangles on the scene—one across the bottom for a floor and one across the top for a ceiling. Just like the `QPainter` class, `QGraphicsScene` has methods to add ellipses, pixmaps, lines, polygons, text, and other such items. Unlike the painter, however, the `QGraphicsScene` methods don't just draw pixels to the screen; instead, they create items of the `QGraphicsItem` class (or a subclass). We can subsequently query or manipulate the items created.

For example, we can add some text items to display our scores as follows:

```
self.top_score = 0
self.bottom_score = 0
score_font = qtg.QFont('Sans', 32)
self.top_score_display = self.addText(
    str(self.top_score), score_font)
self.top_score_display.setPos(10, 10)
self.bottom_score_display = self.addText(
    str(self.bottom_score), score_font)
self.bottom_score_display.setPos(
    SCREEN_WIDTH - 60, SCREEN_HEIGHT - 60)
```

Here, after creating the text items, we are manipulating their properties and setting the position of each text item using the `setPos()` method.

We can also update the text in the items; for example, let's create methods to update our scores:

```
def top_score_increment(self):
    self.top_score += 1
    self.top_score_display.setPlainText(str(self.top_score))

def bottom_score_increment(self):
    self.bottom_score += 1
    self.bottom_score_display.setPlainText(str(self.bottom_score))
```

If you think about `QPainter` as being analogous to painting on paper, adding `QGraphicsItems` to a `QGraphicsScene` class is analogous to placing felt shapes on a flannel-graph. The items are *on* the scene, but they not part of it and, subsequently, they can be altered or removed.

Creating the tanks

Our game will have two tanks, one at the top of the screen and one at the bottom. These will be drawn on the `Scene` object and be animated so that the players can move them left and right. In *Chapter 6, Styling Qt Applications,* you learned that animation can be done using `QPropertyAnimation`, but *only* if the property being animated belongs to a descendant of `QObject`. `QGraphicsItem` is *not* a `QObject` descendant, but the `QGraphicsObject` object combines both to provide us with a graphics item that we can animate.

Therefore, we'll need to build our `Tank` class as a subclass of `QGraphicsObject`:

```
class Tank(qtw.QGraphicsObject):

    BOTTOM, TOP = 0, 1
    TANK_BM = b'\x18\x18\xFF\xFF\xFF\xFF\xFF\x66'
```

This class begins by defining two constants, `TOP`, and `BOTTOM`. These will be used to signify whether we're creating the tank at the top of the screen or the bottom.

`TANK_BM` is a `bytes` object that contains data for an 8 × 8 bitmap of a tank graphic. We'll see how this works shortly.

First, though, let's begin the constructor:

```
    def __init__(self, color, y_pos, side=TOP):
        super().__init__()
        self.side = side
```

Our tank will be given a color, a *y* coordinate, and a `side` value, which will be either `TOP` or `BOTTOM`. We'll use this information to position and orient the tank.

Next, let's use our `bytes` string to create a bitmap for our tank:

```
        self.bitmap = qtg.QBitmap.fromData(
            qtc.QSize(8, 8), self.TANK_BM)
```

A `QBitmap` object is a special case of `QPixmap` for monochromatic images. By passing a size and `bytes` object to the `fromData()` static method, we can generate a simple bitmap object without needing a separate image file.

To understand how this works, consider the `TANK_BM` string. Because we're interpreting it as an 8 × 8 graphic, each byte (which is 8 bits) in this string corresponds to one row of the graphic.

If you were to convert each row to binary numbers and lay them out one byte per line, it would look like this:

```
00011000
00011000
11111111
11111111
11111111
11111111
11111111
01100110
```

The shape created by the ones is essentially the shape that this bitmap will take. Of course, an 8x8 graphic will be quite small, so we ought to enlarge it. Additionally, this tank is clearly pointing up, so if we're the top tank, we need to flip it over.

We can do both of those things using a QTransform object:

```
transform = qtg.QTransform()
transform.scale(4, 4)   # scale to 32x32
if self.side == self.TOP:   # We're pointing down
    transform.rotate(180)
self.bitmap = self.bitmap.transformed(transform)
```

A QTransform object represents a set of transformations to be done on QPixmap or QBitmap. After creating the transform object, we can set the various transformations to be applied, starting with a scaling operation and adding a rotate transformation if the tank is on the top. The QTransform object can be passed to a bitmap transformed() method, which returns a new QBitmap object with the transformations applied.

The bitmap is monochromatic and, by default, it draws in black. To draw in another color, we will need a QPen (not a brush!) object set to the desired color. Let's use our color argument to create this as follows:

```
self.pen = qtg.QPen(qtg.QColor(color))
```

The actual appearance of the QGraphicsObject object is determined by overriding the paint() method. Let's create this as follows:

```
def paint(self, painter, option, widget):
    painter.setPen(self.pen)
    painter.drawPixmap(0, 0, self.bitmap)
```

The first argument to `paint()` is the `QPainter` object, which Qt has created and assigned to paint the object. We simply need to apply commands to that painter, which will draw the image as we desire. We'll start by setting the `pen` property to the pen we've created, and then use the painter's `drawPixmap()` method to draw our bitmap.

Note that the coordinates we pass to `drawPixmap()` do not refer to coordinates of the `QGraphicsScene` class, but coordinates within the bounding rectangle of the `QGraphicsObject` object itself. Because of that, we need to make sure that our object returns a proper bounding rectangle so that our image is drawn correctly.

To do this, we'll need to override the `boundingRect()` method:

```
def boundingRect(self):
    return qtc.QRectF(0, 0, self.bitmap.width(),
                      self.bitmap.height())
```

In this case, we want our `boundingRect()` method to return a rectangle that is the same size as the bitmap.

Back in `Tank.__init__()`, let's position our tank:

```
if self.side == self.BOTTOM:
    y_pos -= self.bitmap.height()
self.setPos(0, y_pos)
```

The `QGraphicsObject.setPos()` method allows you to position the object anywhere on its assigned `QGraphicsScene` using pixel coordinates. Since pixel coordinates always count from the top-left of the object, we need to adjust the *y* coordinate of our object if it is on the bottom of the screen, raising it by its own height so that the *bottom* of the tank is at `y_pos` pixels from the top.

 The position of an object always indicates the position of its upper-left corner.

Now we want to animate our tanks; each tank will move back and forth along the *x* axis, bouncing back when it hits the edge of the screen.

Let's create a `QPropertyAnimation` method to do this:

```
self.animation = qtc.QPropertyAnimation(self, b'x')
self.animation.setStartValue(0)
self.animation.setEndValue(SCREEN_WIDTH - self.bitmap.width())
self.animation.setDuration(2000)
```

The QGraphicsObject object has x and y properties that define its *x* and *y* coordinates on the scene, so animating the object is as simple as directing our property animation to these properties. We're going to animate x starting at 0 and ending at the width of the screen; however, to keep our tanks from going off the edge, we need to subtract the width of the bitmap from the value. Finally, we set duration of two seconds.

A property animation can be run forward or backward. So, to enable the left and right movement, we simply need to toggle the direction in which the animation runs. Let's create some methods to do this:

```python
def toggle_direction(self):
    if self.animation.direction() == qtc.QPropertyAnimation.Forward:
        self.left()
    else:
        self.right()

def right(self):
    self.animation.setDirection(qtc.QPropertyAnimation.Forward)
    self.animation.start()

def left(self):
    self.animation.setDirection(qtc.QPropertyAnimation.Backward)
    self.animation.start()
```

Switching directions is just a matter of setting the animation object's direction property to Forward or Backward, and then calling start() to apply it.

Back in __init__(), let's use the toggle_direction() method to create the *bounce*:

```python
self.animation.finished.connect(self.toggle_direction)
```

To make the game more interesting, we should also start our tanks on opposite ends of the screen:

```python
if self.side == self.TOP:
    self.toggle_direction()
self.animation.start()
```

After setting up the animation, we start it by calling start(). This takes care of the tank animation; now it's time to load our weapons.

Creating the bullets

In this game, each tank will only be allowed one bullet on the screen at a time. This simplifies our game code, but also keeps the game relatively challenging.

To implement these bullets, we'll create another QGraphicsObject object called Bullet, which is animated to move along the *y* axis.

Let's start our Bullet class as follows:

```
class Bullet(qtw.QGraphicsObject):

    hit = qtc.pyqtSignal()

    def __init__(self, y_pos, up=True):
        super().__init__()
        self.up = up
        self.y_pos = y_pos
```

The bullet class starts by defining a hit signal indicating that it has hit an enemy tank. The constructor takes a y_pos argument to define the starting point of the bullet, and a Boolean indicating whether the bullet is to travel up or down. These arguments are saved as instance variables.

Next, let's define the bullet's look as follows:

```
    def boundingRect(self):
        return qtc.QRectF(0, 0, 10, 10)

    def paint(self, painter, options, widget):
        painter.setBrush(qtg.QBrush(qtg.QColor('yellow')))
        painter.drawRect(0, 0, 10, 10)
```

Our bullet will simply be a 10 × 10 yellow square created using the painter's drawRect() method. This is appropriate for a retro game but, just for fun, let's make it a bit more interesting. To do this, we can apply something called a QGraphicsEffect class to the QGraphicsObject. The QGraphicsEffect class can apply a visual effect to the object in real-time. We implement this by creating an instance of one of the QGraphicEffect class's subclasses and assigning it to the bullet's graphicsEffect property, as follows:

```
        blur = qtw.QGraphicsBlurEffect()
        blur.setBlurRadius(10)
        blur.setBlurHints(
            qtw.QGraphicsBlurEffect.AnimationHint)
        self.setGraphicsEffect(blur)
```

This code added to `Bullet.__init__()`, creates a blur effect and applies it to our `QGraphicsObject` class. Note that this is applied at the object level, and not at the painting level, so it is applied to any pixels we draw. We've adjusted the blur radius to 10 pixels and added the `AnimationHint` object, which tells us the effect that is being applied to an animated object and activates certain performance optimizations.

Speaking of animation, let's create the bullet's animation as follows:

```
self.animation = qtc.QPropertyAnimation(self, b'y')
self.animation.setStartValue(y_pos)
end = 0 if up else SCREEN_HEIGHT
self.animation.setEndValue(end)
self.animation.setDuration(1000)
```

The animation is configured so that it takes the bullet one second to go from its current `y_pos` argument to either the top or bottom of the screen, depending on whether the bullet is to shoot up or down. We aren't starting the animation yet, though, because we don't want the bullet to start moving until it's shot.

Shooting will happen in a `shoot()` method, as follows:

```
def shoot(self, x_pos):
    self.animation.stop()
    self.setPos(x_pos, self.y_pos)
    self.animation.start()
```

When a player shoots a bullet, we first stop any animation that might be happening. Since only one bullet is allowed at a time, rapid-firing will just result in the bullet starting over (while this is not terribly realistic, it makes gameplay more challenging).

Then, the bullet is repositioned to the *x* coordinate and passed into the `shoot()` method and the tank's *y* coordinate. Finally, the animation is started. The idea is that we'll pass in the tank's current *x* coordinate when the player shoots and the bullet will fly up or down from that position in a straight line.

Let's go back to our `Tank` class and add a `Bullet` object. In `Tank.__init__()`, add in the following code:

```
bullet_y = (
    y_pos - self.bitmap.height()
    if self.side == self.BOTTOM
    else y_pos + self.bitmap.height()
)
self.bullet = Bullet(bullet_y, self.side == self.BOTTOM)
```

So that we don't hit our own tank with our own bullet, we want the bullet to start at a position just above the bottom tank or just below the top tank, which is what we've calculated in the first statement. Since our tanks don't move up or down, this position is a constant, and we can pass it to the bullet's constructor.

To make the tank shoot the bullet, we'll create a method in the Tank class called shoot():

```
def shoot(self):
    if not self.bullet.scene():
        self.scene().addItem(self.bullet)
    self.bullet.shoot(self.x())
```

The first thing we need to do is to add the bullet to the scene if it's not yet added (or if it's been removed). We can determine this by checking the bullet's scene property, which returns None if the object is not on the scene.

Then, we call the bullet's shoot() method by passing in the tank's *x* coordinate.

Collision detection

Bullets don't do much good if nothing happens when they hit the target. To make something happen when a bullet hits a tank, we need to implement **collision detection**. We will implement this in the Bullet class by asking it to check whether it has hit anything whenever it moves.

Start by creating a method in Bullet called check_colllision():

```
def check_collision(self):
    colliding_items = self.collidingItems()
    if colliding_items:
        self.scene().removeItem(self)
        for item in colliding_items:
            if type(item).__name__ == 'Tank':
                self.hit.emit()
```

QGraphicsObject.collidingItems() returns a list of any QGraphicsItem objects whose bounding rectangles overlap with this item. This includes not only our Tank objects, but also the floor and ceiling items we created in the Scene class, or even the other tank's Bullet object. If our bullet touches any of these items, we need to remove it from the scene; to do this, we call self.scene().removeItem(self) to eliminate the bullet.

Then, we need to check whether any of the items we've collided with are `Tank` objects. This we do by simply checking the type and name of the object hit. If we hit a tank, we emit our `hit` signal. (We can safely assume it's the other tank because of the way our bullets move.)

This method needs to be called every time the `Bullet` object moves, since every movement could result in a collision. Fortunately, the `QGraphicsObject` method has a `yChanged` signal, which is emitted every time its *y* coordinate changes.

So, back in the `Bullet.__init__()` method, we can add a connection, as follows:

```
self.yChanged.connect(self.check_collision)
```

Our tank and bullet objects are now ready, so let's head back to the `Scene` object to finish out our game.

Finishing the game

Back in `Scene.__init__()`, let's create our two tanks:

```
self.bottom_tank = Tank(
    'red', floor.rect().top(), Tank.BOTTOM)
self.addItem(self.bottom_tank)

self.top_tank = Tank(
    'green', ceiling.rect().bottom(), Tank.TOP)
self.addItem(self.top_tank)
```

The bottom tank sits on top of the floor, and the top tank is positioned on the bottom of the ceiling. Now we can connect the `hit` signals of their bullets to the proper score-incrementing methods:

```
self.top_tank.bullet.hit.connect(self.top_score_increment)
self.bottom_tank.bullet.hit.connect(self.bottom_score_increment)
```

At this point, our game is almost done:

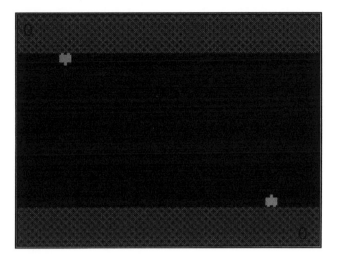

Of course, there is one very important aspect still missing—the controls!

Our tanks will be controlled by the keyboard; we'll assign the bottom player the arrow keys for movement and the return key for firing, while the top player will get *A* and *D* for movement and the spacebar for firing.

To handle keystrokes, we need to override the Scene object's keyPressEvent() method:

```
def keyPressEvent(self, event):
    keymap = {
        qtc.Qt.Key_Right: self.bottom_tank.right,
        qtc.Qt.Key_Left: self.bottom_tank.left,
        qtc.Qt.Key_Return: self.bottom_tank.shoot,
        qtc.Qt.Key_A: self.top_tank.left,
        qtc.Qt.Key_D: self.top_tank.right,
        qtc.Qt.Key_Space: self.top_tank.shoot
    }
    callback = keymap.get(event.key())
    if callback:
        callback()
```

`keyPressEvent()` is called whenever the user presses a key while the `Scene` object is focused. It's the only argument that is a `QKeyEvent` object whose `key()` method returns a constant from the `QtCore.Qt.Key` enum telling us what key was pressed. In this method, we've created a `dict` object that maps certain key constants to methods on our tank objects. Whenever we receive a keystroke, we attempt to fetch a callback method, and if we're successful, we call the method.

The game is now ready to play! Grab a friend (preferably someone you don't mind sharing a keyboard with) and fire it up.

Summary

In this chapter, you learned all about working with 2D graphics in PyQt. We learned how to use the `QPainter` object to edit images and create custom widgets. You then learned how to use a `QGraphicsScene` method in conjunction with the `QGraphicsObject` class to create animated scenes that can be controlled using automated logic or user input.

In the next chapter, we'll add an additional dimension to our graphics as we explore the use of OpenGL 3D graphics with PyQt. You'll learn some of the basics of OpenGL programming and how it can be integrated into a PyQt application.

Questions

Try these questions to test your knowledge from this chapter:

1. Add code to this method to write your name in blue on the bottom of the picture:

```
def create_headshot(self, image_file, name):
    image = qtg.QImage()
    image.load(image_file)
    # your code here

    # end of your code
    return image
```

2. Given a `QPainter` object called `painter`, write a line of code to paint an 80 × 80 pixel octagon in the upper-left corner of the painter's paint device. You can refer to the documentation at `https://doc.qt.io/qt-5/qpainter.html#drawPolygon` for guidance.

3. You're creating a custom widget and can't figure out why the text is showing up in black. The following is your `paintEvent()` method; see whether you can figure out the problem:

```
def paintEvent(self, event):
    black_brush = qtg.QBrush(qtg.QColor('black'))
    white_brush = qtg.QBrush(qtg.QColor('white'))
    painter = qtg.QPainter()
    painter.setBrush(black_brush)
    painter.drawRect(0, 0, self.width(), self.height())
    painter.setBrush(white_brush)
    painter.drawText(0, 0, 'Test Text')
```

4. A deep-fried meme is a style of a meme that uses extreme compression, saturation, and other processing to make the meme image look intentionally low quality. Add a feature to your meme generator to optionally make the meme deep-fried. Some things you can try include reducing the color bit depth and adjusting the hue and saturation of the colors in the image.

5. You'd like to animate a circle moving horizontally across the screen. Change the following code to animate the circle:

```
scene = QGraphicsScene()
scene.setSceneRect(0, 0, 800, 600)
circle = scene.addEllipse(0, 0, 10, 10)
animation = QPropertyAnimation(circle, b'x')
animation.setStartValue(0)
animation.setEndValue(600)
animation.setDuration(5000)
animation.start()
```

6. The following code attempts to set up a `QPainter` object with a gradient brush. Discover what is wrong with it:

```
gradient = qtg.QLinearGradient(
    qtc.QPointF(0, 100), qtc.QPointF(0, 0))
gradient.setColorAt(20, qtg.QColor('red'))
gradient.setColorAt(40, qtg.QColor('orange'))
gradient.setColorAt(60, qtg.QColor('green'))
painter = QPainter()
painter.setGradient(gradient)
```

7. See whether you can implement some of the following improvements to the game we created:

- Pulsating bullets
- Explosions when a tank is hit
- Sounds (see `Chapter 7`, *Working with Audio-Visual Using QtMultimedia*, for guidance)
- Background animation
- Multiple bullets

Further reading

For further information, please refer the following:

- An in-depth discussion of `QPainter` and Qt's paint system can be found at `https://doc.qt.io/qt-5/paintsystem.html`
- An overview of the Qt Graphics View framework can be found at `https://doc.qt.io/qt-5/graphicsview.html`
- An overview of the animation framework can be found at `https://doc.qt.io/qt-5/animation-overview.html`

Creating 3D Graphics with QtOpenGL

13

From games to data visualizations to engineering simulations, 3D graphics and animations are at the heart of many important software applications. For several decades, the de facto standard **Application Programming Interface (API)**
for cross-platform 3D graphics has been OpenGL. Although many Python and C implementations of the API exist, Qt offers one that is directly integrated into its widgets, giving us the capability to embed interactive OpenGL graphics and animations in our GUI.

In this chapter, we'll take a look at those capabilities in the following topics:

- The basics of OpenGL
- Embedding OpenGL drawings with `QOpenGLWidget`
- Animating and controlling OpenGL drawings

Technical requirements

For this chapter, you'll need a basic Python 3 and PyQt5 setup, as we've been using throughout the book, and you might like to download the example code from `https://github.com/PacktPublishing/Mastering-GUI-Programming-with-Python/tree/master/Chapter13`. You will also need to make sure that your graphics hardware and drivers support OpenGL 2.0 or higher, although this is almost certainly true if you are using a conventional desktop or laptop computer made within the last ten years.

Check out the following video to see the code in action: `http://bit.ly/2M5xApP`

The basics of OpenGL

OpenGL is not simply a library; it is a **specification** for an API to interact with your graphics hardware. The implementation of this specification is shared between your graphics hardware, the drivers for that hardware, and the OpenGL software library you choose to use. As a result, the exact behavior of your OpenGL-based code might be slightly different depending on any of those factors, just as, for example, the same HTML code might be slightly differently rendered in different web browsers.

OpenGL is also a **versioned** specification, meaning that the available features and recommended usage of OpenGL changes depending on which version of the specification you're targeting. As new features are introduced and old features deprecated, the best practices and recommendations also evolve, so that code written for OpenGL 2.x systems may look nothing at all like a code written for OpenGL 4.x.

The OpenGL specification is managed by the Khronos Group, an industry consortium that maintains several graphics-related standards. The latest specification at the time of writing is 4.6, released in February 2019, which can be found at `https://www.khronos.org/registry/OpenGL/index_gl.php`. However, it's not always a good idea to follow the latest specification. A computer's ability to run an OpenGL code of a given version is limited by hardware, driver, and platform considerations, so if you want your code to be run by the widest possible array of users, it's better to target an older and more established version. Many common embedded graphics chips from Intel only support OpenGL 3.x or lower, and some low-end devices, such as the Raspberry Pi (which we'll look at in `Chapter 15,` *PyQt on the Raspberry Pi*) only support 2.x.

In this chapter, we'll limit our code to OpenGL 2.1, since it is well supported by PyQt and most modern computers should be able to run it. However, since we're going to be sticking to the basics, everything we'll learn applies equally well to the 4.x version.

The rendering pipeline and drawing basics

Turning code and data into pixels on a screen requires a multi-stage process; in OpenGL, this process is known as the **rendering pipeline.** Some stages in this pipeline are programmable, while others are fixed-function, meaning that their behavior is predetermined by the OpenGL implementation and cannot be altered.

Let's walk through the major stages of this pipeline from start to finish:

1. **Vertex specification**: In the first stage, the **vertices** of the drawing are determined by your application. A **vertex** is essentially a point in a 3D space that can be used to draw a shape. The vertex may also contain metadata about the point, such as its color.

2. **Vertex processing**: This user-definable stage processes each vertex in various ways to calculate the final position of each vertex; for example, in this step you might rotate or move the basic shape defined in the vertex specification.

3. **Vertex post-processing**: This fixed-function stage does some additional processing on the vertices, such as clipping sections that fall outside the viewing space.

4. **Primitive assembly**: In this stage, vertices are composed into primitives. A primitive is a 2D shape, such as a triangle or rectangle, from which more complex 3D shapes are built.

5. **Rasterization**: This stage transforms the primitives into a series of individual pixel points, called fragments, by interpolating between the vertices.

6. **Fragment shading**: The main job of this user-defined stage is to determine the depth and color value for each fragment.

7. **Per-sample operations**: This final stage performs a series of tests on each fragment to determine its final visibility and color.

As programmers using OpenGL, we are mostly concerned with just three stages of this operation – the vertex specification, the vertex processing, and the fragment shading. For the vertex specification, we will simply define some points in Python code to describe a shape for OpenGL to draw; for the other two stages, we will need to learn about creating OpenGL programs and shaders.

Programs and shaders

Despite the name, a **shader** has nothing to do with shadows or shading; it is simply the name for a unit of code that runs on your GPU. In the previous section, we talked about some stages of the rendering pipeline being user-definable; in fact, some of them *must* be defined, as most OpenGL implementations do not provide default behavior for certain stages. To define those stages, we need to write a shader.

At a minimum, we need to define two shaders:

- **The vertex shader:** This shader is the first step of the vertex processing stage. Its main job is to determine the spatial coordinates of each vertex.
- **The fragment shader:** This is the second-to-last stage of the pipeline, and its only required job is to determine the color of an individual fragment.

When we have a collection of shaders that comprise a complete render pipeline, this is called a program.

Shaders cannot be written in Python. They must be written in a language called **GL Shader Language (GLSL)**, a C-like language that is part of the OpenGL specification. It's impossible to create serious OpenGL drawings without some knowledge of GLSL, but fortunately, it is simple enough to write a fairly rudimentary set of shaders good enough for a basic example.

A simple vertex shader

We're going to compose a simple GLSL vertex shader that we can use for our demo; create a file called `vertex_shader.glsl`, and copy in the following code:

```
#version 120
```

We've begun with a comment indicating the version of GLSL we are using. This is important, as each version of OpenGL is only compatible with a particular version of GLSL, and the GLSL compiler will use this comment to check whether we've mismatched those versions.

 A chart showing compatibility between versions of GLSL and OpenGL can be found at `https://www.khronos.org/opengl/wiki/Core_Language_ (GLSL)`.

Next, we will need to make some **variable declarations**:

```
attribute highp vec4 vertex;
uniform highp mat4 matrix;
attribute lowp vec4 color_attr;
varying lowp vec4 color;
```

In C-like languages, variable declarations are used to create the variable, define various attributes about it, and allocate space for it in memory. Each of our declarations has four tokens; let's go through these in order:

- The first token is one of `attribute`, `uniform`, or `varying`. This indicates whether the variable will be distinct for each vertex (`attribute`), each primitive (`uniform`), or each fragment (`varying`). So, our first variable will be different for each vertex, but our second one will be the same for each vertex within the same primitive.
- The second token indicates the basic data type that the variable contains. In this case, it's either `highp` (a high-precision number), `mediump` (a medium-precision number), or `lowp` (a low-precision number). We could have used `float` or `double` here, but these aliases are helpful in making our code cross-platform.
- The third term defines each of these variables as pointing to either a **vector** or a matrix. You can think of a vector like a Python `list` object, and a matrix like a `list` object where each item is a `list` object of the same length. The number at the end indicates the size, so `vec4` is a list of four values, and `mat4` is a 4x4 matrix of values.
- The last token is the variable name. These names will be used through the entire program so we can use them in shaders further down the pipeline to access data from earlier shaders.

These variables can be used to insert data into the program or pass data to other shaders in the program. We'll see how to do that later in this chapter, but for now, understand that, in our shader, `vertex`, `matrix`, and `color_attr` represent data that will be received by the vertex shader from our PyQt application.

After the variable declarations, we will create a function called `main()`:

```
void main(void)
{
  gl_Position = matrix * vertex;
  color = color_attr;
}
```

The primary purpose of the `vertex` shader is to set a variable called `gl_Position` with the coordinates of the `vertex`. In this case, we're setting it to our `vertex` value passed into the shader multiplied by the `matrix` value. As you'll see later, this arrangement will allow us to manipulate our drawing in space.

Matrices and vectors are critical mathematical concepts to understand when creating 3D graphics. While we will remain mostly abstracted from the details of this math in this chapter, it's a good idea to brush up on these concepts if you want to dive deeper into OpenGL programming.

The last line of code in our shader may seem somewhat pointless, but it allows us to specify a color for each vertex in the vertex specification stage and have that color passed along to other shaders later in the pipeline. Variables in a shader are either input or output variables, meaning that they expect to receive data from the previous stage of the pipeline or pass data along to the next stages. Within the vertex shader, declaring a variable with the attribute or uniform qualifiers implicitly marks a variable as an input variable, while declaring it with the varying qualifier implicitly marks it as an output variable. Thus, we are copying the value of our attribute-type color_attr variable to the varying-type color variable in order to pass the value to shaders further down the pipeline; specifically, we want to pass it to the fragment shader.

A simple fragment shader

The second shader we need to create is the fragment shader. Remember that this shader's primary job is to determine the color of each point (or *fragment*) on a primitive.

Create a new file called fragment_shader.glsl and add in this code:

```
#version 120

varying lowp vec4 color;

void main(void)
{
  gl_FragColor = color;
}
```

Just as with our vertex shader, we begin with a comment specifying the version of GLSL we're targeting. Then, we will declare a variable called color.

Because this is the fragment shader, specifying a variable as varying makes it an input variable. Using the name color, which was an output variable from our shader, means that we will receive from that shader the color value it assigned.

Within main(), we then assign that color to the built-in gl_FragColor variable. What this shader effectively does is tell OpenGL to use the color value passed in with the vertex shader to determine the color of an individual fragment.

This is about as simple a `fragment` shader as we can get. A more complex `fragment` shader, such as one that you would find in a game or simulation, might implement textures, lighting effects, or other color manipulations; but this one should suffice for our purposes.

Now that we have our required shaders, we can create a PyQt application to use them.

Embedding OpenGL drawings with QOpenGLWidget

To see how OpenGL works with PyQt, we're going to use our shaders to make a simple OpenGL image, which we will be able to control through a PyQt interface. Create a copy of your Qt application template from `Chapter 4`, *Building Applications with QMainWindow*, and call it `wedge_animation.py`. Put this in the same directory as your `shader` files.

Then, start by adding this code in `MainWindow.__init__()`:

```
self.resize(800, 600)
main = qtw.QWidget()
self.setCentralWidget(main)
main.setLayout(qtw.QVBoxLayout())
oglw = GlWidget()
main.layout().addWidget(oglw)
```

This code creates our central widget and adds a `GlWidget` object to it. The `GlWidget` class is what we'll be creating to display our OpenGL drawing. To create it, we'll need to subclass a widget that can display OpenGL content.

First steps with OpenGLWidget

There are two Qt classes that we can use to display OpenGL content: `QtWidgets.QOpenGLWidget` and `QtGui.QOpenGLWindow`. In practice, they behave almost exactly the same, but `OpenGLWindow` offers slightly better performance and may be a better choice if you don't want to use any other Qt widgets (that is, if your application is just full-screen OpenGL content). In our case, we're going to be combining our OpenGL drawing with other widgets, so we'll use `QOpenGLWidget` as the base for our class:

```
class GlWidget(qtw.QOpenGLWidget):
    """A widget to display our OpenGL drawing"""
```

To create OpenGL content on our widget, we need to override two `QOpenGLWidget` methods:

- `initializeGL()`, which is run once to set up our OpenGL drawing
- `paintGL()`, which is called whenever our widget needs to paint itself (for example, in response to an `update()` call)

We'll start with `initializeGL()`:

```
def initializeGL(self):
    super().initializeGL()
    gl_context = self.context()
    version = qtg.QOpenGLVersionProfile()
    version.setVersion(2, 1)
    self.gl = gl_context.versionFunctions(version)
```

The first thing that we need to do is get access to our OpenGL API. The API is made up of a set of functions, variables, and constants; in an object-oriented platform, such as PyQt, we will be creating a special OpenGL functions object that contains those functions as methods and the variables and constants as properties.

To do this, we first retrieve an OpenGL **context** from the `QOpenGLWidget` method. The context represents our interface to the OpenGL surface on which we're currently drawing. From the context, we can retrieve the object that contains our API.

Because we need access to a specific version of the API (2.1), we will first need to create a `QOpenGLVersionProfile` object with its `version` property set to `(2, 1)`. This can be passed to the context's `versionFunctions()` method, which will return a `QOpenGLFunctions_2_1` object. This is the object that contains our OpenGL 2.1 API.

 Qt defines OpenGL function objects for other versions of OpenGL as well, but be aware that, depending on your platform, your hardware, and how you acquired Qt, a particular version may or may not be supported.

We're saving the `functions` object as `self.gl`; all of our API calls will be done on this object.

Now that we have access to the API, let's start configuring OpenGL:

```
self.gl.glEnable(self.gl.GL_DEPTH_TEST)
self.gl.glDepthFunc(self.gl.GL_LESS)
self.gl.glEnable(self.gl.GL_CULL_FACE)
```

Much like Qt, OpenGL uses defined constants to represent various settings and states. Configuring OpenGL is mostly a matter of passing these constants to various API functions that toggle various settings.

In this case, we're performing three settings:

- Passing `GL_DEPTH_TEST` to `glEnable()` activates **depth testing,** which means that OpenGL will try to figure out which of the points its drawings are in the foreground and which are in the background.
- `glDepthFunc()` sets the function that will determine whether or not a depth-tested pixel will be drawn. In this case, the `GL_LESS` constant indicates that the pixel with the lowest depth (that is, the one closest to us) will be drawn. Generally, this is the setting you want, and it's also the default setting.
- Passing `GL_CULL_FACE` to `glEnable()` activates **face culling**. This simply means that OpenGL will not bother drawing the sides of the object that the viewer can't actually see. It makes sense to enable this as well, as it saves on resources that would otherwise be wasted.

These three optimizations should help to reduce the resources used by our animation; in most cases, you'll want to use them. There are many more options that can be enabled and configured; for a complete list, see `https://www.khronos.org/registry/OpenGL-Refpages/gl2.1/xhtml/glEnable.xml`. Be aware that some options only apply to the older fixed-function method of using OpenGL.

> If you see OpenGL code that uses `glBegin()` and `glEnd()`, it is using the very old OpenGL 1.x fixed-function drawing API. This approach was easier, but much more limited, so this shouldn't be used for modern OpenGL programming.

Creating a program

Our next step in implementing an OpenGL drawing is to create our program. You may remember that an OpenGL program is a collection of shaders that form a complete pipeline.

In Qt, the process to create a program is as follows:

1. Create a `QOpenGLShaderProgram` object
2. Add your shader code to the program
3. Link the code into a complete program

The following code will implement this:

```
self.program = qtg.QOpenGLShaderProgram()
self.program.addShaderFromSourceFile(
    qtg.QOpenGLShader.Vertex, 'vertex_shader.glsl')
self.program.addShaderFromSourceFile(
    qtg.QOpenGLShader.Fragment, 'fragment_shader.glsl')
self.program.link()
```

Shaders can be added from files, as we've done here using `addShaderFromSourceFile()`, or from strings using `addShaderFromSourceCode()`. We're using relative file paths here, but the best approach would be to use Qt resource files (see the *Using Qt Resource Files* section in `Chapter 6`, *Styling Qt Applications*). As the files are added, Qt compiles the shader code and outputs any compilation errors to the Terminal.

 In the production code, you'll want to check the Boolean output of `addShaderFromSourceFile()` to see whether your shader compiled successfully before proceeding.

Note that the first argument to `addShaderFromSourceFile()` specifies what kind of shader we're adding. This is important, as vertex shaders and fragment shaders have very different requirements and functionality.

Once all the shaders are loaded, we call `link()` to link all the compiled code into a ready-to-execute program.

Accessing our variables

Our shader programs contained some variables that we need to be able to access and put values into, so we need to retrieve a handle for those variables. The `QOpenGLProgram` object has two methods, `attributeLocation()` and `uniformLocation()`, which can be used to retrieve a handle for attribute and uniform variables, respectively (there is no such function for the `varying` types).

Let's grab some handles for our `vertex` shader variables:

```
self.vertex_location = self.program.attributeLocation('vertex')
self.matrix_location = self.program.uniformLocation('matrix')
self.color_location = self.program.attributeLocation('color_attr')
```

The values returned from these methods are actually just integers; internally, OpenGL just uses sequential integers to track and reference objects. However, that doesn't matter to us. We can treat this as if they were object handles and pass them into OpenGL calls to access these variables, as you'll see soon.

Configuring a projection matrix

In OpenGL, the **projection matrix** defines how our 3D model is projected to a 2D screen. This is represented by a 4x4 matrix of numbers that can be used to calculate vertex positions. Before we can do any drawing, we need to define this matrix.

In Qt, we can use the QMatrix4x4 object to represent it:

```
self.view_matrix = qtg.QMatrix4x4()
```

A QMatrix4x4 object is very simply a table of numbers arranged in four rows and four columns. However, it has several methods that allow us to manipulate those numbers in such a way that they represent 3D transformations, such as our projection.

OpenGL can use two kinds of projections—**orthographic**, meaning that points at all depths are rendered the same, or **perspective**, meaning that the field of view expands as we move away from the viewer. For realistic 3D drawings, you'll want to use perspective projection. This kind of projection is represented by a **frustum**.

A frustum is a section of a regular geometric solid between two parallel planes, and it's a useful shape for describing a field of vision. To understand this, place your hands on either side of your head. Now, move them forward, keeping them just outside your field of vision. Notice that you must move them outward (to the left and right) in order to do this. Try this again with your hands above and below your head. Once again, you must move them outward vertically to keep them from your field of visions.

The shape that you've just made with your hands is like a pyramid, extending from your eyes, whose point has been sliced off parallel to the base—in other words, a frustum.

To create a matrix that represents a perspective frustum, we can use the matrix object's perspective() method:

```
self.view_matrix.perspective(
    45,   # Angle
    self.width() / self.height(),   # Aspect Ratio
    0.1,   # Near clipping plane
    100.0   # Far clipping plane
)
```

The `perspective()` method takes four arguments:

- The angle, in degrees, at which the frustum expands from the near plane to the far plane
- The aspect ratio of the near and far planes (which are identical)
- The depth into the screen of the near plane
- The depth into the screen of the far plane

Without digging into the complicated math, this matrix effectively represents our field of view relative to our drawing. As we'll see when we start drawing, all we need to do to move our object is to manipulate the matrix.

For example, we should probably back up a bit from where we're going to be drawing so that it's not happening right up in the front of the field of view. This movement can be accomplished by the `translate()` method:

```
self.view_matrix.translate(0, 0, -5)
```

`translate` takes three arguments—an x amount, a y amount, and a z amount. Here, we've specified a z translation of -5, which pushes the object deeper into the screen.

This may all seem a bit confusing now, but, once we start drawing our shape, things will become clearer.

Drawing our first shape

Now that our OpenGL environment is initialized, we can move on to the `paintGL()` method. This method will contain all the code for drawing our 3D object and will be called whenever the widget needs to be updated.

The first thing we'll do when painting is clear the canvas:

```
def paintGL(self):
    self.gl.glClearColor(0.1, 0, 0.2, 1)
    self.gl.glClear(
        self.gl.GL_COLOR_BUFFER_BIT | self.gl.GL_DEPTH_BUFFER_BIT)
    self.program.bind()
```

`glClearColor()` is used to fill the background of the drawing with a solid color, as specified by our arguments. Colors in OpenGL are specified using three or four values. In the case of three values, they represent red, green, and blue. A fourth value, when used, represents the **alpha**, or opacity, of the color. Unlike Qt, where RGB values are integers ranging from 0 to 255, OpenGL color values are floating-point numbers ranging from 0 to 1. Our values in the preceding describe a deep purple-blue color; feel free to experiment with other values.

> You should redraw the background with `glClearColor` on every repaint; if you don't, the previous paint operations will still be visible. This is a problem if you animate or resize your drawing.

The `glClear()` function is used to clean out various memory buffers on the GPU, which we'd like to reset between redraws. In this case, we're specifying some constants that cause OpenGL to clear the color buffer and the depth buffer. This helps to maximize performance.

Finally, we `bind()` the program object. Since an OpenGL application can have multiple programs, we call `bind()` to tell OpenGL that the commands we're about to issue apply to this particular program.

Now we can draw our shape.

Shapes in OpenGL are described using vertices. You may recall that a vertex is essentially a point in 3D space described by *X*, *Y*, and *Z* coordinates, and defines one corner or end of a primitive.

Let's create a list of vertices to describe a triangle that will be the front of a wedge shape:

```
front_vertices = [
    qtg.QVector3D(0.0, 1.0, 0.0),   # Peak
    qtg.QVector3D(-1.0, 0.0, 0.0),  # Bottom left
    qtg.QVector3D(1.0, 0.0, 0.0)   # Bottom right
    ]
```

Our vertex data doesn't have to be grouped into distinct objects of any kind, but, for convenience and readability, we've used the `QVector3D` object to hold the coordinates for each of the vertices in our triangle.

The numbers used here represent points on a grid, where (0, 0, 0) is the center of our OpenGL viewport at the forward-most point. The x axis goes from −1 at the left-hand side of the screen to 1 at the right-hand side, and the y axis goes from 1 at the top of the screen to −1 at the bottom. The z axis is a bit different; if you imagine the field of vision (the frustum we described earlier) as a shape expanding out of the back of your monitor, a negative z value pushes deeper into that field of vision. A positive z value would move out of the screen toward (and eventually behind) the viewer. So, generally, we will be operating with negative or zero z values to stay within the visible range.

By default, OpenGL will draw in black, but it would be far more interesting to have some colors. So, we'll define a `tuple` object containing some colors:

```
face_colors = (
    qtg.QColor('red'),
    qtg.QColor('orange'),
    qtg.QColor('yellow'),
)
```

We've defined three colors here, one for each vertex of the triangle. These are `QColor` objects, though; remember that OpenGL needs colors as vectors of values between 0 and 1.

To address this, we'll create a little method to convert a `QColor` to an OpenGL-friendly vector:

```
def qcolor_to_glvec(self, qcolor):
    return qtg.QVector3D(
        qcolor.red() / 255,
        qcolor.green() / 255,
        qcolor.blue() / 255
    )
```

This code is fairly self-explanatory, it will create another `QVector3D` object with the converted RGB values.

Back in `paintGL()`, we can use a list comprehension to convert our colors to something usable:

```
gl_colors = [
    self.qcolor_to_glvec(color)
    for color in face_colors
]
```

At this point, we've defined some vertex and color data, but we've sent nothing to OpenGL yet; these are just data values in our Python script. To pass these to OpenGL, we'll need those variable handles we grabbed in `initializeGL()`.

The first variable we'll pass to our shaders is the `matrix` variable. We're going to use our `view_matrix` object that we defined in `initializeGL()` for this:

```
self.program.setUniformValue(
    self.matrix_location, self.view_matrix)
```

`setUniformValue()` can be used to set the value of a `uniform` variable; we can simply pass it the handle of the `GLSL` variable that we retrieved using `uniformLocation()` and the `matrix` object we created to define our projection and field of vision.

You can also use `setAttributeValue()` to set the value of `attribute` variables. For instance, if we wanted all our vertices to be red, we could add this:

```
self.program.setAttributeValue(
    self.color_location, gl_colors[0])
```

But let's not do that; it will look much better if each vertex has its own color.

To do this, we need to create some **attribute arrays.** An attribute array is an array of data that will be passed into an attribute-type variable. Remember that variables marked as attributes in GLSL apply a distinct value to each vertex. So effectively we're telling OpenGL, *here are some arrays of data where each item applies to one vertex.*

The code looks like this:

```
self.program.enableAttributeArray(self.vertex_location)
self.program.setAttributeArray(
    self.vertex_location, front_vertices)
self.program.enableAttributeArray(self.color_location)
self.program.setAttributeArray(self.color_location, gl_colors)
```

The first step is to enable an array on the `GLSL` variable by calling `enableAttributeArray()` with the handle for the variable that we want to set the array on. Then, we pass in the data using `setAttributeArray()`. This effectively means that our `vertex` shader is going to be run on each of the items in the `front_vertices` array. Each time that shader runs, it will also grab the next item from the `gl_colors` list and will apply that to the `color_attr` variable.

If you are using multiple attribute arrays like this, you need to make sure that there are enough items in the arrays to cover all the vertices. If we only had two colors defined, the third vertex would pull garbage data for `color_attr`, resulting in an undefined output.

Now that we've queued up all the data for our first primitive, let's draw using the following code:

```
self.gl.glDrawArrays(self.gl.GL_TRIANGLES, 0, 3)
```

`glDrawArrays()` will send all the arrays we've defined into the pipeline. The `GL_TRIANGLES` argument tells OpenGL that it will be drawing triangle primitives, and the next two arguments tell it to start at array item `0` and draw three items.

If you run the program at this point, you should see that we've drawn a red and yellow triangle. Nice! Now, let's make it 3D.

Creating a 3D object

To make a 3D object, we need to draw the back and sides of our wedge object. We'll start by calculating the coordinates for the back of the wedge using a list comprehension:

```
back_vertices = [
    qtg.QVector3D(x.toVector2D(), -0.5)
    for x in front_vertices]
```

To create the back face, we only need to copy each of the front face coordinates and move the z axis back a bit. So, we're using the `QVector3D` object's `toVector2D()` method to produce a new vector with only the x and y axes, then passing that to the constructor of a new `QVector3D` object along with a second argument specifying the new z coordinate.

Now, we'll pass this set of vertices to OpenGL and draw as follows:

```
self.program.setAttributeArray(
    self.vertex_location, reversed(back_vertices))
self.gl.glDrawArrays(self.gl.GL_TRIANGLES, 0, 3)
```

By writing these to `vertex_location`, we've overwritten the vertices for the front face (which are already drawn) and replaced them with the back face vertices. Then, we make the same call to `glDrawArrays()` and the new set of vertices will be drawn, along with the corresponding colors.

You will notice that we will reverse the order of the vertices before drawing. When OpenGL displays a primitive, it only shows one side of that primitive, since it's assumed that the primitive is part of some 3D object whose insides would not need to be drawn. OpenGL determines which side of the primitive should be drawn depending on whether its points are drawn clockwise or counterclockwise. By default, the near face of a primitive drawn counter-clockwise is shown, so we will reverse the order of the back face vertices so that it is drawn clockwise and its far face is shown (which will be the outside of the wedge).

Let's finish our shape by drawing its sides. Unlike the front and back, which are triangles, our sides are rectangles and so will need four vertices each to describe them.

We'll calculate those vertices from our other two lists:

```
sides = [(0, 1), (1, 2), (2, 0)]
side_vertices = list()
for index1, index2 in sides:
    side_vertices += [
        front_vertices[index1],
        back_vertices[index1],
        back_vertices[index2],
        front_vertices[index2]
    ]
```

The `sides` list contains indexes for the `front_vertices` and `back_vertices` lists, which define the sides of each triangle. We iterate this list, and, for each one, define a list of four vertices describing one side of the wedge.

Notice that those four vertices are drawn in counter-clockwise order, just like the front (you may need to sketch this out on paper to see it).

We'll also define a new list of colors since we now need more than three:

```
side_colors = [
    qtg.QColor('blue'),
    qtg.QColor('purple'),
    qtg.QColor('cyan'),
    qtg.QColor('magenta'),
]
gl_colors = [
    self.qcolor_to_glvec(color)
    for color in side_colors
] * 3
```

Our list of side vertices contains a total of 12 vertices (4 for each of the 3 sides), so we need a list of 12 colors to match it. We can do this by just specifying 4 colors and then multiplying the Python `list` object by 3 to produce a repeating list with 12 items in total.

Now, we'll pass these arrays to OpenGL and draw:

```
self.program.setAttributeArray(self.color_location, gl_colors)
self.program.setAttributeArray(self.vertex_location, side_vertices)
self.gl.glDrawArrays(self.gl.GL_QUADS, 0, len(side_vertices))
```

This time, instead of `GL_TRIANGLES`, we're using `GL_QUADS` as the first argument to indicate that we're drawing quadrilaterals.

 OpenGL can draw several different primitive types, including lines, points, and polygons. Most of the time, you should use triangles, because this is the fastest primitive on most graphics hardware.

Now that all our points are drawn, we'll clean up a bit:

```
self.program.disableAttributeArray(self.vertex_location)
self.program.disableAttributeArray(self.color_location)
self.program.release()
```

These calls aren't strictly necessary in our simple little demonstration, but, in a more complex program, they would likely save you some headaches. OpenGL operates as a state machine, where the result of an operation depends on the current state of the system. When we bind or enable a particular object, OpenGL is then pointed *to* that object and certain operations (such as setting array data) will be automatically directed to it. When we've finished a drawing operation, we don't want to leave OpenGL pointed at our object, so it's good practice to release and disable objects when we're finished with them.

If you run the application now, you should see your amazing 3D shape:

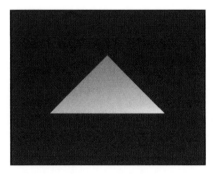

Oops, not so 3D, is it? In fact, we *have* drawn a 3Dshape, but you can't see that, because we're looking directly at it. In the next section, we'll create some code to animate this shape and get a full appreciation of all its dimensions.

Animating and controlling OpenGL drawings

To get a sense of the 3D aspects of our drawing, we're going to build some controls into our GUI that allow us to rotate and zoom around the drawing.

We'll start by adding some buttons in `MainWindow.__init__()` that we can use as controls:

```
btn_layout = qtw.QHBoxLayout()
main.layout().addLayout(btn_layout)
for direction in ('none', 'left', 'right', 'up', 'down'):
    button = qtw.QPushButton(
        direction,
        autoExclusive=True,
        checkable=True,
        clicked=getattr(oglw, f'spin_{direction}'))
    btn_layout.addWidget(button)
zoom_layout = qtw.QHBoxLayout()
main.layout().addLayout(zoom_layout)
zoom_in = qtw.QPushButton('zoom in', clicked=oglw.zoom_in)
zoom_layout.addWidget(zoom_in)
zoom_out = qtw.QPushButton('zoom out', clicked=oglw.zoom_out)
zoom_layout.addWidget(zoom_out)
```

We've created two sets of buttons here; the first set will be a set of radio-style buttons (so only one can be down at a time) that will select the rotation direction of the object – none (no rotation), left, right, up, or down. Each button will call a corresponding method on the `GlWidget` object when activated.

The second set comprises a zoom-in and zoom-out buttons, which calls a `zoom_in()` or `zoom_out()` method on the `GlWidget` respectively. With these buttons added to our GUI, let's hop over to `GlWidget` and implement the callback methods.

Animating in OpenGL

Animating our wedge is purely a matter of manipulating the `view` matrix and redrawing our image. We'll start in `GlWidget.initializeGL()` by creating an instance variable to hold rotation values:

```
self.rotation = [0, 0, 0, 0]
```

The first value in this list represents an angle of rotation; the remaining values are the *X*, *Y*, and *Z* coordinates of the point around which the `view` matrix will rotate.

At the end of `paintGL()`, we can pass these values into the `matrix` object's `rotate()` method:

```
self.view_matrix.rotate(*self.rotation)
```

Right now, this will do nothing, because our rotation values are all `0`. To cause rotation, we will have to change `self.rotation` and trigger a repaint of the image.

So, our rotation callbacks will look like this:

```
def spin_none(self):
    self.rotation = [0, 0, 0, 0]

def spin_left(self):
    self.rotation = [-1, 0, 1, 0]

def spin_right(self):
    self.rotation = [1, 0, 1, 0]

def spin_up(self):
    self.rotation = [1, 1, 0, 0]

def spin_down(self):
    self.rotation = [-1, 1, 0, 0]
```

Each method simply changes the value of our rotation vector. The angle is shifted one degree forward (1) or backward (1) around an appropriate point to produce the rotation desired.

Now, we just need to kick off animation by triggering repeated repaints. At the end of `paintGL()`, add this line:

```
self.update()
```

`update()` schedules a repaint on the `event` loop, which means that this method will be called again and again. Each time, our `view` matrix will be rotated by the amount set in `self.rotation`.

Zooming in and out

We also want to implement zooming. Each time we click the zoom-in or zoom-out buttons, we want the image to get a tiny bit closer or further away.

Those callbacks look like this:

```
def zoom_in(self):
    self.view_matrix.scale(1.1, 1.1, 1.1)

def zoom_out(self):
    self.view_matrix.scale(.9, .9, .9)
```

The `scale()` method of `QMatrix4x4` causes the matrix to multiply each vertex point by the given amounts. Thus, we can cause our object to shrink or grow, giving the illusion that it is nearer or further away.

We could use `translate()` here, but translating in conjunction with rotation can cause some confusing results and we can lose sight of our object quickly.

Now, when you run the application, you should be able to spin your wedge and see it in all its 3D glory:

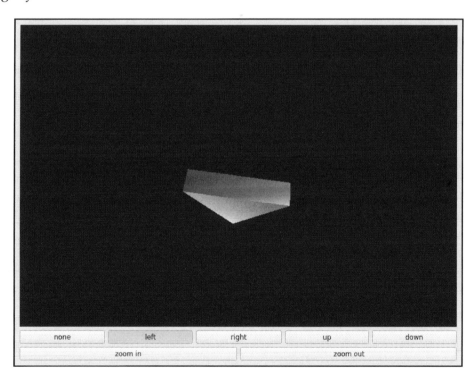

This demonstration is only the beginning of what can be done with OpenGL. While this chapter may not have made you an OpenGL expert, you'll hopefully feel more comfortable digging deeper with the resources at the end of this chapter.

Summary

In this chapter, you have learned about creating 3D animations with OpenGL, and how to integrate them into your PyQt application. We explored the basic principles of OpenGL, such as the render pipeline, shaders, and GLSL. We learned how to use Qt widgets as an OpenGL context to draw and animate a simple 3D object.

In the next chapter, we'll learn to visualize data interactively using the `QtCharts` module. We'll create basic charts and graphs and learn how to build charts using a model-view architecture.

Questions

Try these questions to test your knowledge from this chapter:

1. Which steps of the OpenGL render pipeline are user-definable? Which steps *must* be defined in order to render anything? You may need to reference the documentation at `https://www.khronos.org/opengl/wiki/Rendering_Pipeline_Overview`.

2. You're writing a shader for an OpenGL 2.1 program. Does the following look correct?

```
#version 2.1

attribute highp vec4 vertex;

void main (void)
{
gl_Position = vertex;
}
```

3. Is the following a `vertex` or `fragment` shader? How can you tell?

```
attribute highp vec4 value1;
varying highp vec3 x[4];
void main(void)
{
  x[0] = vec3(sin(value1[0] * .4));
  x[1] = vec3(cos(value1[1]));
  gl_Position = value1;
  x[2] = vec3(10 * x[0])
}
```

4. Given the following `vertex` shader, what code do you need to write to assign simple values to the two variables?

```
attribute highp vec4 coordinates;
uniform highp mat4 matrix1;

void main(void){
   gl_Position = matrix1 * coordinates;
}
```

5. You enable face culling to save some processing power, but find that several of the visible primitives in your drawing are now not rendering. What could the problem be?

6. What does the following code do to our OpenGL image?

```
matrix = qtg.QMatrix4x4()
matrix.perspective(60, 4/3, 2, 10)
matrix.translate(1, -1, -4)
matrix.rotate(45, 1, 0, 0)
```

7. Experiment with the demo and see whether you can add any of the following features:

- A more interesting shape (a pyramid, cube, and so on)
- More controls for moving the object
- Shadows and lighting effects
- Animated shape changes in the object

Further reading

For further information, please refer the following:

- A complete tutorial on modern OpenGL programming can be found at https://paroj.github.io/gltut
- Packt Publications' *Learn OpenGL*, available at https://www.packtpub.com/game-development/learn-opengl, is a good resource for learning the basics of OpenGL
- A free tutorial on matrix mathematics for 3D graphics is available from Central Connecticut State University at https://chortle.ccsu.edu/VectorLessons/vectorIndex.html

14
Embedding Data Plots with QtCharts

The world is full of data. From server logs to financial records, sensor telemetry to census statistics, there seems to be no end to the raw data that programmers are tasked to sift through and extract meaning from. In addition to this, nothing distills a set of raw data into meaningful information as effectively as a good chart or graph. While there are some great charting tools such as `matplotlib` available for Python, PyQt offers its own `QtCharts` library, which is a simple toolkit for constructing charts, graphs, and other data visualizations.

In this chapter, we're going to explore data visualization using `QtCharts` in the following topics:

- Making a simple chart
- Displaying real-time data
- Styling Qt charts

Technical requirements

In addition to the basic PyQt setup we've been using throughout the book, you will need to install PyQt support for the `QtCharts` library. This support is not part of the default PyQt install, but it can be easily installed from PyPI, as follows:

```
$ pip install --user PyQtChart
```

You'll also need the `psutil` library, which can be installed from PyPI. We already used this library in Chapter 12, *Creating 2D Graphics with QPainter*, so if you have been through that chapter, then you should already have it. If not, it can be easily installed using the following command:

```
$ pip install --user psutil
```

Finally, you may want to download the example code for this chapter from https:// github.com/PacktPublishing/Mastering-GUI-Programming-with-Python/tree/master/ Chapter14.

Check out the following video to see the code in action: http://bit.ly/2M5y67f

Making a simple chart

In Chapter 12, *Creating 2D Graphics with QPainter*, we created a CPU activity graph using the Qt graphics framework and the `psutil` library. While that approach to building a chart worked fine, it took a lot of work to create a rudimentary chart that lacked simple niceties such as axis labels, a title, or a legend. The `QtChart` library is also based on the Qt graphics framework, but simplifies the creation of a variety of feature-complete charts.

To demonstrate how it works, we're going to build a more complete system monitoring program that includes several charts derived from data provided by the `psutil` library.

Setting up the GUI

To begin our program, copy the Qt application template from Chapter 4, *Building Applications with QMainWindow*, to a new file called `system_monitor.py`.

At the top of the application, we need to import the `QtChart` library:

```
from PyQt5 import QtChart as qtch
```

We're also going to need the `deque` class and the `psutil` library, just like we needed them in Chapter 12, *Creating 2D Graphics with QPainter*:

```
from collections import deque
import psutil
```

Our program will contain several charts, each in its own tab. So, we will create a tab widget in `MainWindow.__init__()` to hold all the charts:

```
tabs = qtw.QTabWidget()
self.setCentralWidget(tabs)
```

Now that the main framework of the GUI is in place, we'll start creating our chart classes and adding them to the GUI.

Building a disk usage chart

The first chart we'll create is a bar chart for displaying the disk space used by each storage partition on the computer. Each detected partition will have a bar indicating what percentage of its space is being used.

Let's start by creating a class for the chart:

```
class DiskUsageChartView(qtch.QChartView):

    chart_title = 'Disk Usage by Partition'

    def __init__(self):
        super().__init__()
```

The class is subclassed from the `QtChart.QChartView` class; this subclass of `QGraphicsView` is a widget that can display `QChart` objects. Just like the Qt graphics framework, the `QtChart` framework is based on a model-view design. In this case, the `QChart` object is analogous to a `QGraphicsScene` object, which will be attached to the `QChartView` object for display.

Let's create our `QChart` object, as follows:

```
chart = qtch.QChart(title=self.chart_title)
self.setChart(chart)
```

The `QChart` object receives a title but, otherwise, doesn't require a lot of configuration; notice that it says nothing about being a bar chart either. Unlike other charting libraries you may have used, the `QChart` object doesn't determine what kind of chart we're creating. It's simply a container for data plots.

The actual type of chart is determined by adding one or more **series** objects to the chart. A series represents a single set of plotted data on a chart. `QtChart` contains many series classes, all derived from `QAbstractSeries`, each of which represents a different kind of chart style.

Some of these classes are as follows:

Class	Chart type	Useful for
`QLineSeries`	Straight-line plot	Points sampled from continuous data
`QSplineSeries`	Line plot, but with curves	Points sampled from continuous data
`QBarSeries`	Bar chart	Comparing values by category
`QStackedBarSeries`	Stacked bar chart	Comparing subdivided values by category
`QPieSeries`	Pie chart	Relative percentages
`QScatterSeries`	Scatter Plot	Collections of points

A complete list of available series types can be found at `https://doc.qt.io/qt-5/qtcharts-overview.html`. Our chart will be comparing disk usage percentages across multiple partitions, so the most sensible type of series to use from among these options seems to be the `QBarSeries` class. Each partition will be a *category* that will have a single value (the usage percentage) associated with it.

Let's create the `QBarSeries` class, as follows:

```
series = qtch.QBarSeries()
chart.addSeries(series)
```

After creating the series object, we can add it to our chart using the `addSeries()` method. As you might suspect from the name of this method, we can actually add multiple series to the chart, and they don't all need to be of the same type. We could, for example, combine a bar and line series in the same chart. In our case, though, we're only going to have one series.

To append data to our series, we have to create something called a **bar set**:

```
bar_set = qtch.QBarSet('Percent Used')
series.append(bar_set)
```

Qt bar charts are designed to show data in categories, but also allow for different sets of data to be compared across those categories. For instance, if you wanted to compare the relative sales success of several of your company's products in various US cities, you could use the cities as your categories and create a bar set for each product.

In our case, the categories are going to be the partitions on the system, and we have only one set of data that we want to see for each of those partitions – that is, the disk usage percent.

So, we'll create a single bar set to append to our series:

```
bar_set = qtch.QBarSet('Percent Used')
series.append(bar_set)
```

The QBarSet constructor takes a single argument, which represents the label for the dataset. This QBarSet object is the object to which we're going to append our actual data.

So, let's go ahead and retrieve that data:

```
partitions = []
for part in psutil.disk_partitions():
    if 'rw' in part.opts.split(','):
        partitions.append(part.device)
        usage = psutil.disk_usage(part.mountpoint)
        bar_set.append(usage.percent)
```

This code utilizes the disk_partitions() function of pustil to list all the writable partitions on the system (we aren't interested in read-only devices, such as optical drives, since their usage is irrelevant). For each partition, we use the disk_usage() function to retrieve a named tuple of information about disk usage. The percent property of this tuple contains the usage percentage of the disk, so we append that value to our bar set. We also append the device name of the partition to a list of partitions.

At this point, our chart contains a data series and can display the bars for the data. However, it would be difficult to extract much meaning from the chart because there would be no **axes** labeling the data. To fix this, we need to create a couple of axis objects to represent the *x* and *y* axes.

We'll start with the *x* axis, as follows:

```
x_axis = qtch.QBarCategoryAxis()
x_axis.append(partitions)
chart.setAxisX(x_axis)
series.attachAxis(x_axis)
```

`QtCharts` offers different types of axis objects to handle different approaches to organizing data. Our *x* axis is made up of categories—one for each partition found on the computer – so, we've created a `QBarCategoryAxis` object to represent the *x* axis. To define the categories used, we pass a list of strings to the `append()` method.

It's important that the order of our categories matches the order in which data is appended to the bar set, since each data point is categorized according to its position in the series.

Once created, an axis has to be attached both to the chart and to the series; this is because the chart needs to know about the axis object so that it can properly label and scale the axis. This is accomplished by passing the axis object to the chart's `setAxisX()` method. The series also needs to know about the axis object so that it can scale the plots correctly for the chart, which we accomplish by passing it to the series object's `attachAxis()` method.

Our *y* axis represents a percentage, so we'll need an axis type that handles values between 0 and 100. We will use a `QValueAxis` object for this, as follows:

```
y_axis = qtch.QValueAxis()
y_axis.setRange(0, 100)
chart.setAxisY(y_axis)
series.attachAxis(y_axis)
```

`QValueAxis` represents an axis that displays a scale of numeric values, and allows us to set an appropriate range for the values. Once created, we can attach it to both the chart and the series.

At this point, we can create an instance of our chart view object in `MainView.__init__()` and add it to the tab widget:

```
disk_usage_view = DiskUsageChartView()
tabs.addTab(disk_usage_view, "Disk Usage")
```

If you run the application at this point, you should get a display of your partition usage percentages:

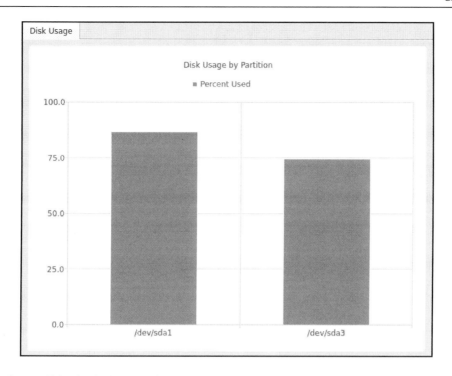

Your display will look slightly different, depending on your OS and drive configurations. The preceding diagram looks pretty good, but one small improvement we can make is to actually put percentage labels on our bars so that readers can see the precise data values. This can be done back in `DiskUsageChartView.__init__()` by adding the following line:

```
series.setLabelsVisible(True)
```

Now when we run the program, we get labeled bars, as follows:

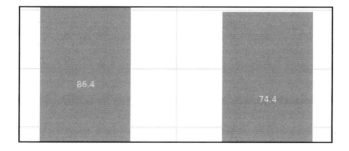

Well, it seems this author is due for a larger hard drive!

Displaying real-time data

Now that we have seen how easy it is to create a static chart, let's take a look at the process of creating a chart that updates in real time. Essentially, the process is the same, but we'll need to periodically update the chart's data series with fresh data. To demonstrate this, let's make a real-time CPU usage monitor.

Building a CPU usage chart

Let's start our CPU monitor in a new class called CPUUsageView:

```
class CPUUsageView(qtch.QChartView):

    num_data_points = 500
    chart_title = "CPU Utilization"

    def __init__(self):
        super().__init__()
        chart = qtch.QChart(title=self.chart_title)
        self.setChart(chart)
```

Just as we did with our disk usage chart, we're basing this class on QChartView and beginning the constructor by creating a QChart object. We've also defined a title, and, just as we did in Chapter 12, *Creating 2D Graphics with QPainter*, configured a number of data points to display at one time. We're going to do a lot more points this time, though, so that we can get a more detailed chart.

After creating the chart object, the next step is to create the series object:

```
        self.series = qtch.QSplineSeries(name="Percentage")
        chart.addSeries(self.series)
```

This time, we're using the QSplineSeries object; we could have also used QLineSeries, but the spline version will connect our data point using cubic spline curves for a smooth appearance, which is similar to what we achieved using Bezier curves in Chapter 12, *Creating 2D Graphics with QPainter*.

Next, we need to populate the series object with some default data, as follows:

```
self.data = deque(
    [0] * self.num_data_points, maxlen=self.num_data_points)
self.series.append([
    qtc.QPoint(x, y)
    for x, y in enumerate(self.data)
])
```

Once again, we're creating a `deque` object to store the data points and filling it with zeros. We then append this data to our series by creating a list of `QPoint` objects from our `deque` object using a list comprehension. Unlike the `QBarSeries` class, data is appended directly to the `QSplineSeries` object; there is nothing analogous to the `QBarSet` class for line-based series.

Now that our series is set up, let's work on the axes:

```
x_axis = qtch.QValueAxis()
x_axis.setRange(0, self.num_data_points)
x_axis.setLabelsVisible(False)
y_axis = qtch.QValueAxis()
y_axis.setRange(0, 100)
chart.setAxisX(x_axis, self.series)
chart.setAxisY(y_axis, self.series)
```

Because our data is mostly (x, y) coordinates, both our axes are `QValueAxis` objects. However, the value of our x axis coordinate is essentially meaningless (it's just the index of the CPU usage value in the `deque` object), so we'll hide those labels by setting the axis's `labelsVisible` property to `False`.

Note that this time, we passed the series object along with the axis when setting the chart's x and y axes with `setAxisX()` and `setAxisY`. Doing this automatically attaches the axis to the series as well, and saves us an extra method call for each axis.

Since we're using curves here, we should make one appearance optimization:

```
self.setRenderHint(qtg.QPainter.Antialiasing)
```

The `QChartView` object's `renderHint` property can be used to activate **anti-aliasing,** which will improve the smoothness of the spline curves.

The basic framework for our chart is now complete; what we need now is a way to collect the data and update the series.

Updating the chart data

Our first step in updating our data is to create a method that calls `psutil.cpu_percent()` and updates the `deque` object:

```
def refresh_stats(self):
    usage = psutil.cpu_percent()
    self.data.append(usage)
```

To update the chart, we only need to update the data in the series. There are a couple of ways to do this; for example, we could completely remove all the data in the chart and `append()` new values.

A better approach is to `replace()` the values, as follows:

```
new_data = [
    qtc.QPoint(x, y)
    for x, y in enumerate(self.data)]
self.series.replace(new_data)
```

First, we generate a new set of `QPoint` objects from our `deque` object using a list comprehension, and then pass the list to the series object's `replace()` method, which swaps out all the data. This method is somewhat faster than wiping out all the data and repopulating the series, although either approach works.

Now that we have the refresh method, we just need to call it periodically; back in `__init__()`, let's add a timer:

```
self.timer = qtc.QTimer(
    interval=200, timeout=self.refresh_stats)
self.timer.start()
```

This timer will call `refresh_stats()` every 200 milliseconds, updating the series and, consequently, the chart.

Back in `MainView.__init__()`, let's add our CPU chart:

```
cpu_view = CPUUsageView()
tabs.addTab(cpu_view, "CPU Usage")
```

Now, you can run the application and click on the **CPU Usage** tab to see a chart that is similar to the following diagram:

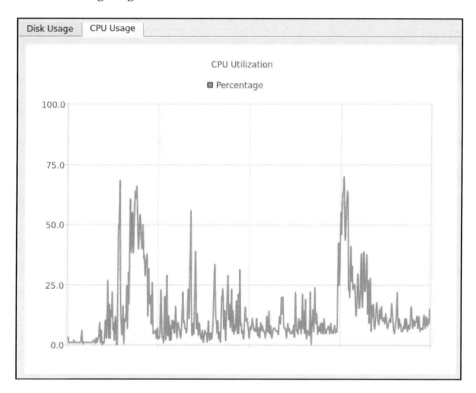

Try doing some CPU-intensive tasks to generate some interesting data for the chart.

Panning and zooming around the chart

With our refresh method being called five times a second, the data in this series is pretty detailed for such a small chart. A dense chart such as this one is something a user might like to explore in more detail. To implement this capability, we can take advantage of the QChart object's methods for panning and zooming around the chart image, and allow the user to get a better view of the data.

To configure interactive controls for the `CPUUsageView` class, we can override the `keyPressEvent()` method, just as we did in our game in `Chapter 12`, *Creating 2D Graphics with QPainter*:

```python
def keyPressEvent(self, event):
    keymap = {
        qtc.Qt.Key_Up: lambda: self.chart().scroll(0, -10),
        qtc.Qt.Key_Down: lambda: self.chart().scroll(0, 10),
        qtc.Qt.Key_Right: lambda: self.chart().scroll(-10, 0),
        qtc.Qt.Key_Left: lambda: self.chart().scroll(10, 0),
        qtc.Qt.Key_Greater: self.chart().zoomIn,
        qtc.Qt.Key_Less: self.chart().zoomOut,
    }
    callback = keymap.get(event.key())
    if callback:
        callback()
```

This code is similar to the code that we used in our tank game—we create a `dict` object to map key codes to callback functions, and then check our event object to see whether one of the mapped keys was pressed. If it was, then we call the `callback` method.

The first of these methods we've mapped is `QChart.scroll()`. `scroll()` takes *x* and *y* values and moves the chart within the chart view by that amount. Here, we've mapped the arrow keys to `lambda` functions, which scroll the chart appropriately.

The other methods we've mapped are `zoomIn()` and `zoomOut()`. These do precisely what their names suggest, each zooming in or out by a factor of two. If we wanted to customize the amount of zoom, then we could alternately call the `zoom()` method, which takes a float value indicating the zoom factor.

If you run this program now, you should find that you can move the chart around using the arrow keys and zoom in or out using the angle brackets (remember to press *Shift* on most keyboards to get an angle bracket).

Styling Qt charts

As good as Qt charts look by default, let's face it—nobody wants to be stuck with defaults when it comes to style. Fortunately, `QtCharts` offers a wide variety of options for styling the different components of our visualizations.

To explore these options, we're going to build a third chart to show physical and swap memory usage, and then style it to our own preferences.

Building the memory chart

We'll start this chart view object just like we started the others in the previous sections:

```
class MemoryChartView(qtch.QChartView):

    chart_title = "Memory Usage"
    num_data_points = 50

    def __init__(self):
        super().__init__()
        chart = qtch.QChart(title=self.chart_title)
        self.setChart(chart)
        series = qtch.QStackedBarSeries()
        chart.addSeries(series)
        self.phys_set = qtch.QBarSet("Physical")
        self.swap_set = qtch.QBarSet("Swap")
        series.append(self.phys_set)
        series.append(self.swap_set)
```

This class starts in a similar way to our disk usage chart – by subclassing QChartView, defining a chart, defining a series, and then defining some bar sets. This time, however, we are going to use QStackedBarSeries. The stacked bar is just like the regular bar chart, except that each bar set is stacked vertically rather than placed side by side. This kind of chart is useful for displaying a series of relative percentages, which is exactly what we're going to display.

In this case, we're going to have two bar sets – one for physical memory usage and the other for swap memory usage, each as a percentage of the total memory (physical and swap). By using a stacked bar, the total memory usage will be represented by the bar height, while the individual segments will show the swap and physical components of that total.

To hold our data, we'll once again set up a deque object with the default data and append the data to the bar sets:

```
        self.data = deque(
            [(0, 0)] * self.num_data_points,
            maxlen=self.num_data_points)
        for phys, swap in self.data:
            self.phys_set.append(phys)
            self.swap_set.append(swap)
```

This time, each data point in the `deque` object needs to have two values: the first for the physical data and the second for the swap. We're representing this by using a two-tuple sequence for each data point.

The next step, once again, is to set up our axes:

```
x_axis = qtch.QValueAxis()
x_axis.setRange(0, self.num_data_points)
x_axis.setLabelsVisible(False)
y_axis = qtch.QValueAxis()
y_axis.setRange(0, 100)
chart.setAxisX(x_axis, series)
chart.setAxisY(y_axis, series)
```

Here, like the CPU usage chart, our *x* axis just represents the somewhat meaningless index number of the data, so we're just going to hide the labels. Our *y* axis, on the other hand, represents a percentage, so we'll set its range from 0 to 100.

Now, we'll create our `refresh` method to update the chart data:

```
def refresh_stats(self):
    phys = psutil.virtual_memory()
    swap = psutil.swap_memory()
    total_mem = phys.total + swap.total
    phys_pct = (phys.used / total_mem) * 100
    swap_pct = (swap.used / total_mem) * 100

    self.data.append(
        (phys_pct, swap_pct))
    for x, (phys, swap) in enumerate(self.data):
        self.phys_set.replace(x, phys)
        self.swap_set.replace(x, swap)
```

The `psutil` library has two functions for examining memory usage: `virtual_memory()`, which returns information about the physical RAM; and `swap_memory()`, which returns information about the swap file usage. We're applying some basic arithmetic to find out the percentage of total memory (swap and physical) used by swap and physical memory. We then append this data to the `deque` object and iterate through it to replace the data in the bar sets.

Finally, we'll add our timer back in `__init__()` to call the refresh method:

```
self.timer = qtc.QTimer(
    interval=1000, timeout=self.refresh_stats)
self.timer.start()
```

The chart view class should now be fully functional, so let's add it to the `MainWindow` class and test it out.

To do this, add the following code in `MainWindow.__init__()`:

```
cpu_time_view = MemoryChartView()
tabs.addTab(cpu_time_view, "Memory Usage")
```

If you run the program at this point, you should have a working memory usage monitor that updates once per second. It's nice, but it looks too default-like; so, let's style things up a bit.

Chart styling

To give our memory chart a healthy dose of individuality, let's head back up to `MemoryChartView.__init__()` and start adding in code to style the various elements of the chart.

One of the easiest, yet most interesting, changes that we can make is to activate the chart's built-in animations:

```
chart.setAnimationOptions(qtch.QChart.AllAnimations)
```

The `QChart` object's `animationOptions` property determines which of the built-in chart animations will be run when the chart is created or updated. The options include `GridAxisAnimations`, which animate the drawing of the axes; `SeriesAnimations`, which animate updates to the series data; `AllAnimations`, which we've used here to activate both grid and series animations; and `NoAnimations`, which, as you might guess, is used to turn all the animations off (this is, of course, the default).

If you run the program now, you'll see that the grid and axes sweep into place and each bar pops up from the bottom of the chart in a smooth animation. The animations themselves are preset for each series type; note that we can't do much to customize them other than set the easing curve and duration:

```
chart.setAnimationEasingCurve(
    qtc.QEasingCurve(qtc.QEasingCurve.OutBounce))
chart.setAnimationDuration(1000)
```

Here, we've set the chart's `animationEasingCurve` property to a `QtCore.QEasingCurve` object with an *out bounce* easing curve. We've also slowed the animation time to a full second. If you run the program now, you'll see the animations bounce and last slightly longer.

Another simple tweak we can make is enabling the chart's drop shadow, as follows:

```
chart.setDropShadowEnabled(True)
```

Setting `dropShadowEnabled` to `True` will cause a drop shadow to be displayed around the chart's plot area, giving it a subtle 3D effect.

A more dramatic change in appearance comes by setting the chart's `theme` property, as follows:

```
chart.setTheme(qtch.QChart.ChartThemeBrownSand)
```

Although this is called a chart theme, it mainly affects the colors used for the plots. Qt 5.12 ships with eight chart themes, which can be found at `https://doc.qt.io/qt-5/qchart.html#ChartTheme-enum`. Here, we've configured the *Brown Sand* theme, which will utilize earth tones for our data plots.

In the case of our stacked bar chart, this means each part of the stack will get a different color from the theme.

Another very noticeable change we can make is done by setting the chart's background. This can be done by setting the `backgroundBrush` property to a custom `QBrush` object:

```
gradient = qtg.QLinearGradient(
    chart.plotArea().topLeft(), chart.plotArea().bottomRight())
gradient.setColorAt(0, qtg.QColor("#333"))
gradient.setColorAt(1, qtg.QColor("#660"))
chart.setBackgroundBrush(qtg.QBrush(gradient))
```

In this case, we've created a linear gradient and used it to create a `QBrush` object for the background (see Chapter 6, *Styling Qt Applications*, for more discussion on this).

The background also has a `QPen` object, which is used to draw the border around the plot area:

```
chart.setBackgroundPen(qtg.QPen(qtg.QColor('black'), 5))
```

If you run the program at this point, you might find the text a little hard to read. Unfortunately, there isn't an easy way to update the look of all the text in the chart at once – we need to do it piece by piece. We can start with the chart's title text by setting the `titleBrush` and `titleFont` properties, as follows:

```
chart.setTitleBrush(
    qtg.QBrush(qtc.Qt.white))
chart.setTitleFont(qtg.QFont('Impact', 32, qtg.QFont.Bold))
```

Fixing the rest of the text cannot be done through the `chart` object. For that, we need to look at styling the other objects in the chart.

Styling axes

The font and color of the labels used on the chart's axes must be set through our axis's objects:

```
axis_font = qtg.QFont('Mono', 16)
axis_brush = qtg.QBrush(qtg.QColor('#EEF'))
y_axis.setLabelsFont(axis_font)
y_axis.setLabelsBrush(axis_brush)
```

Here, we've set the *y* axis font and color by using the `setLabelsFont()` and `setLabelsBrush()` methods, respectively. Note that we could set the *x* axis label font and color as well, but there isn't much point since we're not showing the *x* labels.

The axis objects also give us access to styling our grid lines, using the `gridLinePen` property:

```
grid_pen = qtg.QPen(qtg.QColor('silver'))
grid_pen.setDashPattern([1, 1, 1, 0])
x_axis.setGridLinePen(grid_pen)
y_axis.setGridLinePen(grid_pen)
```

Here, we've set up a dashed silver `QPen` object to draw the grid lines of our *x* and *y* axes. Incidentally, if you want to change how many grid lines are drawn on the chart, that can be done by setting the axis object's `tickCount` property:

```
y_axis.setTickCount(11)
```

The default tick count is 5, and the minimum is 2. Note that this number includes the top and bottom lines, so to have a grid line at every 10 percent, we've set the axis to 11 ticks.

To help users distinguish between tightly-packed grid lines, we can also enable **shades** on the axis object:

```
y_axis.setShadesVisible(True)
y_axis.setShadesColor(qtg.QColor('#884'))
```

As you can see, if you run the application, this causes every alternate region between the grid lines to be shaded according to the configured color rather than using the default background.

Styling the legend

The final thing that we might want to fix in this chart is the **legend**. This is the part of the chart that explains which color goes with which bar set. The legend is represented by a QLegend object, which is automatically created and updated by the QChart object as we add bar sets or series objects.

We can retrieve the chart's QLegend object using the legend() accessor method:

```
legend = chart.legend()
```

By default, the legend doesn't have a background and simply draws directly on the chart background. We can change that to improve readability, as follows:

```
legend.setBackgroundVisible(True)
legend.setBrush(
    qtg.QBrush(qtg.QColor('white')))
```

We first turn on the background by setting backgroundVisible to True and then configuring a brush for the background by setting the brush property to a QBrush object.

The color and font of the text can also be configured, as follows:

```
legend.setFont(qtg.QFont('Courier', 14))
legend.setLabelColor(qtc.Qt.darkRed)
```

We can set the label color using setLabelColor(), or use a brush for finer control using the setLabelBrush() method.

Finally, we can configure the shape of the markers that are used to indicate the colors:

```
legend.setMarkerShape(qtch.QLegend.MarkerShapeCircle)
```

The options here include MarkerShapeCircle, MarkerShapeRectangle, and MarkerShapeFromSeries, the last of which chooses a shape that is appropriate to the series being drawn (for example, a short line for line or spline plots, or a dot for scatter plots).

At this point, your memory chart should look something like this:

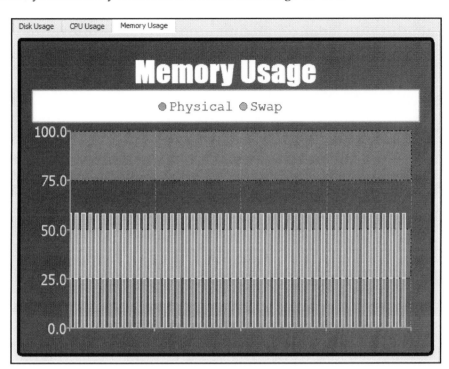

Not bad! Now, try your own color, brush, pen, and font values to see what you can create!

Summary

In this chapter, you learned how to visualize data using `QtChart`. You created a static table, an animated real-time table, and a fancy chart with custom colors and fonts. You also learned how to create bar charts, stacked bar charts, and spline charts.

In the next chapter, we're going to explore the use of PyQt on the Raspberry Pi. You'll learn how to install a recent version of PyQt and how to interface your PyQt applications with circuits and external hardware using the unique capabilities of the Pi.

Questions

Try these questions to test your knowledge on this chapter:

1. Consider the following descriptions of datasets. Suggest a style of chart for each:
   - Web server hit counts by date
   - Sales figures by salesperson per month
   - The percentage of support tickets for the past year by a company department
   - The yield of a plot of bean plants against the plant's height, for several hundred plants

2. Which chart component has not been configured in the following code, and what will the result be?

```
data_list = [
    qtc.QPoint(2, 3),
    qtc.QPoint(4, 5),
    qtc.QPoint(6, 7)]
chart = qtch.QChart()
series = qtch.QLineSeries()
series.append(data_list)
view = qtch.QChartView()
view.setChart(chart)
view.show()
```

3. What's wrong with the following code?

```
mainwindow = qtw.QMainWindow()
chart = qtch.QChart()
series = qtch.QPieSeries()
series.append('Half', 50)
series.append('Other Half', 50)
mainwindow.setCentralWidget(chart)
mainwindow.show()
```

4. You want to create a bar chart comparing Bob and Alice's sales figures for the quarter. What code needs to be added? Note that axes are not required here:

```
bob_sales = [2500, 1300, 800]
alice_sales = [1700, 1850, 2010]

chart = qtch.QChart()
series = qtch.QBarSeries()
chart.addSeries(series)
```

```
# add code here

# end code
view = qtch.QChartView()
view.setChart(chart)
view.show()
```

5. Given a `QChart` object named `chart`, write some code so that the chart has a black background and blue data plots.
6. Style the other two charts in the system monitor script using the techniques you used for the `Memory Usage` chart. Experiment with different brushes and pens, and see whether you can find other properties to set.

7. `QPolarChart` is a subclass of `QChart`, which allows you to construct a polar chart. Investigate the use of the polar chart in the Qt documentation and see whether you can create a polar chart of an appropriate dataset.
8. `psutil.cpu_percent()` takes an optional argument, `percpu`, which will create a list of values showing usage information per CPU core. Update your application to use this option and separately display each CPU core's activity on one chart.

Further reading

For further information, please refer to the following links:

- The `QtCharts` overview can be found at https://doc.qt.io/qt-5/qtcharts-index.html
- More documentation on the `psutil` library can be found at https://psutil.readthedocs.io/en/latest/
- This guide from the University of California at Berkeley offers some guidelines for choosing the right kind of plot for different types of data: http://guides.lib.berkeley.edu/data-visualization/type

15
PyQt Raspberry Pi

The Raspberry Pi is one of the most successful and exciting computers of the past decade. Introduced in 2012 by a British nonprofit organization as a way to teach children about computer science, the tiny **Advanced RISC Machine** (**ARM**)-based computer has become a ubiquitous tool for hobbyists, tinkerers, developers, and IT professionals of all kinds. With Python and PyQt readily available and well supported on its default OS, the Raspberry Pi is a great tool for PyQt developers as well.

In this chapter, we'll look at developing with PyQt5 on the Raspberry Pi in the following sections:

- Running PyQt5 on the Raspberry Pi
- Controlling **General Purpose Input/Output** (**GPIO**) devices with PyQt
- Controlling PyQt with GPIO devices

Technical requirements

In order to follow along with the examples in this chapter, you'll need these items:

- A Raspberry Pi—preferably 3 Model B+ or newer
- A power supply, keyboard, mouse, monitor, and network connection for the Pi
- A micro SD card with Raspbian 10 or later installed; you can refer to the official documentation at `https://www.raspberrypi.org/documentation/installation/` for instructions on how to install Raspbian

At the time of writing, Raspbian 10 has not yet been released, though it is possible to upgrade Raspbian 9 to the testing version. You can refer to `Appendix B`, *Upgrading Raspbian 9 to Raspbian 10*, of this book for instructions on how to upgrade if Raspbian 10 is not available.

To program our GPIO-based projects, you'll also need some electronic components to interface with. These parts are commonly available in electronics starter kits or from your local electronics supply store.

The first project will require the following items:

- A breadboard
- Three identical resistors (between 220 and 1,000 ohms)
- One tri-color LED
- Four female-to-male jumper wires

The second project will require the following items:

- A breadboard
- One DHT11 or DHT22 temperature/humidity sensor
- One push button switch
- One resistor (the value isn't important)
- Three female-to-male jumper wires
- The Adafruit DHT sensor library, which is available from PyPI using the following command:

```
$ sudo pip3 install Adafruit_DHT
```

You can refer to the GitHub repository at `https://github.com/adafruit/Adafruit_Python_DHT` for more information.

You may also want to download the example code from `https://github.com/PacktPublishing/Mastering-GUI-Programming-with-Python/tree/master/Chapter15`.

Check out the following video to see the code in action: `http://bit.ly/2M5xDSx`

Running PyQt5 on the Pi

The Raspberry Pi is capable of running many different operating systems, so installing Python and PyQt is entirely dependent on which operating system you choose. In this book, we're going to focus on **Raspbian**—the official (and most commonly used) operating system for the Pi.

Raspbian is based on the stable release of Debian GNU/Linux, which, at the time of publication, is Debian 9 (Stretch). Unfortunately, the versions of Python and PyQt5 available for this release of Debian are too old for the code in this book. If, as you read this book, Raspbian 10 has not yet been released, please consult Appendix B, *Upgrading Raspbian 9 to Raspbian 10*, for instructions on how to upgrade Raspbian 9 to Raspbian 10.

Raspbian 10 comes with Python 3.7 preinstalled, but we'll need to install PyQt5 ourselves. Note that you cannot use pip to install PyQt5 on the Raspberry Pi, as the required Qt binary files are not available from PyPI for the ARM platform (on which the Pi is based). However, a version of PyQt5 is available from the Raspbian software repositories. This will *not* be the latest version of PyQt5, but a version that was chosen during the Debian development process to be the most stable and compatible with the release. For Debian/Raspbian 10, this version is PyQt 5.11.

To install it, first make sure that your device is connected to the internet. Then, open a command-line Terminal and enter the following command:

```
$ sudo apt install python3-pyqt5
```

The **Advanced Packaging Tool** (APT) utility will download and install PyQt5 and all of the necessary dependencies. Note that this command only installs the main modules of PyQt5 for Python 3. Certain modules, such as QtSQL, QtMultimedia, QtChart, and QtWebEngineWidgets, are packaged separately and will need to be installed using an additional command:

```
$ sudo apt install python3-pyqt5.qtsql python3-pyqt5.qtmultimedia python3-
pyqt5.qtchart python3-pyqt5.qtwebengine
```

There are many more optional libraries packaged for PyQt5. To obtain a complete list, you can use the apt search command, as follows:

```
$ apt search pyqt5
```

 APT is the primary way in which software is installed, removed, and updated on Raspbian, Debian, and many other Linux distributions. While similar to pip, APT is used for the whole operating system.

Editing Python on the Pi

Although you can edit Python on your own computer and copy it to the Raspberry Pi for execution, you will likely find it more convenient to edit your code directly on the device. If your favorite code editor or **Integrated Development Environment (IDE)** is not available for Linux or ARM, never fear; Raspbian offers several alternatives:

- The **Thonny** Python IDE comes preloaded with the default Raspbian image and is perfectly suitable for the examples in this chapter
- **IDLE**, Python's default programming environment is also preinstalled
- **Geany**, a generic programming text editor suitable for many languages, is also preinstalled
- Traditional code editors such as **Vim** and **Emacs** and Python IDEs, such as **Spyder**, **Ninja IDE**, and **Eric**, can be installed from the package repository using the **Add/Remove Software** tool (found under **Preferences** in the **Programs** menu) or using the `apt` command

Whatever application or approach you choose, make sure that you back up your files to another device, as Raspberry Pi's SD card storage is not the most robust.

Running PyQt5 applications on the Pi

Once Python and PyQt5 are installed on your Raspberry Pi, you should be able to run any of the applications we've written so far in this book. Essentially, the Pi is a computer running GNU/Linux, with which all of the code in this book is compatible. With this in mind, you *could* simply use it as a small, energy-efficient computer for running your PyQt applications.

However, the Raspberry Pi has some distinctive features of its own, most notably, its GPIO pins. These pins enable the Pi to communicate with external digital circuits in a very simple and accessible way. Raspbian comes with software libraries preinstalled, which allows us to control these pins using Python.

To take full advantage of the unique platform that this feature offers us, we're going to spend the rest of this chapter focused on using PyQt5 in combination with the GPIO features of the Raspberry Pi to create GUI applications that interact with real-world circuitry in a way that only a device like the Pi can.

Controlling GPIO devices with PyQt

For our first project, we're going to learn how we can control an external circuit from a PyQt application. You'll be wiring up a multicolor LED and controlling its color using QColorDialog. Gather the components listed in the *Technical requirements* section for the first project and let's get started.

Connecting the LED circuit

Let's begin this project by connecting the components of our circuit on the breadboard. Power off the Pi and disconnect the power, and then place it near your breadboard.

 It's always a good idea to shut down your Raspberry Pi and disconnect the power before connecting circuits to the GPIO pins. This will reduce the risk of destroying your Raspberry Pi in the event that you connect something incorrectly, or if you accidentally touch the component leads.

The main component in this circuit is the tri-color LED. Although these vary slightly, the most common pinout for this component is as follows:

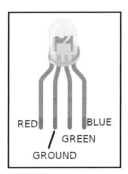

Essentially, a tri-color LED is a red LED, a green LED, and a blue LED combined into one package. It provides separate input leads to send current into each color separately and a fourth lead for the common ground. By feeding different voltages into each pin, we can mix red, green, and blue light to create a wide variety of colors, just as we mix these three elements to create RGB colors in our applications.

Add the LED to your breadboard so that each pin is on a separate row in the board. Then, connect the remaining components as follows:

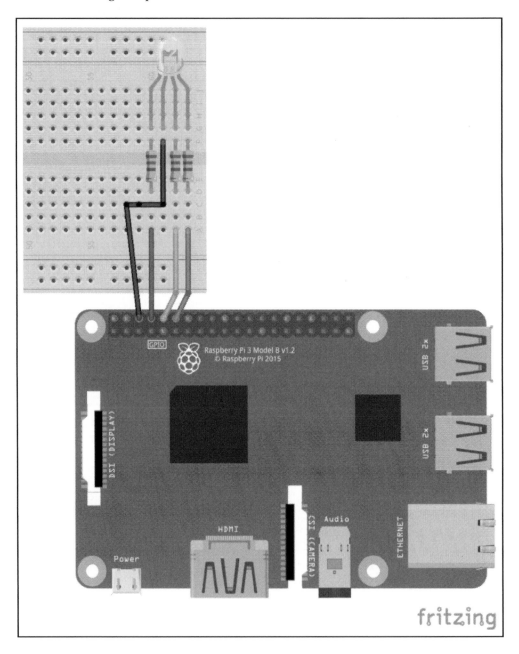

As you can see in the preceding diagram, we're making the following connections:

- The ground pin on the LED is connected directly to the third outside pin from the left on the Raspberry Pi
- The red pin on the LED is connected to one of the resistors, which is then connected to the next pin to the right (that is, pin 8)
- The green pin on the LED is connected to another resistor, which is then connected to the next free pin to the right (that is, pin 10)
- The blue pin on the LED is connected to the last resistor, which is connected to the next free pin to the right on the Pi (pin 12)

It is important to double-check your circuit and make sure that you've connected the wires to the correct pins on the Raspberry Pi. Not all GPIO pins on the Raspberry Pi are the same; some of them are programmable, while others have a hardcoded purpose. You can view a listing of the pins on your Pi by running the `pinout` command in the Terminal; you should see the following output:

```
   3V3  (1) (2)  5V
 GPIO2  (3) (4)  5V
 GPIO3  (5) (6)  GND
 GPIO4  (7) (8)  GPIO14
   GND  (9) (10) GPIO15
GPIO17 (11) (12) GPIO18
GPIO27 (13) (14) GND
GPIO22 (15) (16) GPIO23
   3V3 (17) (18) GPIO24
GPIO10 (19) (20) GND
 GPIO9 (21) (22) GPIO25
GPIO11 (23) (24) GPIO8
   GND (25) (26) GPIO7
 GPIO0 (27) (28) GPIO1
 GPIO5 (29) (30) GND
 GPIO6 (31) (32) GPIO12
GPIO13 (33) (34) GND
GPIO19 (35) (36) GPIO16
GPIO26 (37) (38) GPIO20
   GND (39) (40) GPIO21
```

The preceding screenshot shows the layout of the pins as if you were holding the Pi in front of you with the USB ports down. Note that several of the pins are marked **GND**; these are always the ground pins so you can connect the ground of your circuit to any of those pins. Other pins are labeled **5V** or **3V3**; these are always 5 volts or 3.3 volts, respectively. The remaining pins with the GPIO labels are programmable pins. Your wires should be connected to pins 8 (**GPIO14**), 10 (**GPIO15**), and 12 (**GPIO18**).

Double-check your circuit connections, and then boot the Raspberry Pi. It's time to start coding!

Writing a driver library

Now that our circuit is connected, we need to write some code to control it. To do this, we're going to make use of the GPIO library on the Pi. Create a copy of your PyQt application template from Chapter 4, *Building Applications with QMainWindow*, and call it three_color_led_gui.py.

We'll start by importing the GPIO library:

```
from RPi import GPIO
```

What we want to do first is to create a Python class that will serve as an API for our circuit. We'll call it ThreeColorLed, and then start it as follows:

```
class ThreeColorLed():
    """Represents a three color LED circuit"""

    def __init__(self, red, green, blue, pinmode=GPIO.BOARD, freq=50):
        GPIO.setmode(pinmode)
```

Our __init__() method takes five arguments: the first three arguments are the pin numbers for the red, green, and blue LED connections; the fourth argument is the **pin mode** used to interpret the pin numbers; and the fifth argument is a frequency, which we'll discuss later. First, let's talk about the pin mode.

If you look at the output from the pinout command, you'll notice that there are two ways to describe a pin on the Pi using integers. The first is by its position on the board, from 1 to 40. The second is by its GPIO number (that is, the number following GPIO in the pin description). The GPIO library allows you to specify pins using either number, but you have to tell it which method you're going to use by passing one of two constants to the GPIO.setmode() function. GPIO.BOARD specifies that you're using the positional numbers (such as 1 to 40), while GPIO.BCM means you want to use the GPIO names. As you can see, we default here to using BOARD.

 Whenever you write a class that takes GPIO pin numbers as arguments, be sure to allow the user to specify the pin mode as well. The numbers themselves are meaningless without the context of the pin mode.

Next, our __init__() method needs to set up the output pins:

```
self.pins = {
    "red": red,
    "green": green,
    "blue": blue
    }
for pin in self.pins.values():
    GPIO.setup(pin, GPIO.OUT)
```

A GPIO pin can be set to the IN or OUT mode, depending on whether you want to read from the pin's state or write to it. In this project, we're going to be sending information from the software to the circuit, so we need all of the pins in the OUT mode. After storing our pin numbers in a dict object, we have iterated through them and set them to the appropriate mode using the GPIO.setup() function.

Once set up, we can tell an individual pin to go high or low using the GPIO.output() function, as follows:

```
# Turn all on and all off
for pin in self.pins.values():
    GPIO.output(pin, GPIO.HIGH)
    GPIO.output(pin, GPIO.LOW)
```

This code simply turns each pin on and immediately off again (probably faster than you can see). We could use this approach to set the LED to a few simple colors; for example, we could make it red by setting the red pin HIGH and the others LOW, or cyan by setting the blue and green pins HIGH and the red LOW. Of course, we want to produce a much wider variety of colors, but we can't do that by simply turning the pins fully on or off. We need some way to vary the voltage of each pin between the minimum (0 volts) and the maximum (5 volts) smoothly.

Unfortunately, the Raspberry Pi cannot do this. The outputs are digital, not analog, so they can only be fully on or fully off. However, we can *simulate* varying voltage by using a technique called **Pulse Width Modulation (PWM)**.

PWM

Find a light switch in your house with reasonably responsive bulbs (LED bulbs work best). Then, try turning them on and off once per second. Now flick the switch faster and faster until the light in the room appears almost constant. You should notice that it seems dimmer in the room than when you had the light on all of the time, even though the bulb is only ever completely on or completely off.

PWM works in the same way, except that, with the Pi, we can turn the voltage on and off so quickly (and quietly, of course) that the toggling between on and off appears seamless. Additionally, by varying the ratio of how long the pin is on to how long it is off in each cycle, we can simulate varying voltages between zero voltage and the maximum voltage. This ratio is known as the **duty cycle**.

 More information about the concept and use of pulse width modulation can be found at `https://en.wikipedia.org/wiki/Pulse-width_modulation`.

To use PWM on our pins, we have to set them up first by creating a `GPIO.PWM` object on each pin:

```
self.pwms = dict([
    (name, GPIO.PWM(pin, freq))
    for name, pin in self.pins.items()
])
```

In this case, we're using a list comprehension to produce another `dict` that will contain the name of each pin along with a `PWM` object. The `PWM` object is created by passing in a pin number and a frequency value. This frequency will be the rate at which the pin is toggled on and off.

Once we've created our `PWM` objects, we need to start them up:

```
for pwm in self.pwms.values():
    pwm.start(0)
```

The `PWM.start()` method begins the flicking of the pin from on to off. The argument passed to `start()` indicates the duty cycle as a percentage; here, `0` means that the pin will be on 0% of the time (so, basically, it's off). A value of 100 will keep the pin completely on all of the time, and values in between indicate the amount of on time the pin receives per cycle.

Setting a color

Now that our pins are configured for PWM, we need to create a method that will allow us to set the LED to a specific color by passing in red, green, and blue values. Most software RGB color implementations (including `QColor`) specify these values as 8-bit integers (0 to 255). Our PWM values, however, represent a duty cycle, which is expressed as a percentage (0 to 100).

Therefore, since we're going to need to convert numbers from the 0 to 255 range into the 0 to 100 range several times, let's start with a static method that will do such a conversion:

```
@staticmethod
def convert(val):
    val = abs(val)
    val = val//2.55
    val %= 101
    return val
```

This method ensures that we'll get a valid duty cycle regardless of the input by using simple arithmetic:

- First, we use the absolute value of the number to prevent passing any negative values.
- Second, we divide the value by 2.55 to find the percentage of 255 that it represents.
- Finally, we get the modulus of 101 for the number, so that percentages higher than 100 will cycle around and remain in range.

Now, let's write our set_color() method, as follows:

```
def set_color(self, red, green, blue):
    """Set color using RGB color values of 0-255"""
    self.pwms['red'].ChangeDutyCycle(self.convert(red))
    self.pwms['green'].ChangeDutyCycle(self.convert(green))
    self.pwms['blue'].ChangeDutyCycle(self.convert(blue))
```

The PWM.ChangeDutyCycle() method takes a value from 0 to 100 and adjusts the duty cycle of the pin accordingly. In this method, we're simply converting our input RGB values into the proper scale and passing them into the corresponding PWM objects.

Cleaning up

The last method we need to add to our class is a clean-up method. The GPIO pins on the Raspberry Pi can be thought of as a state machine, in which each pin has a state of high or a state of low (that is, on or off). When we set these pins in our program, the state of those pins will remain set after our program exits.

Note that this could cause a problem if we're connecting a different circuit to our Pi; having a pin set to HIGH at the wrong moment while connecting a circuit could fry some of our components. For that reason, we want to leave everything off when we exit the program.

This can be done using the `GPIO.cleanup()` function:

```
def cleanup(self):
    GPIO.cleanup()
```

By adding this method to our LED driver class, we can easily clean up the state of the Pi after each use.

Creating the PyQt GUI

Now that we've taken care of the GPIO side, let's create our PyQt GUI. In `MainWindow.__init__()`, add in the following code:

```
self.tcl = ThreeColorLed(8, 10, 12)
```

Here, we're creating a `ThreeColorLed` instance using the pin numbers that we connected to our breadboard. Remember that the class uses the BOARD numbers by default, so 8, 10, and 12 are the correct values here. If you want to use the BCM numbers, be sure to specify this in the constructor arguments.

Now let's add a color picker dialog:

```
ccd = qtw.QColorDialog()
ccd.setOptions(
    qtw.QColorDialog.NoButtons
    | qtw.QColorDialog.DontUseNativeDialog)
ccd.currentColorChanged.connect(self.set_color)
self.setCentralWidget(ccd)
```

Typically, we invoke a color dialog by calling `QColorDialog.getColor()`, but in this case, we want to use the dialog as if it were a widget. So, we're instantiating one directly and setting the `NoButtons` and `DontUseNativeDialog` options. By taking away the buttons and using the Qt version of the dialog, we can prevent the user from canceling or submitting the dialog. This allows us to treat it as a regular widget and assign it as the main window's central widget.

We've connected the `currentColorChanged` signal (which is emitted whenever the user selects a color) to a `MainWindow` method called `set_color()`. We'll add this next, as follows:

```
def set_color(self, color):
    self.tcl.set_color(color.red(), color.green(), color.blue())
```

The `currentColorChanged` signal includes a `QColor` object representing the color selected, so we can simply dissect that into red, green, and blue values using the `QColor` property accessors, and then pass that information to our `ThreeColorLed` object's `set_color()` method.

Now the script is complete. You should be able to run it and light up your LED—give it a try!

 Note that the color you pick won't exactly match the color output for the LED due to differences in the relative brightness of different colored LEDs. However, they should be reasonably close.

Controlling PyQt with GPIO devices

Controlling circuits from Python using GPIO pins is fairly straightforward. It's simply a matter of calling the `GPIO.output()` function with the appropriate pin number and high or low value. Now, however, we're going to look at the opposite situation, that is, controlling or updating a PyQt GUI from GPIO input.

To demonstrate this, we're going to build a temperature and humidity readout. Just as before, we'll start by connecting the circuit.

Connecting the sensor circuit

The DHT 11 and DHT 22 sensors are both temperature and humidity sensors that can easily work with the Raspberry Pi. Both are packaged as four-pin components, but only three of the pins are actually used. Some component kits even mount the DHT 11/22 on a small PCB with only the active three pins for output.

In either case, if you're looking at the DHT's front (that is, the grill side), then the pins from left to right are as follows:

- The input voltage—either 5 or 3 volts
- The sensor output
- The dead pin (on a 4-pin configuration)
- Ground

Either the DHT 11 or the DHT 22 will work equally well for this project. The 11 is smaller and cheaper, but slower and less accurate than the 22. Otherwise, they are functionally the same.

Plug your sensor into the breadboard so that each pin is in its own row. Then, connect it to the Raspberry Pi using jumper wires, as demonstrated in the following screenshot:

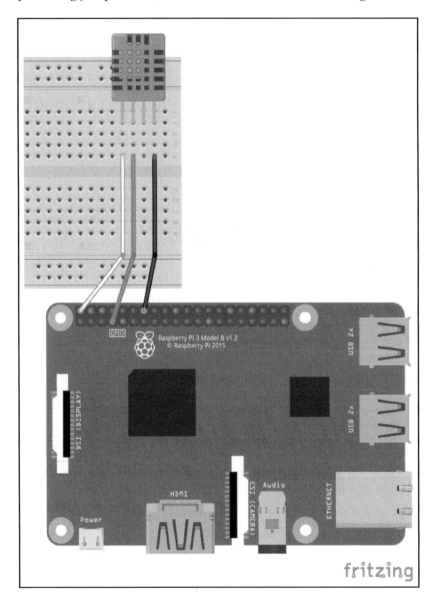

The sensor's voltage input pin can be connected to either of the 5V pins, and the ground can be connected to any of the GND pins. Additionally, the data pin can be connected to any GPIO pin on the Pi, but in this case, we'll use pin 7 (once again, going by the BOARD numbers).

Double-check your connections to make sure everything is correct, then power on the Raspberry Pi, and we'll start coding.

Creating the sensor interface

To begin our sensor interface software, first, create another copy of your Qt application template and call it temp_humid_display.py.

The first thing we'll do is import the necessary libraries, as follows:

```
import Adafruit_DHT
from RPi import GPIO
```

Adafruit_DHT will encapsulate all of the complicated bits required to talk to the DHT unit so that we only need to work with high-level functions to control and read data from the device.

Underneath the imports, let's set up a global constant:

```
SENSOR_MODEL = 11
GPIO.setmode(GPIO.BCM)
```

We're setting up a global constant indicating which model of DHT we're working with; if you have the DHT 22, then set this value to 22. We're also setting up the Pi's pin mode. But this time, we're going to use the BCM mode to specify our pin numbers. The Adafruit library only takes BCM numbers, so it makes sense to be consistent across all of our classes.

Now, let's start our sensor interface class for the DHT:

```
class SensorInterface(qtc.QObject):

    temperature = qtc.pyqtSignal(float)
    humidity = qtc.pyqtSignal(float)
    read_time = qtc.pyqtSignal(qtc.QTime)
```

This time, we're going to base our class on `QObject` so that we can emit signals when the values are read from the sensor and run the object in its own thread. The DHT units are a bit slow and can take a full second or more to respond when we request a reading. For that reason, we'll want to run its interface in a separate thread of execution. As you may remember from Chapter 10, *Multithreading with QTimer and QThread*, this is easily done when we can interact with the object using signals and slots.

Now, let's add the __init__() method, as follows:

```
def __init__(self, pin, sensor_model, fahrenheit=False):
    super().__init__()
    self.pin = pin
    self.model = sensor_model
    self.fahrenheit = fahrenheit
```

The constructor will take three arguments: the pin connected to the data line, the model number (11 or 22), and a Boolean indicating whether we want to use the Fahrenheit or Celsius scale. We'll simply save all of these arguments to instance variables for the time being.

Now we want to create a method to tell the sensor to take a reading:

```
@qtc.pyqtSlot()
def take_reading(self):
    h, t = Adafruit_DHT.read_retry(self.model, self.pin)
    if self.fahrenheit:
        t = ((9/5) * t) + 32
    self.temperature.emit(t)
    self.humidity.emit(h)
    self.read_time.emit(qtc.QTime.currentTime())
```

As you can see, the `Adafruit_DHT` library takes all of the complications out of reading this sensor. We simply have to call `read_entry()` with the model and pin numbers of our sensor and it returns a tuple containing the humidity and temperature values. The temperature is returned in degrees Celsius, so for American users, we're doing a calculation to convert this into Fahrenheit if the object is configured to do so. Then, we emit our three signals—one each for temperature, humidity, and the current time.

Note that we have wrapped this function using the `pyqtSlot` decorator. Again, recall from Chapter 10, *Multithreading with QTimer and QThread,* that this will remove some of the complications of moving this class to its own thread.

This takes care of our sensor driver class, so now, let's build the GUI.

Displaying the readings

By this point in this book, creating a PyQt GUI to display a couple of numbers should be a walk in the park. Just to make things interesting and to create a stylish look, we're going to use a widget that we haven't talked about yet—QLCDNumber.

First, create a base widget in MainWindow.__init__(), as follows:

```
widget = qtw.QWidget()
widget.setLayout(qtw.QFormLayout())
self.setCentralWidget(widget)
```

Now, let's apply some of the styling skills that we learned in Chapter 6, *Styling Qt Applications*:

```
p = widget.palette()
p.setColor(qtg.QPalette.WindowText, qtg.QColor('cyan'))
p.setColor(qtg.QPalette.Window, qtg.QColor('navy'))
p.setColor(qtg.QPalette.Button, qtg.QColor('#335'))
p.setColor(qtg.QPalette.ButtonText, qtg.QColor('cyan'))
self.setPalette(p)
```

Here, we're creating a custom QPalette object for this widget and its children, giving it a color scheme that is reminiscent of a blue-backlit LCD screen.

Next, let's create widgets to display our readings:

```
tempview = qtw.QLCDNumber()
humview = qtw.QLCDNumber()
tempview.setSegmentStyle(qtw.QLCDNumber.Flat)
humview.setSegmentStyle(qtw.QLCDNumber.Flat)
widget.layout().addRow('Temperature', tempview)
widget.layout().addRow('Humidity', humview)
```

The QLCDNumber widget is a widget for displaying numbers. It resembles an eight-segment LCD display, such as you might find on an instrument panel or digital clock. Its segmentStyle property switches between a couple of different visual styles; in this case, we're using Flat, which draws the segments filled in with the foreground color.

With the layout now configured, let's create a sensor object:

```
self.sensor = SensorInterface(4, SENSOR_MODEL, True)
self.sensor_thread = qtc.QThread()
self.sensor.moveToThread(self.sensor_thread)
self.sensor_thread.start()
```

Here, we've created a sensor connected to pin GPIO4 (that is, pin 7), which passes in the `SENSOR_MODEL` constant that we defined earlier and sets Fahrenheit to `True` (feel free to set it to `False` if you prefer Celsius). After that, we create a `QThread` object and move the `SensorInterface` object to it.

Next, let's connect our signals and slots, as follows:

```
self.sensor.temperature.connect(tempview.display)
self.sensor.humidity.connect(humview.display)
self.sensor.read_time.connect(self.show_time)
```

The `QLCDNumber.display()` slot can be connected to any signal that emits a number, so we connect our temperature and humidity signals directly. The `QTime` object sent with the `read_time` signal will need some parsing, however, so we'll connect it to a `MainWindow` method called `show_time()`.

That method looks like the following code block:

```
def show_time(self, qtime):
    self.statusBar().showMessage(
        f'Read at {qtime.toString("HH:mm:ss")}')
```

This method will take advantage of the `MainWindow` object's convenient `statusBar()` method to show the time of the last temperature reading in the status area.

So, that takes care of our GUI output display; we now need a way to trigger the sensor to take readings. One approach we could take is to create a timer to do it periodically:

```
self.timer = qtc.QTimer(interval=(60000))
self.timer.timeout.connect(self.sensor.take_reading)
self.timer.start()
```

In this case, this timer will call `sensor.take_reading()` every minute, ensuring that our readings are regularly updated.

We can also add `QPushButton` to the interface so that the user can get fresh readings on demand:

```
readbutton = qtw.QPushButton('Read Now')
widget.layout().addRow(readbutton)
readbutton.clicked.connect(self.sensor.take_reading)
```

This is fairly trivial, as we just need to connect the button's `clicked` signal to the sensor's `take_reading` slot. But what about a hardware control? How might we implement something external to trigger a temperature reading? We'll explore that in the next section.

Adding a hardware button

Reading values from a sensor can be useful, but what would be even more useful is being able to respond to events that happen in a circuit and take action as a result. To demonstrate this process, we'll add a hardware button to our circuit and monitor its state so that we can take temperature and humidity readings at the push of a button.

Expanding the circuit

To begin, power off the Raspberry Pi and let's add some components to the circuit, as shown in the following diagram:

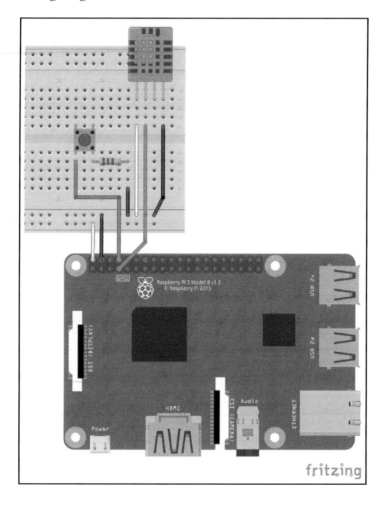

Here, we've essentially added a button and a resistor. The button needs to be connected to pin 8 on the Pi on one side, and the resistor, which is connected to ground, on the other. To keep the wiring clean, we've also taken advantage of the common ground and common voltage rails on the side of the breadboard, although this is optional (you can just connect things directly to the appropriate GND and 5V pins on the Pi, if you prefer).

 The push buttons that are often found in starter kits have four connectors—two for each side of the switch. Make sure that your connections are not connected until the button is pushed. If you find that they are always connected even without the button being pushed, then you probably need to rotate your button by 90 degrees in the circuit.

The button in this circuit will simply connect our GPIO pin to ground when pushed, which will allow us to detect a button push. We'll see how that works in more detail when we write the software.

Implementing the button driver

Start a new class at the top of your script to be the driver for our push button:

```
class HWButton(qtc.QObject):

    button_press = qtc.pyqtSignal()
```

Once again, we're using `QObject` so that we can emit Qt signals, which we'll do when we detect that the button has been pushed down.

Now, let's write the constructor, as follows:

```
def __init__(self, pin):
    super().__init__()
    self.pin = pin
    GPIO.setup(pin, GPIO.IN, pull_up_down=GPIO.PUD_UP)
```

The first thing our `__init__()` method does after calling `super().__init__()` is configure our button's GPIO pin to be an input pin by passing the `GPIO.IN` constant to the `setup()` function.

The pull_up_down value we've passed here is very important. Because of the way we've connected this circuit, the pin will be connected to the ground whenever the button is pushed. But what happens when the button is not pushed? Well, in that case, it's in a state called **float**, in which the input will be unpredictable. In order to keep the pin in a predictable state when the button is not pushed, the pull_up_down argument will cause it to be pulled either HIGH or LOW when it is not otherwise connected. In our case, we want it pulled HIGH because our button will be pulling it LOW; passing in the GPIO.PUD_UP constant will do this.

> This could work in a reverse fashion as well; for example, we could have connected the other side of the button to 5V, and then set pull_up_down to GPIO.PUD_DOWN in the setup() function.

Now, we need to figure out how to detect when the button is being pressed so that we can emit our signal.

One simple approach to this task is **polling**. Polling simply means that we're going to check the button at a regular interval and emit a signal if something changes from the last check.

To do this, we first need to create an instance variable to save the last known state of the button:

```
self.pressed = GPIO.input(self.pin) == GPIO.LOW
```

We can check the current state of the button by calling the GPIO.input() function with the pin number. This function will return either HIGH or LOW, indicating whether the pin is at 5V or ground. If the pin is LOW, then that means the button is pressed down. We'll save that result to self.pressed.

Next, we'll write a method to check the state of the button for changes:

```
def check(self):
    pressed = GPIO.input(self.pin) == GPIO.LOW
    if pressed != self.pressed:
        if pressed:
            self.button_press.emit()
        self.pressed = pressed
```

This check method will take the following steps:

1. First, it compares the output of input() to the LOW constant to see whether the button is pressed
2. Then, we compare the current state of the button to the saved state to see whether the button's state has changed
3. If it has, we then need to check whether the change of state is a press or a release
4. If it is a press (pressed is True), then we emit the signal
5. In either case, we update self.pressed with the new state

Now, all that remains is to call this method on a regular basis to poll for changes; back in __init__(), we can do this with a timer, as follows:

```
self.timer = qtc.QTimer(interval=50, timeout=self.check)
self.timer.start()
```

Here, we've created a timer that times out every 50 milliseconds, calling self.check() when it does so. This should be often enough to catch even the fastest button push that a human being can execute.

Polling works well, but there is a cleaner way to do this by using the GPIO library's add_event_detect() function:

```
# Comment out timer code
#self.timer = qtc.QTimer(interval=50, timeout=self.check)
#self.timer.start()
GPIO.add_event_detect(
    self.pin,
    GPIO.RISING,
    callback=self.on_event_detect)
```

The add_event_detect() function will start monitoring the pin in another thread for either a RISING event or a FALLING event, and call the configured callback method when such an event is detected.

In this case, we just call the following instance method:

```
def on_event_detect(self, *args):
    self.button_press.emit()
```

We could pass our emit() method directly as a callback, but add_event_detect() will call the callback function with the pin number as an argument, which emit() will not accept.

The downside of using `add_event_detect()` is that it introduces another thread, using the Python `threading` library, which can lead to subtle problems with the PyQt event loop. Polling is a perfectly workable alternative that allows you to avoid this complication.

Either approach will work for our simple script, so let's head back to `MainWindow.__init__()` to add support for our button:

```
self.hwbutton = HWButton(8)
self.hwbutton.button_press.connect(self.sensor.take_reading)
```

All we need to do is create an instance of our `HWButton` class with the right pin number and connect its `button_press` signal to the sensor's `take_reading()` slot.

Now, if you fire everything up on the Pi, you should be able to see an update when you push the button.

Summary

The Raspberry Pi is an exciting technology, not only because of its small size, low cost, and low resource usage, but because it makes connecting the world of programming to real-world circuitry simple and accessible in a way that nothing had before. In this chapter, you learned how to configure the Raspberry Pi to run PyQt applications. You also learned how to control circuits using PyQt and Python, and how circuits could control actions in your software.

In the next chapter, we're going to bring the World Wide Web into our PyQt applications using `QtWebEngineWidgets`, a full Chromium-based browser inside a Qt Widget. We'll build a functional browser, and we'll learn about the ins and outs of the web engine library.

Questions

Try answering the following questions to test your knowledge from this chapter:

1. You have just bought a Raspberry Pi with Raspbian preinstalled to run your PyQt5 application. When you try to run your application, you get an error trying to import `QtNetworkAuth`, which your application depends on. What is likely to be the problem?

2. You have written a PyQt frontend for a legacy scanner device. Your code talks to the scanner through a proprietary driver utility called scanutil.exe. It is currently running on a Windows 10 PC, but your employer wants to save money by moving it to a Raspberry Pi. Is this a good idea?

3. You've acquired a new sensor and want to try it out with the Raspberry Pi. It has three connections, labeled Vcc, GND, and Data. How would you connect this to the Raspberry Pi? Is there more information you need?

4. You're trying to light an LED connected to the fourth GPIO pin from the left on the outside. What is wrong with this code?

```
GPIO.setmode(GPIO.BCM)
GPIO.setup(8, GPIO.OUT)
GPIO.output(8, 1)
```

5. You are trying to dim an LED connected to GPIO pin 12. Does the following code work?

```
GPIO.setmode(GPIO.BOARD)
GPIO.setup(12, GPIO.OUT)
GPIO.output(12, 0.5)
```

6. You have a motion sensor with a data pin that goes HIGH when motion is detected. It's connected to pin 8. The following is your driver code:

```
class MotionSensor(qtc.QObject):

    detection = qtc.pyqtSignal()

    def __init__(self):
        super().__init__()
        GPIO.setmode(GPIO.BOARD)
        GPIO.setup(8, GPIO.IN)
        self.state = GPIO.input(8)

    def check(self):
        state = GPIO.input(8)
        if state and state != self.state:
            detection.emit()
        self.state = state
```

Your main window class creates a `MotionSensor` object and connects its `detection` signal to a callback method. However, nothing is being detected. What is missing?

7. Combine the two circuits in this chapter in a creative way; for example, you might create a light that changes color depending on humidity and temperature.

Further reading

For further information, please refer to the following:

- More documentation for the Raspberry Pi's `GPIO` library can be found at `https://sourceforge.net/p/raspberry-gpio-python/wiki/Home/`
- Packt offers many books covering the Raspberry Pi in detail; you can find more information at `https://www.packtpub.com/books/content/raspberry-pi`

16
Web Browsing with QtWebEngine

In Chapter 8, *Networking with QtNetwork*, you learned how to interact with systems over a network using sockets and HTTP. The modern web is much more than just networking protocols, however; it's a programming platform built on the combination of HTML, JavaScript, and CSS, and working with it effectively requires a complete web browser. Fortunately for us, Qt provides us with the QtWebEngineWidgets library, which gives our application a full web browser in a widget.

In this chapter, we're going to learn how to access the web with Qt in the following section:

- Building a basic browser with QWebEngineView
- Advanced QtWebEngine usage

Technical requirements

In addition to the basic PyQt5 setup that we've used in this book, you will need to make sure you have the PyQtWebEngine package installed from PyPI. You can do this using the following command:

```
$ pip install --user PyQtWebEngine
```

You may also want the example code for this chapter, and this is available from https://github.com/PacktPublishing/Mastering-GUI-Programming-with-Python/tree/master/Chapter16.

Check out the following video to see the code in action: http://bit.ly/2M5xFtD

Building a basic browser with QWebEngineView

The primary class used from `QtWebEngineWidgets` is the `QWebEngineView` class; this class provides a nearly complete Chromium-based browser in a `QWidget` object. Chromium is the open source project that underpins much of Google Chrome, the newest versions of Microsoft Edge, and many other browsers.

 Qt also has a deprecated `QtWebKit` module based on the **Webkit** rendering engine used in Safari, Opera, and some older browsers. There are some significant differences between the API and the rendering behavior of `QtWebKit` and `QtWebEngineWidgets`, with the latter being preferred for newer projects.

In this section, we'll see how easy it is to include web content in your Qt application by building a simple web browser using `QtWebEngineWidgets`.

Using the QWebEngineView widget

We need to make a copy of our Qt application template from `Chapter 4`, *Building Applications with QMainWindow,* and call it `simple_browser.py`; we're going to develop a rudimentary browser with tabs and a history display.

We start by importing the `QtWebEngineWidgets` library as follows:

```
from PyQt5 import QtWebEngineWidgets as qtwe
```

 Note that there is also a `QtWebEngine` module, but it is for use with the **Qt Modeling Language (QML)** declarative framework, not the Qt Widgets framework covered by this book. `QtWebEngineWidgets` contains the widgets-based browser.

In our `MainWindow` class constructor, we'll start the GUI by defining a navigation toolbar:

```
navigation = self.addToolBar('Navigation')
style = self.style()
self.back = navigation.addAction('Back')
self.back.setIcon(style.standardIcon(style.SP_ArrowBack))
self.forward = navigation.addAction('Forward')
self.forward.setIcon(style.standardIcon(style.SP_ArrowForward))
self.reload = navigation.addAction('Reload')
```

```
self.reload.setIcon(style.standardIcon(style.SP_BrowserReload))
self.stop = navigation.addAction('Stop')
self.stop.setIcon(style.standardIcon(style.SP_BrowserStop))
self.urlbar = qtw.QLineEdit()
navigation.addWidget(self.urlbar)
self.go = navigation.addAction('Go')
self.go.setIcon(style.standardIcon(style.SP_DialogOkButton))
```

Here, we've defined toolbar buttons for standard browser actions, as well as a `QLineEdit` object for the URL bar. We've also extracted icons for these actions from the default style, just as we did in the *Adding toolbars* section of `Chapter 4`, *Building Applications with QMainWindow*.

Now we'll create a `QWebEngineView` object:

```
webview = qtwe.QWebEngineView()
self.setCentralWidget(webview)
```

A `QWebEngineView` object is a (mostly, as you'll see) fully functional and interactive web widget, capable of retrieving and rendering HTML, CSS, JavaScript, images, and other standard web content.

To load a URL in the view, we pass `QUrl` to its `load()` method:

```
webview.load(qtc.QUrl('http://www.alandmoore.com'))
```

This will prompt the web view to download and render the page just like a normal web browser would.

Of course, as good as that website is, we'd like to be able to navigate to others, so we'll add the following connection:

```
self.go.triggered.connect(lambda: webview.load(
    qtc.QUrl(self.urlbar.text())))
```

Here, we've connected our `go` action to a `lambda` function that retrieves the text of the URL bar, wraps it in a `QUrl` object, and sends it to the web view. If you run the script at this point, you should be able to type a URL into the bar, hit **Go,** and browse the web just like any other browser.

QWebView has slots for all the common browser navigation actions, which we can connect to our navigation bar:

```
self.back.triggered.connect(webview.back)
self.forward.triggered.connect(webview.forward)
self.reload.triggered.connect(webview.reload)
self.stop.triggered.connect(webview.stop)
```

With these signals connected, our script is well on its way to being a fully functional web-browsing experience. However, we're currently limited to a single browser window; we want tabs, so let's implement that in the following section.

Allowing multiple windows and tabs

In MainWindow.__init__(), delete or comment-out the web view code you just added (going back to the creation of the QWebEngineView object). We're going to move that functionality to a method instead, so that we can create multiple web views in a tabbed interface. We will do this as follows:

1. To begin, we'll replace our QWebEngineView object with a QTabWidget object as our central widget:

```
self.tabs = qtw.QTabWidget(
    tabsClosable=True, movable=True)
self.tabs.tabCloseRequested.connect(self.tabs.removeTab)
self.new = qtw.QPushButton('New')
self.tabs.setCornerWidget(self.new)
self.setCentralWidget(self.tabs)
```

This tab widget will have movable and closable tabs, and a **New** button in the left corner for adding new tabs.

2. To add a new tab with a web view, we'll create an add_tab() method:

```
def add_tab(self, *args):
    webview = qtwe.QWebEngineView()
    tab_index = self.tabs.addTab(webview, 'New Tab')
```

This method begins by creating a web view widget and adding it to a new tab in the tab widget.

3. Now that we have our web view object, we need to connect some signals:

```
webview.urlChanged.connect(
    lambda x: self.tabs.setTabText(tab_index, x.toString()))
webview.urlChanged.connect(
    lambda x: self.urlbar.setText(x.toString()))
```

The `QWebEngineView` object's `urlChanged` signal is emitted whenever a new URL is loaded into the view, and it sends with it the new URL as a `QUrl` object. We're connecting this signal to a `lambda` function that sets the tab title text to the URL, as well as another function that sets the contents of the URL bar. This will keep the URL bar in sync with the browser when the user navigates using hyperlinks in the web page, rather than directly using the URL bar.

4. We can then add default content to our web view using its `setHtml()` method:

```
webview.setHtml(
    '<h1>Blank Tab</h1><p>It is a blank tab!</p>',
    qtc.QUrl('about:blank'))
```

This sets the content of the browser window to whatever HTML string we give to it. If we also pass a `QUrl` object, it will be used as the current URL (and published to the `urlChanged` signal, for example).

5. To enable navigation, we need to connect our toolbar actions to the browser widget. Since our browser has one global toolbar, we can't just directly connect these to the web view widgets. We'll need to connect them to methods that pass the signals on to the slots in the currently active web view. Start by creating the callback methods as follows:

```
def on_back(self):
    self.tabs.currentWidget().back()

def on_forward(self):
    self.tabs.currentWidget().forward()

def on_reload(self):
    self.tabs.currentWidget().reload()

def on_stop(self):
    self.tabs.currentWidget().stop()

def on_go(self):
    self.tabs.currentWidget().load(
        qtc.QUrl(self.urlbar.text()))
```

These methods are essentially the same as those used with the single-pane browser, but with one crucial change—they use the tab widget's `currentWidget()` method to retrieve the `QWebEngineView` object for a currently visible tab, then call the navigation methods on that web view.

6. Back in `__init__()`, connect the following methods:

```
self.back.triggered.connect(self.on_back)
self.forward.triggered.connect(self.on_forward)
self.reload.triggered.connect(self.on_reload)
self.stop.triggered.connect(self.on_stop)
self.go.triggered.connect(self.on_go)
self.urlbar.returnPressed.connect(self.on_go)
self.new.clicked.connect(self.add_tab)
```

For convenience and keyboard-friendliness, we've also connected the URL bar's `returnPressed` signal to the `on_go()` method. We've also connected our **New** button to the `add_tab()` method.

Give the browser a try now, and you should be able to add multiple tabs and browse independently in each one.

Adding a tab for pop-up windows

Currently, there is a problem with our script in that if you *Ctrl* + click on a hyperlink, or open a link that is configured to open a new window, nothing happens. By default, `QWebEngineView` is incapable of opening new tabs or windows. In order to enable this, we have to override its `createWindow()` method with a function that creates and returns a new `QWebEngineView` object.

We can do this fairly easily by updating our `add_tab()` method:

```
webview.createWindow = self.add_tab
return webview
```

Rather than subclassing `QWebEngineView` to override the method, we'll just assign our `MainWindow.add_tab()` method to its `createWindow()` method. Then we just need to make sure that we return the created web view object at the end of the method.

Note that it's not our responsibility to load the URL in the `createWindow()` method; we only need to create the view and add it appropriately to the GUI. Qt will take care of doing what needs to be done browsing-wise in the web view object that we return.

Now when you try the browser, you should find that a *Ctrl* + click opens a new tab with the requested link.

Advanced QtWebEngine usage

While we have implemented a basic, serviceable browser, it leaves much to be desired. In this section, we're going to explore some of the more advanced features of `QtWebEngineWidgets` by fixing some pain points in our user experience and implementing useful tools such as history and text search.

Sharing a profile

Although we can view multiple tabs in our browser, there is a small problem in the way they work with authenticated websites. Visit any website where you have a login account; log in, then *Ctrl* + click on a link within the site to open it in a new tab. You'll find that you aren't authenticated in the new tab. This can be a real problem with sites that use multiple windows or tabs to implement their user interface. We'd like authentication and other session data to be browser-wide, so let's fix this.

Session information is stored in a **profile** that is represented by a `QWebEngineProfile` object. This object is autogenerated for each `QWebEngineWidget` object, but we can override it with an object of our own.

Start by creating one in `MainWindow.__init__()`:

```
self.profile = qtwe.QWebEngineProfile()
```

We will need to associate this profile object with each new web view as we create them in `add_tab()`. Profiles, however, are not actually a property of the web view; they're the property of the web page object. The page, represented by a `QWebEnginePage` object, can be thought of as the *model* for the web view. Each web view generates its own `page` object, which acts as an interface to the browsing engine.

To override the web view's profile, we need to create a page object, override its profile with our own, then override the web view's page with our new page, like this:

```
page = qtwe.QWebEnginePage(self.profile)
webview.setPage(page)
```

The profile *must* be passed as an argument to the QWebEnginePage constructor, as there is no accessor function to set it afterward. Once we've got a new QWebEnginePage object that uses our profile, we can call QWebEngineView.setPage() to assign it to our web view.

Now when you test the browser, your authentication status should remain intact across all tabs.

Viewing history

Each QWebEngineView object manages its own browsing history, which we can access to allow the user to view and navigate the URLs visited.

To build this feature, let's create an interface that displays the history of the current tab and allows the user to click history items to navigate back to:

1. Start by creating a dock widget for history in MainView.__init__():

```
history_dock = qtw.QDockWidget('History')
self.addDockWidget(qtc.Qt.RightDockWidgetArea, history_dock)
self.history_list = qtw.QListWidget()
history_dock.setWidget(self.history_list)
```

   The history dock just contains a QListWidget object, which will display the history of the currently selected tab.

2. Since we'll need to refresh this list when the user switches tabs, connect the tab widget's currentChanged signal to a callback that can do this:

```
self.tabs.currentChanged.connect(self.update_history)
```

3. The update_history() method looks like this:

```
def update_history(self, *args):
    self.history_list.clear()
    webview = self.tabs.currentWidget()
    if webview:
        history = webview.history()
        for history_item in reversed(history.items()):
            list_item = qtw.QListWidgetItem()
```

```
list_item.setData(
    qtc.Qt.DisplayRole, history_item.url())
self.history_list.addItem(list_item)
```

First, we clear the list widget and retrieve the web view for the currently active tab. If a web view exists (it might not if all the tabs are closed), we retrieve the web view's history using the `history()` method.

This history is a `QWebEngineHistory` object; this object is a property of the web page object and tracks the browsing history. When the `back()` and `forward()` slots are called on a web view, this object is consulted to find the correct URL to load. The `items()` method of the history object returns a list of `QWebEngineHistoryItem` objects detailing the entire browsing history of the web view object.

Our `update_history` method iterates this list and adds a new `QListWidgetItem` object for each item in the history. Note that we're using the list widget item's `setData()` method rather than `setText()`, as it allows us to store the `QUrl` object directly instead of having to convert it to a string (`QListWidget` will automatically convert the URL to a string for display, using the URL's `toString()` method).

4. In addition to calling this method whenever the tabs are switched, we also need to call it when a web view navigates to a new page, in order to keep the history current as the user browses. To make this happen, add a connection to each newly generated web view in the `add_tab()` method:

```
webview.urlChanged.connect(self.update_history)
```

5. To finish our history feature, we'd like to be able to double-click an item in the history and navigate to its URL in the currently open tab. We'll start by creating a `MainWindow` method to do the navigation:

```
def navigate_history(self, item):
    qurl = item.data(qtc.Qt.DisplayRole)
    if self.tabs.currentWidget():
        self.tabs.currentWidget().load(qurl)
```

We're going to be using the `itemDoubleClicked` signal within `QListWidget` to trigger this method, which passes the `QListItemWidget` object that was clicked to its callback. We simply retrieve the URL from the list item by calling its `data()` accessor method, then pass the URL to the currently visible web view.

6. Now, back in `__init__()`, we'll connect the signal to the callback as follows:

```
self.history_list.itemDoubleClicked.connect(
    self.navigate_history)
```

This completes our history functionality; launch the browser and you'll find you can view and navigate using the history list in the dock.

Web settings

The `QtWebEngine` browser, just like the Chromium browser that it's based on, offers a very customizable web experience; we can edit many of its settings to implement various security, functionality, or appearance changes.

To do this, we need to access the following default `settings` object:

```
settings = qtwe.QWebEngineSettings.defaultSettings()
```

The `QWebEngineSettings` object returned by the `defaultSettings()` static method is a global object referenced by all web views in our program. We do not have to (nor can we) explicitly assign it to the web views after changing it. Once we've retrieved it, we can configure it in various ways and our settings will be respected by all the web views we create.

For example, let's alter the fonts a bit:

```
# The web needs more drama:
settings.setFontFamily(
    qtwe.QWebEngineSettings.SansSerifFont, 'Impact')
```

In this case, we're setting the default font family for all sans-serif fonts to `Impact`. In addition to setting the font family, we can also set a default `fontSize` object and a `defaultTextEncoding` object.

The `settings` object also has a number of attributes, which are Boolean switches that we can toggle; for example:

```
settings.setAttribute(
    qtwe.QWebEngineSettings.PluginsEnabled, True)
```

In this example, we're enabling the use of Pepper API plugins, such as Chrome's Flash implementation. There are 29 attributes that we can toggle, a few examples of which are listed in the following table:

Attribute	Default	Description
JavascriptEnabled	True	Allow running JavaScript code.
JavascriptCanOpenWindows	True	Allow JavaScript to open new pop-up windows.
FullScreenSupportEnabled	False	Allow the browser to be fullscreen.
AllowRunningInsecureContent	False	Allow running HTTP content on HTTPS pages.
PlaybackRequiresUserGesture	False	Don't play back media until the user interacts with the page.

To alter settings for an individual web view, access its `QWebEngineSettings` object using `page().settings()`.

Building a text search feature

So far, we've loaded and displayed content in our web view widget, but we haven't really done much with the actual content. One of the powerful features that we get with `QtWebEngine` is the ability to manipulate the contents of web pages by injecting our own JavaScript code into those pages. To see how this works, we're going to use the following instructions to develop a text search feature that will highlight all instances of a search term:

1. We'll start by adding the GUI components to `MainWindow.__init__()`:

```
find_dock = qtw.QDockWidget('Search')
self.addDockWidget(qtc.Qt.BottomDockWidgetArea, find_dock)
self.find_text = qtw.QLineEdit()
find_dock.setWidget(self.find_text)
self.find_text.textChanged.connect(self.text_search)
```

The search widget is just a `QLineEdit` object that is embedded in a dock widget. We've connected the `textChanged` signal to a callback function that will perform the search.

2. To implement the search functionality, we need to write some JavaScript code that will locate and highlight all the instances of a search term for us. We could add this code as a string, but for clarity let's write it in a separate file; open a file called `finder.js` and add in this code:

```
function highlight_selection(){
    let tag = document.createElement('found');
    tag.style.backgroundColor = 'lightgreen';
    window.getSelection().getRangeAt(0).surroundContents(tag);}

function highlight_term(term){
    let found_tags = document.getElementsByTagName("found");
    while (found_tags.length > 0){
        found_tags[0].outerHTML = found_tags[0].innerHTML;}
    while (window.find(term)){highlight_selection();}
    while (window.find(term, false, true)){highlight_selection();}}
```

This book isn't a JavaScript text, so we won't get into the dirty details of how this code works, other than to summarize what's happening:

1. The `highlight_term()` function takes a single string as a search term. It begins by cleaning up any HTML `<found>` tags; this isn't a real tag—it's one we've invented for this functionality so that it won't conflict with any real tags.
2. The function then searches forward and backward through the document looking for instances of the search term.
3. When it finds one, it wraps it in a `<found>` tag with the background color set to light green.

3. Back in `MainWindow.__init__()`, we'll read in this file and save it as an instance variable:

```
with open('finder.js', 'r') as fh:
    self.finder_js = fh.read()
```

4. Now, let's implement our search callback method under `MainWindow`:

```
def text_search(self, term):
    term = term.replace('"', '')
    page = self.tabs.currentWidget().page()
    page.runJavaScript(self.finder_js)
    js = f'highlight_term("{term}");'
    page.runJavaScript(js)
```

To run JavaScript code in our current web view, we need to get a reference to its `QWebEnginePage` object. Then we can call the page's `runJavaScript()` method. This method simply takes a string containing JavaScript code and executes it on the web page.

5. In this case, we first run the contents of our `finder.js` file to set up the functions, then we call the `highlight_term()` function with the search term inserted. As a quick-and-dirty security measure, we're also stripping all the double quotes from the search term; therefore, it can't be used to inject arbitrary JavaScript. If you run the application now, you should be able to search for strings on the page, like this:

This works pretty well, but it is not very efficient to redefine those functions every time we update the search term, is it? It would be great if we could just define those functions once and then have access to them on any page that we navigate to.

6. This can be done using the `QWebEnginePage` object's `scripts` property. This property stores a collection of `QWebEngineScript` objects, which contain JavaScript snippets to be run each time a new page is loaded. By adding our scripts to this collection, we can ensure that our function definitions are run only on each page load, rather than every time we try to search. To make this work, we'll start back in `MainWindow.__init__()` by defining a `QWebEngineScript` object:

```
self.finder_script = qtwe.QWebEngineScript()
self.finder_script.setSourceCode(self.finder_js)
```

7. Each script in the collection is run in one of 256 **worlds**, which are isolated JavaScript contexts. For us to have access to our functions in subsequent calls, we need to make sure our `script` object is executed in the main world by setting its `worldId` property:

```
self.finder_script.setWorldId(qtwe.QWebEngineScript.MainWorld)
```

`QWebEngineScript.MainWorld` is a constant that points to the main JavaScript execution context. If we did not set this, our script would run, but the functions would run in their own world, and wouldn't be available in the web page context for us to use for searching.

8. Now that we have our `script` object, we need to add it to the web page object. This should be done in `MainWindow.add_tab()`, when we create our `page` object:

```
page.scripts().insert(self.finder_script)
```

9. Finally, we can shorten the `text_search()` method:

```
def text_search(self, term):
    page = self.tabs.currentWidget().page()
    js = f'highlight_term("{term}");'
    page.runJavaScript(js)
```

Apart from just running scripts, we can also retrieve data back from the scripts and send it to a callback method within our Python code.

For example, we can make the following change to our JavaScript to return the number of matches from our function:

```
function highlight_term(term){
    //cleanup
    let found_tags = document.getElementsByTagName("found");
    while (found_tags.length > 0){
        found_tags[0].outerHTML = found_tags[0].innerHTML; }
    let matches = 0
    //search forward and backward
    while (window.find(term)){
        highlight_selection();
        matches++;
    }
    while (window.find(term, false, true)){
        highlight_selection();
        matches++;
    }
```

```
                    return matches;
            }
```

This value is *not* returned from `runJavaScript()` as the JavaScript code is executed asynchronously.

To access the return value, we need to pass a reference to a Python callable as a second argument to `runJavaScript()`; Qt will call that method with the return value of the called code:

```python
def text_search(self, term):
    term = term.replace('"', '')
    page = self.tabs.currentWidget().page()
    js = f'highlight_term("{term}");'
    page.runJavaScript(js, self.match_count)
```

Here, we're going to pass the output of the JavaScript call to a method called `match_count()`, which looks like the following code snippet:

```python
def match_count(self, count):
    if count:
        self.statusBar().showMessage(f'{count} matches ')
    else:
        self.statusBar().clearMessage()
```

In this case, we'll just show a status bar message if there are any matches found. Try the browser again and you'll see that the message should successfully be conveyed.

Summary

In this chapter, we explored the possibilities made available to us by `QtWebEngineWidgets`. You implemented a simple browser, then learned how to utilize features such as browsing history, profile sharing, multiple tabs, and common settings. You also learned to inject arbitrary JavaScript into web pages and retrieve the results of those calls.

In the next chapter, you'll learn how to prepare your code for sharing, distribution, and deployment. We'll discuss how to structure your project directory properly, how to distribute Python code using official tools, and how to create standalone executables for various platforms using PyInstaller.

Questions

Try these questions to test your knowledge from this chapter:

1. The following code is giving you an attribute error; what's wrong?

```
from PyQt5 import QtWebEngine as qtwe
w = qtwe.QWebEngineView()
```

2. The following code should connect this `UrlBar` class with a `QWebEngineView` so that the entered URL is loaded when the *return/Enter* key is pressed. It doesn't work, though; what is wrong?

```
class UrlBar(qtw.QLineEdit):

    url_request = qtc.pyqtSignal(str)

    def __init__(self):
        super().__init__()
        self.returnPressed.connect(self.request)

    def request(self):
        self.url_request.emit(self.text())

mywebview = qtwe.QWebEngineView()
myurlbar = UrlBar()
myurlbar.url_request(mywebview.load)
```

3. What is the result of the following code?

```
class WebView(qtwe.QWebEngineView):

    def createWindow(self, _):

        return self
```

4. Check out the documentation for QWebEngineView at https://doc.qt.io/qt-5/qwebengineview.html. How would you implement a zoom feature in your browser?

5. As the name implies, QWebEngineView represents the view portion of a model-view architecture. What class represents the model in this design?

6. Given a QWebEngineView object that is named webview, write code to determine whether JavaScript is enabled on webview.

7. You saw in our browser example that runJavaScript() can pass an integer value to a callback function. Write a simple demo script to test what other kinds of JavaScript objects can be returned, and how they would appear in Python code.

Further reading

For further information, please refer to the following:

- **QuteBrowser** is an open source web browser written in Python using QtWebEngineWidgets. You can find its source code at https://github.com/qutebrowser/qutebrowser.

- **ADMBrowser** is a browser that is based on QtWebEngineWidgets, which was created by the author of this book, and can be used with kiosk systems. You can find it at https://github.com/alandmoore/admbrowser.

- QtWebChannel is a feature that allows for more robust communication between your PyQt application and web content. You can start exploring this advanced feature at https://doc.qt.io/qt-5/qtwebchannel-index.html.

Preparing Your Software for Distribution

17

Up to this point in the book, we have primarily been concerned with writing a working piece of code. Our projects have all been single scripts with, at most, a handful of supporting data files. Producing a finished project doesn't end with writing the code, however; we also need our projects to be easily distributable so that we can share them with (or sell them to) other people.

In this chapter, we're going to look at ways to prepare our code for sharing and distribution.

We'll cover these topics:

- Structuring a project
- Distributing with `setuptools`
- Compiling with PyInstaller

Technical requirements

For this chapter, you will need the basic Python and PyQt setup we have used throughout the book. You will also need the `setuptools`, `wheel`, and `pyinstaller` libraries available from PyPI with this command:

```
$ pip install --user setuptools wheel pyinstaller
```

Windows users will want to install the 7-Zip program from `https://www.7-zip.org/` so that they can work with `tar.gz` files, and users on all platforms should install the UPX utility from `https://upx.github.io/`.

Finally, you will want the example code from the repository at `https://github.com/PacktPublishing/Mastering-GUI-Programming-with-Python/tree/master/Chapter17`.

Check out the following video to see the code in action: `http://bit.ly/2M5xH4J`

Structuring a project

So far in this book, we've been putting all the Python code in each example project into a single file. Real-world Python projects, however, benefit from better organization. While there are no official standards on how to structure a Python project, there are some conventions and general concepts we can apply to our project structure that will not only keep things organized, but encourage others to contribute to our code.

To see how this works, we're going to create a simple tic-tac-toe game in PyQt, then spend the rest of the chapter getting it ready for distribution.

Tic-tac-toe

Our tic-tac-toe game is made up of three classes:

- An engine class that manages the logic of the game
- A board class that provides a view of the game state and a way to make plays
- The main window class that brings the other two together into a GUI

Open a new copy of the application template from `Chapter 4`, *Building Applications with QMainWindow*, and call it `ttt-qt.py`. Now let's create these classes.

The engine class

Our game engine object's main responsibility is to keep track of plays and to check whether there is a winner or whether the game is a draw. The players will be represented simply by the `'X'` and `'O'` strings, and the board will be modeled as a list of nine items that will either be a player or `None`.

It begins like this:

```
class TicTacToeEngine(qtc.QObject):

    winning_sets = [
        {0, 1, 2}, {3, 4, 5}, {6, 7, 8},
        {0, 3, 6}, {1, 4, 7}, {2, 5, 8},
        {0, 4, 8}, {2, 4, 6}
    ]
    players = ('X', 'O')

    game_won = qtc.pyqtSignal(str)
    game_draw = qtc.pyqtSignal()

    def __init__(self):
        super().__init__()
        self.board = [None] * 9
        self.current_player = self.players[0]
```

The `winning_sets` list contains `set` objects with every combination of board indexes that constitutes a win. We'll be using that list to check whether a player won. We've also defined signals to be emitted when the game is won or when there is a draw (that is, all the squares are filled and nobody won). The constructor populates the board list and sets the current player to `X`.

We'll need a method to update the current player after each turn, which looks like this:

```
def next_player(self):
    self.current_player = self.players[
        not self.players.index(self.current_player)]
```

Next, we'll add a method for marking a square:

```
def mark_square(self, square):
    if any([
            not isinstance(square, int),
            not (0 <= square < len(self.board)),
            self.board[square] is not None
    ]):
        return False
    self.board[square] = self.current_player
    self.next_player()
    return True
```

This method first checks for any reason the given square shouldn't be marked, returning `False` if there is a reason; otherwise, we mark the square, swap to the next player, and return `True`.

The last method in this class will check the state of the board to see whether there is a winner or a draw:

```
def check_board(self):
    for player in self.players:
        plays = {
            index for index, value in enumerate(self.board)
            if value == player
        }
        for win in self.winning_sets:
            if not win - plays:  # player has a winning combo
                self.game_won.emit(player)
                return
    if None not in self.board:
        self.game_draw.emit()
```

This method uses some set operations to check each player's currently-marked squares against the list of winning combinations. If any match is found, the game_won signal is emitted and the method returns. If nobody has won yet, we also check to see whether there are any unmarked squares; if there aren't, the game is a draw. If neither of these cases is true, we do nothing.

The board class

For the board GUI, we'll use a QGraphicsScene object just as we did for our tank game in Chapter 12, *Creating 2D Graphics with QPainter*.

We'll start with some class variables:

```
class TTTBoard(qtw.QGraphicsScene):

    square_rects = (
        qtc.QRectF(5, 5, 190, 190),
        qtc.QRectF(205, 5, 190, 190),
        qtc.QRectF(405, 5, 190, 190),
        qtc.QRectF(5, 205, 190, 190),
        qtc.QRectF(205, 205, 190, 190),
        qtc.QRectF(405, 205, 190, 190),
        qtc.QRectF(5, 405, 190, 190),
        qtc.QRectF(205, 405, 190, 190),
        qtc.QRectF(405, 405, 190, 190)
    )

    square_clicked = qtc.pyqtSignal(int)
```

The `square_rects` tuple defines a `QRectF` object for each of the nine squares on the board, and a `square_clicked` signal is emitted whenever a square is clicked on; the accompanying integer will indicate which square (0-8) was clicked on.

Here is the `=__init__()` method:

```
def __init__(self):
    super().__init__()
    self.setSceneRect(0, 0, 600, 600)
    self.setBackgroundBrush(qtg.QBrush(qtc.Qt.cyan))
    for square in self.square_rects:
        self.addRect(square, brush=qtg.QBrush(qtc.Qt.white))
    self.mark_pngs = {
        'X': qtg.QPixmap('X.png'),
        'O': qtg.QPixmap('O.png')
    }
    self.marks = []
```

This method sets the scene size and paints a cyan background, and then it draws each of the squares in `square_rects`. We then load up the `QPixmap` objects for the `'X'` and `'O'` images that will be used to mark the squares, and we create an empty list to keep track of the `QGraphicsSceneItem` objects for our marks.

Next, we'll add a method to draw the current state of the board:

```
def set_board(self, marks):
    for i, square in enumerate(marks):
        if square in self.mark_pngs:
            mark = self.addPixmap(self.mark_pngs[square])
            mark.setPos(self.square_rects[i].topLeft())
            self.marks.append(mark)
```

This method will take a list of the marks on our board and draw the appropriate pixmap in each square, keeping track of the `QGraphicsSceneItems` objects created.

Now we'll need a method to clear the board:

```
def clear_board(self):
    for mark in self.marks:
        self.removeItem(mark)
```

This method simply iterates through the saved pixmap items and removes them all.

The last thing we need to do is handle mouse clicks:

```
def mousePressEvent(self, mouse_event):
    position = mouse_event.buttonDownScenePos(qtc.Qt.LeftButton)
    for square, qrect in enumerate(self.square_rects):
        if qrect.contains(position):
            self.square_clicked.emit(square)
            break
```

The `mousePressEvent()` method is called by `QGraphicsScene` whenever the user makes a mouse click. It includes a `QMouseEvent` object that contains details about the event, including the position of the mouse click. We can check whether this click is inside any of our `square_rects` objects, and if so, we'll emit the `square_clicked` signal and exit the method.

The main window class

In `MainWindow.__init__()`, we'll start by creating a board and a `QGraphicsView` object to display it:

```
self.board = TTTBoard()
self.board_view = qtw.QGraphicsView()
self.board_view.setScene(self.board)
self.setCentralWidget(self.board_view)
```

Now we need to create an instance of the game engine and connect its signals. In order to allow us to start games over and over, we'll create a separate method for this:

```
def start_game(self):
    self.board.clear_board()
    self.game = TicTacToeEngine()
    self.game.game_won.connect(self.game_won)
    self.game.game_draw.connect(self.game_draw)
```

This method clears the board, and then it creates an instance of the game engine object, connecting the engine's signals to `MainWindow` methods to handle the two game-over scenarios.

Back in __init__(), we'll go ahead and call this method to set up the first game automatically:

```
self.start_game()
```

Next, we need to enable player input. We'll need a method that will try to mark the square in the engine and then check the board for a win or a draw if the mark was successful:

```
def try_mark(self, square):
    if self.game.mark_square(square):
        self.board.set_board(self.game.board)
        self.game.check_board()
```

That method can be connected to the board's `square_clicked` signal; back in __init__(), add this code:

```
self.board.square_clicked.connect(self.try_mark)
```

Finally, we need to handle the two game-over scenarios:

```
def game_won(self, player):
    """Display the winner and start a new game"""
    qtw.QMessageBox.information(
        None, 'Game Won', f'Player {player} Won!')
    self.start_game()

def game_draw(self):
    """Display the lack of a winner and start a new game"""
    qtw.QMessageBox.information(
        None, 'Game Over', 'Game Over.  Nobody Won...')
    self.start_game()
```

In both cases, we're just going to display an appropriate message in `QMessageBox` and then restart the game.

This completes our game. Take a moment to run the game and make sure you understand how it responds when working correctly (maybe get a friend to play a few rounds with you; it helps if your friend is quite young or not particularly bright).

Now that we have a working game, it's time to prepare it for distribution. The first thing we'll do is structure our project in a way that will make it easier for us to maintain and expand, and for other Python programmers to collaborate on.

Module-style structure

As programmers, we tend to think of applications and libraries as two very different things, but, in truth, well-structured applications aren't that different from libraries. A library is just a collection of ready-made classes and functions. Our application is mostly just class definitions as well; it just happens to have a few lines of code at the end that allow it to be executed as an application. When we see things this way, structuring our application as a Python library module makes a lot of sense. To do this, we're going to convert our single Python file to a directory full of files, each containing an individual unit of code.

The first step is to consider our project's name; right now, that name is `ttt-qt.py`. It's not uncommon to come up with a quick and short name when you first start hacking on a project, but that doesn't need to be the name you stick with. In this case, our name is rather cryptic and doesn't work as a Python module name due to the hyphen. Instead, let's call it `qtictactoe`, a name that is more explicit and avoids the hyphen.

To begin, create a new directory called `QTicTacToe`; this will be our **project root**. The project root is the directory under which all our project files will go.

Inside that directory, we'll create a second directory called `qtictactoe`; this will be the **module directory** inside which the bulk of our source code will live.

Structuring the module

To begin our module, we're going to start by adding the code for our three classes. We're going to put each one in a separate file; this isn't strictly necessary, but it will help us to keep our code decoupled and make it easier to find the class we want to edit.

Therefore, under `qtictactoe`, create three files:

- `engine.py` will hold our game engine class. Copy in the `TicTacToeEngine` definition along with the necessary `PyQt5` import statements for the classes it uses. In this case, you only need `QtCore`.
- `board.py` will hold the `TTTBoard` class. Copy in that code as well as the full set of `PyQt5` import statements.
- Finally, `mainwindow.py` will hold the `MainWindow` class. Copy in the code for that class as well as the `PyQt5` imports.

`mainwindow.py` also needs access to the `TicTacToeEngine` and `TTTBoard` classes from the other files. To provide this access, we need to use **relative imports**. A relative import is a way of importing submodules from the same module.

At the top of `mainwindow.py`, add this:

```
from .engine import TicTacToeEngine
from .board import TTTBoard
```

The dot in the import indicates that this is a relative import, and refers specifically to the current container module (in this case, `qtictactoe`). By using relative imports like this, we can ensure that we're importing these modules from our own project and not from some other Python library on the end user's system.

The next code we need to add to our module is code to make it actually run. This is the code we usually put under our `if __name__ == '__main__'` block.

In the module, we'll put it in a file called `__main__.py`:

```
import sys
from PyQt5.QtWidgets import QApplication
from .mainwindow import MainWindow

def main():
    app = QApplication(sys.argv)
    mainwindow = MainWindow()
    sys.exit(app.exec())

if __name__ == '__main__':
    main()
```

The `__main__.py` file serves a special purpose in a Python module. It is executed whenever our module is run using the `-m` switch, like so:

```
$ python3 -m qtictactoe
```

Essentially, `__main__.py` is the module equivalent of the `if __name__ == '__main__':` block in a Python script.

Note that we have placed our three main lines of code inside a function called `main()`. The reason for that will become apparent when we discuss the use of `setuptools`.

The last file we need to create inside our module is an empty file called __init__.py. The __init__.py file of a Python module is analogous to the __init__() method of a Python class. It is executed whenever the module is imported, and anything in its namespace is considered to be in the root namespace of the module. In this case, though, we're going to just leave it empty. That may seem pointless, but without this file many of the tools we're going to be working with won't recognize this folder of Python files as an actual module.

At this point, your directory structure should look like this:

```
QTicTacToe/
├── qtictactoe
        ├── board.py
        ├── engine.py
        ├── __init__.py
        ├── __main__.py
        └── mainwindow.py
```

Now we can execute our program using python3 -m qtictactoe, but that's not terribly intuitive for most users. Let's help out a little by creating an obvious file for executing the application.

Directly under the project root (outside the module), create a file called run.py:

```
from qtictactoe.__main__ import main
main()
```

This file's only purpose is to load the main() function from our module and execute it. Now you can execute python run.py and you'll find it launches just fine. However, there's a problem—when you click a square, nothing happens. That's because our image files are missing. We'll need to deal with those next.

Non-Python files

In a PyQt program, the best way to deal with files such as our X and O images is to use the pyrcc5 tool to generate a resources file that can then be added to your module like any other Python file (we learned about this in Chapter 6, *Styling Qt Applications*). However, in this case, we're going to keep our images as PNG files so that we can explore our options for dealing with non-Python files.

There is little consensus on where these kinds of files should live inside a project directory, but since these images are a required component of the TTTBoard class, it makes sense to put them inside our module. For the sake of organization, put them in a directory called images.

Your directory structure should now look like this:

```
QTicTacToe/
├── qtictactoe
│   ├── board.py
│   ├── engine.py
│   ├── images
│   │   ├── O.png
│   │   └── X.png
│   ├── __init__.py
│   ├── __main__.py
│   └── mainwindow.py
└── run.py
```

The way we have written `TTTBoard`, you can see that each image is loaded using a relative file path. In Python, relative paths are always relative to the current working directory—that is, the directory from which the user launched the script. Unfortunately, this is a rather brittle design, as we have no control over this directory. We also can't hardcode an absolute file path since we don't know where our application might be stored on a user's system (see our discussion of this problem in Chapter 6, *Styling Qt Applications*, under the *Using Qt Resource files* section).

 The ideal way to solve this problem in a PyQt application is to use Qt Resource files; however, we're going to try a different approach just to illustrate how to solve this problem in cases where that isn't an option.

To get around this, we need to modify the way `TTTBoard` loads the images so that it's relative to the location of our module, rather than the user's current working directory. This will require us to use the `os.path` module from the Python standard library, so add this at the top of `board.py`:

```
from os import path
```

Now, down in `__init__()`, we'll modify the lines that load in the images:

```
directory = path.dirname(__file__)
self.mark_pngs = {
    'X': qtg.QPixmap(path.join(directory, 'images', 'X.png')),
    'O': qtg.QPixmap(path.join(directory, 'images', 'O.png'))
}
```

The __file__ variable is a built-in variable that always contains the absolute path to the current file (board.py, in this case). Using path.dirname, we can find the directory that contains this file. Then, we can use path.join to assemble a path that looks for the files under a folder called images in the same directory.

If you run the program now, you should find that it works perfectly, just as before. We're not quite done yet, though.

Documentation and metadata

Working and well-organized code is a great start for our project; however if you want others to use or contribute to your project, you'll need to address some of the questions they're likely to have. For example, they'll need to know how to install the program, what its prerequisites are, or what the legal terms of use or distribution are.

To answer these questions, we'll include a series of standard files and directories: the LICENSE file, the README file, the docs directory, and the requirements.txt file.

The LICENSE file

When you share code, it's important to spell out exactly what others can or cannot do with that code. In most countries, a person who creates a piece of work such as a program is automatically the copyright holder of that work; that means you exercise control over the copying of your work. If you want others to contribute to or use what you've created, you need to grant them a **license** to do so.

The license that governs your project is usually provided in a plain-text file in the project root called LICENSE. In our example code, we've included such a file that contains a copy of the **MIT license**. The MIT license is a permissive open source license which basically allows anyone to do anything with the code as long as they retain our copyright notice. It also states that we aren't responsible for anything terrible that happens as a result of someone using our code.

 This file is sometimes called COPYING, and may have a file extension such as txt as well.

You are certainly free to put any conditions you wish in your license; however, for PyQt applications, you need to make sure your license is compatible with the terms of PyQt's **General Public License** (**GPL**) GNU and Qt's **Lesser General Public License** (**LGPL**) GNU. If you intend to release commercial or restrictively-licensed PyQt software, remember from Chapter 1, *Getting Started with PyQt,* that you will need to purchase commercial licenses from both the Qt company and Riverbank Computing.

For open source projects, the Python community strongly recommends you stick with well-known licenses such as the MIT, BSD, GPL, or LGPL. A list of recognized open source licenses can be found on the website of the Open Source Initiative at `https://opensource.org/licenses`. You may also want to consult `https://choosealicense.com`, a site that offers guidance on selecting a license that best matches your intentions.

The README file

The `README` file is one of the oldest traditions in software distribution. Dating back to the mid 1970s, this plain-text file is usually meant to convey the most basic set of instructions and information to users of the program before they install or run the software.

Although there is no standard for what a `README` file should contain, there are certain things a user would expect to find; some of these include the following:

- The name and home page of the software
- The author of the software (with contact information)
- A short description of the software
- Basic usage instructions, including any command-line switches or arguments
- Instructions for reporting bugs or contributing to the project
- A list of known bugs
- Notes such as platform-specific issues or instructions

Whatever you include in the file, you should aim to keep it concise and organized. To facilitate some organizations, many modern software projects employ a markup language when writing a `README` file; this allows us to use elements such as headers, bullet lists, and even tables.

In Python projects, the preferred markup language is the **ReStructured Text** (**RST**). This language is part of the `docutils` project, which provides documentation utilities for Python.

We'll take a brief look at RST as we walk through creating a `README.rst` file for `qtictactoe`. Start with a title:

```
=============
 QTicTacToe
=============
```

The equals signs around the top line indicate that it is a title; in this case, we've just used the name of our project.

Next, we'll create a couple of sections for basic information about the project; we indicate section headers by simply underlining a line of text with symbols, like this:

```
Authors
=======
By Alan D Moore -  https://www.alandmoore.com

About
=====

This is the classic game of **tic-tac-toe**, also known as noughts and
crosses.  Battle your opponent in a desperate race to get three in a line.
```

The symbols used for underlining section headers must be one of the following:

```
= - ` : ' " ~ ^ _ * + # < >
```

The order in which we use them isn't important, as RST interpreters will assume the first symbols used as an underline representing a top-level header, the next type of symbol is a second-level header, and so on. In this case, we're using the equals sign first, so it will indicate a level-one header wherever we use it throughout this document.

Note the double asterisks around the words `tic-tac-toe`; this indicates bold text. RST can also indicate underlines, italics, and similar typographic styles.

For example, we can indicate monospaced code text by using the backtick:

```
Usage
=====

Simply run `python qtictactoe.py` from within the project folder.

- Players take turns clicking the mouse on the playing field to mark
squares.
- When one player gets 3 in a row, they win.
- If the board is filled with nobody getting in a row, the game is a draw.
```

This example also shows a bullet list: each line is prefixed with a dash and space. We can alternately use the + or * symbols as well, and create subpoints by indenting.

Let's finish our README.rst file with some information about contributing and some notes:

```
Contributing
============

Submit bugs and patches to the
`public git repository <http://git.example.com/qtictactoe>`_.

Notes
=====

    A strange game.  The only winning move is not to play.

    *—Joshua the AI, WarGames*
```

The Contributing section shows how to create a hyperlink: put the hyperlink text inside backticks, with the URL inside angle brackets, and add an underscore after the closing backtick. The Notes section demonstrates a block quote, which is accomplished by simply indenting the line four spaces.

Although our file is perfectly readable as text, many popular code-sharing sites will translate RST and other markup languages to HTML. For example, on GitHub this file will appear in the browser like this:

QTicTacToe

Authors

By Alan D Moore - https://www.alandmoore.com

About

This is the classic game of **tic-tac-toe**, also known as noughts and crosses. Battle your opponent in a desperate race to get three in a line.

Usage

Simply run python qtictactoe.py from within the project folder.

- Players take turns clicking the mouse on the playing field to mark squares.
- When one player gets 3 in a row, they win.
- If the board is filled with nobody getting in a row, the game is a draw.

Contributing

Submit bugs and patches to the public git repository.

Notes

> A strange game. The only winning move is not to play.
>
> —*Joshua the AI, WarGames*

This simple `README.rst` file is sufficient for our small application; as an application grows, it will warrant further expansion to document added features, contributors, community policies, and more. This is why we prefer to use a plain-text format such as RST and why we make it part of the project repository; it should be updated along with the code.

 A quick reference for RST syntax can be found at `docutils.sourceforge.net/docs/user/rst/quickref.html`.

The docs directory

While this README file is sufficient documentation for QTicTacToe, a more complex program or library may demand more robust documentation. The standard place to put such documentation is in the docs directory. This directory should be right under our project root, and can contain any sort of additional documentation, including the following:

- Sample configuration files
- User manuals
- API documentation
- Database diagrams

Since our program doesn't need any of these things, we don't need to add a docs directory to this project.

The requirements.txt file

Python programs often require packages outside the standard library to operate, and users will need to know what to install in order for your project to run. You can (and probably should) put this information in the README file, but you should also put it in requirements.txt.

The format for requirements.txt is one library per line, like so:

```
PyQt5
PyQt5-sip
```

The library names in this file should match what is used in PyPI, as this file can then be used by pip to install all the required libraries for the project, like so:

```
$ pip  install --user -r requirements.txt
```

We don't actually have to specify PyQt5-sip since it's a dependency of PyQt5 and will be installed automatically. We added it here to show how multiple libraries are specified.

If specific versions of libraries are required, this can also be noted using version specifiers:

```
PyQt5 >= 5.12
PyQt5-sip == 4.19.4
```

In this case, we are specifying PyQt5 version 5.12 or greater, and only version 4.19.4 of PyQt5-sip.

More information about the requirements.txt file can be found at https://pip.readthedocs.io/en/1.1/requirements.html.

Other files

These are the bare essentials of project documentation and metadata, but you may find some additional files useful in certain situations:

- TODO.txt: A shortlist of bugs or missing features that need work
- CHANGELOG.txt: A log of the history of major project changes and releases
- tests: A directory containing unit tests for your module
- scripts: A directory containing Python or shell scripts that are useful to, but not part of, your module
- Makefile: Some projects benefit from a scripted build process, and for that, a utility such as make can be helpful; alternatives include CMake, SCons, or Waf

At this point, though, your project is ready to upload to your favorite source code-sharing site. In the next section, we'll look at getting it ready for PyPI.

Distributing with setuptools

Many times throughout this book, you have installed Python packages using pip. You probably know that pip downloads these packages from PyPI and installs them to your system, Python virtual environment, or user environment. What you may not know is that the tool used to create and install these packages is called setuptools, and it's readily available to us if we want to make our own packages for PyPI or for personal use.

Although `setuptools` is the officially recommended tool for creating Python packages, it is not part of the standard library. However, it *is* included in the default distributions for most **operating systems** (**OS**es) if you elect to include `pip` during installation. If for some reason you don't have `setuptools` installed, consult the documentation at `https://setuptools.readthedocs.io/en/latest/` to see how you can install it on your platform.

The main task involved in using `setuptools` is writing a `setup.py` script. In this section, we'll learn how to write and use our `setup.py` script to generate distributable packages.

Writing the setuptools configuration

The primary purpose of `setup.py` is to call the `setuptools.setup()` function with keyword arguments, which will define our project's metadata as well as how our project should be packaged and installed.

So, the first thing we'll do is import that function:

```
from setuptools import setup

setup(
    # Arguments here
)
```

The remaining code in `setup.py` will be keyword arguments to `setup()`. Let's go through the different categories of those arguments.

Basic metadata arguments

The simplest arguments involve the basic metadata about the project:

```
name='QTicTacToe',
version='1.0',
author='Alan D Moore',
author_email='alandmoore@example.com',
description='The classic game of noughts and crosses',
url="http://qtictactoe.example.com",
license='MIT',
```

Here, we've described the package name, version, short description, project URL, and license, as well as the author's name and email. This information will be written to the package metadata and used by sites such as PyPI to build a profile page for your project.

For example, look at the PyPI page for PyQt5:

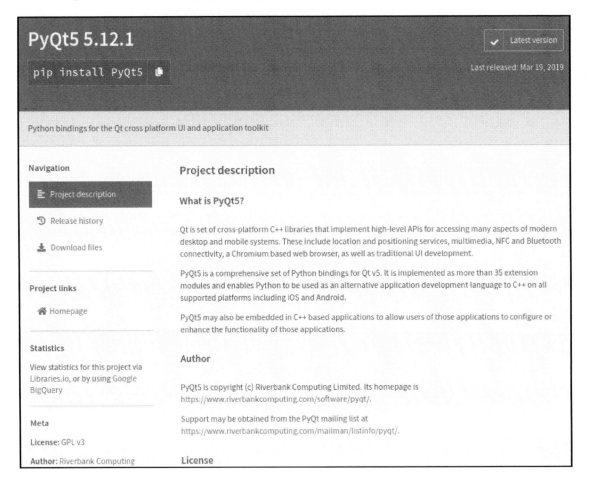

Along the left-side of the page, you'll see a link to the project's home page, the author (with a hyperlinked email address), and the license. At the top, you see the project name and version, as well as a short description of the project. All of this kind of data can be extracted from a project's `setup.py` script.

 If you plan to submit a package to PyPI, please see PEP 440 at https://www.python.org/dev/peps/pep-0440/ for how your version number should be specified.

The long text you see in the main body of this page comes from the `long_description` argument. We could just put a long string directly into this argument, but since we already have such a nice `README.rst` file, why not use that here? Since `setup.py` is a Python script, we can just read in the file's contents, like so:

```
long_description=open('README.rst', 'r').read(),
```

One advantage of using RST here is that PyPI (and many other code-sharing sites) will automatically render your markup into nicely-formatted HTML.

If we wish to make our project easier to search for, we can include a string of space-separated keywords:

```
keywords='game multiplayer example pyqt5',
```

In this case, a person who searched for "multiplayer pyqt5" in PyPI should find our project.

Finally, you can include a dictionary of project-related URLs:

```
project_urls={
    'Author Website': 'https://www.alandmoore.com',
    'Publisher Website': 'https://packtpub.com',
    'Source Code': 'https://git.example.com/qtictactoe'
},
```

The format is `{'label': 'URL'}`; examples of things you might include here are the project's bug tracker, documentation site, Wiki page, or source repository, especially if any of those are different to the home URL.

Packages and dependencies

Apart from establishing the basic metadata, `setup()` needs information about the actual code that needs to be included, or the environment that needs to be present on the system for this package to be executed.

The first keyword we need to deal with here is `packages`, which defines the modules in our project that need to be included:

```
packages=['qtictactoe', 'qtictactoe.images'],
```

Note that we need to include both the `qtictactoe` module and the `qtictactoe.images` module explicitly; even though the `images` directory is under `qtictactoe`, it will not be included automatically.

If we had a lot of submodules and didn't want to explicitly list them, `setuptools` offers an automatic solution as well:

```
from setuptools import setup, find_package

setup(
    #...
    packages=find_packages(),
)
```

> If you want to use `find_packages`, make sure each submodule has an `__init__.py` file in it so that `setuputils` can identify it as a module. In this case, you'd need to add an `__init__.py` file to the `images` folder or it will be ignored.

Both approaches have advantages and drawbacks; the manual approach is more work, but `find_packages` may sometimes fail to identify a library in certain circumstances.

We also need to specify the external libraries that are needed for this project to run—in this case, `PyQt5`. That can be done with the `install_requires` keyword:

```
install_requires=['PyQt5'],
```

This keyword takes a list of names for packages that must be installed for the program to be installed. When your program is installed using `pip`, it will use this list to install all dependency packages automatically. You should include anything that isn't part of the standard library in this list.

Just like the `requirements.txt` file, we can even be explicit about the version number of each dependency required:

```
install_requires=['PyQt5 >= 5.12'],
```

In this case, `pip` would make sure a version of PyQt5 greater than or equal to 5.12 is installed. If no version is specified, `pip` will install the latest version available from PyPI.

In some cases, we might require a certain version of Python as well; for example, our project uses f-strings, a feature only found in Python 3.6 or greater. We can specify that with the `python_requires` keyword:

```
python_requires='>=3.6',
```

We can also specify dependencies for optional features; for example, if we added an optional network-play feature to `qtictactoe`, which required the `requests` library, we would specify that like so:

```
extras_require={
    "NetworkPlay": ["requests"]
}
```

The `extras_require` keyword accepts a mapping of feature names (which can be anything you want) to lists of package names. These modules won't be automatically installed when your package is, but other modules can depend on these subfeatures. For example, another module can specify a dependency on our project's `NetworkPlay` extra keywords like so:

```
install_requires=['QTicTacToe[NetworkPlay]'],
```

This would trigger a cascade of dependencies that would result in the `requests` library being installed.

Non-Python files

By default, `setuptools` will package the Python files it finds in our project, and other file types will be ignored. In almost any project, however, there are going to be non-Python files that we're going to want to include in our distribution package. These files fall generally into two categories: those that are part of a Python module, such as our PNG files, and those that are not, such as the README file.

To incorporate files that are *not* part of a Python package, we need to create a file called `MANIFEST.in`. This file contains `include` directives for file paths underneath the project root. For example, if we want to include our documentation files, ours should look like the following:

```
include README.rst
include LICENSE
include requirements.txt
include docs/*
```

The format is simple: the word `include` followed by a filename, path, or pattern that will match a set of files. All paths are relative to the project root.

To include files that are part of a Python package, we have two choices.

One way is to include them in the MANIFEST.in file, and then set
include_package_data to True in setup.py:

```
include_package_data=True,
```

Another way to include non-Python files is to use the package_data keyword argument in setup.py:

```
package_data={
    'qtictactoe.images': ['*.png'],
    '': ['*.txt', '*.rst']
},
```

This argument takes a dict object, where each item is a module path and a list of patterns that match the files included. In this case, we want to include all PNG files found in the qtictactoe.images module, and any TXT or RST files anywhere in the package. Keep in mind this argument only applies to files *in the module directory* (that is, files under qtictactoe). If we want to include files such as README.rst or run.py, those should be put in the MANIFEST.in file.

> You can use either approach to including files, but you cannot use *both* approaches in the same project; if you enable include_package_data, the package_data directives will be ignored.

Executables

We tend to think of PyPI as a tool to install Python libraries; in fact, it works well for installing applications as well, and many Python applications are available from it. Even if you are creating a library, it's likely your library will ship with executable utilities, such as the pyrcc5 and pyuic5 utilities that come with PyQt5.

To accommodate these, setuputils gives us a way to specify particular functions or methods as console scripts; when the package is installed, it will create a simple executable file, which will call that function or method when executed from the command line.

This is specified using the entry_points keyword:

```
entry_points={
    'console_scripts': [
        'qtictactoe = qtictactoe.__main__:main'
    ]
}
```

The `entry_points` dictionary has other uses, but the one we're most concerned with is the `'console_scripts'` key. This key points to a list of strings that specify the functions we want set up as command-line scripts. The format for these strings is as follows:

```
'command_name = module.submodule:function'
```

You can add as many console scripts as you wish; they just need to point to a function or method in the package that can be run directly. Note that you *must* specify an actual callable here; you can't just point to a Python file to run. This is why we've put all the execution code under a `main()` function inside `__main__.py`.

`setuptools` contains many more directives to deal with less common situations; for a complete list, see `https://setuptools.readthedocs.io/en/latest/setuptools.html`.

Source distributions

Now that `setup.py` is ready to go, we can use it to actually create our package distributions. There are two basic types of package distributions: `source` and `built`. In this section, we'll talk about how to use **source distributions**.

A source distribution is a bundle of all the source code and extra files needed to build our project. It includes the `setup.py` file and is useful for distributing your project in a cross-platform way.

Creating a source distribution

To build a source distribution, open Command Prompt in your project root and enter this command:

```
$ python3 setup.py sdist
```

This will create a couple of directories and many files:

- The `ProjectName.egg-info` directory (in our case, the `QTicTacToe.egg-info` directory) will contain several files of metadata generated from our `setup.py` arguments.
- The `dist` directory will contain the `tar.gz` archive file containing our distribution. Ours is called `QTicTacToe-1.0.tar.gz`.

Take a few minutes to explore the contents of QTicTacToe.egg-info; you'll see that all the information we specified in setup() is there in some form. This directory is also included inside the source distribution.

Also, take a moment to open the tar.gz file and see what it contains; you'll see all the files we specified in MANIFEST.in, as well as the qtictactoe module and all the files from QTicTacToe.egg-info. Essentially, this is a complete copy of our project directory.

 Linux and macOS have native support for tar.gz archives; on Windows, you can use the free 7-Zip utility. See the *Technical requirements* section for information about 7-Zip.

Installing a source distribution

A source distribution can be installed using pip; to see how this works in a clean environment, we'll install our library in a Python **virtual environment**. Virtual environments are a way to create an isolated Python stack in which you can add or remove libraries independently of your system Python installation.

In a console window, create a new directory and then make it a virtual environment:

```
$ mkdir test_env
$ virtualenv -p python3 test_env
```

The virtualenv command copies the necessary files into the given directory so that Python can be run, as well as some scripts to activate and deactivate the environment.

To start using your new environment, run this command:

```
# On Linux and Mac
$ source test_env/bin/activate
# On Windows
$ test_env\Scripts\activate
```

Depending on your platform, your command-line prompt may change to indicate that you're in a virtual environment. Now when you run python or Python-related tools such as pip, they will do all the operations in the virtual environment rather than in your system Python.

Let's install our source distribution package:

```
$ pip install QTicTacToe/dist/QTicTacToe-1.0.tar.gz
```

This command will cause `pip` to extract our source distribution and execute `python setup.py install` inside the project root. The `install` directive will download any dependencies, build an entry point executable, and copy the code into the directory where your Python libraries are stored (in the case of our virtual environment, that would be `test_env/lib/python3.7/site-packages/`). Notice that a fresh copy of `PyQt5` is downloaded; your virtual environment has nothing but Python and the standard library installed, so any dependencies we listed in `install_requires` will have to be installed anew.

After `pip` finishes, you should be able to run the `qtictactoe` command and launch the application successfully. This command is stored in `test_env/bin`, in case your OS does not automatically append the virtual environment directories to your `PATH`.

To remove the package from the virtual environment, you can run the following:

```
$ pip uninstall QTicTacToe
```

This should clean up the sources and all the generated files.

Built distributions

Source distributions are essential for developers, but they often contain many elements that aren't necessary for an end user, such as unit tests or example code. In addition to this, if the project contains compiled code (such as Python extensions written in C), that code will require compilation before it can be used on the target. To address this, `setuptools` offers a variety of **built distribution** types. A built distribution provides a ready-made set of files, which only need to be copied to the appropriate directories to use.

In this section, we'll talk about how to work with built distributions.

Types of built distributions

The first step in creating a built distribution is determining the type of built distribution we want. The `setuptools` library offers a few different built distribution types, and we can install other libraries to add more options.

The built-in types are as follows:

- **Binary distribution**: This is a `tar.gz` file just like a source distribution, but unlike the source distribution it contains precompiled code (for example, the `qtictactoe` executable) and omits certain types of files (such as tests). The contents of a built distribution need to be extracted and copied to an appropriate location to be run.
- **Windows installer**: This is just like the binary distribution, except that it's an executable that will launch an install wizard on Windows. The wizard merely serves to copy the files to the proper location for execution or library use.
- **RPM Package Manager (RPM) installer**: Again, this one is just like the binary distribution, except that it packages code in an RPM file. RPM files are used by package management utilities on several Linux distributions (such as Red Hat, CentOS, Suse, Fedora, and more).

While you may find these distribution types useful in certain situations, they are all a bit dated in 2019; the standard way to distribute Python today is using a **wheel distribution**. These are the binary distribution packages you'll find on PyPI.

Let's look at creating and installing wheel packages.

Creating a wheel distribution

To create a wheel distribution, you first need to make sure the `wheel` library is installed from PyPI (see the *Technical requirements* section). After that, `setuptools` will have an additional `bdist_wheel` option.

You can use that to create your wheel file like this:

```
$ python3 setup.py bdist_wheel
```

Just as before, this command will create the `QTicTacToe.egg-info` directory and populate it with files containing your project metadata. It also creates a `build` directory, where compiled files are staged before being compacted into the `wheel` file.

Under `dist`, we'll find our completed `wheel` file. In our case, it's called `QTicTacToe-1.0-py3-none-any.whl`. The format for the filename is as follows:

- The project name (`QTicTacToe`).
- The version (1.0).
- The version of Python that is supported, whether 2, 3, or `universal` (py3).

- The `ABI` tag, which indicates a specific release of Python on whose binary interface our project depends (`none`). This will only be used if we have compiled the code.
- The platform (OS and CPU architecture). Ours is any because we aren't including any platform-specific binaries.

Binary distributions come in three types:

- A **Universal** type has only Python and is compatible with Python 2 or 3
- A **Pure Python** type has only Python but is compatible with Python 2 or Python 3
- A **Platform** type includes a compiled code that only runs on a particular platform

As reflected in the distribution name, our package is of the pure Python variety since it contains no compiled code and only supports Python 3. PyQt5 is an example of a platform package type since it includes the Qt libraries compiled for specific platforms.

Recall from `Chapter 15`, *PyQt on the Raspberry Pi*, that we could not install PyQt from PyPI on the Raspberry Pi because there was no `wheel` file for the Linux ARM platform. Since PyQt5 is a platform package type, it can only be installed on platforms for which this `wheel` file has been generated.

Installing a built distribution

Just as with source distributions, we can install our wheel file using `pip`:

```
$ pip install qtictactoe/dist/QTicTacToe-1.0-py3-none-any.whl
```

If you try this in a fresh virtual environment, you should find that, once again, PyQt5 is downloaded from PyPI and installed and that you have the `qtictactoe` command available afterward. There isn't much difference to the end user in the case of a program such as `QTicTacToe`, but in the case of a library with binary files to compile (such as PyQt5), it makes the set up considerably less problematic.

Of course, even a `wheel` file requires that the target system have Python and `pip` installed, as well as access to the internet and PyPI. This is still a lot to ask of many users or computing environments. In the next section, we're going to explore a tool that will allow us to create a standalone executable from our Python projects, which can run without any prerequisites.

Compiling with PyInstaller

After successfully writing their first application, the most common question many Python programmers have is *How do I make this code into an executable?*. Unfortunately, there isn't a single, official answer to this question. Over the years, many projects have been launched to address this task (such as Py2Exe, cx_Freeze, Nuitka, and PyInstaller to name a few), with varying degrees of support, simplicity of use, and consistency of results. In terms of these qualities, the current best option is **PyInstaller**.

PyInstaller overview

Python is an interpreted language; instead of being compiled to machine code the way C or C++ is, your Python code (or an optimized version of it called **bytecode**) is read and executed by the Python interpreter each time you run it. This allows Python to have some features that make it very easy to use, but also make it hard to compile into machine code to provide a traditional standalone executable.

PyInstaller steps around this problem by packaging your script with a Python interpreter, as well as any libraries or binaries required for it to run. These things are bundled together into either a directory or a single file to provide a distributable application that can be copied over to any system and executed, even if that system doesn't have Python.

To see how this works, make sure you have PyInstaller installed from PyPI (see the *Technical requirements* section) and let's create an executable for `QTicTacToe`.

 Note that the application packages created by PyInstaller are platform-specific and can only be run on an OS and CPU architecture compatible with that on which it was compiled. For example, if you build your PyInstaller executable on 64-bit Linux, it will not run on 32-bit Linux or 64-bit Windows.

Basic command-line usage

In theory, using PyInstaller is as simple as opening Command Prompt and typing this:

```
$ pyinstaller my_python_script.py
```

In fact, let's try this with our `qt_template.py` file from Chapter 4, *Building Applications with QMainWindow*; copy it to an empty directory, and run `pyinstaller qt_template.py` in that directory.

You'll get a great deal of output to the console and find that several directories and files were generated:

- The `build` and `__pycache__` directories mainly contain intermediate files generated during the build process. These may be helpful during debugging, but they are not part of the end product.
- The `dist` directory contains our distributable output.
- The `qt_template.spec` file holds the configuration data generated by PyInstaller.

By default, PyInstaller produces a directory containing the executable file plus all the libraries and data files required for it to work. The entire directory must be copied over to another computer if you want to run the executable.

Enter this directory and look for an executable file called `qt_template`. If you run it, you should see a blank `QMainWindow` object pop open.

If you'd rather just have a single file, PyInstaller can compress this directory into a single executable, which when run, extracts itself into a temporary location and runs the main executable.

This can be accomplished with the `--onefile` argument; delete the contents of `dist` and `build`, and then run this command:

```
$ pyinstaller --onefile qt_template.py
```

Now, under `dist`, you'll just find a single `qt_template` executable file. Again, run it and you'll see our blank `QMainWindow`. Keep in mind, while this approach is tidier, it increases the start-up time (since the application needs to be extracted) and may create some complications if your application opens up local files, as we'll see next.

> If you make significant changes to your code, environment, or build specifications, it's a good idea to delete the `build` and `dist` directories, and possibly the `.spec` file.

Before we attempt to package `QTicTacToe`, let's take a deeper look into the `.spec` file.

The .spec file

The .spec file is a Python-syntax config file that contains all the metadata about our build. You can think of it as PyInstaller's answer to a setup.py file. Unlike setup.py, however, the .spec file is automatically generated. This happens whenever we run pyinstaller, using a combination of detected data from our script and data passed in through command-line switches. We can also just generate the .spec file (and not start the build) using the pyi-makespec command.

Once generated, a .spec file can be edited and then passed back to pyinstaller to rebuild the distribution without having to specify command-line switches every time:

```
$ pyinstaller qt_template.spec
```

To see what kind of things we might edit in this file, run pyi-makespec qt_template.py again and open up qt_template.spec in your editor. Inside the file, you'll find four kinds of objects being created: Analysis, PYZ, EXE, and COLLECT.

The Analysis constructor receives information about our script, data files, and libraries. It uses this information to analyze the dependencies of the project and produces five tables of paths pointing to the files that should be included in the distribution. The five tables are:

- scripts: The Python files that serve as entry points and will be converted into executables
- pure: The pure Python modules required by the scripts
- binaries: The binary libraries required by the scripts
- datas: The non-Python data files, such as text files or images
- zipfiles: Any zipped Python .egg files

In our file, the Analysis portions look something like this:

```
a = Analysis(['qt_template.py'],
             pathex=['/home/alanm/temp/qt_template'],
             binaries=[],
             datas=[],
             hiddenimports=[],
             hookspath=[],
             runtime_hooks=[],
             excludes=[],
             win_no_prefer_redirects=False,
             win_private_assemblies=False,
             cipher=block_cipher,
             noarchive=False)
```

You see the name of the Python script, the path, and a lot of empty keyword arguments. Most of these arguments correspond to the output tables and are used to manually supplement the results of the analysis with things that PyInstaller fails to detect, including the following:

- `binaries` correspond to the `binaries` table.
- `datas` corresponds to the `datas` table.
- `hiddenimports` corresponds to the `pure` table.
- `excludes` allows us to leave out modules that may have been automatically included but aren't really needed.
- `hookspath` and `runtime_hooks` allow you to manually specify PyInstaller **hooks**; hooks allow you to override aspects of the analysis. They're typically used for dealing with troublesome dependencies.

The next object created is the `PYZ` object:

```
pyz = PYZ(a.pure, a.zipped_data,
            cipher=block_cipher)
```

A `PYZ` object represents a compressed archive of all the pure Python scripts detected in the analysis phase. All the pure Python scripts in our project will be compiled to bytecode (`.pyc`) files and packed into this archive.

Note the `cipher` argument present in both `Analysis` and `PYZ`; this argument can be used to obfuscate our Python bytecode further using AES256 encryption. While it doesn't fully prevent decryption and decompiling of the code, it can be a useful deterrent to the curious if you plan to distribute your code commercially. To use this option, specify an encryption string using the `--key` argument when creating the file, like so:

```
$ pyi-makespec --key=n0H4CK1ngPLZ qt_template.py
```

After the `PYZ` section, an `EXE()` object is generated:

```
exe = EXE(pyz,
            a.scripts,
            [],
            exclude_binaries=True,
            name='qt_template',
            debug=False,
            bootloader_ignore_signals=False,
            strip=False,
            upx=True,
            console=True )
```

The EXE object represents the executable file. The positional arguments here represent all the file tables we're bundling into the executable. Right now, this is just the compressed Python libraries and the main scripts; if we had specified the --onefile option, the other tables (binaries, zipfiles, and datas) would also be included here.

The keyword arguments to EXE allow us to control aspects of the executable file:

- name is the filename of the executable
- debug toggles the debugging output for the executable
- upx toggles whether the executable will be compressed with **UPX**
- console toggles whether to run the program in console or GUI mode in Windows and macOS; in Linux, it has no effect

 UPX is a free executable packer available for multiple platforms from https://upx.github.io/. If you have it installed, enabling this argument can make your executables smaller.

The final phase in the process is generating a COLLECT object:

```
coll = COLLECT(exe,
               a.binaries,
               a.zipfiles,
               a.datas,
               strip=False,
               upx=True,
               name='qt_template')
```

This object gathers all the necessary files into the final distribution directory. It only runs in one-directory mode, and its positional arguments include the components to be included in the directory. We can also override a few other aspects of the folder, such as whether to use UPX on the binaries and the name of the output directory.

Now that we understand a bit more about how PyInstaller works, let's package QTicTacToe.

Preparing QTicTacToe for PyInstaller

PyInstaller is simple enough when working with a single script, but how does it work with our module-style project arrangement? We cannot point PyInstaller at our module, as it will return an error; it needs to be pointed at a Python script that serves as the entry point, such as our run.py file.

This seems to work:

```
$ pyinstaller run.py
```

However, the resulting distribution and executable are now called run, which is not so great. You might be tempted to change run.py to qtictactoe.py; in fact, some tutorials on Python packaging recommend this arrangement (that is, having the run script the same name as the main module).

If you attempt this, however, you may find you got an error such as this:

```
Traceback (most recent call last):
  File "qtictactoe/__init__.py", line 3, in <module>
    from .mainwindow import MainWindow
ModuleNotFoundError: No module named '__main__.mainwindow'; '__main__' is
not a package
[3516] Failed to execute script qtictactoe
```

Because a Python module can be either a .py file or a directory, PyInstaller can't be sure which one constitutes the qtictactoe module, so having the same name for both will fail.

The correct approach is to use the --name switch when creating our .spec file or running pyinstaller:

```
$ pyinstaller --name qtictactoe run.py
# or, to just create the spec file:
# pyi-makespec --name qtictactoe run.py
```

This will create qtictactoe.spec and set the name arguments of EXE and COLLECT to qtictactoe, like so:

```
exe = EXE(pyz,
          #...
          name='qtictactoe',
          #...
coll = COLLECT(exe,
               #...
               name='qtictactoe')
```

This can, of course, be done manually by editing the .spec file as well.

Dealing with non-Python files

Our program runs, but we're back to the old problem of the 'X' and 'O' images not showing up. There are two problems here: first, our PNG files aren't being made part of the distribution and, second, the program can't find them even when they are.

To deal with the first problem, we have to tell PyInstaller to include our files in the `datas` table during the `Analysis` phase of the build. We can do that in the command line, like so:

```
# On Linux and macOS:
$ pyinstaller --name qtictactoe --add-data qtictactoe/images:images run.py
# On Windows:
$ pyinstaller --name qtictactoe --add-data qtictactoe\images;images run.py
```

The `--add-data` argument takes a source path and a destination path separated by either a colon (on macOS and Linux) or a semicolon (on Windows). The source path is relative to the project root where we're running `pyinstaller` (QTicTacToe, in this case), and the destination path is relative to the distribution root folder.

If we don't want to make a long, complex command line, we can also update the `Analysis` section of the `qtictactoe.spec` file:

```
a = Analysis(['run.py'],
             #...
             datas=[('qtictactoe/images', 'images')],
```

Here, the source and destination paths are just a tuple inside the `datas` list. The source value can also be a pattern such as `qtictactoe/images/*.png`. If you run `pyinstaller qtictactoe.spec` with these changes, you should find an `images` directory in `dist/qtictactoe`, which contains our PNG files.

This has solved the first problem with the images, but we still need to solve the second. In the *Distributing with setuptools* section, we solved the problem of locating our PNG files by using the `__file__` built-in variable. However, when you are running from a PyInstaller executable, the value of `__file__` is *not* the path to the executable; it's actually a path to a temporary directory where the executable unpacks the compressed bytecode. The location of this directory changes depending on whether we are in one-file or one-directory mode as well. To work around this problem, we'll need to update our code to detect whether the program has been made into an executable and, if so, use a different method to locate the files.

When we run PyInstaller executables, PyInstaller adds two properties to the `sys` module to help us:

- The `sys.frozen` property, which is given a value of `True`
- The `sys._MEIPASS` property, which stores the path to the executable directory

Thus, we can update our code in `board.py` to something like this:

```
if getattr(sys, 'frozen', False):
    directory = sys._MEIPASS
else:  # Not frozen
    directory = path.dirname(__file__)
self.mark_pngs = {
    'X': qtg.QPixmap(path.join(directory, 'images', 'X.png')),
    'O': qtg.QPixmap(path.join(directory, 'images', 'O.png'))
}
```

Now, when executing from a frozen PyInstaller environment, our code will be able to locate the files correctly. Re-run `pyinstaller qtictactoe.spec` and you should find that the X and O graphics display correctly. Hooray!

 As mentioned before, the far better solution in a PyQt5 application is to use the Qt Resource files discussed in Chapter 6, *Styling Qt Applications*. For non-PyQt programs, the `setuptools` library has a tool called `pkg_resources` that might be helpful.

Further debugging

If your build continues to have trouble, there are a couple of ways to get more information about what's going on.

First, make sure your code runs correctly as a Python script. If there is a syntax error or other code problem in any of your module files, the distribution will be built without them. These omissions will neither halt the build nor be mentioned in the command-line output.

After confirming that, check the build directory for details on what PyInstaller is doing. Under `build/projectname/`, you should see a number of files that can help you debug, including these:

- `warn-projectname.txt`: This contains warnings output by the `Analysis` process. Some of these are meaningless (often just failures to locate platform-specific libraries that don't exist on your platform), but if libraries have errors or are not being found, those issues will be logged here.
- `.toc` files: These contain the tables of contents created during the phases of the build process; for example, `Analysis-00.toc` shows the tables found in `Analysis()`. You can examine these to see whether the project's dependencies are being incorrectly identified or pulled from an incorrect location.
- `base_library.zip`: This archive should contain Python bytecode files for all the pure Python modules used by your application. You can inspect this to see whether anything is missing.

If you need more verbose output, you can use the `--log-level` switch to increase the detail of the output to `warn-projectname.txt`. A setting of `DEBUG` will provide more details:

```
$ pyinstaller --log-level DEBUG my_project.py
```

More debugging tips can be found at `https://pyinstaller.readthedocs.io/en/latest/when-things-go-wrong.html`.

Summary

In this chapter, you learned how to share your projects with others. You learned the optimal layout for your project directory to enable you to collaborate with other Python coders and Python tools. You learned how to work with `setuptools` to make distributable Python packages for sites such as PyPI. Finally, you learned how to convert your code into executables using PyInstaller.

Congratulations! You have finished this book. By now, you should feel confident in your ability to develop a compelling GUI application from scratch using Python and PyQt5. From basic input forms to advanced network, database, and multimedia applications, you now have the tools to create and distribute amazing programs. Even with all the topics we've covered, there's still much more to discover inside PyQt. Keep learning, and make great things!

Questions

Try answering these questions to test your knowledge from this chapter:

1. You have written a PyQt application in a file called Scan & Print Tool-box.py. You want to convert this into a module-style organization; what change should you make?

2. Your PyQt5 database application has a set of .sql files containing queries used by the application. It worked when your app was a single script in the same directories as the .sql files, but now that you've converted it to a module-style organization, the queries can't be found. What should you do?

3. You're writing a detailed README.rst file to document your new application before uploading it to a code-sharing site. What characters should be used to underline your level 1, 2, and 3 headings, respectively?

4. You're creating a setup.py script for your project so that you can upload it to PyPI. You would like to include a URL for the project's FAQ page. How can you accomplish this?

5. You have specified include_package_data=True in your setup.py file, but for some reason, the docs folder is not being included in your distribution package. What's wrong?

6. You ran pyinstaller fight_fighter3.py to package your new game as an executable. Something went wrong, though; where can you find a log of the build process?

7. Despite the name, PyInstaller cannot actually generate installer programs or packages for your application. Research some options for your platform of choice.

Further reading

For further information, please refer to the following:

- A tutorial on ReStructuredText markup can be found at http://docutils. sourceforge.net/docs/user/rst/quickstart.html.
- More information on designing, structuring, documenting, and packaging Python GUI applications can be found in this author's first book, *Python GUI programming with Tkinter*, available from *Packt Publications*.

- If you're interested in publishing a package to PyPI, see `https://blog.jetbrains.com/pycharm/2017/05/how-to-publish-your-package-on-pypi/` for a tutorial on the process.
- A better solution to the problem of including images in a Python library for a non-PyQt code is the `pkg_resources` tool provided by `setuptools`. You can read about it at `https://setuptools.readthedocs.io/en/latest/pkg_resources.html`.
- Advanced usage of PyInstaller is documented in the PyInstaller manual found at `https://pyinstaller.readthedocs.io/en/stable/`.

Answers to Questions

Chapter 1

1. **Qt is written in C++, a language that is very different from Python. What are some of the major differences between the two languages? How might these differences come across as we use Qt in Python?**

    The C++ language differences impact PyQt in several ways, for example:

    - Its static typing and type-safe functions mean that PyQt is fairly strict about which functions can be called and which variables can be passed, in some circumstances.
    - The relative lack of built-in data types in C++ means that Qt provides a rich selection of data types, many of which we must use in Python due to type safety.
    - The use of `enum` types, common in C++ but rare in Python, is pervasive in Qt.

2. **GUIs are composed of widgets. Open some GUI applications on your computer and try to identify as many widgets as you can.**

    Some examples might include the following:

    - Buttons
    - Checkboxes
    - Radio buttons
    - Labels
    - Text edits
    - Sliders
    - Image areas
    - Comboboxes

3. **Suppose that the following program crashes. Figure out why, and fix it so that it shows a window:**

```
from PyQt5.QtWidgets import *
app = QWidget()
app.show()
QApplication().exec()
```

The code should read as follows:

```
from PyQt5.QtWidgets import *

app = QApplication([])
window = QWidget()
window.show()
app.exe()
```

Remember that a `QApplication()` object must exist before any `QWidget` objects, and it must be created with a list as an argument.

4. **The** `QWidget` **class has a property called** `statusTip`**. Which of these are most likely to be the names of the accessor methods for this property:**

   a. `getStatusTip()` and `setStatusTip()`
   b. `statusTip()` and `setStatusTip()`
   c. `get_statusTip()` and `change_statusTip()`

The answer **b** is correct. In most cases, the accessors for `property` are `property()` and `setProperty()`.

5. `QDate` **is a class for wrapping a calendar date. In which of the three main Qt modules would you expect to find it?**

`QDate` is in `QtCore`. `QtCore` holds data type classes for things not necessarily related to a GUI.

6. `QFont` **is a class that defines a screen font. In which of the three main Qt modules would you expect to find it?**

`QFont` is in `QtGui`. Fonts relate to GUIs but aren't widgets or layouts, so you would expect it to be in `QtGui`.

7. **Can you recreate** `hello_world.py` **using Qt Designer? Make sure to set** `windowTitle`**.**

    Create a new project based on `QWidget`. Then select the main widget and set `windowTitle` in the **Properties** pane.

Chapter 2

1. **How would you create a** `QWidget` **that is fullscreen, has no window frame, and uses the hourglass cursor?**

    The code looks like this:

    ```
    widget = QWidget(cursor=qtc.Qt.WaitCursor)
    widget.setWindowState(qtc.Qt.WindowFullScreen)
    widget.setWindowFlags(qtc.Qt.FramelessWindowHint)
    ```

2. **Suppose that you're asked to design a data-entry form for a computer inventory database. Choose the best widget to use for each of the following fields:**

    - **Computer make**: One of eight brands that your company purchases
    - **Processor speed**: The CPU speed in GHz
    - **Memory amount**: The amount of RAM, in whole MB
    - **Hostname**: The computer's hostname
    - **Video make**: Whether the video hardware is Nvidia, AMD, or Intel
    - **OEM license**: Whether the computer uses an OEM license

    This table lists some possible answers:

Field	Widget(s)	Explanation
Computer make	QComboBox	For choosing between a list of many values, a combobox is ideal
Processor Speed	QDoubleSpinBox	Best choice for decimal values
Memory Amount	QSpinBox	Best choice for integer values
Hostname	QLineEdit	A hostname is just a one-line text string
Video Make	QComboBox, QRadioButton	Combobox would work, but with only three choices, radio buttons are an option, too

Field	Widget(s)	Explanation
OEM License	QCheckBox	QCheckBox is a good choice for Boolean values

3. **The data entry form includes an** `inventory number` **field that requires the** `XX-999-9999X` **format, where** `X` **is an uppercase letter from** `A` **to** `Z`, **excluding** `O` **and** `I`, **and** `9` **is a number from** `0` **to** `9`. **Can you create a validator class to validate this input?**

   See `inventory_validator.py` in the example code.

4. **Check out the following calculator form:**

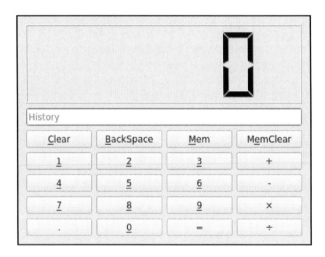

   What layouts may have been used to create it?

   It is most likely either a `QVBoxLayout` with a nested `QGridLayout` layout for the button area, or a single `QGridLayout` layout using a column span for the first two rows.

5. **Referring to the preceding calculator form, how would you make the button grid take up any extra space when the form is resized?**

   Set the `sizePolicy` property on each widget to `QtWidgets.QSizePolicy.Expanding` for both vertical and horizontal.

6. **The topmost widget in the calculator form is a** QLCDNumber **widget. Can you find the Qt documentation on this widget? What unique properties does it have? When might you use it?**

   The QLCDNumber documentation is at https://doc.qt.io/qt-5/ qlcdnumber.html. Its unique properties are digitCount, intValue, mode, segmentStyle, smallDecimalPoint, and value. It's useful for displaying any kind of number, including octal, hexadecimal, and binary.

7. **Starting with your template code, build the calculator form in code.**

   See calculator_form.py in the example code.

8. **Build the calculator form in Qt Designer.**

   See calculator_form.ui in the example code.

Chapter 3

1. **Look at the following table and determine which of the connections could actually be made, and which would result in an error. You may need to look up the signatures of these signals and slots in the documentation:**

#	Signal	Slot
1	QPushButton.clicked	QLineEdit.clear
2	QComboBox.currentIndexChanged	QListWidget.scrollToItem
3	QLineEdit.returnPressed	QCalendarWidget.setGridVisible
4	QLineEdit.textChanged	QTextEdit.scrollToAnchor

   The answers are as follows:

   1. Yes, because the Boolean argument of clicked can be ignored by clear
   2. No, because currentIndexChanged sends int, but scrollToItem expects an item and a scroll hint
   3. No, because returnPressed sends no arguments and setGridVisible expects one
   4. Yes, because textChanged sends a string, which scrollToAnchor accepts

2. **The** `emit()` **method does not exist on a signal object until the signal has been bound (that is, connected to a slot). Rewrite the** `CategoryWindow.onSubmit()` **method from our first** `calendar_app.py` **file to protect against the possibility of** `submitted` **being unbound.**

We need to catch an `AttributeError`, like so:

```
def onSubmit(self):
    if self.category_entry.text():
        try:
            self.submitted.emit(self.category_entry.text())
        except AttributeError:
            pass
    self.close()
```

3. **You find an object in the Qt documentation with a slot that requires** `QString` **as an argument. Can you connect your custom signal that sends a Python** `str` **object?**

Yes, because PyQt automatically converts between `QString` and Python `str` objects.

4. **You find an object in the Qt documentation with a slot that requires** `QVariant` **as an argument. What built-in Python types could you sent to this slot?**

Any of them can be sent. `QVariant` is a generic object container that can hold any other type of object.

5. **You're trying to create a dialog window that takes time and emits it when the user has finished editing the value. You're trying to use automatic slot connections, but your code isn't doing anything. Determine what is missing from the following:**

```
class TimeForm(qtw.QWidget):

    submitted = qtc.pyqtSignal(qtc.QTime)

    def __init__(self):
        super().__init__()
        self.setLayout(qtw.QHBoxLayout())
        self.time_inp = qtw.QTimeEdit(self)
        self.layout().addWidget(self.time_inp)
```

```
def on_time_inp_editingFinished(self):
    self.submitted.emit(self.time_inp.time())
    self.destroy()
```

First, you're missing a call to `connectSlotsByName()`. Also, you have not set the object name of `self.time_inp`. Your code should look like this:

```
class TimeForm(qtw.QWidget):

    submitted = qtc.pyqtSignal(qtc.QTime)

    def __init__(self):
        super().__init__()
        self.setLayout(qtw.QHBoxLayout())
        self.time_inp = qtw.QTimeEdit(
            self, objectName='time_inp')
        self.layout().addWidget(self.time_inp)
        qtc.QMetaObject.connectSlotsByName(self)

    def on_time_inp_editingFinished(self):
        self.submitted.emit(self.time_inp.time())
        self.destroy()
```

6. **You've created a `.ui` file in Qt Designer for a calculator application, and you're trying to get it working in code, but it's not. What are you doing wrong? See the following source code:**

```
from calculator_form import Ui_Calculator

class Calculator(qtw.QWidget):
    def __init__(self):
        self.ui = Ui_Calculator(self)
        self.ui.setupGUI(self.ui)
        self.show()
```

There are four things wrong here:

- First, you've forgotten to call `super().__init__()`
- Second, you're passing `self` to `Ui_Calculator`, which doesn't need any arguments
- Third, you're calling `self.ui.setupGUI()`; it should be `self.ui.setupUi()`
- Finally, you're passing `self.ui` into `setupUi()`; you should be passing in a reference to the containing widget, in this case, `self`

7. **You're trying to create a new button class that emits an integer value when clicked; unfortunately, nothing happens when you click on the button. Look at the following code and try to make it work:**

```
class IntegerValueButton(qtw.QPushButton):

    clicked = qtc.pyqtSignal(int)

    def __init__(self, value, *args, **kwargs):
        super().__init__(*args, **kwargs)
        self.value = value
        self.clicked.connect(
            lambda: self.clicked.emit(self.value))
```

The answer is to change the last line of __init__() to the following:

```
super().clicked.connect(
    lambda: self.clicked.emit(self.value))
```

Because we've overridden the built-in `clicked` property with our own signal, `self.clicked` no longer points to the signal emitted when the button is clicked. We have to call `super().clicked` to get a reference to the parent class's `clicked` signal.

Chapter 4

1. **You want to use** `QMainWindow` **with the** `calendar_app.py` **script from** Chapter 3, *Handling Events with Signals and Slots.* **How would you go about converting it?**

The easiest approach would be the following:

- Rename `MainWindow` to something like `CalendarForm`
- Create a new `MainWindow` class based on `QMainWindow`
- Create an instance of `CalendarForm` inside `MainWindow` and set it as the central widget

2. **You're working on an app and have added the sub-menu names to the menu bar but have not populated any of them with items. Your coworker says that none of the menu names are appearing on his desktop when he tests it. Your code looks correct; what is probably going on here?**

   Your coworker is using a platform (such as macOS) that doesn't display empty menu folders by default.

3. **You're developing a code editor and want to create a sidebar panel for interacting with a debugger. Which** QMainWindow **feature would be most appropriate for this task?**

   QDockWidget would be most appropriate, since it allows you to build any kind of widget into a dockable window. The toolbar wouldn't be a good choice, since it's mainly designed for buttons.

4. **The following code isn't working correctly; it proceeds no matter what is clicked. Why doesn't it work, and how can you fix it?**

   ```
   answer = qtw.QMessageBox.question(
       None, 'Continue?', 'Run this program?')
   if not answer:
       sys.exit()
   ```

   QMessageBox.question() does not return a Boolean; it returns a constant matching the type of button that was clicked. The actual integer value of the constant matching the No button is 65536, which evaluates to True in Python. The code should read as follows:

   ```
   answer = qtw.QMessageBox.question(
       None, 'Continue?', 'Run this program?')
   if answer == qtw.QMessageBox.No:
       sys.exit()
   ```

5. **You're building a custom dialog by subclassing** QDialog. **You need to get the information entered into the dialog back to the main window object. Which of the following approaches will not work?**

   a. **Pass in a mutable object and use the dialog's** accept() **method to alter its values.**

   b. **Override the objects** accept() **method and have it return a** dict **of the entered values.**

c. **Override the dialog's** `accepted` **signal with one that passes along a** `dict` **of the entered values. Connect this signal to a callback in your main window class.**

Answers **a** and **c** will work. Answer **b** will not work, because the return value of `accept` is not returned by the dialog when `exec()` is called. `exec()` only returns a Boolean value indicating whether the dialog was accepted or rejected.

6. **You're writing a photo editor called SuperPhoto on Linux. You've written the code and saved the user settings, but looking in** `~/.config/`, **you can't find** `SuperPhoto.conf`. **Look at the code and determine what went wrong:**

```
settings = qtc.QSettings()
settings.setValue('config_file', 'SuperPhoto.conf')
settings.setValue('default_color', QColor('black'))
settings.sync()
```

The configuration file (or registry key, on Windows) used by `QSettings` is determined by the company name and app name passed in as arguments to the constructor. The code should read as follows:

```
settings = qtc.QSettings('My Company', 'SuperPhoto')
settings.setValue('default_color', QColor('black'))
```

Also, note that `sync()` doesn't need to be called explicitly. It's automatically called by the Qt event loop.

7. **You're saving preferences from a settings dialog, but for some reason, the settings being saved are coming back very strangely. What is wrong here? See the following code:**

```
settings = qtc.QSettings('My Company', 'SuperPhoto')
settings.setValue('Default Name',
dialog.default_name_edit.text)
    settings.setValue('Use GPS', dialog.gps_checkbox.isChecked)
    settings.setValue('Default Color', dialog.color_picker.color)
```

The problem is that you're not actually calling the accessor functions for the widgets. As a result, `settings` is storing a reference to the accessor function. On the next program launch, these are meaningless, since new objects are created at new memory locations. Be aware that `settings` won't complain if you save function references.

Chapter 5

1. **Assuming we have a well-designed model-view application, is the following code part of a model or a view?**

```
def save_as(self):
    filename, _ = qtw.QFileDialog(self)
    self.data.save_file(filename)
```

It's view code, since it creates a GUI element (the file dialog) and seems to call back to what might be a model (`self.data`).

2. **Can you name at least two things that a model should never do, and two things that a view should never do?**

Examples of things models should never do are create or directly alter GUI elements, format data for presentation, or close the application. Examples of things views should never do are save data to disk, perform transformations on the stored data (such as sorting or arithmetic), or read data from anything other than the model.

3. `QAbstractTableModel` **and** `QAbstractTreeModel` **both have abstract in the name. What does abstract mean in this context? Does it mean something different in C++ from what it means in Python?**

In any programming language, abstract classes are classes that are not intended to be instantiated into objects; they should only be used by subclassing them and overriding required methods. In Python, this is implied but not enforced; in C++, classes marked `abstract` will fail to instantiate.

4. **Which model type—list, table, or tree—would best suit the following collections of data?**

   1. **The user's recent files**
   2. **A Windows registry hive**
   3. **Linux** `syslog` **records**
   4. **Blog entries**
   5. **Personal salutations (for example, Mr., Mrs., or Dr.)**
   6. **Distributed version control history**

Although it's debatable, the most likely answers are as follows:

1. List
2. Tree
3. Table
4. Table
5. List
6. Tree

5. **Why is the following code failing?**

```
class DataModel(QAbstractTreeModel):
    def rowCount(self, node):
        if node > 2:
            return 1
        else:
            return len(self._data[node])
```

The argument for `rowCount()` is a `QModelIndex` object pointing to a parent node. It cannot be compared to an integer (`if node > 2`).

6. **Your table model isn't working quite right when inserting columns. What is wrong with your** `insertColumns()` **method?**

```
def insertColumns(self, col, count, parent):
    for row in self._data:
        for i in range(count):
            row.insert(col, '')
```

You've neglected to call `self.beginInsertColumns()` before altering the data, and `self.endInsertColumns()` after doing it.

7. **You would like your views to display the item data as a tooltip when hovered. How would you accomplish this?**

You need to handle `QtCore.Qt.TooltipRole` in the model's `data()` method. An example of the code would be as follows:

```
def data(self, index, role):
    if role in (
        qtc.Qt.DisplayRole,
        qtc.Qt.EditRole,
        qtc.Qt.ToolTipRole
    ):
        return self._data[index.row()][index.column()]
```

Chapter 6

1. **You are preparing to distribute your text editor application and want to ensure that the user is given a monospaced font by default, no matter what platform they use. What two methods can you use to accomplish this?**

   The first way is to set the `styleHint` of the default font to `QtGui.QFont.Monospace`. The second is to find an appropriately-licensed, monospaced font, bundle it in a Qt Resource file, and set the font to your bundled font.

2. **As closely as possible, try to mimic the following text using** `QFont`:

   The code is as follows:

   ```
   font = qtg.QFont('Times', 32, qtg.QFont.Bold)
   font.setUnderline(True)
   font.setOverline(True)
   font.setCapitalization(qtg.QFont.SmallCaps)
   ```

3. **Can you explain the difference between** `QImage`, `QPixmap`, **and** `QIcon`?

   `QPixmap` and `QImage` both represent a single image, but `QPixmap` is optimized for display, while `QImage` is optimized for image manipulation in memory. `QIcon` is not a single image, but a collection of images that can be tied to a widget or action's state.

4. **You have defined the following** `.qrc` **file for your application, run** `pyrcc5`, **and imported the resource library in your script. How would you load this image into** `QPixmap`?

   ```
   <RCC>
     <qresource prefix="foodItems">
       <file alias="pancakes.png">pc_img.45234.png</file>
     </qresource>
   </RCC>
   ```

   The code should look like this:

   ```
   pancakes_pxm = qtg.QPixmap(":/foodItems/pancakes.png")
   ```

5. **Using** QPalette, **how would you tile the background of a** QWidget **object with the** tile.png **image?**

    The code should look like this:

    ```
    widget = qtw.QWidget()
    palette = widget.palette()
    tile_brush = qtg.QBrush(
        qtg.QColor('black'),
        qtg.QPixmap('tile.png')
    )
    palette.setBrush(qtg.QPalette.Window, tile_brush)
    widget.setPalette(palette)
    ```

6. **You are trying to make a delete button pink using QSS, but it's not working. What is wrong with your code?**

    ```
    deleteButton = qtw.QPushButton('Delete')
    form.layout().addWidget(deleteButton)
    form.setStyleSheet(
        form.styleSheet() + 'deleteButton{ background-color: #8F8; }'
    )
    ```

    There are two problems with your code. First, your deleteButton does not have an objectName assigned. QSS does not know anything about your Python variable names; it only knows Qt object names. Second, your style sheet doesn't prefix the object name with a # symbol. The corrected code should look like this:

    ```
    deleteButton = qtw.QPushButton('Delete')
    deleteButton.setObjectName('deleteButton')
    form.layout().addWidget(deleteButton)
    form.setStyleSheet(
        form.styleSheet() +
        '#deleteButton{ background-color: #8F8; }'
    )
    ```

7. **Which style sheet string will turn the background colors of your** QLineEdit **widget black?**

    ```
    stylesheet1 = "QWidget {background-color: black;}"
    stylesheet2 = ".QWidget {background-color: black;}"
    ```

    stylesheet1 will turn the background of any QWidget child class black, including QLineEdit. stylesheet2 will only turn the background of actual QWidget objects black; child classes will remain unaffected.

8. **Build a simple app with a combobox that allows you to change the Qt style to any style installed on your system. Include some other widgets so that you can see how they look in the different styles.**

   See `question_8_answer.py` in the example code included for this chapter.

9. **You feel very happy about learning how to style PyQt apps and want to create a** `QProxyStyle` **class that will force all pixmaps in a GUI to be** `smile.gif`. **How would you do this? Hint: You will need to research some drawing methods of** `QStyle` **other than the ones discussed in this chapter.**

   The class looks like this:

   ```
   class SmileyStyley(qtw.QProxyStyle):

       def drawItemPixmap(
           self, painter, rectangle, alignment, pixmap):
           smile = qtg.QPixmap('smile.gif')
           super().drawItemPixmap(
               painter, rectangle, alignment, smile)
   ```

10. **The following animation doesn't work; figure out why it doesn't work:**

    ```
    class MyWidget(qtw.QWidget):
        def __init__(self):
            super().__init__()
            animation = qtc.QPropertyAnimation(
                self, b'windowOpacity')
            animation.setStartValue(0)
            animation.setEndValue(1)
            animation.setDuration(10000)
            animation.start()
    ```

    The short answer is that `animation` should be `self.animation`. Animations do not have parent objects and do not get **re-parented** like widgets do when they're added to a layout. Hence, when the constructor exits, `animation` goes out of scope and gets destroyed. The moral of the story is, save your animations as instance variables.

Chapter 7

1. **Using** QSoundEffect, **you've written a utility for a call center that allows them to review recorded phone calls. They're moving to a new phone system that stores the audio calls as MP3 files. Do you need to make any changes to your utility?**

   Yes. You'll need to use QMediaPlayer instead of QSoundEffect, or write a layer to decode the MP3 to WAV, because QSoundEffect cannot play compressed audio.

2. cool_songs **is a Python list containing path strings to your favorite songs. What do you need to do to play these songs back in a random order?**

   You need to convert the paths into QUrl objects, add them to QMediaPlaylist, set playbackMode to Random, then pass it to QMediaPlayer. The code looks like this:

   ```
   playlist = qtmm.QMediaPlaylist()
   for song in cool_songs:
       url = qtc.QUrl.fromLocalFile(song)
       content = qtmm.QMediaContent(url)
       playlist.addMedia(content)
   playlist.setPlaybackMode(qtmm.QMediaPlaylist.Random)
   player = qtmm.QMediaPlayer()
   player.setPlaylist(playlist)
   player.play()
   ```

3. **You have installed the** audio/mpeg **codec on your system, but the following code isn't working. Find out what's wrong with it:**

   ```
   recorder = qtmm.QAudioRecorder()
   recorder.setCodec('audio/mpeg')
   recorder.record()
   ```

   QAudioRecorder **doesn't have a** setCodec method. The codec used in the recording is set on the QAudioEncoderSettings object. The code should read as follows:

   ```
   recorder = qtmm.QAudioRecorder()
   settings = qtmm.QAudioEncoderSettings()
   settings.setCodec('audio/mpeg')
   recorder.setEncodingSettings(settings)
   recorder.record()
   ```

4. **Run** `audio_test.py` **and** `video_test.py` **on several different Windows, macOS, and Linux systems. How is the output different? Are there any items supported across all systems?**

   The answers will depend on the systems you choose.

5. **The properties of the** `QCamera` **class include several control objects, which allow you to manage different aspects of the camera. One of these is** `QCameraFocus`**. Investigate** `QCameraFocus` **in the Qt documentation at** `https://doc.qt.io/qt-5/qcamerafocus.html` **and write a simple script that shows a viewfinder and lets you adjust the digital zoom.**

   See `question_5_example_code.py` in the included code examples.

6. **You've noticed the audio being recorded to your Captain's Log video log is quite loud. You want to add a control to adjust it; how would you do this?**

   `QMediaRecorder` has a `volume()` slot, just like `QAudioRecorder`. You need to create a `QSlider` (or any other control widget) and connect its `valueChanged` or `sliderMoved` signal to the recorder's `volume()` slot.

7. **Implement a dock widget in** `captains_log.py` **that allows you to control as many aspects of the audio and video recording as you can. You can include things such as the focus, zoom, exposure, white balance, framerate, resolution, audio volume, audio quality, and more.**

   You're on your own here!

Chapter 8

1. **You are designing an application that will emit a status message to the local network, which you will monitor with administrator tools. What kind of socket object would be a good choice?**

   `QUdpSocket` would be best here, since it allows for broadcasting packets, and the status packets do not need the overhead of TCP.

2. **Your GUI class has a** `QTcpSocket` **object called** `self.socket`. **You've connected its** `readyRead` **signal to the following method, but it's not working. What's happening, and how can you fix it?**

```
def on_ready_read(self):
    while self.socket.hasPendingDatagrams():
        self.process_data(self.socket.readDatagram())
```

`QTcpSocket` does not have a `hasPendingDatagrams()` or `readDatagram()` method. TCP sockets work with data streams, not datagrams. This method needs to be rewritten to extract data using a `QDataStream` object.

3. **Use** `QTcpServer` **to implement a simple service that listens on port** 8080 **and prints any requests received. Make it reply to the client with a byte string of your choice.**

See `question_3_tcp_server.py` in the example code. Test it by running the script and pointing a web browser to `http://localhost:8080`.

4. **You're creating a download function for your application to retrieve a large data file for import into your application. The code does not work. Read the code and decide what you're doing wrong:**

```
def download(self, url):
    self.manager = qtn.QNetworkAccessManager(
        finished=self.on_finished)
    self.request = qtn.QNetworkRequest(qtc.QUrl(url))
    reply = self.manager.get(self.request)
    with open('datafile.dat', 'wb') as fh:
        fh.write(reply.readAll())
```

You're trying to use `QNetworkAccessManager.get()` synchronously, but it is designed to be used asynchronously. Instead of retrieving a reply object from `get()`, you need to connect a callback to the network access manager's `finished` signal, which carries the finished reply with it.

5. **Modify your** `poster.py` **script so that it sends the key-value data as JSON, rather than HTTP form data.**

See the `question_5_json_poster.py` file in the example code.

Chapter 9

1. **Compose an SQL CREATE statement that builds a table to hold television schedule listings. Make sure it has fields for the date, time, channel, and program name. Also, make sure it has a primary key and constraints to prevent nonsensical data (such as two shows at the same time on the same channel, or a show with no time or date).**

    An example might look like this:

    ```
    CREATE TABLE tv_schedule AS (
        id INTEGER PRIMARY KEY,
        channel TEXT NOT NULL,
        date DATE NOT NULL,
        time TIME NOT NULL,
        program TEXT NOT NULL,
        UNIQUE(channel, date, time)
    )
    ```

2. **The following SQL query is returning a syntax error; can you fix it?**

    ```
    DELETE * FROM my_table IF category_id == 12;
    ```

    There are several problems here:

    - DELETE does not take a field list, so * must be removed.
    - IF is the wrong keyword. It should use WHERE.
    - == is not an SQL operator. Unlike Python, SQL uses a single = for both assignment and comparison operations.

    The resulting SQL should read as follows:

    ```
    DELETE FROM my_table WHERE category_id = 12;
    ```

3. **The following SQL query doesn't work correctly; can you fix it?**

    ```
    INSERT INTO flavors(name) VALUES ('hazelnut', 'vanilla',
    'caramel', 'onion');
    ```

    Each set of parentheses in the VALUES clause represents a single row. Since we are only inserting one column, each row should have only one value in it. Hence, our statement should look like this:

    ```
    INSERT INTO flavors(name) VALUES ('hazelnut'), ('vanilla'),
    ('caramel'), ('onion');
    ```

4. **The documentation for** QSqlDatabase **can be found at** https://doc.qt.io/qt-5/qsqldatabase.html. **Read up on how you can work with multiple database connections, for example, a read-only and read/write connection to the same database. How would you create two connections and make specific queries to each?**

The key is to call addDatabase() multiple times with unique connection names; an example is as follows:

```
db1 = qts.QSqlDatabase.addDatabase('QSQLITE', 'XYZ read-only')
db1.setUserName('readonlyuser')
# etc...
db1.open()
db2 = qts.QSqlDatabase.addDatabase('QSQLITE', 'XYZ read-write')
db2.setUserName('readwriteuser')
# etc...
db2.open()

# Keep the database reference for querying:
query = qts.QSqlQuery('SELECT * FROM my_table', db1)

# Or retrieve it using its name:
db = qts.QSqlDatabase.database('XYZ read-write')
db.exec('INSERT INTO my_table VALUES (1, 2, 3)')
```

5. **Using** QSqlQuery, **write code to safely insert the data in the** dict **object into the** coffees **table:**

```
data = {'brand': 'generic', 'name': 'cheap coffee', 'roast':
    'light'}
# Your code here:
```

To be safe, we'll use the prepare() method of QSqlQuery:

```
data = {'brand': 'generic', 'name': 'cheap coffee', 'roast':
    'Light'}
query = QSqlQuery()
query.prepare(
    'INSERT INTO coffees(coffee_brand, coffee_name, roast_id) '
    'VALUES (:brand, :name,
    '(SELECT id FROM roasts WHERE description == :roast))'
)
query.bindValue(':brand', data['brand'])
query.bindValue(':name', data['name'])
query.bindValue(':roast', data['roast'])
query.exec()
```

6. **You've created a** `QSqlTableModel` **object and attached it to** `QTableView`. **You know there is data in the table, but it is not showing in the view. Look at the code and decide what is wrong:**

```
flavor_model = qts.QSqlTableModel()
flavor_model.setTable('flavors')
flavor_table = qtw.QTableView()
flavor_table.setModel(flavor_model)
mainform.layout().addWidget(flavor_table)
```

You have not called `select()` on your model. Until you do so, it will be empty.

7. **The following is a callback attached to the** `textChanged` **signal of** `QLineEdit`. **Explain why this is not a good idea:**

```
def do_search(self, text):
    self.sql_table_model.setFilter(f'description={text}')
    self.sql_table_model.select()
```

The problem here is that you're taking arbitrary user input and passing it to a table model's `filter()` string. This string is appended literally to the table model's internal SQL query, opening up your database to SQL injection. To make this safe, you would need to take steps to sanitize `text` or switch the SQL table model for a `QSqlQueryModel` and use `prepare()` to create a prepared statement.

8. **You decide you'd rather have colors than names in the roasts comboboxes in your coffee list. What changes would you need to make to accomplish this?**

You would need to change the display field used by the `QSqlRelation` set on `roast_id` to `color`. Then, you would need to create a custom delegate for `coffee_list` that creates color icons (see Chapter 6, *Styling Qt Applications*) and uses them instead of text labels in the combobox.

Chapter 10

1. **Create code to call the** `self.every_ten_seconds()` **method every ten seconds.**

   Assuming we're in the `__init__()` method of a class, it looks like this:

   ```
   self.timer = qtc.QTimer()
   self.timer.setInterval(10000)
   self.timer.timeout.connect(self.every_ten_seconds)
   ```

2. **The following code uses** `QTimer` **incorrectly. Can you fix it?**

   ```
   timer = qtc.QTimer()
   timer.setSingleShot(True)
   timer.setInterval(1000)
   timer.start()
   while timer.remainingTime():
       sleep(.01)
   run_delayed_command()
   ```

   `QTimer` is being used synchronously with the `while` loop. This creates blocking code. The same can be done asynchronously, like so:

   ```
   qtc.QTimer.singleShot(1000, run_delayed_command)
   ```

3. **You've created the following word-counting worker class and want to move it to another thread to prevent large documents from slowing the GUI. It's not working, however; what do you need to change about this class?**

   ```
   class Worker(qtc.QObject):

       counted = qtc.pyqtSignal(int)

       def __init__(self, parent):
           super().__init__(parent)
           self.parent = parent

       def count_words(self):
           content = self.parent.textedit.toPlainText()
           self.counted.emit(len(content.split()))
   ```

The class relies on accessing a widget through a common parent because the `Worker` class must be parented by the GUI class containing the widget. You'll need to change this class so that the following applies:

- It doesn't have a parent widget.
- It accesses the content some other way, such as through a slot.

4. **The following code is blocking, rather than running in a separate thread. Why is this so?**

```
class Worker(qtc.QThread):

    def set_data(data):
        self.data = data

    def run(self):n
        start_complex_calculations(self.data)

class MainWindow(qtw.QMainWindow):

    def __init__(self):
        super().__init__()
        form = qtw.QWidget()
        self.setCentralWidget(form)
        form.setLayout(qtw.QFormLayout())

        worker = Worker()
        line_edit = qtw.QLineEdit(textChanged=worker.set_data)
        button = qtw.QPushButton('Run', clicked=worker.run)
        form.layout().addRow('Data:', line_edit)
        form.layout().addRow(button)
        self.show()
```

The button callback is pointed at `Worker.run()`. It should point to the `start()` method of the `QThread` object.

5. **Will this worker class run correctly? If not, why?**

```
class Worker(qtc.QRunnable):

    finished = qtc.pyqtSignal()

    def run(self):
        calculate_navigation_vectors(30)
        self.finished.emit()
```

No. `QRunnable` objects cannot emit signals, because they do not descend from `QObject` or have an event loop. You would be better off using `QThread`, in this case.

6. **The following code is a** `run()` **method from a** `QRunnable` **class designed for processing large data file output from scientific equipment. The files consist of millions of long rows of space-delimited numbers. Is this code likely to be slowed down by the Python GIL? Could you make it less likely that the GIL will interfere?**

```
def run(self):
    with open(self.file, 'r') as fh:
        for row in fh:
            numbers = [float(x) for x in row.split()]
            if numbers:
                mean = sum(numbers) / len(numbers)
                numbers.append(mean)
            self.queue.put(numbers)
```

Reading in the file is an I/O-bound operation, which does not require acquiring the GIL. However, doing mathematical calculations and type conversions is a CPU-bound task and will require the acquisition of the GIL. This could be mitigated by doing the calculations in a non-Python math library, such as NumPy.

7. **The following is a** `run()` **method from** `QRunnable` **in a multithreaded TCP Server application you're writing. All threads share a server socket instance accessed through** `self.datastream`**. This code is not thread-safe, though. What do you need to do to fix it?**

```
def run(self):
    message = get_http_response_string()
    message_len = len(message)
    self.datastream.writeUInt32(message_len)
    self.datastream.writeQString(message)
```

Since you don't want two threads writing to the data stream at the same time, you'll want to use `QMutex` to ensure that only one thread has access. After defining a shared mutex objected called `qmutex`, the code would look like this:

```
def run(self):
    message = get_http_response_string()
    message_len = len(message)
    with qtc.QMutexLocker(self.qmutex):
```

```
self.datastream.writeUInt32(message_len)
self.datastream.writeQString(message)
```

Chapter 11

1. **The following HTML isn't displaying like you wanted. Find as many errors as you can:**

```
<table>
<thead background=#EFE><th>Job</th><th>Status</th></thead>
<tr><td>Backup</td><font text-
color='green'>Success!</font></td></tr>
<tr><td>Cleanup<td><font text-
style='bold'>Fail!</font></td></tr>
</table>
```

There are several errors here:

- The `<thead>` section is missing a `<tr>` tag around the cells.
- In the next row, the second cell is missing the opening `<td>` tag.
- Also, there's no `text-color` attribute. It's just `color`.
- In the next row, the first cell is missing a closing `</td>` tag.
- Also, there's no `text-style` attribute. The text should just be wrapped in a `<b>` tag.

2. **What is wrong with the following Qt HTML snippets?**

```
<p>There is nothing <i>wrong</i> with your television
<b>set</p></b>
<table><row><data>french fries</data>
<data>$1.99</data></row></table>
<font family='Tahoma' color='#235499'>Can you feel the
<strikethrough>love</strikethrough>code tonight?</font>
<label>Username</label><input type='text'
name='username'></input>
<img source=':://mypix.png'>My picture</img>
```

The problems are as follows:

1. The last two closing tags are switched. Nested tags must be closed before the outer tags.
2. There is no such tag as `<row>` or `<data>`. The correct tags should be `<tr>` and `<td>`, respectively.
3. There are two problems—`<font>` has no `family` attribute, and it should be `face`; also, there is no `<strikethrough>` tag, and it should be `<s>`.
4. Qt doesn't support the `<label>` or `<input>` tags. Also, `<input>` does not use a closing tag.
5. `<img>` has no `source` attribute; it should be `src`. It also does not use a closing tag and cannot enclose text content.

3. **This snippet is supposed to implement a table of contents. Why doesn't it work right?**

```
<ul>
  <li><a href='Section1'>Section 1</a></li>
  <li><a href='Section2'>Section 2</a></li>
</ul>
<div id=Section1>
  <p>This is section 1</p>
</div>
<div id=Section2>
  <p>This is section 2</p>
</div>
```

This is not how document anchors work. The correct code is as follows:

```
<ul>
  <li><a href='#Section1'>Section 1</a></li>
  <li><a href='#Section2'>Section 2</a></li>
</ul>
<a name='Section1'></a>
<div id=Section1>
  <p>This is section 1</p>
</div>
<a name='Section2'></a>
<div id=Section2>
  <p>This is section 2</p>
</div>
```

Note the pound sign (#) before `href`, indicating that this is an internal anchor, and the `<a>` tags above the sections, with a `name` attribute containing the section name (without the pound sign!).

4. **Using** `QTextCursor`**, you need to add a sidebar on the right-hand side of your document. Explain how you would go about this.**

   The steps to do this are as follows:

   1. Create a `QTextFrameFormat` object
   2. Configure your frame format's `position` property to float right
   3. Position your text cursor in the root frame
   4. Call `insertFrame()` on your cursor with the frame object as the first argument
   5. Insert the sidebar contents using cursor insert methods

5. **You are trying to create a document with** `QTextCursor`**. It should have a top and bottom frame; in the top frame, there should be a title, and in the bottom frame, an unordered list. Correct this code so that it does that:**

```
document = qtg.QTextDocument()
cursor = qtg.QTextCursor(document)
top_frame = cursor.insertFrame(qtg.QTextFrameFormat())
bottom_frame = cursor.insertFrame(qtg.QTextFrameFormat())

cursor.insertText('This is the title')
cursor.movePosition(qtg.QTextCursor.NextBlock)
cursor.insertList(qtg.QTextListFormat())
for item in ('thing 1', 'thing 2', 'thing 3'):
    cursor.insertText(item)
```

   The main problem with this code is that it fails to move the cursor correctly, so content is not being created in the right spots. This is the corrected code:

```
document = qtg.QTextDocument()
cursor = qtg.QTextCursor(document)
top_frame = cursor.insertFrame(qtg.QTextFrameFormat())
cursor.setPosition(document.rootFrame().lastPosition())
bottom_frame = cursor.insertFrame(qtg.QTextFrameFormat())

cursor.setPosition(top_frame.lastPosition())
cursor.insertText('This is the title')
# This won't get us to the next frame:
#cursor.movePosition(qtg.QTextCursor.NextBlock)
cursor.setPosition(bottom_frame.lastPosition())
```

```
            cursor.insertList(qtg.QTextListFormat())
            for i, item in enumerate(('thing 1', 'thing 2', 'thing 3')):
                # don't forget to add a block for each item after the
    first:
                if i > 0:
                    cursor.insertBlock()
                cursor.insertText(item)
```

6. **You're creating your own** QPrinter **subclass to add a signal when the page size changes. Will the following code work?**

```
class MyPrinter(qtps.QPrinter):

    page_size_changed = qtc.pyqtSignal(qtg.QPageSize)

    def setPageSize(self, size):
        super().setPageSize(size)
        self.page_size_changed.emit(size)
```

Unfortunately, it won't. Since QPrinter is not derived from QObject, it cannot have signals. You will get an error like this:

```
TypeError: MyPrinter cannot be converted to PyQt5.QtCore.QObject
in this context
```

7. QtPrintSupport **contains a class called** QPrinterInfo. **Using this class, print a list of the names, make and model, and default page size of all of the printers on your system.**

The code looks like this:

```
for printer in qtps.QPrinterInfo.availablePrinters():
    print(
        printer.printerName(),
        printer.makeAndModel(),
        printer.defaultPageSize())
```

Chapter 12

1. **Add code to this method to write your name in blue on the bottom of the picture:**

```
def create_headshot(self, image_file, name):
    image = qtg.QImage()
    image.load(image_file)
```

```
# your code here
# end of your code
return image
```

Your code will need to create `QPainter` and `QPen`, then write to the image:

```
def create_headshot(self, image_file, name):
    image = qtg.QImage()
    image.load(image_file)
    # your code here
    painter = qtg.QPainter(image)
    pen = qtg.QPen(qtg.QColor('blue'))
    painter.setPen(pen)
    painter.drawText(image.rect(), qtc.Qt.AlignBottom, name)
    # end of your code
    return image
```

2. **Given a** `QPainter` **object called** `painter`, **write a line of code to paint an 80 × 80 pixel octagon in the upper-left corner of the painter's paint device. Refer to the documentation at** `https://doc.qt.io/qt-5/qpainter.html#drawPolygon`.

   There are a few ways to create and draw a polygon, but the simplest is to pass a series of `QPoint` objects to `drawPolygon()`:

   ```
   painter.drawPolygon(
       qtc.QPoint(0, 20), qtc.QPoint(20, 0),
       qtc.QPoint(60, 0), qtc.QPoint(80, 20),
       qtc.QPoint(80, 60), qtc.QPoint(60, 80),
       qtc.QPoint(20, 80), qtc.QPoint(0, 60)
   )
   ```

   Of course, you could also use a `QPainterPath` object, as well.

3. **You're creating a custom widget and can't figure out why the text is showing up in black. The following is your** `paintEvent()` **method; see if you can figure out the problem:**

   ```
   def paintEvent(self, event):
       black_brush = qtg.QBrush(qtg.QColor('black'))
       white_brush = qtg.QBrush(qtg.QColor('white'))
       painter = qtg.QPainter()
       painter.setBrush(black_brush)
       painter.drawRect(0, 0, self.width(), self.height())
       painter.setBrush(white_brush)
       painter.drawText(0, 0, 'Test Text')
   ```

The problem is that you've set `brush`, but the text is drawn with a `pen`. The default pen is black. To fix this, create a `pen` set to white and pass it to `painter.setPen()` before drawing the text.

4. **A deep-fried meme is a style of meme that uses extreme compression, saturation, and other processing to make the meme image look intentionally low quality. Add a feature to your meme generator to optionally make the meme deep-fried. Some things you can try include reducing the color bit depth and adjusting the hue and saturation of the colors in the image.**

   Be creative here, but for an example, see the `question_4_example_code.py` file in the included source code.

5. **You'd like to animate a circle moving horizontally across the screen. What do you need to change in the following code to animate the circle?**

   ```
   scene = QGraphicsScene()
   scene.setSceneRect(0, 0, 800, 600)
   circle = scene.addEllipse(0, 0, 10, 10)
   animation = QPropertyAnimation(circle, b'x')
   animation.setStartValue(0)
   animation.setEndValue(600)
   animation.setDuration(5000)
   animation.start()
   ```

   Your `circle` object cannot be animated as it is, since it is a `QGraphicsItem`. To animate an object's properties with `QPropertyAnimation`, it must be a `QObject` descendant. You need to build your circle as a subclass of `QGraphicsObject`; then, you can animate it.

6. **What's wrong with the following code, which attempts to set up** `QPainter` **with a gradient brush?**

   ```
   gradient = qtg.QLinearGradient(
       qtc.QPointF(0, 100), qtc.QPointF(0, 0))
   gradient.setColorAt(20, qtg.QColor('red'))
   gradient.setColorAt(40, qtg.QColor('orange'))
   gradient.setColorAt(60, qtg.QColor('green'))
   painter = QPainter()
   painter.setGradient(gradient)
   ```

There are two problems here:

1. The first argument to `setColorAt` is not a pixel location, but rather, it's a percentage expressed as a float between `0` and `1`.
2. There is no `QPainter.setGradient()` method. The gradient must be passed into the `QPainter` constructor.

7. **See if you can implement some of the following improvements to the game we created:**

   - **Pulsating bullets**
   - **Explosions when a tank is hit**
   - **Sounds (see** `Chapter 7`**,** *Working with Audio-Visual Using QtMultimedia,* **for help here)**
   - **Background animation**
   - **Multiple bullets**

   You're own your own here. Have fun!

Chapter 13

1. **Which steps of the OpenGL render pipeline are user-definable? Which steps must be defined in order to render anything? You may need to reference the documentation at** `https://www.khronos.org/opengl/wiki/Rendering_Pipeline_Overview`**.**

   The vertex processing and fragment shader steps are user-definable. At a minimum, you must create a vertex shader and a fragment shader. Optional steps include the geometry shader and tessellation steps, which are part of vertex processing.

2. **You're writing a shader for an OpenGL 2.1 program. Does the following look correct?**

```
#version 2.1

attribute highp vec4 vertex;

void main (void)
{
gl_Position = vertex;
}
```

Your version string is wrong. It should read #version 120, since it specifies the version of GLSL, not the version of OpenGL. Versions are also specified as a three-digit number with no period.

3. **Is the following a vertex or fragment shader? How can you tell?**

```
attribute highp vec4 value1;
varying highp vec3 x[4];
void main(void)
{
   x[0] = vec3(sin(value1[0] * .4));
   x[1] = vec3(cos(value1[1]));
   gl_Position = value1;
   x[2] = vec3(10 * x[0])
}
```

This is a vertex shader; there are a couple of clues:

- It has an attribute variable, which it assigns to gl_Position.
- It has a varying variable to which it's assigning values.

4. **Given the following vertex shader, what code do you need to write to assign simple values to the two variables?**

```
attribute highp vec4 coordinates;
uniform highp mat4 matrix1;

void main(void){
   gl_Position = matrix1 * coordinates;
}
```

Assuming that your `QOpenGLShaderProgram` object is saved as `self.program`, the following code is needed:

```
c_handle = self.program.attributeLocation('coordinates')
m_handle = self.program.uniformLocation('matrix1')
self.program.setAttributeValue(c_handle, coordinate_value)
self.program.setUniformValue(m_handle, matrix)
```

5. **You enable face culling to save some processing power, but find that several of the visible primitives in your drawing are not rendering now. What could be the problem?**

   The vertices were drawn in the wrong order. Remember that drawing a primitive counterclockwise will cause the far face to be culled; drawing it clockwise will cause the near face to be culled.

6. **What does the following code do to our OpenGL image?**

```
matrix = qtg.QMatrix4x4()
matrix.perspective(60, 4/3, 2, 10)
matrix.translate(1, -1, -4)
matrix.rotate(45, 1, 0, 0)
```

   By itself, nothing. This code simply creates a 4 x 4 matrix and runs some transform operations on it. If, however, we passed this into a shader that applied its values to a vertex, it would create a perspective projection, move our object in space, and rotate the image. The actual `matrix` object is nothing more than a matrix of numbers.

7. **Experiment with the demo and see whether you can add any of the following features:**

   - **A more interesting shape (pyramid, cube, and so on)**
   - **More controls for moving the object**
   - **Shadows and lighting effects**
   - **Animating shape changes in the object**

   You're on your own here!

Chapter 14

1. **Consider the following descriptions of datasets. What style of chart would you suggest for each?**

    1. **Web server hit counts by date**
    2. **Sales figures by salesperson per month**
    3. **Percentages of support tickets for the past year by company department**
    4. **The yield of a plot of bean plants against the plant's height, for several hundred plants**

    The answers are subjective, but the author suggests the following:

    1. A line or spline chart, as it would illustrate traffic trends
    2. A bar or stacked by chart, as this would allow you to compare salespeople over time
    3. A pie chart, since it represents a set of percentages adding up to 100
    4. A scatter plot, since you want to show a general trend of a large set of data

2. **Which chart component has not been configured in the following code, and what will the result be?**

    ```
    data_list = [
        qtc.QPoint(2, 3),
        qtc.QPoint(4, 5),
        qtc.QPoint(6, 7)]
    chart = qtch.QChart()
    series = qtch.QLineSeries()
    series.append(data_list)
    view = qtch.QChartView()
    view.setChart(chart)
    view.show()
    ```

    The axes have not been configured. This chart can be displayed, but will not have reference marks on the axes, and may not be scaled intuitively.

3. **What's wrong with the following code?**

```
mainwindow = qtw.QMainWindow()
chart = qtch.QChart()
series = qtch.QPieSeries()
series.append('Half', 50)
series.append('Other Half', 50)
mainwindow.setCentralWidget(chart)
mainwindow.show()
```

QChart is not a widget and cannot be added to a layout or set as a central widget. It must be attached to QChartView.

4. **You want to create a bar chart comparing Bob and Alice's sales figures for the quarter. What code needs to be added? (Note that axes are not required here.):**

```
bob_sales = [2500, 1300, 800]
alice_sales = [1700, 1850, 2010]

chart = qtch.QChart()
series = qtch.QBarSeries()
chart.addSeries(series)

# add code here

# end code
view = qtch.QChartView()
view.setChart(chart)
view.show()
```

We need to create bar sets for Bob and Alice and append them to the series:

```
bob_set = qtch.QBarSet('Bob')
alice_set = qtch.QBarSet('Alice')
bob_set.append(bob_sales)
alice_set.append(alice_sales)
series.append(bob_set)
series.append(alice_set)
```

5. **Given a** QChart **object named** chart, **write code so that the chart has a black background and blue data plots.**

To do this, set the backgroundBrush and theme properties:

```
chart.setBackgroundBrush(
    qtg.QBrush(qtc.Qt.black))
chart.setTheme(qtch.QChart.ChartThemeBlueIcy)
```

6. **Style the other two charts in the system monitor script using the techniques you used on the last chart. Experiment with different brushes and pens, and see whether you can find other properties to set.**

   You're on your own here!

7. `QPolarChart` **is a subclass of** `QChart` **that allows you to construct a polar chart. Investigate the use of the polar chart in the Qt documentation and see whether you can create a polar chart of an appropriate dataset.**

   You're on your own here!

8. `psutil.cpu_percent()` **takes an optional argument,** `percpu`**, that will create a list of values showing usage information per CPU core. Update your application to use this option and separately display each CPU core's activity on one chart.**

   You're still on your own here; don't worry, though, you can do it!

Chapter 15

1. **You have just bought a Raspberry Pi with Raspbian preinstalled to run your PyQt5 application. When you try to run your application, you get an error trying to import** `QtNetworkAuth`**, which your application depends on. What is likely the problem?**

   Possibly, your Raspbian installation is version 9. Version 9 has Qt 5.7, which does not have the `QtNetworkAuth` module. You need to upgrade to a newer release of Raspbian.

2. **You have written a PyQt frontend for a legacy scanner device. Your code talks to the scanner through a proprietary driver utility called** `scanutil.exe`**. It is currently running on a Windows 10 PC, but your employer wants to save money by moving it to a Raspberry Pi. Is this a good idea?**

   Unfortunately, it isn't. If your application relies on a proprietary Windows x86 binary, that program will not run on the Pi. To switch to the Pi, you would need a binary compiled for the ARM platform that can run on one of the Pi's supported operating systems (also, that OS needs to be able to run Python and Qt).

3. **You've acquired a new sensor and want to try it out with the Raspberry Pi. It has three connections, labeled Vcc, GND, and Data. How would you connect this to the Raspberry Pi? Is there more information you need?**

   You really need more information, but here's enough to get started:

   - **Vcc** is an abbreviation that means input voltage. You will have to connect this to either a 5V or 3V3 pin on the Pi. You will need to consult the manufacturer's documentation to determine which connection will work.
   - **GND** means ground, and you can connect this to any ground pin on the Pi.
   - **Data** is presumably a connection you would want to make to one of the programmable GPIO pins. It's very likely that, you'll need some kind of library to make it work, so you should check with the manufacturer for that.

4. **You're trying to light an LED connected to the fourth GPIO pin from the left on the outside. What is wrong with this code?**

   ```
   GPIO.setmode(GPIO.BCM)
   GPIO.setup(8, GPIO.OUT)
   GPIO.output(8, 1)
   ```

   The GPIO pin mode is set to BCM, which means you have the wrong number for the pin you're using. Set the mode to BOARD or use the correct BCM number for your pin (14).

5. **You are trying to dim an LED connected to GPIO pin 12. Does this code work?**

   ```
   GPIO.setmode(GPIO.BOARD)
   GPIO.setup(12, GPIO.OUT)
   GPIO.output(12, 0.5)
   ```

   This code doesn't work, because pins can only be either on or off. To simulate half voltage, you need to use pulse width modulation, as shown in the following example:

   ```
   GPIO.setmode(GPIO.BOARD)
   GPIO.setup(12, GPIO.OUT)
   pwm = GPIO.PWM(12, 60)
   pwm.start(0)
   pwm.ChangeDutyCycle(50)
   ```

6. **You have a motion sensor with a data pin that goes** HIGH **when motion is detected. It's connected to pin** 8. **The following is your driver code:**

```
class MotionSensor(qtc.QObject):

    detection = qtc.pyqtSignal()

    def __init__(self):
        super().__init__()
        GPIO.setmode(GPIO.BOARD)
        GPIO.setup(8, GPIO.IN)
        self.state = GPIO.input(8)

    def check(self):
        state = GPIO.input(8)
        if state and state != self.state:
            detection.emit()
        self.state = state
```

Your main window class creates a MotionSensor **object and connects its** detection **signal to a callback method. However, nothing is being detected. What is missing?**

You are not calling MotionSensor.check(). You should implement polling by adding a QTimer object that calls check() periodically.

7. **Combine the two circuits in this chapter in a creative way; for example, you might create a light that changes color depending on the humidity and temperature.**

You're on your own here!

Chapter 16

1. **The following code is giving you an attribute error; what's wrong?**

```
from PyQt5 import QtWebEngine as qtwe
w = qtwe.QWebEngineView()
```

You want to import QtWebEngineWidgets, not QtWebEngine. The latter is for use with Qt's QML frontend.

2. **The following code should connect this** `UrlBar` **class with** `QWebEngineView`, **so that the entered URL is loaded when the** *return/Enter* **key is pressed. It doesn't work, though; what is wrong?**

```
class UrlBar(qtw.QLineEdit):

    url_request = qtc.pyqtSignal(str)

    def __init__(self):
        super().__init__()
        self.returnPressed.connect(self.request)

    def request(self):
        self.url_request.emit(self.text())

mywebview = qtwe.QWebEngineView()
myurlbar = UrlBar()
myurlbar.url_request(mywebview.load)
```

`QWebEngineView.load()` requires a `QUrl` object, not a string. The `url_request` signal sends the text of the bar as a string directly to `load()`. It should wrap it in a `QUrl` object first.

3. **What is the result of the following code?**

```
class WebView(qtwe.QWebEngineView):

    def createWindow(self, _):

        return self
```

`QWebEngineView.createWindow()` is called whenever a browser action requests a new tab or window to be created, and is expected to return a `QWebEngineView` object, which will be used for the new window or tab. By returning `self`, this subclass forces any links or calls that try to create a new window to just navigate in the same window, instead.

4. **Check out the documentation for** `QWebEngineView` **at** https://doc.qt.io/qt-5/qwebengineview.html. **How would you implement a zoom feature in your browser?**

First, you'd need to implement callback functions on the `MainWindow` to set the `zoomFactor` property on the current web view:

```
def zoom_in(self):
    webview = self.tabs.currentWidget()
```

```
        webview.setZoomFactor(webview.zoomFactor() * 1.1)

    def zoom_out(self):
        webview = self.tabs.currentWidget()
        webview.setZoomFactor(webview.zoomFactor() * .9)
```

Then, in `MainWindow.__init__()`, you would just need to create controls to call those methods:

```
navigation.addAction('Zoom In', self.zoom_in)
navigation.addAction('Zoom Out', self.zoom_out)
```

5. **As the name implies,** `QWebEngineView` **represents the view portion of a model-view architecture. What class represents the model in this design?**

   `QWebEnginePage` seems to be the clearest candidate here, since it stores and controls the rendering of the web content.

6. **Given a** `QWebEngineView` **named** `webview`, **write code to determine whether JavaScript is enabled on** `webview`.

   The code must query the view's `QWebEngineSettings` object, like this:

```
webview.settings().testAttribute(
    qtwe.QWebEngineSettings.JavascriptEnabled)
```

7. **You saw in our browser example that** `runJavaScript()` **can pass an integer value to a callback function. Write a simple demo script to test what other kinds of JavaScript objects can be returned, and how they appear in Python code.**

   See `chapter_7_return_value_test.py` in the example code.

Chapter 17

1. **You have written a PyQt application in a file called** Scan & Print Tool-box.py. **You want to convert this into module-style organization; what change should you make?**

   The name of the script should change, since spaces, ampersands, and dashes are not valid characters to use in a Python module name. You might change the module name to `scan_and_print_toolbox`, for example.

2. **Your PyQt5 database application has a set of** `.sql` **files containing queries used by the application. It worked when your app was a single script in the same directories as the** `.sql` **files, but now that you've converted it into module-style organization, the queries can't be found. What should you do?**

   The best thing to do is to put your `.sql` files into a Qt resource file and make that part of your Python module. If you are unable to use Qt resource files, you will need to convert your relative paths to absolute paths using the `path` module and the built-in `file` variable

3. **You're writing a detailed** `README.rst` **file to document your new application before uploading it to a code-sharing site. What characters should be used to underline your level 1, 2, and 3 headings, respectively?**

   It actually doesn't matter, as long as you use characters from the list of acceptable characters:

   ```
   = - ` : ' " ~ ^ _ * + # < >
   ```

An RST interpreter should consider the first header character encountered to mean level one; the second, level two; and the third, level three.

4. **You're creating a** `setup.py` **script for your project so that you can upload it to PyPI. You would like to include a URL for the project's FAQ page. How can you accomplish this?**

   You need to add a `key: value` pair to the `project_urls` dict, like so:

   ```
   setup(
       project_urls={
           'Project FAQ': 'https://example.com/faq',
       }
   )
   ```

5. **You have specified** `include_package_data=True` **in your** `setup.py` **file, but for some reason, the** `docs` **folder is not being included in your distribution package. What's wrong?**

   `include_package_data` only affects data files inside packages (modules). If you want to include files outside your modules, you need to use the `MANIFEST.in` file for these.

6. **You ran** `pyinstaller fight_fighter3.py` **to package your new game as an executable. Something went wrong, though; where can you find a log of the build process?**

   You need to look at `build/fight_fighter3/warn-fight_fighter3.txt`, for a start. You might need to increase the debugging output by calling PyInstaller with the `--log-level DEBUG` argument.

7. **Despite the name, PyInstaller cannot actually generate installer programs or packages for your application. Research some options for your platform of choice.**

   You're on your own here, although a popular option is the **Nullsoft Scriptable Install System (NSIS)**.

Upgrading Raspbian 9 to Raspbian 10

In Chapter 15, *PyQt Raspberry Pi*, Raspbian 10 is required so that you can have a sufficiently recent version of Python and PyQt5. At the time of publication, the current release of Raspbian is version 9, with version 10 expected in mid-to-late 2019. You can, however, upgrade to the testing version of Raspbian 10, which will work correctly for the purposes of this book.

To do so, follow these steps:

1. First, verify that you're using Raspbian 9 by checking the contents of /etc/issue. It should read as follows:

   ```
   $ Rasbpian GNU/Linux 9 \n \l
   ```

2. Open Command Prompt and, using sudo, edit /etc/apt/sources.list:

   ```
   $ sudo -e /etc/apt/sources.list
   ```

3. Change every instance of stretch to buster. For example, the first line should read as follows:

   ```
   deb http://raspbian.raspbrrypi.org/raspbian/
    buster main contrib non-free rpi
   ```

4. Run the sudo apt update command and make sure you don't have any errors.
5. Now run the sudo apt upgrade command. This command may take a long time to complete, as it will need to download an updated copy of every package on the system and install it. After the download phase ends, there will be some questions to answer as well. Generally speaking, take the default answer for these questions.
6. Finally, restart your Raspberry Pi. To clean up old packages, run this command:

   ```
   $ sudo apt autoremove
   ```

That's it; you should now be running Raspbian 10. If you run into difficulties, consult the Raspbian community at https://www.raspberrypi.org/forums/.

Other Books You May Enjoy

If you enjoyed this book, you may be interested in these other books by Packt:

Qt5 Python GUI Programming Cookbook
B.M. Harwani

ISBN: 9781788831000

- Use basic Qt components, such as a radio button, combo box, and sliders
- Use QSpinBox and sliders to handle different signals generated on mouse clicks
- Work with different Qt layouts to meet user interface requirements
- Create custom widgets and set up customizations in your GUI
- Perform asynchronous I/O operations and thread handling in the Python GUI
- Employ network concepts, internet browsing, and Google Maps in UI
- Use graphics rendering and implement animation in your GUI
- Make your GUI application compatible with Android and iOS devices

Mastering OpenCV 4 with Python

Alberto Fernández Villán

ISBN: 9781789344912

- Handle files and images, and explore various image processing techniques
- Explore image transformations, including translation, resizing, and cropping
- Gain insights into building histograms
- Brush up on contour detection, filtering, and drawing
- Work with Augmented Reality to build marker-based and markerless applications
- Work with the main machine learning algorithms in OpenCV
- Explore the deep learning Python libraries and OpenCV deep learning capabilities
- Create computer vision and deep learning web applications

Leave a review - let other readers know what you think

Please share your thoughts on this book with others by leaving a review on the site that you bought it from. If you purchased the book from Amazon, please leave us an honest review on this book's Amazon page. This is vital so that other potential readers can see and use your unbiased opinion to make purchasing decisions, we can understand what our customers think about our products, and our authors can see your feedback on the title that they have worked with Packt to create. It will only take a few minutes of your time, but is valuable to other potential customers, our authors, and Packt. Thank you!

Index

Printed in Great Britain
by Amazon

67970075R00307